PRAISE FOR
JOHN M. CLUM'S *SOMETHING FOR THE BOYS*

"Clum is laudably refreshing . . ."—*New York Times* Book Review

"It's true! The gay scene does include a musical-theater chromosome . . . John Clum . . . pays tribute to the quintessential American art form—the Broadway musical . . . smart and affectionate . . ."—*Metrosource*

"Any diva's best-loved audience is the gay one—the guys and gals who adore us most. John Clum's analysis of the long love affair between musicals and gay culture is a fascinating read. I especially recommend pp. 170-172. Thank you, John, with all my heart. Love, Betty Buckley."

"[Clum offers] perceptive comments about gender roles on stage and alternative ways of looking at shows . . ."—*Choice*

"[a] fascinating new book on musical theater and gay culture."—*The Advocate*

"[Clum's] thoughts on the enduring appeal of Ethel Merman and Carol Channing, the lives of composers Cole Porter and Lorenz Hart, and the subtexts of countless musicals such as *Gypsy* . . . are worth pondering by all readers."
—*Dallas Morning News*

"entertaining . . . Mixing personal anecdote with scholarly analysis, Clum takes his readers into a world where, despite homophobia and plots that seemed basically heterosexual, life could be fabulous."—*Library Journal*

FOR BOB WEST
"DR. SHOWBIZ"

SOMETHING FOR THE BOYS

Musical Theater and Gay Culture

John M. Clum

palgrave

for St. Martin's Griffin

First published 1999 by
PALGRAVE™
175 Fifth Avenue, New York, N.Y. 10010.
Companies and representatives throughout the world.

PALGRAVE is the new global publishing imprint of St. Martin's Press LLC Scholarly and Reference Division and Palgrave Publishers Ltd (formerly Macmillan Press Ltd).

ISBN 0-312-21058-2 hardback
ISBN 0-312-23832-0 paperback

Library of Congress Cataloging-in-Publication Data

Clum, John M.
Something for the boys : musical theater and gay culture / John M. Clum.
    p. cm.
  Discography: p.
  Includes bibliographical references and index.
    ISBN 0-312-21058-2 (hardback) 0-312-23832-0 (paperback)
    1. Gay men and musicals.   I. Title.
ML 1700.C581999
782.1'4'086642—dc21   99-25435
                                                       CIP

Designed by Acme Art, Inc.

First paperback edition: May 2001

10 9 8 7 6 5 4 3 2 1

Printed in the United States of America.

PERMISSIONS CREDITS

CONTENTS

Two pages of photos appear between pages 30 and 31 and between pages 196 and 197.

The big surprise is
When the curtain rises
We're up here dressed as YOU.

—*Neil Bartlett,* Night After Night

ACKNOWLEDGMENTS

Many people figured in the forty-plus-year gestation of this book. My mother and late father, who took me to musicals from an early age, beginning with something called *Texas Li'l Darlin'* in 1949; my sister, who helped produce my first musical in my teen years; my early friend and collaborator on our teenage extravaganzas, the knowledgeable Stephen Holden, with whom I still carry on conversations about musical theater; and my more recent mentors, particularly the book's dedicatee, Bob West (Dr. Showbiz), a living history of British musical theater. Also Anthony Lyn, Hector Lugo, Sam Adamson, Richard Porter, Susannah Waters, Wayland Wong, and Glenn and Jane Cee Redbord.

Thanks to my colleague, chairperson, and friend, Richard Riddell, who gave me the time and funding I needed to write this as well as considerable moral support. To my right hand, colleague, and friend, Jon D. Rossini, for careful reading and suggestions. To my assistant, Kevin Dwayne Poole, for minding the store while I went into hiding to write this.

Thanks to my agent, Gordon Massman, for encouraging me to write the book my way; and to Michael Flamini, my editor, who could write this book himself. Special thanks to Fred Ebb, Rose Marie Gawelko at Warner Chappell, Robin Walton and Flora Griggs with the Rodgers and Hammerstein Organization, and Jeni Elliott at Hal Leonard Corporation. Very special thanks for service above and beyond the call of duty to Paul McKibbins at Rilting Music.

In addition to those thanked above, let me add Boze Hadleigh, Eric Hendricks, Linda Fresia, Larry Moore, and divo Craig Rubano for their useful and informative correspondence, tapes, and CDs. Thanks too to Jamie Brickhouse and Jennifer Simington at Palgrave for all their help.

And, of course, thanks and thanks again to my companion in theatergoing and life, Walter Melion.

PREFACE TO THE PAPERBACK EDITION

At the Prince Charles Cinema off Leicester Square in London during the Spring of 2000, a new phenomenon began that once again proved the connection between musical theater and gay culture. An enterprising theater manager came up with the idea of superimposing the Oscar Hammerstein lyrics onto a print of the Robert Wise film of *The Sound of Music*. Late night singalong screenings introduced by local gay celebrities are packed with folks in costume. Nuns' habits predominate, but there are also lots of imitation Trapp children, baronesses, Marias, and even people dressed as their favorite thing—some dressed, for instance as a brown paper package tied up with string. During the screenings audience members boisterously sing along and add their witty contributions to the dialogue scenes. Gay people are not the only participants at this weekly rite, but they are the core audience. This local London phenomenon has been covered by the American media. A picture of Bob West, the dedicatee of this book, as Uncle Max flanked by friends dressed as nuns appeared in the Los Angeles *Times*. By the time this edition comes out, there will be *Sound of Music* singalongs in cities across the United States.

At a time when only cartoon characters sing on the screen and the only musicals garnering any enthusiasm on Broadway were written before *The Sound of Music,* these singalong screenings at the Prince Charles are a reminder that the musical still has a special place in the imaginations of a lot of gay men. Some in the audience may remember when they first saw that aerial shot zoom in on Julie Andrews on the hilltop singing that famous opening line. They may recall feeling that inchoate but powerful sense of difference, may begin wishing that the world were indeed one big song cue and that they were taught by the sixties' favorite governess, Julie Andrews, to sing and dance their way down the street. How bad a threat can Nazis of various kinds be when your life is a musical? How dangerous can life be when you have a diva as your surrogate mother? Perhaps these future queens were even then drawn to the silliness of *The Sound of Music,* all the more attractive for being unintentional.

Many of us have had our epiphanies, our moments of awareness of difference combined with a special exhilaration, inspired by musicals on stage or screen. I remember at age nine or ten watching Gene Kelly and Leslie Caron dance to Gershwin's "Our Love Is Here to Stay" on the banks of a very artificial Seine in *An American in Paris* and realizing for the first time that, yes, there is something different about me and that song and dance world on the screen has more power for me than the things I'm supposed to like (baseball?). At thirteen I saw Julie Andrews on stage in Sandy Wilson's *The Boy Friend* and experienced, though I didn't know the word yet, the special delight of camp—and of cute chorus boys!

Some of us also love the arcana of musical theater the way other men love baseball statistics and recognize our membership in an elite club when others join us in celebrating our esoteric knowledge. For me, the little references dropped into the scripts of *Will and Grace* are the best thing about that delightful sitcom. "You ain't gettin' eighty-eight cents from me, Rose," says one character to another in the 2000 season finale. If you don't know where that comes from, you may have picked up the wrong book.

We come together in a theater to enjoy musicals, but for many of us they are an intensely personal experience. As much as I may try to generalize in the following pages, this is a very personal book, as much memoir as history or criticism. For all my academic training, I could not write an objective book on the musical; nor could most of the authors who have preceded me in celebrating this most illogical of art forms. So I should not have been surprised by the fact that *Something for the Boys* has garnered such passionate positive and negative responses, particularly in forums like the amazon.com Web site. At the same time, since the book's publication, my email and snailmail have been filled with fascinating and often informative communiqués. I've picked up lots of juicy gossip I wish I could print here (that would take more concrete evidence than I now have) and some helpful corrections that have been incorporated into this edition.

Baltimore, 2000

MUSICAL THEATER AND GAY CULTURE

Something for the Boys: Musical Theater and Gay Culture is part exploration, part history, and always, I hope, celebration: of musical theater itself, but particularly of the gayness that circulates through the best and worst of musical theater. *Something for the Boys* is a study of the relationship of American and British musical theater and a specific sense of what might be called "gay culture." Since the golden era of the American musical ended as gay liberation began, the bulk of this book will focus on the period between the end of World War I and the early 1970s, the first era of gay liberation. This will not be a conventional history: there are a number of decent histories of musical theater.[1] Rather it will be a series of related essays that explore different aspects of the relationship, building on my knowledge of musical theater and gay cultural history. Perforce this book will be autobiographical, not sociological or anthropological. My fieldwork is impressionistic more than statistical. My more theoretical colleagues would rightly call the book a performance. It focuses, as any study of the dynamics and erotics of theater must, on what happens in the audience as well as what happens on stage. It has usually been the gay audience member, "out there in the dark," who queers the musical, who finds or invents a gay reading to the spectacle presented to him. Andrew Lloyd Webber, Don Black, and Trevor Nunn may be straight, but *Sunset Boulevard* worked best for those who could appreciate its camp elements, particularly a love of the genre of women's pictures of the late 1940s and early 1950s and diva worship.

Something for the Boys is an antidote to the many books on musical theater that avoid or attack the elements gay men celebrate. Journalist Mark Steyn's *Broadway Babies Say Goodnight: Musicals Then and Now* is basically a kvetch about how musicals have deteriorated since the good ole days of Rodgers and Hammerstein. Believe it or not, there is a chapter entitled "The Fags," in which Steyn addresses the issue of gay influence on the theater and gay reception of musicals, pointing out that "The Broadway musical encompassed everything except the one subject its creators were specially expert in."[2] He doesn't realize, as D. A. Miller, a noted literary critic, does, that none "who saw the closet at work on the musical stage, least of all ourselves, failed to witness this double operation: not only of 'hiding' homosexual desire, but also of manifesting, across all manner of landscapes, an extensive network of hiding places—call them latencies—apparently ready-made for the purpose."[3] Like the doors in a French farce, the closets of gay America, the sexuality they hid, and the aesthetic that, for many, accompanied that sexuality, were visible in the musical for all who were able to see them. We all know that some of the defining aspects of past musicals were gay created and were expressions of that fictional entity, the "gay sensibility," which might better be called "mastery of the closet," accompanied as it was by the impulse to keep the subject matter of the musical closeted, a reflection of American society's hatred of homosexuality and homosexuals. Throughout its history, the musical accommodated itself to this mainstream prejudice, while managing at the same time to reflect the changing styles of its closeted gay creators and earn the enthusiastic support of the gay men in the audience. That "era of the closet," like the current era of gay identity, is an historical moment.

This book is an antidote to heterosexist works like Steyn's, which argue for a return to the days when gay men knew their place in the theater (essential but invisible) and the world view and style of the musical existed, as the world did, to please straight men. The "tired businessman" (straight white male after martinis and dinner) was once the target audience for the musical, though I wonder how much he really delighted in gay-infused postwar musicals. Now the target audience seems to be the suburban family, but behind even a family entertainment like *The Lion King,* there's Elton John (even if his songs for this kiddie show are below acceptable Broadway quality), a queeny villain, and a fabulously refurbished New Amsterdam Theater that only a show queen can truly appreciate. *Something for the Boys* is more in tune with Ethan Mordden's many invaluable books on musical theater. Mordden, a gay writer who is celebrated for his fine novels on gay life in New York, sees the musical from the point of view of a show queen, but he doesn't discuss what makes a gay writer wax rhapsodic over musicals like *Goldilocks* (1958). Like Mordden, I was there for many of these fifties musicals, including *Goldilocks*. They shaped my aesthetic as a director and writer and my sense of gayness. In his book *Coming Up Roses: The Broadway Musical in the 1950s*, Mordden responds to the gayness of the fifties musicals without naming it. Like many creators of musicals, Mordden is reluctant to lose a wider audience by being too parochial— appealing too overtly to his gay audience.

Gay men could see that gayness seemed barely contained by the musicals of the era of the closet. Neil Bartlett's 1993 musical, *Night After Night* (music by Nicolas Bloomfield), celebrates the notion that every man involved in a supporting position in a London West End musical in 1958 (the year Bartlett was born)—the chorus boys, ushers, bartender, program sellers, cloakroom attendants—was a gay man for whom the theater was a redeeming fantasy. While the United States was hardly gay friendly in 1958, England was particularly Draconian in its policing of gays, so the theater seemed even more of a sanctuary. In *Night After Night*, Bartlett, accurately, focuses on musical theater in particular as a refuge. A friend who works in the British theater tells me that even now the percentage of gay nonmusical actors is relatively small; the gays are in musical theater. One song, "There You Are," tells the mainly heterosexual audience that their heterosexual, heterosexist fantasies are being provided by gay men:

> The one who sold your ticket
> The one who poured your drink
> The one who stood there smiling—
> Well, he's not what you might think.
> The smart one selling programs
> "That will be one shilling, ta,"
> Those two who stood behind you
> While you waited at the bar
> Those three who seem to, well, stand out
> Those four who we're not sure about—
> Look, surely that's a bit too far—
> And what about you—
> Well
> There (*indicating boys*)
> You (*indicating audience*)
> Are!!![4]

Night After Night is a witty, cogent picture of the marriage of gay culture and musical theater, even though in 1958 that theater was devoted (as it still is, with rare exceptions) to heterosexual fantasy. At the beginning of the musical,

Bartlett's father, Trevor, waits at the theater for his wife, pregnant with Neil. While he waits, the participants in the musical and the theater workers show him that, for heterosexuals, the musical is a saving fantasy of optimism and romance, yet every song has particular meaning for gay men. When a surprised, baffled Trevor is brought up on the stage to replace the absent leading man, the chorus boys give him advice:

> When you're just starting out you'll find
> That knowing which step to take—
> And knowing what Place is your proper place—
> And showing the World that Make-
> Up's not something you put on your face
> But something you do with your mind . . .
> Knowing just which way in Life to turn
> Isn't something you know . . . but . . . Learn![5]

The song may be advice for an insecure, unwilling understudy; it's also advice on performing straightness, something all men must learn:

> The only thing that really proves
> If he has got it is how he moves.

"It" may betoken sex appeal or star charisma; "it" also could denote homosexuality. Every lyric in *Night After Night* contains this sort of gay/straight double entendre. Like gay readings of older "straight" musicals, *Night After Night* demonstrates the way gay men read their own lives into musicals. What could not be envisioned in 1958, before Neil Bartlett was born, was that a musical might celebrate the gayness of even straight fantasies, how those fantasies unite gay and straight people.

    Night After Night is highly theatrical and metatheatrical, a celebration of what some might call kitsch. Here is a mainstream work, performed at the prestigious Royal Court Theatre in London, that asserts that musical theater is not only gay now, but that it was gay even when it seemed most straight. Those gay men in a more oppressive age, whose lives were built on performance, had the greatest investment in the theatricality of and romantic hope offered by those musical fantasies.

    Something for the Boys is a meditation on the same themes as *Night After Night*. It weaves together two related topics. The first is the stereotype and reality of the "show queen." Why is it that a stereotypical signifier of gayness is a love of musical theater and a collection of original cast albums? Like all stereotypes, it is problematic, at best partially accurate, and it may be generational, though if my students are any indicator, it continues to have some validity. To what extent has musical theater been a particularly safe place for gay men to work and to congregate? Has musical theater really been as much a focus of the fantasy life of young gay men as plays like Larry Kramer's *The Destiny of Me,* for example, suggest? In that play the young Alexander's "difference" is tied to his love for musical theater. When viciously assaulted by his father for being a "sissy," Alexander counters by singing "I'm Gonna Wash That Man Right Outa My Hair" from *South Pacific* (it is 1949). Alexander's love of musical theater is tied as well to his youthful, defiant willingness to operate outside of conventional gender formulations, which is what his father most hates. As Alexander is, through family pressures and years of psychotherapy, "normalized" into a self-hating adult, he stops being a show queen and becomes a disillusioned, lonely, angry man. At the end, he comes to terms with his past and sings a show tune, "Make Believe" (from *Show Boat*), with his young, former self. There is some unintentional irony in Kramer's choice of Oscar Hammerstein as the voice through which young Alexander expresses his rebellion. As I will discuss in chapter three, Hammerstein was the bard of heterosexism in the musical, writing shows that allowed minimal space for any sort of gay reading. Yet Kramer has hit on something crucial about the relationship of gays to musical theater. A young man has taken on a male-created female voice to protect himself from patriarchal brutality. A heterosexist text has been queered to create a song of gay resistance and self-assertion. My survey is as informal and subjective as Kramer's. I do know the show queen is, like the opera queen, a real *genus* (often, like me, they are the same person), more abundant in an earlier age, when he was in some ways a product of a more universally policed closet. As recent events in Wyoming and elsewhere and recent utterances from one of our political parties demonstrate, there are still powerful institutions intent on maintaining the closet, the breeding ground for show queens.

What aspects of musical theater are particularly powerful for the show queen? Musicals are, to use Tony Kushner's term, "Fabulous," which for him should be the essence of gay theater:

> What are the salient features of Fabulousness? Irony. Tragic history. Defiance. Gender-fuck. Glitter Drama. It is not butch. It is not hot. The cathexis surrounding Fabulousness is not necessarily erotic. The Fabulous is not delimited by age or beauty. Style has a dialectical relationship to physical reality. The body is the Real. Style is Theater. The raw materials are reworked into illusion. [6]

Musicals are for eye and ear. They are about the exposure and ornamentation of the body; handsome chorines and lithe dancers, svelte bodies ornamented by gorgeous clothes, women flamboyantly decked out like drag queens. Musicals celebrate sensual pleasure, not deadly passion. Even when a musical is serious— and in the past fifteen years, musicals have turned from laughter to sentiment— its goal is entertainment and sheer dazzlement. Their heightened theatricality, their exaggerated, often parodic presentation of gender codes, and their lyrical romantic fantasies offered my generation of cocooned gay adolescents an escape from the masculine rites that disinterested and threatened us. Musicals are trips to Oz, that place celebrated in the 1939 film that had such metaphoric power for gay men.

Musicals problematize the body and gender. They have a different relationship to the body than opera does, though, as writers like Wayne Koestenbaum have explained, opera has its own special fascination for gay men. Opera is about the transcendence of the body through music. I have strong memories of the first *Aida* I ever saw as a kid in 1954, from somewhere in the upper reaches of the old Met on Thirty-ninth Street. Once I had overcome my acrophobia and performed some major contortions of body, neck, and head to see the stage, what I saw was flimsy, tacky scenery lit by what seemed to be floodlights, in front of which were oddly costumed unglamorous people. If memory serves me right, Zinka Milanov's massive, matronly slave girl sported lavender gowns with long trains and Fedora Barbieri's Amneris looked like a giant, round, green-sequined Christmas ornament. The men were equally ungainly, with an ugly, fat, middle-aged Radames looking more like General Norman Schwarzkopf than a stage hero. No one did anything that my young mind associated with acting, but I was mesmerized by the ethereal noises they made. Zinka Milanov, the Met's reigning diva in the fifties, was the greatest living example of the magic of opera: heavy, ungainly, hilariously melodramatic in her acting, but on a good night capable of the most beautiful sounds it is possible for a human being to make. In great operatic performances we accept or forget that we are watching homely, overweight men and women who often cannot act because their voices and the music they sing make our ears master our eyes. There's a video of Birgit Nilsson's last *Elektra* at the Met with the great Leonie Rysanek as Chrysothemis. What one sees in cruel close-up is a middle-aged Nilsson working at singing and acting this great, demented role, with Rysanek, another middle-aged lady in an ugly dress, running around being equally demented. One misses entirely the visceral experience of hearing those two great voices in the theater and the distance that allows the audience to imagine these women are what the script calls for. Television also makes surreal the grand gesture opera requires. At the end of *Elektra* the audience went berserk, as it does at a great operatic or musical performance, but the small screen version doesn't show why. Opera needs some distance and an adoring audience.

Musicals require a similar imaginative projection. The object of adoration is not an attractive male, an erotic object, but, as in opera, the diva, the woman who defies conventional notions of gender and plays out the parodic, larger-than-life performance of gender the musical privileges. British musicals have historically focused on men, from Ivor Novello and Noël Coward to Jean Valjean and the Phantom. American musicals focus on women, from Ethel Merman to Bernadette Peters and Betty Buckley. Why are/were gay men uninterested in leading men, while they identify with and shower adulation upon women who play caricatures of women? What do the Broadway divas have in common? Chapters four and five will address these questions.

As opera triumphs over the flesh, the musical triumphs over mortality. In opera, the soprano dies at the end. In a musical, the leading lady who is killed in Act I comes back to sing in Act II (*Les Misérables, Ragtime*). Broadway's Mimi, unlike her namesake in *La Bohème,* comes back to life. The hero can be shot, but return to see his daughter's high school graduation (*Carousel*). The passengers who sink on the *Titanic* are back for the final chorus. What greater magic can theater offer to a culture obsessed with eternal life, in which people try to sue doctors if a relative dies of a fatal disease, than resurrection for the final curtain? Above all, musicals are about defiant survival. No wonder show queens so adore Carlotta Campion's anthem in that greatest of all musicals, *Follies,* "I'm Still Here." It not only celebrates the survival of two divas, Carlotta and the aging diva playing her— Yvonne De Carlo, Carol Burnett, Dolores Gray, Eartha Kitt, Ann Miller—it celebrates the survival of gay men. We made it through J. Edgar Hoover, Joseph McCarthy, Stonewall, HIV, Jesse Helms, Pat Robertson, and we're still here.

The gay voice in the musical's spectacle and presentation speaks with some irony, some awareness of its artificiality. In discussing that gay voice one must discuss camp, an over-theorized but crucial term that explains many of the links between musical theater and gay culture. At their best, and sometimes their worst, musicals are camp. In recent years, a number of books have been written about camp that often confuse more than clarify.[7] David Bergman synthesizes much of what has been written to give the essentials:

> Camp is a style that favors "exaggeration," "artifice," and "extremity" . . . the person who can recognize camp, who sees things as campy, or who can camp [perform in an artificial or exaggerated or mock effeminate way] is a person outside the cultural mainstream . . . camp is affiliated with homosexual culture, or at least with a self-conscious eroticism that throws into question the naturalization of desire.[8]

Ragtime and *Titanic* aren't camp, but *Hello, Dolly!,* with its cartoon heroine, is. Vanessa Williams playing the sex symbol Aurora in *Kiss of the Spider Woman* isn't camp, but sixty-something Chita Rivera playing her is. Not everyone seeing these performances would perceive them as camp. It is a gay way of seeing. Eve Sedgwick sums it up this way:

> The typifying gesture of camp is really something amazingly simple, the moment at which a consumer of culture makes the wild surmise: "What if whoever made this was gay too?" Unlike kitsch-attribution, camp recognition doesn't ask, "What kind of debased creature could possibly be the right audience for this spectacle?" Instead, it says *what if:* What if the right audience for this were exactly *me?*[9]

For all the current writing on camp, it may be, like show queens and the shows and divas we adore, a thing of the past, a gesture toward gay culture and solidarity when members of that culture felt decidedly out of the mainstream. It may seem silly to feel nostalgia for an age that carried so much negative baggage, but in the era of the closet gay men could find joy in a shared alternative reading of mainstream culture.

Camp allows gay spectators to find gayness in shows that are ostensibly heterosexual and heterosexist. It allows us to identify with the indomitable, odd women, whom Ethan Mordden calls "amiable freaks," who are often at the center of musicals. For show queens, the musical offers a reading against its own ostensible heterosexuality. As the opera lover's imagination, with Verdi's help, could turn Zinka Milanov into a beautiful Ethiopian princess (though an opera queen would revel in the discrepancy between signifier and signified), the show queen could see *Company* as a coming-out story and *Mame* a celebration of fabulous queerness. In doing so, we were not imagining something that wasn't there, but seeing an implicit narrative its closeted creators deny, the way Josh, on the aptly named sitcom *Veronica's Closet,* denies the stereotypical signs of his gayness.

Oddly, the musical doesn't give us much to identify with among the men onstage. The male object of desire in the musical is seldom the leading man, often stolid and unerotic, crippled by his society's rigid definition of masculinity, but the gypsy, the chorus boy, who is allowed a freedom of expression and an overt sexiness denied the male star. The chorus boy carries the erotic charge of the show for the gay men in the audience. He carried connotations of gayness and has been depicted as gay as far back as the 1920s, offering to gay audiences a queer presence.

The 1996 film version of *Evita* showed how Hollywood has captured and made even more literal the allure of the diva and the erotic appeal of the chorus boy. Gay audiences were offered not only Madonna, the latest female icon for many gay men, in a diva musical, but a shower scene in which handsome young men, singing of their disdain for Mrs. Peron, barely covered their crotches with white towels held close enough to their genitals to reveal their size and shape.

In offering this moment of spectatorial pleasure that queers an already queer musical, the film of *Evita* is only making more literal what stage musicals have done for years.

In addition to discussing gay spectatorship, *Something for the Boys* will examine the gayness, closeted and uncloseted, of the musical, from the work of great writers like Lorenz Hart to the emergence of the gay musical in its Broadway and gay theatrical incarnations. I am particularly interested in musicals and songs that in some way depict the experience of gay men, from the lyrics of Hart, Porter, and Coward to the openly gay musicals of the 1990s. Two recent musicals (*When Pigs Fly* in New York and Neil Bartlett's *Night After Night* in London) dramatize their authors' very personal takes on the relationship of musical theater and gay culture. My take will be, perforce, equally personal if only slightly flamboyantly theatrical.

Musicals were always gay. They always attracted a gay audience, and, at their best, even in times of a policed closet, they were created by gay men. Case in point: Cole Porter's most celebrated musical was *Kiss Me, Kate* (1948), something of a comeback for a composer the show's producers initially didn't want because they thought he was "washed up." It proved Porter could be a contender in the post-*Oklahoma!* arena of "integrated" musicals. This smash hit backstage-cum-Shakespeare musical speaks volumes about the musical as a gay art form. Its producer, Arnold Saint Subber, was not only openly gay for 1948 but owned a gay bar. Its director was John C. Wilson, who had been Noël Coward's lover for many years and was still his manager. Music and lyrics were by gay Cole Porter and among the stars was randily bisexual Harold Lang. Few shows are more irrefutable proof of D. A. Miller's claim that:

> the Broadway musical, with "disproportionate numbers" of gay men among its major architects, is determined from the inside out by an Open Secret whose fierce cultural keeping not all the irony on a show queen's face can ever quite measure, nor all his flamboyance of carriage undo.[10]

I will argue that Lorenz Hart's lyrics, written in the 1930s and 1940s, create a very specific gay narrative, though, unlike Noël Coward, Hart never openly acknowledges the existence of gay desire. Lorenz Hart's lyrics create another story than that which is literally told in his musicals: a story of self-hate and desire for caddish men. After Stonewall, the gay subtext started to become the text in some shows, but, in another strange irony, Stephen Sondheim, who is considered to be the contemporary icon for show queens, is leerier of anything gay in his shows than Porter or Coward were. Yet his shows lend themselves to gay readings and the Sondheim cult is one of the most enthusiastic ones in contemporary musical theater, with its own very active e-mail discussion groups. Why should Sondheim be such a gay icon when he never writes about gayness? Despite his denials, his lyrics are open to queer readings.

Openly gay musicals have evolved since the Stonewall rebellion and have become part of the repertory of the commercial and fringe theater in the United States. In this era of regional and local theater, gay theater is produced in every major city and even backwaters like Durham, North Carolina. I will explore the considerable difference between Broadway's notion of a gay musical and that found in smaller gay-oriented theaters across the country. Broadway's version of a gay musical is always problematic—foregrounding a comforting, stereotypical version of gayness for the bridge-and-tunnel crowd. However, in the background something much more consonant with contemporary gay culture may be going on that highlights some of the problems of contemporary gay culture. The uncloseted gay musical, however earnestly it attempts to recreate gay experience, is not as complex or captivating as earlier closeted musicals. In fact, it often reflects the less attractive elements of contemporary gay culture. The few gay musical films actually are more complex and challenging, particularly *Zero Patience* and *Stonewall*.

Throughout the book, I discuss performances as much as scripts and scores. The allure of musical theater is in its performances, particularly its diva performances. I am interested in the interaction of performer, text, and audience, particularly gay audience, that makes a diva performance.

In a rare scientific mood, I begin by defining my terms, particularly the vague and politically charged nouns in my title.

MUSICAL THEATER. Let me take the easier part first. I mean musical theater in the broadest sense: musical comedy, musical plays, revue, some opera—though queer reception of opera has been written about quite a lot by now.[11] Throughout the book I will also discuss some Hollywood musicals. For many gay men, they were the only available form of musical theater. The gay national anthem is still "Over the Rainbow": the gay flag is a rainbow, as gay life is seen as a technicolor Oz, far away from the oppressive, homophobic black-and-white world in which many gay men were raised. Oz has dangers, as does living in the urban gay ghetto, but they're mitigated by the fabulousness of the place. There Dorothy and her queer friends can build their own family. Yes, our seminal work is a film, not a Broadway musical, but the cross-fertilization between Hollywood and Broadway is important. I agree with the historians who say that Hollywood in the 1930s gave the musical comedy a plot coherence it seldom had on stage previously and thus raised standards of narrative coherence for the stage musical.[12] It is in the Hollywood musicals of the 1930s, particularly the Fred Astaire–Ginger Rogers classics, that one also finds some fascinating sexual ambiguity as part of the comic sophistication. More recently, gay musical films have given us complex, fabulous recreations of our history.

There are subdivisions of musical theater that are important to understand in the context of this study.

MUSICAL COMEDY is a genre involving comedy, song, and dance that treats its subject matter through the lenses of burlesque, parody, or satire. It is usually a vehicle for star performances by male comics and/or Broadway divas, women stars who may be singers (Ethel Merman, Mary Martin, Julie Andrews, Barbara Cook), dancers who also are distinctive singers (Gwen Verdon or Chita Rivera), comics or actresses who can sing (Angela Lansbury or Carol Channing), or, occasionally, actresses who can't sing or dance (Lauren Bacall, Shirley Booth). Musical numbers exist to further the plot and/or to showcase the stars. They also exist to showcase the song itself. In the heyday of musical comedy from the end of World War I to the 1950s, hit tunes and Broadway theater music were synonymous. Musical comedy died out on Broadway and in Hollywood in the 1960s. In the 1990s, with very few exceptions and most of them unsuccessful (*The Goodbye Girl, Victor/Victoria, Big, The Life*), the musical comedy is extinct. Revivals of "classic" musical comedies (*A Funny Thing Happened on the Way to the Forum, Damn Yankees, Chicago, Cabaret*) do better business than new ones. Like many aspects of musical theater on this bridge to the twenty-first century, musical comedy has become an exercise in nostalgia. For show queens, the musical has become what opera was in my youth. Instead of comparing Tebaldi and Callas as Tosca, we compare Tyne Daly and Betty Buckley as Mama Rose with our memory of Ethel Merman and Angela Lansbury, or Bernadette Peters as Annie Oakley with our memory of Ethel Merman. Such nostalgia can work against a revival as easily as for it. Sarah Jessica Parker foundered on comparisons with Carol Burnett in *Once Upon a Mattress*. You've got to be a diva to compete with the memory of one.

The book of a musical comedy is funny, fast-moving, and contemporary, and often sharply satiric or at least topical. It could be about something prosaic like racketeering in the jukebox industry (*Do Re Mi*) or strikes in the garment industry (*The Pajama Game*), so long as it offers good ballads for the romantic leads, opportunities for song, dance, and jokes for the comic leads, a bit of ribaldry, and good dancing. If the musical takes place in the past, it is a spoof of a mythic past in which absurd anachronisms are part of the humor (*The Boys from Syracuse, A Connecticut Yankee, A Funny Thing Happened on the Way to the Forum, Out of This World*). If it seems to be fantasy, it allows for oblique social satire (*Finian's Rainbow, Flahooley*). If it verges on classical territory, like Shakespeare, it does so with tongue firmly in cheek (*The Boys from Syracuse*).

In addition to the stars, there were two crucial figures in the creation of a musical comedy: the composer (obviously) and the lyricist. The heyday of musical comedy was the heyday of witty, brilliantly crafted lyrics written by masters like Lorenz Hart, Ira Gershwin, Cole Porter, and Yip Harburg. Hart's ballads were achingly beautiful and often heart-rending. Gershwin and Porter wrote brilliant patter songs filled with verbal invention.

Musical comedy has died out for a number of reasons. The surfeit of television situation comedy has pretty much killed stage comedy. When you can get crypto-gay *Frasier* free every week, who needs the gag-rich musical comedy? Musical comedy used to be a vehicle for introducing popular music. For economic and cultural reasons more than artistic ones, current hit songwriters aren't interested in musical comedy. Burt Bacharach wrote one of the strongest scores for a 1968 musical comedy, *Promises, Promises,* but quickly returned to Hollywood. Now he writes for the agonizing postmodern whine of rock star Elvis Costello. The financial returns of writing for Broadway aren't as great or as instantaneous; the pressure is greater and artistic control less than pop composers accustomed to performing their own music are now used to. Randy Newman and Paul Simon have written (unsuccessful) musicals and Elton John has begun writing original musicals (if you can call a musical of *Aida* original!) in addition to the staged version of his scores for Disney cartoons, but these are middle-aged songwriter-performers who have had long, lucrative careers and can afford to devote some time to a less profitable effort. Moreover, few stars of film or television are interested in performing eight times a week for salaries considerably lower than those offered by Hollywood. Occasionally a Matthew Broderick, Sarah Jessica Parker, Whoopi Goldberg, or Lou Diamond Phillips will star in a musical, but Broadway is not their bread and butter. Nor is it the most efficient form of star exposure in the age of film and television. What is left are feeble attempts to turn comic films into musical comedies (*Victor/Victoria* and *Big*) and the Disney mass-produced live versions of their cartoons, an artistically pointless but financially successful enterprise.

Burt Bacharach may also be indirectly responsible for the end of the possibility of the Broadway musical-comedy star. He insisted that *Promises, Promises* (1968) sound like a good stereo recording, which began the wholesale miking of cast and band and the prominence of the "sound designer." I don't want to be too rough on the wireless microphone. I remember straining to hear in the upper balconies of the St. James and Shubert theaters before sound technology was developed. Nor do I think miking has killed good singing. There is a greater supply of good singers now than in the heyday of the musical, and they can now act and move as well. The megamusical demands good singing, itself a nostalgic contrast to the minimal musical competence of many rock singers. The music now is more difficult than it was forty years ago. However, sound technology does get in the way of the star turn. Like opera singers, Broadway stars are larger-than-life creatures meant to be captured live. Microphones domesticate them, reduce them. Would Merman or Channing have blossomed with a mike taped to her forehead? Would the distinctive quaver of Gwen Verdon work in the age of homogenized, miked Broadway soubrettes? There is an odd disproportion in the more distant reaches of a large Broadway theater between the tiny faces and bodies and the amplified sound more appropriate to magnified cinematic images, as there is a frustration with sitting close to the stage and hearing sound emanate not from the performer but rather from a nearby loudspeaker. Miked sound works better for large, serious musicals than for performer-centered musical comedies. The loud, odd belt voice of an Elaine Stritch or Ethel Merman made them androgynous, queer. The grand gesture that went with the big noise made them theatrical rather than realistic. These qualities, unnecessary with a mike taped to one's hairline, attracted the devotion of show queens.

Not all musicals are worthy of full-scale revivals. Though their scores may be brilliant, their books, once wittily timely, are now dated or clearly clumsy grout to hold the songs together. How can these less coherent musical comedies of the past be kept alive?

On Sunday afternoons from May through September, in a smallish cinema in the bowels of the Barbican Centre in London, impresario Ian Marshall Fisher produces his series "Discover the Lost Musicals." Talented casts perform semi-staged readings of musical comedies to piano accompaniment. After an informative fifteen-minute introduction, often by the composer or lyricist, if he is still alive, the shows are presented complete, featuring comics who know how to add the right amount of schtick to the comic scenes as well as singers whose voices may be smaller than those of the pre-microphone era, but who have sure technique and personal charm. There are no microphones here. Fisher alternates true novelties such as the 1951 flop *Flahooley* (music by Fain, lyrics by Harburg) with hits that are never revived like *Bloomer Girl* (Arlen, Harburg), *Plain and Fancy* (Hague, Horwitt), or *Music in the Air* (Kern, Hammerstein) and better known "classics" like the Gershwin brothers' *Of Thee I Sing* and *Strike Up the Band*. "Discover the Lost Musicals" is one of the hottest tickets in London and for good reason. In this intimate, no-frills setting, with the right performers, one appreciates not only the music and lyrics, but the books of these shows. One might not want to see a full-blown production of *Flahooley*, but in these circumstances the show is charming and touching, a document of Harburg's social conscience and anger at the McCarthy era. If a show's book is utterly incoherent, like Alan Jay Lerner's for *On a Clear Day You Can See Forever*, one doesn't mind as much in these modest surroundings and for about twenty dollars a ticket. The audience for these shoestring revivals is older straight couples and gay men. For all of us, this is an exercise in nostalgia, a show of love for an adored lost art form.

The American version of "Discover the Lost Musicals," "Encores! Great American Musicals in Concert," is, of course, bigger. The shows are performed with full orchestra in the 2,684-seat New York City Center. Star-studded casts (miked, of course) perform a condensed version of the book and more elaborately staged and choreographed musical numbers. The performances are as much about star turns as about the shows (Patti LuPone in *Pal Joey*, Tyne Daly in *Call Me Madam*) and are often immortalized on CD like full Broadway productions. There is nothing wrong with this. The original shows themselves were often star vehicles. One of these simpler productions, *Chicago*, moved onto Broadway in 1996 and has been far more successful than its over-produced original version. Now other cities are beginning series of musicals in concert.

"Discover the Lost Musicals" proves the vitality and durability of musical comedy. These shows were never built on spectacle, and while sentiment was one ingredient, tears were never the goal of their creators. They were, in the best sense, entertainment, but they depended on real talents: lyricists with a gift for language; melodists who knew how to write a tune that was memorable in its own right, not because you were sure you had heard it before, and probably had; and book writers who knew how to tie the songs and story together economically. The concert revivals demonstrate how good even unsuccessful musicals can be without the trappings that might have overwhelmed them. In 1996, the London series presented the Harold Rome/Jerome Weidman show, *I Can Get It for You Wholesale* (1962). In this simple environment, the mother-son relationship, which seemed stereotypical when originally played in the cavernous Shubert Theater in New York by Lillian Roth and Elliott Gould, was both touching and frightening when distinguished actress Sara Kestelman and talented young television star Andrew Lincoln were only a few feet away. The original show is only remembered because it introduced Barbra Streisand in the one-song role of Miss Marmelstein. She was the only performer large enough for the surroundings. What we saw in this concert version in 1996 was a better show than David Merrick produced in 1961, partly because *I Can Get It for You Wholesale* is really an intimate show. The play's the thing, and the concert version of the Broadway non-hit had a dramatic coherence and musical inventiveness not available in the megamusicals on the West End. Why aren't people writing shows like this? Because book writers are writing sitcoms, good pop composers are too greedy, and audiences want spectacle and sentiment.

If musical comedy is dead, the surviving (for a while) form of musical theater is that hybrid the MUSICAL PLAY, now less a play than it was in the days of its inventor, Oscar Hammerstein, because it has been shorn of most, if not all, of its dialogue. Only Sondheim, Hammerstein's protégé, remains committed to the combination of song and dialogue known as the BOOK MUSICAL, and I wonder if that isn't one of the reasons why he has never had a major hit. Yet Sondheim's *Sweeney Todd* is a primary influence on all the serious musicals that followed in its quasi-operatic sweep, the darkness of its story line, the uniqueness of its staging and scenery. One can see mementos of Hal Prince's staging of *Sweeney Todd* in *Les Misérables* and *Ragtime*. One hears echoes of its music everywhere. *Sweeney Todd* fathered the nineteenth-century megamusical. Its children include *Phantom of the Opera* (also directed by Prince), *Les Miserables, Titanic,* and *Ragtime;* and bastard spawn like *Jekyll and Hyde* and *The Scarlet Pimpernel* (although this show's real ancestor is *The Desert Song*). All the children lost the mordant wit of their forebear, the musical comedy, in favor of the sentiment of Oscar Hammerstein II. The current hit musical plays are, like their predecessors created by Hammerstein (*Show Boat, Carousel, South Pacific,* etc.), set in the past and based on "serious" romantic stories. They demand stage spectacle and are usually through sung with music that has its roots in Puccini and contemporary soft rock more than Gershwin or Porter.[13] What dialogue there is is underscored and spoken with orchestral accompaniment like a Hollywood movie (there were only three minutes in *Titanic* when the orchestra was silent). Indeed, the orchestrator is a crucial member of the creative team, giving each musical a characteristic sound.

What these musicals lack—other than the wit of the great musical comedies—is the space for a star turn. The script, score, and scenery are the stars, and the performers are interchangeable. The scenery doesn't stop moving long enough for a performer to make the kind of impression necessary for real audience excitement. There is certainly no room for improvisation. The megamusical is a theatrical machine in which the performers are the replaceable parts. As long as they sing well, look good, and get out of the way of the scenery, they are doing their job. It is interesting that the one recent Andrew Lloyd Webber megamusical that called for a star turn, *Sunset Boulevard,* was the least successful and most problematic of his shows (though also, in the hands of divas and divos like Betty Buckley and John Barrowman, the best). There are moments in *Ragtime* in which the leading performers are allowed to sing their hearts out on an empty stage, and for all the scenic and directorial brilliance of that production, those are the moments the audience cheers. Star turns work if a show allows them, and there are probably more brilliantly talented performers now than in the heyday of musical theater, but they have to compete with spectacle and technology and appear in works that are essentially ensemble pieces designed to outlast their original casts. *Ragtime* and the hit revivals of *Chicago* and *Cabaret,* filled with star turns, may turn the tide somewhat, but the hugely successful Disney extravaganzas allow even less humanity and individuality than *Phantom* or *"Les Miz."* Moreover, Broadway does not make stars anymore; television and film do. Unless hugely talented performers such as Brian Stokes Mitchell, Marin Mazzie, Judy Kaye, Audra McDonald, Judith Blazer, David Garrison, Rebecca Luker, Kevin Gray, Terrence Mann, Scott Jacoby, and Sam Harris leave the musical theater to star in a sitcom (as Malcolm Gets and Faith Prince have) or film, they won't gain the real glory of American stardom. The singers I name are the real singing actors. The last surviving Broadway clowns are already in Hollywood. They'll do a few weeks on Broadway during their vacation from their sitcom, but unlike Phil Silvers, Zero Mostel, or even Jackie Gleason, they won't stay long enough to recoup a show's investment.

The real star of the musical play is its director, who provides the show's look. Can one separate *West Side Story* or *Fiddler on the Roof* from the "look" Jerome Robbins gave those shows? Can one imagine *Les Miserables* without its staging, lighting, or revolving stage? The most recent Boubil-Schonberg musical, *Martin Guerre,* failed to attract audiences despite its lovely music and rich story, because it was not effectively staged and designed. Paul Simon's *The Capeman* foundered in great part because novice director Mark Morris knew how to design a tableau but not how to create dramatic moments, and he (or someone on the creative team) was reluctant to play to his strengths as a choreographer. He also didn't—or couldn't—do what any star director of a musical would do—demand radical changes in an incoherent, undramatic book. The directors of 1997 flops *Side Show, The Triumph of Love,* and *The Scarlet Pimpernel* received the lion's share of abuse from the critics. Spectacle is now a major part of musical theater. Look at photographs of musicals before the 1980s and compare those flat, simple settings to what audiences expect and get now. This is possible because of advanced technology, but such spectacle also expands the payroll of a musical. There are over forty people backstage in the London company of *Miss Saigon.*

The core of these musicals is also nostalgia—for a lost era, for past opulence, for the musical itself and the kind of music it celebrates. Show music no longer is contemporary pop music as it was in the pre-rock days. Now it is a hybrid of past forms, a soup of Puccini, Kern, Sondheim, and Barry Manilow.

Basically, the composers are experts at pastiche, imitations of earlier musical styles: Lloyd Webber's evocation of Lehár in the backstage scenes of *Phantom of the Opera;* Maury Yeston's panoply of pre–World War I music, particularly Elgar, for *Titanic;* Boublil and Schonberg's mix of Verdi, Lionel Bart, and French pop for *Les Miserables.* Sometimes the imitations are of other imitations. Stephen Flaherty's score for *Ragtime* sounds like Sondheim's *Assassins* and *Sweeney Todd* mixed with Charles Strouse's score for *Rags,* all three also pastiches. Its final rousing number is straight out of *"Les Miz."* That's OK; it works. Sondheim admits to a love for 1940s Hollywood film music, particularly the work of Bernard Herrmann. No composers were greater synthesizers of past music than the best film composers in the studio era: Korngold (a distinguished composer before he fled Europe), Steiner, Rozsa, Herrmann. Such melding of older musical styles, sometimes adding rock inflection, is exactly what composers of show music now do. Current musical scores are love songs to musical styles no longer central to our culture, except in the theater. At their best, the shows aim for a version of the transcendent power of opera. At their weakest, as in the scores of Frank Wildhorn, one feels that performers are singing along to parodies of pastiches. Yet this hybrid genre, theater music, has the power to move audiences. It is theatrical, though it no longer is "Top 40" popular music. What makes contemporary popular music successful doesn't always work in the theater. Paul Simon's score for *The Capeman* sounds terrific on the album released in advance of the first previews, but it isn't theatrical. Though brilliantly sung in the musical by three Latino singing stars, the songs seem to work against dramatic movement or involvement with character. The simple, sometimes nonexistent accompaniment doesn't work as well in the theater as a lush pit orchestra. On the few occasions one really hears a band, the audience wakes up. Jonathan Larson's score for *Rent* works because, though the trappings are rock, the score is solidly rooted in theater music. It wears its heart on its sleeve. There are young composers who could bridge the old forms and contemporary pop in new, exciting ways. Young singer-songwriter Rufus Wainwright was born to write musicals, but kids like him don't see the theater as part of their culture, however much they love theater music of the past. They're into clubs and concerts and, like most of the major composers of the past generation, performing their own music.

The quasi-operatic megamusical has until recently been a British form, though often directed and choreographed by Americans and equally successful in the United States. One of the most successful songwriting teams is the French duo Alain Boubil and Claude-Michel Schonberg. A number of new musicals began in Canada via Garth Drabinsky and his now defunct Livent organization.

The classic American musical was often written by immigrants or children of immigrants. So I am interested in the musical as an international form, but an English-language form.

REVUE—song and dance combined with satiric or parodic monologues and sketches—has been reborn particularly in gay theater. The grand, heterosexual-oriented *Ziegfeld Follies* of yore have been replaced by the fabulously tacky *Whoop-Dee-Doo!* and its successors. Sondheim's *Assassins* is a topical revue complete with comic skits, serious monologues, and song-and-dance numbers. In the 1950s, when I first became aware of theater, revue was still a common Broadway form. Its last great expression was Leonard Sillman's *New Faces of 1952,* which introduced performers such as Eartha Kitt, Paul Lynde, and Robert Clary. The latter two moved on to Hollywood and television, which co-opted and destroyed the stage revue format. Now intimate revue—cabaret—is having a resurgence. Its most successful incarnation is Gerald Alessandrini's *Forbidden Broadway,* a series of fabulously bitchy cabarets that parody Broadway shows and performers, of particular interest to people who still care passionately about such things (show queens). The revue is the perfect form for small theaters. It is also the ideal form for theatrical satire. Now that television no longer has classic variety shows like *The Carol Burnett Show,* which was in essence a revue, there may be a place for it again in theater.

GAY. Here we get into semantics. In that highly celebrated bit of recent gay/lesbian television history, Ellen DeGeneres and her writers confused things by having Ellen Morgan/Ellen DeGeneres come out as a "gay" character/performer, not a lesbian. For her and her collaborators (writers, producers, skittish folks at Disney and the ABC network), the term "lesbian" excluded gay men from her narrative, but the current umbrella word, "queer" (which covers gay/lesbian/bisexual/transgendered, and, to theorists like Eve Kosofsky Sedgwick, other categories like fat people), was too confrontative and connoted a type of radical politics the "real" and fictional Ellens and their creators and handlers and prospective sponsors did not want to be associated with. I use "gay" here meaning gay male, partly because, as a gay male, I feel more comfortable writing about gay males, and because musical theater has been the province of gay men more than lesbians (despite the rumors about some of the more celebrated musical divas).

I also use "gay" in a cultural/political sense. "Queer" has come to suggest a certain poststructuralist theoretical position (as in Queer Theory), a politics of difference that is one of the last bastions of sixties radicalism, and an opposition to bourgeois art forms like musical theater. I agree with the queer concern over the high cost of uneasy, somewhat fictive assimilation, but I disagree with the notion that sexual dissidence is the only important difference between gays and straights. As contemporary theater studies are being overshadowed by the quasi-anthropological, quasi-autobiographical, quasi-philosophical performance studies, this book will look reactionary to some of my colleagues, particularly those who see any Broadway offering as "bourgeois claptrap." This book and its author are proudly "gay," not angrily or deconstructively "queer," but that is a function of my age, my cultural education, and my social group. A graduate student of mine who is actually as "gay" as I told me that he had to use the language of queer theory because that was the language he came out into. I came out into the language of camp, the argot of an earlier, closeted time. Yet I am aware that what "gay" means to gay people and to heterosexuals has changed enormously, particularly in the past thirty years since Stonewall, and that there is no monolithic definition of gayness anymore than there is, as the fanatics of the Christian Right would have the world believe, one "gay lifestyle." Indeed, the binary opposition of gay/straight has always been a fiction: back in 1948, Kinsey had seven points on his gay–straight scale. In acknowledging homosexuality, most Western societies police a rigid formulation, gay or straight, though desire is usually far less definable and much more fluid. Gay people have done as much to police this formulation as straights. Calling someone gay when they desire both men and women is as inaccurate as calling them straight. For me, being gay has as much to do with an investment in certain kinds of culture as it has with my sexual proclivities.

GAY CULTURE. Is there an indigenous gay culture? Literally, the answer is no. Gayness is not like ethnicity. We do not share a language, race, or religion. Homosexuality, as a matter of fact, is different from most cultural markers in that one seldom shares it with his or her parents. A black kid is usually raised in a black family. A Jewish kid is usually raised in a Jewish family. A gay kid is usually raised in a straight family. Conversely, the gay parents I have known raised straight kids.

Moreover, if there is anything that could be called gay culture it is ever-changing, even from that time a century ago when, according to social constructionists, individuals first thought of themselves as having a sexual orientation and identity. Indeed, one could say there is now less gay culture in all meanings of the term than there once was—the price of assimilation that every minority group has paid.

Before the relative openness of today, lesbians and gay men created elements of a culture—an argot, patterns of dress from drag to the pansy look of the twenties to the clone look of the late seventies and early eighties, a history of sorts, a shared group of cultural icons—partly as a means of self-defense, partly to develop the protection of a tribe.

There may not have been a gay language, but there was gay slang. Men learned to switch pronouns in order to talk about homosexual relationships and to develop slang names for places for sex ("t rooms" for public toilets, "Ruth Ann's" for highway rest areas). One was taught these by gay mentors when one "came out" into gay culture. Coming out was not a public announcement of one's homosexuality, but an entry into the closeted gay world. The term came from the debutante's introduction to her exclusive social world. One was "out" to gay folk, not to straights. One's outness declared one's social and sometimes sexual availability. It declared one's solidarity with other gay men and lesbians. It also tacitly meant that one would protect the closeted status of others. "Outing" in the contemporary sense, even in private conversation, was a powerful taboo. To the extent one can talk about a gay culture, it was on one hand a culture of protection against oppression and, on the other, limited resistance—a way to survive and live out a sexual and social life in the face of legal constraints and the threat of social ostracism.

It is true that many "out" (in the old sense) gay men were involved in professions and avocations that fit under the general rubric "aesthetic": the arts, interior decoration and related fields like antique sales, clothes design, and hairdressing. People who are victims of prejudice tend to go into professions where they will be accepted. A hundred years ago Jewish people went into retail sales (clothing stores, for instance) and later into showbusiness. The film studios were run by Jewish men. Popular music in this country was composed by Jewish men and women. Film and other divisions of showbusiness were considered not respectable, so it was OK for Jewish folks, when they were less welcome in respectable professions, to enter and triumph in those riskier enterprises. There is actually more validity to the analogy of Jews to gays than blacks to gays. Like Jews, gay men have slowly, generation by generation, moved into "respectable" positions once forbidden them, so that there are now openly gay (in our contemporary sense) doctors, lawyers, and stockbrokers as well as hairdressers and interior decorators. In the old days when Jews ran Hollywood studios, they were very closeted about their Jewishness. Hollywood made few films with Jewish characters. Jewish actors changed their names and often their physiognomy. Now Hollywood, with many gay producers, writers, and agents, is slowly becoming less closeted about its homosexual writers, producers, and directors. Actors and their handlers (agents, lawyers, publicists) are still paranoid, but that will change as the Rupert Everetts and Ann Heches of this world have successful careers.

It is not surprising that, one way or another, pop and rock singers are leading the way in coming out of the closet. George Michael outed himself in his songs long before his star turn in a Los Angeles men's room. The role play and drag of much rock performance has always had much in common with gay performance. Actors worry that people will not be able to separate gay performer from straight role. Rock stars' personae have always been a bit queer.

There is a stereotype of gay culture. I don't mean the sexual stereotypes that we are all sexually promiscuous and predatory or that, like vampires, we are impelled to recruit children and seduce straight men, no matter how homely. I mean the cultural stereotype that gay men are all at least as good-looking as Rupert Everett, that we all have impeccable taste in our clothes and home furnishings, that we're all affluent enough to support these tastes, that we love opera and musical theater and collect recordings of same, that we worship homely female singers, particularly those with a self-destructive bent. That, with the exception of our love for Liza Minnelli, we deserve to be arbiters of exquisite taste, and that we are genetically programmed to deliver brilliant epigrams as often as possible.

For my generation of gay men, for those of us who came out before Stonewall, I think there is truth that many found our self-expression through culture and art. We were the heirs of Oscar Wilde. Beauty was our way of carving a niche for ourselves and of achieving some pride when we were considered tawdry, sick, and/or immoral. Some of us even aspired to the stereotype I describe.

In his confused but interesting book, *The Rise and Fall of Gay Culture*, journalist Daniel Harris describes the high value formerly placed on high culture by gay men as a means of signing their gayness to other gay men at a time when open communication was dangerous, but also as "a means for compensating for social disenfranchisement," a problem we solve through "the aestheticism of maladjustment":

> While the need for retaliation would seem to be too petty and mean spirited a
> motive for the creation of significant art, the aestheticism of maladjustment is

the source of some of the most valuable contributions that homosexuals have made to American society. It is this unconscious act of revenge and not a gay soul that is the secret to our creativity, the reason so many of us flock to the arts, why we become choreographers, playwrights, actors, and writers, why we are so disproportionately represented at music conservatories, why we staff the major theater companies, why we design the most famous lines of fashion, why we are antique collectors, opera queens, and gallery directors. Without the aestheticism of maladjustment, the American cultural landscape would be, if not altogether barren, at least considerably less interesting, with far fewer ballet companies, more bad films, tackier styles of clothing, and uglier inner-city neighborhoods full of the crumbling tenements that homosexuals gentrify . . .[14]

Harris has a point, however negatively stated. A lot of queens of my era created a world apart from the "manly" straight world. We didn't do well in sports, so screw sports. Gyms were not places we cared to spend hours in. We didn't have to join the military, so the hell with that. There were no noble wars to be fought anyway. So we went into the arts or into academia. We may have pined for a straight guy or two, but we had given up on their world as much as they had given up on us. Straights were dull; we were "pretty, witty, and gay." Many young men of my generation who came out into academia or the arts believed that being gay allowed us unlimited access to the world of the arts that we loved most. That was our notion of gay culture. Being gay meant being cultured.

Gay men of my generation were expected to be in the arts. That was sissy stuff anyway. There gay men could avoid the domination and loathing of the straight guys we still feared, as we had feared them in junior high. However, Daniel Harris doesn't realize that it was also a site of joy, of celebration, not merely a place of exile from the straight world. One could also add that the arts were a refuge only for those of us who found support for our interests at home and/or at school, and who could afford the training necessary to do what we wanted to do. We didn't think of it as revenge. We were the lucky ones.

What happened to us gay boys in the age of gay high culture? If we were lucky we made close friends with other guys who shared our interests and, it turns out, were also gay. If we were lucky we found older mentors. What may be difficult for younger gay men to understand is that homosexuality was not often discussed, nor was there necessarily any sex. But there was a support system and a social world of common interests, a major one being musical theater in all its manifestations, from Callas to Channing.

When, during my adolescence, I became aware of myself as a gay cocoon, a pre-emergent but self-aware gay male, in the bad old 1950s in New Jersey, certain aspects of what would now be called high culture—theater, particularly musical theater, and opera—were connected to the ways in which one could be "gay." That is, gayness was not only a sexual preference (the sex didn't exist for me and my friends until much later) but a cultural milieu. My fellow gay cocoons and I went to musicals and fell in love with Gwen Verdon's comic version of a temptress, or Judy Holliday belting "I'm going back / Where I can be me / At the Bonjour Tristesse brassiere factory," or Barbara Cook symbolically "coming out" as a sexual rebel in *Plain and Fancy*. We also fell in love with opera and knew that when we ran into another person from our university at the bar of the old Met, that person shared with us certain cultural and, in all likelihood, sexual preferences. At the quasi-mythical New Jersey Ivy League university I attended (because I didn't want to be too far from New York theaters and the Met), I became friends and shared a suite with a group of men who shared my love for musical theater. The closest friends of that group were gay or bisexual, though we never acknowledged that to each other until later. For many of us there was something called "gay culture" and it involved camp as a discourse and musical theater as an object of adoration. We knew statistics about opera and musicals the way straight kids knew baseball statistics. One of my roommates bridged both worlds—he watched baseball on television with the volume off while listening to opera. Perhaps musical theater was a safe way to express our difference. Perhaps it was a manifestation of the closet. I know that I could not fully connect with, accept or express my gayness until I also committed myself to working in and writing about theater, which is a much more religious site for me than church.

For many of us who moved to New York or San Francisco in the heady days after Stonewall, there was a new, far more sexual gay culture, a form of musical theater in which everyone could be a performer. Yes, I agree with performance-studies folk that many aspects of gay culture (in an anthropological sense) are performances that took a certain affinity for the theatrical into everyday life—the bars, the discos, the baths, the parades and protests and costumes. Unlike most parades, Gay Pride events are witty, ironic events, filled with inventive costumes and hilarious banners. I am neither drag queen nor leather queen, but I have friends who are and we can engage in verbal play because at heart we know what every gay man learns by puberty—everything involved with gender and sex is role-playing one way or another. That's what unites gay men.

I am particularly interested in a certain historical investment in what is now called high culture, though the Broadway musical had a complex connection to high culture. "I belong to a culture that isn't just sexual," Larry Kramer's Ned Weeks proclaims in *The Normal Heart:*

I belong to a culture that includes Proust, Henry James, Tchaikovsky, Cole Porter, Plato, Socrates, Aristotle, Alexander the Great, Michelangelo, Leonardo da Vinci, Christopher Marlowe, Walt Whitman, Herman Melville, Tennessee Williams, Byron, E. M. Forster, Lorca, Auden, Francis Bacon, James Baldwin, Harry Stack Sullivan, John Maynard Keynes, Dag Hammarskjold.[15]

One could add most American classical composers from Aaron Copland to Ned Rorem, David Diamond, Samuel Barber, and Gian Carlo Menotti; a number of our conductors from Dimitri Mitropoulos to Leonard Bernstein, Thomas Schippers, and Michael Tilson Thomas; our composers of musical theater including Hart, Porter, Coward, Ivor Novello, Bernstein, Sondheim, Jerry Herman, Stephen Flaherty, and, of course, *The Lion King*'s Elton John; our great stage directors and choreographers. Though they are less eager to admit it, one must acknowledge the number of gay performers as well.

This is not to say that there is a monolithic gay culture, but that gay men have in many ways controlled and defined American culture; that culture was a place where we could achieve power. There was always a mixed attitude toward the gay shapers of our culture. Some paranoids and homophobes see this cultural power as a threat to a healthy society—hence the witch hunts against the arts these days. Perhaps the ultimate extreme of this backlash is a recent sexual discrimination lawsuit pursued against the Metropolitan Opera by a heterosexual woman who says that only gay men can be promoted at the Met, even in backstage jobs. *Quel surprise!!!*

What Larry Kramer is doing with his list of gay greats, most of whom are artists, is appealing to history for contemporary validation. There is a gay history or, for the queer theorists, a history of same-sex desire and acts and oppression of them. In the early years of gay liberation that history empowered, but we live in an ahistoric, apolitical time and young gay men don't know or care about Stonewall or what went before it. They've got lots of nightclubs and all the sex they want. They don't care about oppression, even though what they do in bed is still illegal in twenty-one states (including the two in which my partner and I have homes), and the Supreme Court ruled that states still have a right to put homosexuals in jail for consensual private acts performed in their own bedrooms.

Daniel Harris's central thesis in his book *The Rise and Fall of Gay Culture* is that as homosexuality has become more acceptable, the urban gay man has become not a creator in the mold of Copland, Hart, Tennessee Williams, Merce Cunningham, Gianni Versace, or even the men who gentrified and restored urban areas and turned them into chic gay ghettos in New York, Chicago, D.C., and Miami, but that he has become the ultra consumer. He has become perhaps a more chic version of the rest of society. In *Plays Well With Others*, gay novelist Allan Gurganus makes this sad commentary about the decline of American cultural history:

Robert pointed out how, in the last boom of such proportions—the 1880s. . . .
New York society offered thanks for its good luck. Thanks registered as civic
tenderness. The earlier high-rollers founded the Metropolitan Museum, the
Museum of Natural History, the Metropolitan Opera, and on and on. But during
these gusher [nineteen] eighties, where did most of the good fortune go?
Directly up about sixty rebuilt noses.[16]

For many affluent folks, gay and straight, aestheticism was replaced by
hedonism. The creation of culture and taste was replaced by consumption. Porter
and Hart were replaced by jet-setting superstar Elton John sitting with the late
Princess Diana at Versace's funeral. The most displayed gay cultural product is
not a play, musical, painting, ballet, or symphony, but underwear.

Is there a gay culture? Not exactly. But gays have shaped American
culture in profound ways. The exclusive world of high culture of the thirties
and forties that I shall write about has exploded into gay men's taste, shaping
much of the nineties. In 1947, Tennessee Williams wrought a revolution in
American drama by making a male character, Stanley Kowalski as played by
Marlon Brando, the object of the gaze and of desire. A man was placed in the
specular position heretofore held by women. A man was looked at, admired,
lusted after. In the fifties, a generation of gay actors—Tab Hunter, Sal Mineo,
James Dean—offered an alternative to the rugged masculine ideal of
Humphrey Bogart and John Wayne. Another gay actor, Cary Grant, defined
elegant aging, as, twenty years before, he had been the first movie star to utter
the word "gay" in our sense of the word in a film. Calvin Klein's giant photos
of beautiful near-naked men on billboards sell underwear, but they also sell
the right for everyone to look at and admire the bodies of buff young men.
Which is to say that gay men have changed the way America looks at men.
This is as important in many ways to our society as the revolution wrought by
straight Bill Gates and other computer wizards.

To me and many of my peers, gay culture meant music, opera, the theater.
That is true for some of my gay students, but not for all. Many are more interested
in joining fraternities and sharing the culture of their straight peers. Some can
still do an Ethel Merman imitation, but as they have been assimilated into the
larger culture, they have absorbed much more of straight culture than my peers
cared to or could. Moreover, the culture productions we loved have become
straighter. Opera is now more popular than ever, but gay men make up a much
smaller proportion of its audience. Musical theater is also more a mass
entertainment than ever and offers less of the grand flamboyance and wit that
made it popular with gay men. There's nothing gay about *"Les Miz"* or *Titanic,*
except many of the guys onstage, of course.

In the early nineties, in my book *Acting Gay,* I could write that theater was important to gay men because it was the place where we could see ourselves, our lives and our problems, dramatized. We were seldom on television or in film. Now there is a gay character on just about every sitcom, and every adult Hollywood comedy has a cute, if sexless, gay male who, stereotypically, is the voice of morality and fair play in the movie. None of these television shows or films show the lives we really lead, the problems we really have. They certainly never show our love lives. Gay men are still the witty, elegant sidekicks. In 1949, in the classic Katharine Hepburn–Spencer Tracy film *Adam's Rib,* David Wayne played a clever, artistic crypto-gay next-door neighbor. He was a clever composer of pop tunes. In 1997, Rupert Everett and Greg Kinnear played clever, artistic, openly gay next-door neighbors with no more connection to a love life or a gay social life than Wayne had fifty years before. However, though limited, the films and television shows offer the kind of validation gay men got only from theater five or ten years ago.

Gay drama has dwindled in the past five years despite the success of *Angels in America* and *Love! Valour! Compassion!* Most recent successful gay plays have been parades of nude men. Total male nudity is the only taboo left, after all, in television and film. And gay plays with naked male bodies sell out. Plays without them don't. But gay theater survives in small fringe playhouses where actors make little or no money and playwrights receive paltry royalties, if any.

A character in one of my plays says, "You know what we gay men have earned from Stonewall, liberation, survival of AIDS? We've earned the right to be the two things we ran screaming from. We've earned the right to be suburban and boring." It is interesting that at the end of the twentieth century, gay and straight writers are writing plays and films about Oscar Wilde. Celebrating Wilde one hundred years after his death is celebrating not only a martyr, but the representative of what we are quickly losing: aestheticism, flamboyance, elegance, and deconstructive wit. For my generation, that was what we called gay culture and we found it in the musical—by being either onstage or its most devoted audience. As I elaborate in the next and also in the last chapter, that culture may be on the wane and we remaining show queens a vestige of a past that wasn't all bad.

LINE DANCERS
AND SHOW QUEENS

What do you do with queens?
Stand them around a piano and play selections from Gypsy.
—*The Nanny*

In this chapter, I want to focus on the gay men in the audience at musical theater and on the relationship of the stereotype of the "show queen" to gay self-definitions at the end of the twentieth century. I don't want to suggest that all show queens are alike or that no show queens are "straight looking and acting." I will suggest that show queens predominated at a moment in gay history when the closet was still an operative principle for gay men.

Like most current mainstream representations of homosexuality, the NBC sitcom *Will and Grace* demonstrates television's anxieties about presenting homosexuals at all, but something else is going on that is pertinent to my project. *Will and Grace* sums up some of the tensions gay men now have about their relationship to codes of masculinity. Will, the gay lead character, has no identifying sign of gayness other than the assertion that he is gay. He even lives with a (particularly irritating) straight woman, his college pal, Grace. Both have the generic upper-middle-class professions of current sitcom characters: he's a lawyer; she's an interior decorator. Will is generically good-looking, no more flamboyant than most sitcom straight heroes. Compared to the Crane brothers on *Frasier* or supposedly straight Richard on *Caroline in the City,* he's super butch. Will is, of course, played by an openly straight actor. In the coding of the show, Will is a "normal" gay, "easily assimilated" as the song goes, "straight looking and acting," and, like a good gay boy, sexless and uninterested in the gay "scene." Will has no love life and only one gay friend, Jack, whom he mocks mercilessly. Jack (played by the wonderful Sean Hayes) is a real queen. He's cute rather than handsome, flamboyant, and a tad bitchy. He also is unemployed, reinforcing the old stereotype that queens can't fit into the bourgeoisie. You laugh at Jack—he has the lines—but wonder at his friendship with Will. In the first scene of the first episode of *Will and Grace,* Will and Jack are playing poker with straight friends of Will's. Will mocks Jack's obvious gayness, to the amusement of the straights.

Jack is important so that viewers see what Will isn't. The show would be funnier and more real if it were about Jack (though humorless gays would scream "stereotype"). It's OK to be gay like Will, but part of being gay like Will is that you "dis" queens like Jack. *Will and Grace* represents a current tension in gay culture, particularly among younger men. On a recent string on Duke's lesbian-gay-bisexual e-mail list, gay fraternity boys spoke of how it was all right to be openly gay in a fraternity as long as you played by the rules of gender appropriate behavior. No sissies or queens, please. Give me Jack any day! Jack, by the way, plays the piano and sings show tunes, including Sondheim. Among other things, he's a show queen.

In his history of gay culture in New York City in the first half of this century, George Chauncey notes that effeminacy was for many men an empowering and identifiable sign of gayness. A "fairy culture existed in New York from the 1890's and came to represent all homosexuals in the public mind."[1] In the twenties, this culture centered in and around the theater district. This fairy or pansy stereotype made it possible for less flamboyant gay men to "pass" more easily. Though the battles at Stonewall Inn were fought by drag queens, the post-Stonewall period has been marked by gay men's discomfort with signs of effeminacy. However, effeminacy and its sister, aestheticism, were connected to the gay man's identification with various aspects of high culture and with camp, the common language of pre-liberation gay men. In the period George Chauncey treats (1890-1940), even "queers" who eschewed the fairy image were connected to fairies by their investment in the arts:

> The boundaries between the styles of fairies and queers were permeable, not
> only because both groups sometimes engaged in similar forms of behavior, but
> also because queer culture encouraged a style of dress and demeanor and an
> interest in the arts, decor, fashion, and manners that were often regarded by
> outsiders as effete, if not downright effeminate.[2]

One common language for gay men was musical theater, less rarified than opera or ballet, but equally larger than life. Musical theater may be heterosexist, focusing traditionally on female display, but it is also flamboyant and excessive. What could be more camp than the costumes of the Ziegfeld chorines or the androgyny of female musical divas? It is a stereotype that gay men have been particularly invested in musical theater, indeed that love of musical theater is a sign of gayness. Now, when the boundaries between "straight looking and acting" gay men and queens are much more definite, musical theater itself becomes an area of contention.

LINE DANCERS

On a warm summer Sunday, we emerge from the Washington, D.C., underground, the Metro, at Federal Triangle, near the new Ronald Reagan Building (how straight can you get!), to confront not the usual Sunday quiet, but crowds, music, tents. Pennsylvania Avenue and a number of the adjacent side streets have been closed to traffic. It is D.C. Gay Pride day, but this particular manifestation of the annual celebration of gay survival in the face of homophobia and official oppression demonstrates not the celebration of a coherent, separate culture but the lack of one. At the large stage at one end, gay community leaders are introduced, but no one in the crowd seems particularly interested in politics. Entertainers perform who demonstrate a lack of a culture different from the mainstream. A loud girl band plays loudly, and the lead "singer" proudly imitates the foul-mouthed banter of male punk rockers of the eighties. Being able to shout "fuck" seems to be some sort of liberation for her. Since the word is no longer forbidden as it was in my youth, but a staple of film and cable television, her shouts seem only quaint. Janis Joplin did it better twenty years ago. What we see is typical of pride celebrations around the world; they are now a combination of carnival and shopping mall, a far cry from the political events they once were. At this Washington celebration, twice the D.C. Cowboys were brought on the stage to do their sexually suggestive country-and-western routines. They strike a more responsive chord in the mostly male audience, but they're playing out a parody of what is happening down the street.

At the largest tent at the festival hundreds of guys line dance. The crowd thins when the emcee tries to teach a Macedonian folk dance. That's not butch enough and doesn't go with the line dancing drag also being sold at booths around the festival—cowboy boots, ten-gallon hats, fancy shirts. The fact that line dancing drag was also Ronald Reagan's favorite costume as he rode his horse around his California estate is not without its ironies. Line dancing has become a way gay men can perform musical numbers when they're past the age of the buff young dancing boys at the gay nightclubs. More important, it allows gay men to perform musical numbers without entering into the old-fashioned, bourgeois, effeminate (God forbid!) world of musical theater.

I observe the same phenomenon in other cities: giant London, where AIDS charities like CRUSAID sponsor line dancing nights. In cities across the United States, gay bars with names like Stagecoach and Corral bring in droves by having line dancing nights and even, on slow nights, offering dancing lessons. What can be said of line dancing? It is American, though with European roots. It is democratic—anyone can do it, though you need to be able to afford the costume, which is its own form of drag. It is masculine and built on a homoerotic mythos of the Old West where cowboys formed a male culture that must have had its erotic moments—it was your fellow cowboy or your horse on those lonely, horny nights on the range. Insofar as there is a gay culture now, for line dancers it seems to connect with myths of the manly West. John Wayne must be spinning in his grave! Gay rodeos are extremely popular events all over America. I wish I heard more irony from the folks who attend them.

Line dancing is a recent and no doubt temporary manifestation of participatory musical theater for gay men. Gay culture is built in part on musical spectacle: drag shows, pride parades, disco (the most fabulous musical production number fifteen years ago was a disco full of queens dancing to "It's Raining Men." It put Busby Berkeley to shame!), and the high-techno dance clubs that have replaced disco. In the past, we worshiped the most flamboyant of musical divas. Disco allowed us to believe we were the divas. Why pay to see a musical when we could star in our own? Line dancing, however, seems to contain the most specific political message. Line dancing and western drag say "I'm gay, but I'm no sissy," which is the watchword of the majority of gay men these days.

But, honey, all this is a macho drag act, as real as *Oklahoma!* Less real, actually. *Oklahoma!* (1943) was a deliberate act of nostalgia for the homespun, simple, nineteenth-century America we were fighting to maintain in World War II. There, in the cavernous St. James Theater, a block from Times Square, was presented a view of people in touch with nature, a coherent community in which gender roles were clear. Good men were sensitive and could sing "Oh, What a Beautiful Mornin'." Sexually active women were funny, as always on Broadway ("I Cain't Say No"), and the good fella got his girl. This picture of homespun western America was written by New Yorkers. A few years ago, at Atlanta's Actor's Express, director Chris Coleman attempted a revisionist *Oklahoma!* set in a New York rehearsal hall in 1941. A flamboyantly gay director begins a rehearsal when news of the Pearl Harbor attack comes over the radio. In this environment, *Oklahoma!* becomes a show about reinforcing a mythical America at a specific moment in history, a myth that tries, among other things, to erase homosexuality, which, according to historians like Allan Bérubé, was exploding

1. Can a show queen be a cowboy? Michael West as Howard in his "Dream Curly" costume. *When Pigs Fly.* Photo by Gerry Goodstein.

2. (Next page) John Kriza as Billy the Kid. Courtesy Dance Collection, The New York Public Library for the Performing Arts, Astor, Lenox and Tilden Foundations

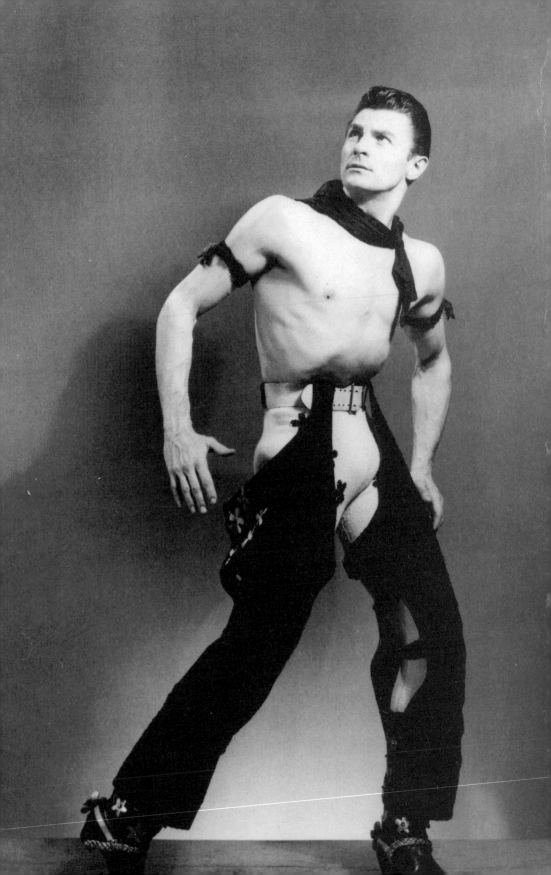

in port cities like New York during World War II.[3] The worst thing for a character in *Oklahoma!* is not to fit in to a specific code of masculinity that includes sexual repression. The Rodgers and Hammerstein folks told Coleman to cease and desist. Do *Oklahoma!* straight, in all senses of the word, or don't do it at all![4] They were within their rights, but I would much rather see Coleman's rethink of *Oklahoma!* than a mindless revival of the original. When the lumbering film version premiered in 1955, the war was long over, but *Oklahoma!* had resonance for America in the era of the Cold War and the House Un-American Activities Committee and the McCarthy witch-hunts. A happy, dancing community cheerfully purged its alien element.

By the time *Oklahoma!* opened in 1943, composer Aaron Copland had already created a nostalgic "western" music for his ballet scores for Agnes de Mille's *Rodeo* and Eugene Loring's *Billy the Kid,* and he later did the same for the Shaker world of Martha Graham's *Appalachian Spring* by combining traditional folk melodies with his sophisticated Stravinskian rhythms and brash dissonances. The Billy the Kid of Copland's score and Eugene Loring's choreography is a strange Freudian creation—the outlaw who loves his mother. He is also, for the early 1940s, an eroticized, one could say homo-eroticized, figure whose fetishizing costume—no shirt, armbands, cuffs, and chaps over tights—is a queerer version of the butch cowboy image than contemporary gay men consume and perform. Billy is an outlaw and a narcissist. He dances alone and he seems to be turned on by his isolated dancing. In his duets, he tends to face away from the woman, and his scenes of violence with other men seem more erotic than his moments with women. Like *Oklahoma!*, *Billy the Kid* is framed by a vision of a frontier community, but in the ballet it is a line of dour people violently working the land, not happy folk going to a picnic. Billy seeks a space of freedom and pleasure outside that community, in contrast to its harsh, angular, downward-directed movements. *Billy the Kid* opens up the possibility of gay readings. Billy has a girlfriend, but his strongest relationships are his violent ones with men. Ironically, the score for *Billy the Kid,* which defines western music and is imitated in the scores of dozens of western films, was written by a Brooklyn-born, Jewish, gay composer in Paris.

There were postwar versions of the western musical. Lerner and Loewe's *Paint Your Wagon* (1951) in which the chorus men sing the haunting hit "They Call the Wind Maria" as well as the exuberantly silly "Hand Me Down That Can o' Beans." Or Harold Rome's *Destry Rides Again* (1959) with Andy Griffith in the Jimmy Stewart role and Dolores Gray in a brassy, more innocent version of Marlene Dietrich's diva of the saloon. Or Cy Coleman's *Wildcat* (1960) with Lucille Ball and the chorus boys digging oil wells. Viennese Loewe and New Yorkers Rome and Coleman actually have a better handle on Coplandy western sounds than Rodgers. The western musical was an Eastern urban fabrication killed by the proliferation of westerns produced by Hollywood for the big screen and for television.

The most successful recent western films have been about urban Jewish guys (the type that might have written a western musical fifty years ago) going out West and finding out that they are "men" after all, worthy of Jack Palance's respect. To test one's manhood, one must leave one's women in the city and go into rugged terrain and confront nature and one's own wussiness. Only by connecting to the old western mythos can middle-class men, straight and gay, avoid being sissies.

Howard Crabtree's hilarious gay musical revue, *When Pigs Fly* (1996), opens with Howard appearing in his high school guidance counselor's office dressed in his "Dream Curly" costume—not the Curly who sings the love songs, but the Curly of the Agnes de Mille dream ballet. Howard dreams of a show created by all the guys who wanted to be Dream Curlys, guys who were too sissy to play the faux macho Curly, but who could dance the dream ballet (real men don't dance). The opening number is sung by five Dream Curlys in flamboyant versions of cowboy drag. This is an old-time, outrageous vision of gayness: flamboyant, effeminate, ironic, and mocking of straight icons and values. Above all, *When Pigs Fly* defies the anti-sissiness of many contemporary gay men—the anti-sissiness at the heart of gay line dancing.

I'm a kid from the suburbs who dreamed of getting to the city and got instead to Durham, North Carolina, where country-and-western dancing was definitely a heterosexual ritual that smacked of Jesse Helms and the Religious Right. For some reason, I had never worried about whether or not I was a sissy. I had built my self-image and my life on the certainty that I was. And a six-foot-five sissy to boot! The Big Bad Bullies knew I was a sissy before I did. They knew I wouldn't want to get in trouble with the teacher by fighting back. But if one got really good at something sissy, if one knew more about opera than anyone else and did theater really well, it didn't matter. Then one discovered kindred spirits and discovered that at least a few of them were also gay:

> There's a place for us,
> Somewhere a place for us.

I never dreamed that place was the Wild West. No irony there, darling. Nor is there any irony in line dancing. These guys are serious. They aren't even smiling. I did dream the place for me might be musical theater.

Recent Pride celebrations I have attended have been more like frat parties than gay gatherings. There has been little outrageousness beyond some water-pistol fights. There were a lot of pierced nipples and navels, a bit of leather, but mostly buff young guys in T-shirts and shorts showing off their well-sculpted bodies. There were also a fair amount of middle-aged men looking at but not interacting with the buff young men. Age is their greatest fear. There were lots of booths selling gay paraphernalia—gay pride T-shirts, hats, bumper stickers, rainbow tchotchkes. There was a booth offering gay matrimonial planning. United Airlines was giving away discount coupons and brochures for gay trips. Various gay and gay-friendly religious organizations had booths. The Log Cabin Republicans were there—their booth was manned (personneled?) by the dourest-looking guys I saw, but that seemed appropriate. In the age of Trent Lott and Jesse Helms, it takes either a surfeit or a total lack of irony to be a Log Cabin Republican.

The most interesting little drama I saw at this Washington Pride celebration involved a young family of tourists; blond mother and father and their blond children. They had somehow gotten lost in their sightseeing and had found themselves in the middle of Gay Pride. The looks on their faces showed that they knew they weren't in Kansas anymore. The father had his back to the festivities on Pennsylvania Avenue (not that anything obscene was going on, but he simply didn't know how to process the event). The mother said to the gay man who gave them directions how to get out of there: "If there are this many gay people in this one city, how many must there be in the country?" And numbers were the point of the whole affair—to show ourselves and any tourists who strayed upon the scene how many of us there are. But it showed no more of a "community" or a "culture" than any shopping mall. Folks talked to the people they came with and with friends they ran into. They didn't talk to strangers. They bought things. D.C. is a predominantly black city, but this was a very white gathering. A separate Black Pride had been held a few weeks before.

Feeling outside of groups is usual for me, and I certainly felt outside of this one, partly because I didn't see an inside. Assimilation seems to have won. We're just like everybody else. Not that I am a Radical Queer. Their difference is not mine either. But I look for some irony, some wit, some flamboyance, some theatricality.

The western end of the D.C. Pride festival was right in front of the National Theater where a touring company of *Chicago* was playing. Even in its 1996 pared-down, black-box revival, *Chicago* is a grand blend of real life and flamboyant theatricality. The show captures brilliantly the self-promotion and cult of celebrity that travesties even justice. What an irony that Madonna, the ultimate self-promoter, is rumored to star in the movie. She may be gay-friendly and a gay icon, but it is too much a case of typecasting. In the decade of O.J., Jon-Benét Ramsey, and Jerry Springer, what could be more timely than

Chicago? But the marquee for *Chicago* seemed like an artifact, a surreal detail in the backdrop for this non-carnival. It was specific but irrelevant. Musical theater, once central to gay culture, is now a remnant of the past.

I remember Pride celebrations in the early 1980s when there were hundreds there, not thousands, and the rousing moment came when some cabaret divo sang "I Am What I Am" from *La Cage aux Folles.* The hymn of gay pride came from a musical! In the late 1990s, we get the D.C. Cowboys doing a dance that looks like a mad Agnes de Mille dream ballet made out of the raping of Ned Beatty in *Deliverance.* Whahoo!

Oh, dear, this is turning into a lament, one of those "whatever happened to the good old days" things. I am aware that my good old days were supposedly days of oppression, though I didn't feel oppressed. Daniel Harris tells us in a very camp sentence: "The grain of sand, our oppression, that irritated the gay imagination to produce the pearl of camp, has been rinsed away, and with it, there has been a profound dilution of the once concentrated gay sensibility."[5] Camp is a language of the closet, we are told, and most great gay art came from closeted gay men. I don't want the closet back, but I want some fabulousness. I guess I want gay culture, if there is such a thing, to be more like a musical and less like a shopping mall or a gym or the Nashville Channel.

I know folks on the queer left hate it, but I loved Terrence McNally's *Love! Valour! Compassion!* I loved the ad for the movie with the eight guys in their *Swan Lake* drag, with its link of gay culture and high culture. These guys weren't just watching *Swan Lake.* They were dancing it. It was lovely, camp, ironic, wistful—fabulous! Since then we've had an even more fabulous *Swan Lake* with sexy male swans and homoerotic pas de deux in London, L.A., on Broadway; on the BBC as Christmas entertainment and even broadcast on ever-cautious-about-gay-stuff PBS.

I ponder recent Pride celebrations I have attended and wonder what it means to be gay now. It meant something very specific to me (beyond the sexual stuff). Does it now mean only the sexual stuff? Or a masculine image to be consumed with the tiniest dash of irony: buff gym boy, leatherman, line dancer, bear? "Straight looking and acting?"

In 1998 *The New Yorker* ran an interview with brilliant American countertenor David Daniels. The writer, Mark Levine, was interested in the queerness of the countertenor voice, a female-gendered voice emanating from a male body. Daniels grew up imitating the sopranos of his youth, Leontyne Price and Montserrat Caballé, though he aspired to be the next Franco Corelli, the most flamboyant tenor of the 1960s. However, according to Levine's article, Daniels seems most concerned with projecting a masculine image. The article notes:

> Offstage, Daniels, who is thirty-one, turns out to be comfortably and unmistak-
> ably a *guy*. He is polite to his elders, but out of their presence he can discharge
> a stream of raunchy comments. He wears jeans and gym socks almost
> everywhere he goes, and he likes dining out at Burger King. During a week of
> opera performances in Miami, he invited me to his hotel one evening to watch
> college basketball—fortified by warm beer and pizza from the box.[6]

However much Levine found Daniels to be a *guy,* his article presented himself
and Daniels as two men deeply conflicted about masculinity and gayness.
Daniels does not want to be read as a eunuch (a stereotype about men with high
voices), so he sports a growth of beard. He is very cagey about his gayness and
the assumption (often correct) that countertenors are gay:

> Inevitably, Daniels must contend with other questions about "masculinity." "The
> only expectation people have of a countertenor is that he's gay," Daniels tells
> me over breakfast one morning. The subject was bound to come up, and when
> it does, Daniels's charming professional manner becomes edgy. "Straight
> countertenors are few and far between, but they do exist," he says.[7]

Is it Daniels or Levine who sees masculinity and gayness as opposites? Later,
Levine reluctantly admits that Daniels is gay but "remains guarded about his
private life." Clearly David Daniels above all wants to be seen as "straight
looking and acting." Heaven forbid that this countertenor who spends his
professional time singing falsetto, and does imitations of star sopranos at parties,
should be thought a sissy! I found Levine's article on Daniels a fascinating study
of an extreme case of the anxiety about masculinity contemporary gay men feel.
"'I'm a man,' Daniels says, sounding weary from having to insist on the
obvious." And we get weary from listening. Recently novelist John Rechy,
longtime chronicler of the darker side of urban gay life, wrote:

> The physical appearance of gay men is determined by considerations of sexual
> attraction. A new breed of gay men is being shaped by its aversion to
> "femmishness." The trend is toward a body with tight muscles formed by
> machines that will not disturb hairstyle. The walk is becoming a strut in equal
> parts Madonna and Clint Eastwood. Hands increasingly cling to the wrist in
> horror that idle hands may relax into a limp wrist, that hips may swish. . . . If
> that direction is pursued, there will emerge a figure of effeminate masculinity,
> a new, conforming "stereotype" as identifiably gay as drag or leather—created
> to avoid looking gay.[8]

Before one starts lamenting current trends, it is important to note that the history of the majority of post-Stonewall gay culture has been one of avoiding looking like a sissy. The clone look of the liberated 70s—T-shirt, jeans, work boots— was an attempt to look straight but be recognizably gay at the same time. In his essential study, *Gay New York,* George Chauncey notes about turn-of-the-century relations between fairies and other men:

> Becoming a fairy offered men a way to make sense of their feeling sexually different from other men and to structure their relations with other men. Because the fairy was the central pejorative category against which men had to measure themselves as they developed their gender and sexual style, all men had to position themselves in relation to it.[9]

Now gay men, as well as straight men, have positioned themselves against the image of the fairy and its tamer form, the sissy. If the fairy and the sissy allowed straight men a model of straightness—being not sissy—it also allowed gay men a version of gay normalcy and the possibility of assimilation. Non-sissies can be doctors, lawyers, stockbrokers. Sissies remain in the traditionally gay occupations that give them less resources for consuming the American dream.

In McNally's *Love! Valour! Compassion!,* Buzz, the show queen, is the most flamboyant of the gay men, the one who wears a "Nancy" T-shirt or an ensemble consisting entirely of an apron and high heels. Buzz is the most negative of stereotypes for the play and film's detractors. Yet musical theater is in the best sense the queerest of art forms, the one in which gender is most clearly a performance that can be exploded or radically altered, the form in which everything can be seen as drag. It is the most openly flamboyant of art forms. It may be the art form of choice for the few courageous enough to be sissies at the turn of the twenty-first century, who are willing to be other than "straight looking and acting."

SHOW QUEENS

An exhilarating moment. It is a couple of minutes before a rehearsal of *Twelfth Night.* I am talking to one of my student cast members who is playing Fabian, who in my production is the flamboyant hairdresser to Olivia. For some reason, this twenty-year-old goes into a perfect imitation of Ethel Merman doing "You Can't Get a Man with a Gun." He is enthusiastically joined by a heretofore quiet freshman sitting twenty feet away. Ethel Merman was not on television or film during these kids' lifetimes, but they can do Ethel Merman imitations and know all the lyrics to the song. I know one of these kids is gay and assume from this performance and other clues that the other is as well. In fact, this joint Ethel Merman imitation is a kind of signaling and bonding ritual for the two young men. This, too, is gay culture, the maintaining of a flamboyant tradition of musical theater and musical divas these kids have never experienced first hand, but somehow know. Perhaps Billy in the 1998 film *Billy's Hollywood Screen Kiss* is right. Perhaps some gay men do have a show tune gene. At the dress rehearsal of *Twelfth Night* a gay student not in the cast comes backstage in full Carol Channing regalia to wish the cast well. Some young gays are not line dancing, nor are they buying into the cultural assumptions of line dancing. They're doing musicals, and for them doing musicals is in some way part of their gayness.

> Predictive sign: a fondness for musical comedy. I worried, listening to records
> of *Darling Lili, Oklahoma!,* and *No, No, Nanette,* that I would end up gay: I
> didn't know the word "gay," I knew about homosexuality only from *Time* feature
> stories about liberation, but I had a clear impression (picked up where?) that
> gays liked musical comedy.[10]

For Wayne Koestenbaum, musical comedy was a way station to opera. Musical comedy evoked a closeted boy's fear of something for which he had no word but homosexuality, though even that word was linked to liberation. Like the progression from marijuana to heroin, listening to Carol Channing and Julie Andrews would escalate to listening to Renata Tebaldi and Koestenbaum's beloved Anna Moffo. Opera and coming out are equated for Koestenbaum, but musicals were the sign that one was gay. Where did the young Koestenbaum get the idea that a fondness for musical comedy was a symptom, an early warning sign, of gayness? It was, as one of my professors used to say about certain prevailing cultural patterns, "in the air." Even D. A. Miller, in a book-length essay on the subject, has to accept the link between musical theater and gayness as a given: "it is impossible to describe the appeal—let me insist: the *organized* appeal—made to gay men by the post-war Broadway musical,"[11] which addressed gay men "as directly as if it had been calling out our names."[12] Gay men and the musical was a stereotype so prevalent and, for some, so true that a source becomes undetectable. One cannot possibly find patient zero.

In Paul Rudnick's script for the 1997 film *In and Out,* Howard's love for musical theater is, along with his tidiness and limp wrists, a sign of his closeted homosexuality. Howard plays the Merman cast album of *Gypsy* in his private moments at home and worships Barbra Streisand. He only gets physically violent when friends say Streisand was no good in *Yentl.* The audience laughs in recognition. Musicals = gay is a stereotype. To exist as such, it must have some familiarity for an audience. Where do such stereotypes come from? *In and Out* was written by a gay satirist, and for the film's iconography to work for a mass audience, its stereotypes had to have some popular currency, but it is not necessarily true that the stereotype has been imposed from the outside as a means of defining and marginalizing gay men.[13] It could be that the currency of the stereotype came from gay writers in the popular media. Recently I saw a rerun of a classic *Golden Girls* episode. Blanche's brother has come to visit, and, in the course of the episode, he comes out to his sister and her housemates. Earlier, Sophia announces that she is sure he's gay: "I heard him singing in the shower. He's the only man I know who knows all the lyrics to 'Send In the Clowns.' The guy's as gay as a fruit basket." In the days before the proliferation of gay characters on sitcoms, few shows were as gay-friendly or as open to gay readings as *Golden Girls,* which is still in syndication on Lifetime, the cable channel a *Saturday Night Live* skit called "the channel for women and gay men." *Golden Girls* was, after all, Battling Divas, starring an aging butch diva with a monster Jewish mother masquerading as an Italian, an aging Blanche DuBois, and an aging dumb blonde. Sophia's quip about Blanche's brother ties gayness generally to musical theater and specifically to Sondheim. Sophia's stereotype is defining, limiting, but not demeaning. It does tie the gay man to an artistic, esoteric milieu different from that of the characters or many of the viewers. Like *In and Out,* it suggests that knowledge of musicals, or of some musicals (what if Blanche's brother had sung a number from *Cats?*) is a signifier of gayness. On an episode of the sitcom *Will and Grace,* flamboyant Jack sings "Nothing's Going to Harm You" from *Sweeney Todd.*

Is this a valid signifier? An informal survey of my gay students who are most passionate about musicals would seem to support the stereotype. Not all gay men are show queens; not all men who love musicals are gay. But there is a phenomenon, the show queen, for whom gayness and musical theater are connected. One student of mine wrote:

> I think among gay actors, musical theater is definitely a cohesive bond for various reasons. First, I think many gay men simply grew up listening to, and sometimes impersonating, musical theater greats, such as good ol' Ethel. I became interested in musical theater before the ugly stick of puberty smacked me across the face. Throughout childhood, you could find me prancing around in my briefs singing "Look at me I'm Sandra Dee" at the top of my lungs whenever I was home alone. . . . It is strange to note that coming out coincided almost perfectly with my involvement in musical theater here at Duke . . . hmmm

. . . INTERESTING. . . . On the flip side I think musical theater for many gay men is so stereotypically gay that they shy away from it. I've had numerous gay friends of mine say, "Oh, you do musical theater . . . that's so GAY! I would never be in a musical."[14]

This kid is from a small town in the Deep South, not New York City. His comments demonstrate both the importance of musical theater to him as a gay man and the power of the stereotype for those who prefer to be "straight looking and acting." It could be that show queens are liberating themselves by consciously asserting a form of flamboyant theatricality instead of accepting traditional masculine codes of appearance and behavior. Reintegrating the show queen could be a means of locating the possibility of joy.

BUSSING TO JULIE

At 9 A.M. on a chilly, sunny Saturday a few years ago, two busloads of gay men leave from a parking lot in a northern suburb of Baltimore for a trip to New York to see Julie Andrews in the musical *Victor/Victoria*. The trip is arranged by a gay couple who run a local theater-party service. Many of the people on the buses know each other from Baltimore gay social life or from other excursions planned by this couple. It costs $125 for the orchestra seats and the three-hour bus ride to and from Times Square. The bus is equipped with a VCR so we can watch a tape of a PBS documentary on Julie Andrews and selected films. Light refreshments are served. My partner and I are part of a mini-party of half a dozen close friends who have arranged to have this day together. We're even going to squeeze in a matinee before seeing Julie. We gather a bit early so we can sit together on one of the buses.

One of our party is a doctor whose avocation is seeing, listening to, and reading about musical theater. He is a true show queen. As am I. As are at least half of the men on the busses. The rest are friends or partners of show queens. My friend the doctor read *Theatre Week* religiously (is it coincidence that *Theatre Week* was published by the same company that published the *New York Native,* the city's major gay newspaper?) before its demise and has seen all the hit musicals multiples of times. His partner, a stockbroker, is a more casual fan. He still hasn't warmed up to Sondheim, but it's OK, he feels guilty about it.

In front of my partner and me is a nineteen-year-old who works in a fast-food restaurant in downtown Baltimore and whose coming out is linked to his adoration of musicals. I am told by others who have been on previous trips with this young man that he has had a hard time coming out in his working-class,

Catholic section of Baltimore. He has saved up for months for this trip. His mother is with him—the only woman on the bus—but she seems to be having a ball. She also seems to understand the culture her son has joined and supports him in it. This is a lonely boy who does not have the support system the gay boys his age that I teach have. He does not have a musical-comedy club to perform with and socialize with. He gets the phone numbers of the men around him on the bus and calls them, not for sexual assignations, but for conversation and companionship. His fellow workers and neighbors aren't into musicals. How did this kid get to be a show queen? How does his love of musicals and his gayness connect?

Everyone on the bus has seen the film of *Victor/Victoria*. For us older folk, it was, for its time, a rare glimpse at a sympathetic gay character, played brilliantly by Robert Preston. Preston's Toddy was shamelessly, proudly gay and, unlike most early gay representations in film, he didn't remain unattached. He got Mr. Bernstein, played in a delightfully deadpan style by former football star Alex Karras. The film begins and ends with Toddy, the gay entertainer who becomes Victoria's best friend and her impresario. The final musical number in the film is Toddy hilariously sending up the dull Spanish number we have twice seen Victoria perform, and the film closes on Toddy receiving the rapturous applause of Victoria and Toddy's new beau, Mr. Bernstein. An audience who supposedly came to see Victoria is even more pleased to see Toddy. During the ovation, Toddy throws a rose from his bouquet to Mr. Bernstein who, with tears of joy, catches it.

Preston's performance—his last on screen or stage—was brilliant. The former Hollywood supporting player had, like Angela Lansbury, had a second career when he starred in a musical (*The Music Man*). Unfortunately, he never found another successful vehicle and bravely appeared in flop after flop, some of which died on the road before they ever reached Broadway. Show queens treasure the cast album of Jerry Herman's *Mack and Mabel* starring Preston and Bernadette Peters, but a recent London revival proved why the show didn't make it—great tunes, but an incoherent bummer of a book. *Victor/Victoria* was another comeback for Preston, and the greatest joy of the film is watching the fun he is having. Is it Toddy or Preston howling with delight during his final drag number? Preston played Toddy without any stereotypical mannerisms; no limp wrists, excessive swishing, or eyeball rolling. In *Victor/Victoria,* it is the straights who insist on playing stereotypes. Still, Toddy is the film's show queen.

Meanwhile, King, the stolid hero (played by James Garner), like Shakespeare's Orsino and Orlando, has to come to terms with the fact that the object of his desire was pretending to be a man, thus making his desire a matter of confusion of sexuality, but raising important questions about gender identity.

To love Victoria, he must love Victor. To gain the female object of his affections, he must not be ashamed to love a man. The beauty of the movie is its critique of American conventions of masculinity and their attendant homophobia. Victor says to King, "You're one kind of man, I'm another." "What kind are you?" King queries. "One who doesn't have to prove it to anyone." King already knows that Victor is Victoria, but he has to learn that there's no tragedy in being thought to be gay. The contrast between the men lovingly dancing together in the gay bar and the violent bonding King prefers in the waterfront dive shows the silliness of macho violence. King challenges a boxer at the gym to a fight to prove his heterosexuality. His opponent is both middleweight champion and gay. King loses on both counts.

For those of us old enough to have seen the film when it was first released, *Victor/Victoria* was a rare affirmation from cautious Hollywood. Critics praised the film and Robert Preston, but a number of critics felt that Andrews's performance was too chilly for the farce surrounding her. She was Mrs. Blake Edwards and that's why she was at the center of a Blake Edwards film. I read Andrews's stolidity as integrity. She was the still center of the farcical world. The androgyne, the character who embodied the gender instability, was the strongest, most stable character in the film. *Victor/Victoria* was as much Shakespearean comedy as farce. Andrews's Victoria was Viola and Rosalind, self-aware while others are deluded. In *Victor/Victoria,* it's the men and women, straight and gay, who believe in stable, conventional definitions of gender and sexuality who are the targets of the comedy.

A musical of *Victor/Victoria* was bound to be a hit with show queens. More than *La Cage aux Folles* (1983), the previous hit gay musical, the subject matter offered the possibility of deconstructing stereotypes of gender and sexuality. One could worry that, unlike *La Cage aux Folles, Victor/Victoria* was being written and directed by heterosexuals. Still, it was a show that seemed to be aimed at us.

Part of that "aim" was a knowledge on the part of the producers and makers of the show that gay people are a sizeable core audience for theater and that this audience of gay theatergoers will go to any show with gay subject matter and characters. There is a significant body of serious gay theater and, as with mainstream theater, a significant amount of gay fluff. For every *Love! Valour! Compassion!* there are a number of plays like *Making Porn* and *Two Boys on a Bed on a Cold Winter's Night,* which seem to exist for the nudity. But gay folks didn't have, until recently, television shows about us, and even now when we do the gay characters have to be sexless.[15] Our appearance in movies is still rare. Gay people are the only core audience left who need theater to see ourselves, which is why many small theaters across the country attract their largest audiences for gay-oriented plays. Seeing ourselves on Broadway at $75 a seat (if you want to see anything but Lilliputians)[16] is a luxury gay men are willing to pay for.

Victor/Victoria was an event for some of us guys on the bus because it was a return to the diva musical. For show queens, musicals are about divas, about Ethel Merman, Mary Martin, Carol Channing, Gwen Verdon, Barbara Cook, Angela Lansbury, and a handful of other women who have that larger-than-life quality that the theater demands. Betty Buckley has it. So does Bernadette Peters. The great attraction of seeing Victor/Victoria on stage was seeing diva Julie Andrews return to Broadway at age sixty. My boyhood best friend and I went to New York to see Julie Andrews in The Boy Friend the summer after eighth grade. We thought the show was hilarious. Already at age thirteen, I had an enormous love of camp and The Boy Friend was as camp as they came. The original cast album was the first I ever bought. For me, seeing My Fair Lady was seeing Julie Andrews. The thrill of the show was watching and hearing her sing "I Could Have Danced All Night" from my perch in the balcony of the Mark Hellinger Theater. I wore out my album of the Rodgers and Hammerstein musical for television, Cinderella, in which Julie was radiant even when she was supposed to be impoverished.[17] I even suffered through the insufferable Camelot to see her make her way through that mess of Arthurian inanity with charm and dignity. I saw her return to the New York stage the year before Victor/Victoria in the Sondheim revue Putting It Together, at the Manhattan Theater Club. Somehow she got a stain on the chic silk aqua pants suit she wore in the show. It was so out of character for the immaculate Julie Andrews to be so sullied that it became my most vivid memory of a decidedly unmemorable show. Everything about Julie has a kind of cleanliness about it: the purity of her soprano voice, now a baritone, but memory overrides physical fact; the purity of her delivery. She has her mannerisms, particularly that characteristic expressive slide on and off of notes for emphasis (she shares that with Leontyne Price). But with her crisp BBC diction and a general air of caution, there is an old-fashioned strength and serenity in Andrews's work. When she sang the acerbic Sondheim songs in Putting It Together, one missed some of the cynicism and anger Diana Rigg gave them in London. Rigg can't hit all the notes, but she acts the songs. When Andrews said "Fuck" one laughed at the incongruousness of it. Still, Andrews is a true Broadway diva, the grand, poised Tebaldi rather than the intense, passionate Callas.

Few, if any, of my other companions had seen Julie Andrews live before. A star was going to appear on Broadway, which had become starless in recent years. Few of the current crop of performers have the discipline or desire to give eight performances a week for a year. Starring on Broadway is the exception, not the rule, and it now has an aura of heroism, of sacrifice. The press surrounding *Victor/Victoria* was about Julie nobly coming to Broadway and signing a long-term contract so that her husband's project would break even. Starring on Broadway used to be the goal of performers, not an act of financial and personal sacrifice. We would be seeing a real star in the flesh sacrificing and working for us.

This star was sixty years old, so starring in this musical was not only sacrifice, but endurance, a sign that one could age gracefully and indefatigably. The remaining Broadway divas are now middle-aged or older. The recent revival of *Hello, Dolly!* offered Carol Channing in her late seventies doing an imitation of a drag queen doing Carol Channing. Not a pretty sight, but an act of endurance. Barbara Cook is over seventy. Bernadette Peters, Betty Buckley, and Liza Minnelli are in their fifties. Gregory Hines, the one real male musical divo of the past twenty years, is middle-aged and a sitcom star. Like everything else about the Broadway musical, these stars now evoke nostalgia more than raging passion.

For most of the guys on the bus seeing Julie was seeing Maria in *The Sound of Music* on video, not a film I associate with show queens, though in the 1997 film *Kiss Me Guido,* it is a favorite of the gay leading character, Warren. Maybe they had seen *Mary Poppins* on video as well. If they were lucky or true show queens, they had seen a video of the wonderfully camp *Thoroughly Modern Millie* in which Andrews shares top billing with Mary Tyler Moore, Carol Channing, and Bea Lillie. *Thoroughly Modern Millie* is a show queen's delight. As in a Broadway musical of the twenties and thirties or the classic postwar MGM musicals produced by Arthur Freed, the plot is simply there to offer the stars a chance to do star turns. Carol Channing was seldom in film and her performance as an eccentric and charmingly promiscuous millionairess here is appropriately wacky. She's game for anything, including being shot out of a cannon or performing with a circus acrobatic team. You see in *Millie* much more than in later revivals of *Hello, Dolly!* how radiantly off-the-wall Channing could be. Beatrice Lillie, fresh from her last Broadway musical, *High Spirits,* is more subdued than in her stage appearance, but funny as the part-Chinese hotel manager and white slave trader (the racial stereotypes in the film are far from politically correct). In her heyday, Lillie was one of the few divas who acknowledged the existence of homosexuality. Her rendition of "There Are Fairies at the Bottom of My Garden," signaling at every line exactly what kind of fairies she was singing about, became her most famous number. Mary Tyler Moore plays the dizzy, soft-voiced ingenue who gets the caricature of the stolid leading man, played stolidly by John Gavin. Julie ends up with Jimmy, the devil-may-care young millionaire, played by the young James Fox, and that gives the film its touch of sexual transgression. Fox is cute and charming and works hard, but in the film he just doesn't seem very, well, heterosexual. Millie (Andrews) discovers at the end that Fox is Carol Channing's son and heir. He acts like he should be Carol Channing's son! I can see why some folks find *Thoroughly Modern Millie* curiously uninvolving. There is absolutely no sexual electricity between anyone in the film, but it has its own camp pleasures.

In the 1960s, Julie Andrews presided over the last triumphs (*Mary Poppins* and *The Sound of Music*) and death throes (*Star!*) of the big Hollywood musical while she carved a niche as a film actress. She is videotape, memories, and legend. The T-shirt for *Victor/Victoria* was not the usual show logo, but a large color photo of Julie in male drag. When Julie was too ill or tired to go on, the majority of the audience asked for a refund or tickets to a later performance. They came to see Julie, and when she went on vacation, they got Liza Minnelli to come in for a few weeks and do her star thing, another piece of nostalgia for a performer who had her heyday over twenty-five years ago. Minnelli is the opposite of Julie, all desperation and total lack of control. For some reason, a number of show queens love her. When Julie finally left the show, the title role went to Raquel Welch, a signifier of nostalgia for a very different branch of show business.[18] Welch may be an aged imitation of her former glory, but she hasn't succeeded in becoming either revered like Julie or camp like Liza. The show closed in a couple of weeks.

Shortly before eight o'clock, we, with the rest of the sold-out audience, take the escalators up to the Marquis Theater, ensconced in the Marriott Marquis Hotel on Times Square. Like many of the new theaters built for Broadway musicals in the past thirty years, the Marquis is characterless. At least, unlike the older theaters, it has lobby space to walk around and spacious bathrooms (if you can find them). But the theater itself does nothing to enhance the sense of an event. Entering it is more like entering a nightclub in a Las Vegas hotel than entering the special world of theater. Large souvenir stands flank the doors to the auditorium. Buying an overpriced memento is part of the experience of seeing a musical now. "See, I paid my $75 to see this, plus my $25 to park and the price of dinner." Such cynicism didn't stop me from buying a Julie Andrews T-shirt I will never wear. The young man in front of us on the bus buys loads of souvenirs.

Our group sits together in the orchestra section. Until the 1999 revival of *Annie Get Your Gun,* there has never been a hit show in the Marquis Theater, and it doesn't take longer than a few seconds to figure out why. It's a cold space. One not only feels distant from the stage, a problem in many new theaters, but doesn't feel the proper sense of closeness with the rest of the audience. A bit of claustrophobia is necessary for theater. In the old Broadway houses, you are always aware of the rest of the audience as you watch the stage, of the communal experience of theater, which adds to the excitement of the event. The Marquis is built like a mall movie theater, offering distance from fellow audience members so that you can ignore their eating and talking. The old theaters aren't always user-friendly. They lack public space, lobbies, and adequate restrooms, but the auditoria make you feel like you are in a theater. They add to the excitement of the event. From row U of the Marquis, I felt miles away from the stage. From row U of the tatty old Neil Simon Theater, where I recently saw *The King and I,* I could see the performers' faces. The Marquis is not a space for a star turn, for a real rapport between performer and audience.

What *Victor/Victoria* had going for it was Julie Andrews and its sexual politics. Unfortunately, the musical was a pale reminder of the film, a lesson in the sort of compromise one has to make to do what shouldn't be done. Songs were added that over-simplified the characters. The first of these, a duet for Victoria and Toddy, "If I Were a Man," moves Toddy from the rich character he was in the film to the Broadway gay stereotype à la *La Cage aux Folles.* Toddy on stage is not a gay man, but a man who wants to be a woman, the oldest Broadway stereotype of a gay man. Toddy never gets the final star turn he got in the film. The finale is an old-fashioned, everybody-on-stage singing of the title tune. "King's Dilemma," his song about his fears of homosexuality, is no replacement for the desperate macho behaviors of King in the film. The musical, to its credit, waits much longer for King to discover Victor is Victoria. The duet for King and Victoria, "Almost a Love Song," is the most dramatically successful song in the show, though like most of the score, it is a bit too low-key for a stage musical. The lyrics aren't witty enough or the music dynamic enough. I thought Victoria's song, "Living in the Shadows" (by Frank Wildhorn, who completed the score after Henry Mancini died), would replace "I Am What I Am" as the gay anthem to be sung at every Gay Pride occasion, but it didn't happen. It's too sweet, too placid. It's a film ballad, not a rousing show tune.

Like the stars of the good old days, Judy Holliday or Ethel Merman, Julie Andrews bravely stuck with *Victor/Victoria* through two theater seasons, over seven hundred performances. She and her husband are not only star and writer/ director; they are also producers and investors and they know, no Julie, no show. The show weathered its lack of a Tony nomination for Best Musical, and Julie tried to capitalize on that disaster (the Tonys are the best publicity a Broadway show gets) by publicly boycotting the Tonys and refusing her own award. The fact is, by the standards of the 1950s, *Victor/Victoria* isn't a very good show.

Yet there we were and we wouldn't have missed it for the world. A diva in a gay-affirming musical was enough to draw busloads from as far as Baltimore. A friend told me that when he saw the show, there was a large lesbian contingent in the audience to cheer the tango Julie Andrews dances with Rachel York (Norma). Such moments of female-female contact are far rarer than male-male moments on Broadway.

I would think there is little in *Victor/Victoria* for what Broadway used to call the "tired businessman," the straight man who comes to the theater for some naughty humor, a few good tunes, and pretty chorines. Norma's number, "Chicago, Illinois" (also in the film), is a caricature of such a number, an echo of the Hot Box numbers in *Guys and Dolls*. Throughout the show, Julie Andrews is backed up by a gaggle of hard-working gypsies. Choreographer Rob Marshall is far more interested in placing his male dancers front and center than in spotlighting the chorines, and his aggressive choreography for his male dancers contains more than a "hint of mint." Since Tony Roberts, who plays Toddy with his usual charmless efficiency, makes Toddy straighter than King, the gypsies give the show its real gay presence.

Julie was given a thundering ovation at the end. Our group escalated out of the theater happy, if not overwhelmed. The bus ride back offered us renditions of "Happy Birthday" to my partner and the other birthday boy on the bus. It also offered a screening of *The Adventures of Priscilla, Queen of the Desert,* that joyous Australian quasi-musical about the trek of a drag troupe across the outback, which has a gay fabulousness totally missing from the show we had just seen. Everyone on the bus knew the film by heart and laughed before things happened. The post-Julie screening of *Priscilla* reminded me that being a show queen is also being something of an anachronism. The kind of musical show queens love is a thing of the past. Watching a mediocre show like *Victor/Victoria* only reminds us that we are show queens without shows, left to reminisce or wait for the next revival to rekindle our passion. *Priscilla,* available on video for repeated viewing, is some solace. Instead of drag queens imitating divas, straight actors imitate drag queens, but there is the tacky joy, the liberation, that we loved in the musicals we remember.

The show queen was adept at the imaginative leap of reading his gayness into the musical, particularly in reading his gayness into the flamboyance of the divas. Why bother reading gayness into a musical when there are gay characters on NBC almost every night? Why dare read gayness into a musical when queer theorists proclaim such a reading is a symptom of the repression and misery of the closet? Why read gayness into musicals when musicals are too gay for comfort for "straight looking and acting" gay men? The true show queen would answer, "Because it's theater!" Because the most theatrical of forms can be an expression of all that is best about gayness in all senses of the word: "keenly alive and exuberant: having or inducing high spirits." Because for some of us gayness and theater are inextricably linked. They are also linked for the line dancers doing their uniform steps and turns, but for the true show queen that's too much like being in the chorus. It doesn't compare with the thrill of calling out: "Here she is, boys! Here's Rose!"

I will argue throughout this book that we show queens found more cause for joy, more recognition, in our readings of shows of the past than in more recent, more ostensibly gay musicals. What could possibly be gay about Tony Roberts's dreary impersonation of a gay man? The irony of theater—and of NBC sitcoms—is that there is often more gayness to be read in ostensibly straight characters. Because of that, much of my history takes place in the bad old days before Stonewall.

GAY LYRICS, GAY ICONS

In the late nineties, as the Broadway musical became transformed into mass entertainment by the Disney kingdom and movie-theater mogul Garth Drabinski, the "gay presence" in musical theater was taken for granted. The megahit *The Lion King* was created from a score by flamboyantly gay rock star Elton John. *Ragtime* has a book and score by openly gay artists. The hit revival of John Kander and Fred Ebb's *Chicago* provided another triumph for gay creators, a counter to the disaster that befell their 1997 show, *Steel Pier.* The ill-fated musical about Siamese twins, *Side Show* (1997), tried unsuccessfully to stay alive by presenting itself in the gay press as an allegory of queerness. Essentially the open gayness of the creators of these shows elicits a big "so what" from most of the populace, a sign of how far we have come in this century.

Some recordings in the 1990s signaled a nostalgia for the musical creators of a more closeted, if gayer, era when musicals were witty, sophisticated comedies instead of heterosexist tragedies. In 1997, EMI released a beautifully packaged four-CD set of all the recordings Noël Coward made for that organization between the 1920s and 1950s. A series of compilations of the work of Cole Porter was released, and *High Society,* a musical based on the 1955 film with lots of Porter songs added, opened at the American Conservatory Theater in San Francisco and eventually moved to Broadway. Soprano Dawn Upshaw recorded an album of Rodgers and Hart songs, accompanied in some by gay jazz pianist Fred Hersh, while Livent commissioned gay playwright Terrence McNally to revise John O'Hara's book for *Pal Joey* for megamusical treatment. The continued currency of the songs of Coward, Porter, and Hart depend on recordings, compilation revues like *Cowardy Custard, Oh Coward!,* and *Cole;* and heavily revised productions to keep their work alive. The dated, lightweight books of the musicals that contained their great songs seldom are more than threads to hold the songs together and won't satisfy a Broadway audience used to through-sung shows or shows with fast-moving books. Many of the musicals of the thirties are more plays with music, much heavier on words than tunes. Contemporary audiences want something more like a movie on stage than a play with tunes.

The age of Coward, Porter, and Hart was one in which the wit of the lyrics was one of the key elements of musical comedy. Except for Sondheim, brilliant lyric writing is a lost art. The loss of interest in language has taken half the joy out of the songs in musicals. *Les Misérables* is marvelous in its grand epic way, but if one listens to the words, it sounds like one of those bad English translations of operas one heard before surtitles; forced rhymes, lines in which notes and syllables don't seem to match, and no wit. It's not a show for folks who care about felicities of language, who care about wit. This was gay men's great contribution to the musical—wit, joy in wordplay. Even without microphones, audiences listened for the words of a Porter or Hart song. Audiences went to the theater for words and music, not scenery, not even for the plots which were at best serviceable and often purposely inane.

In his very straight book on musical theater, Mark Steyn notes, "With Hart, as with Cole Porter, you hear the lyricist, not the character,"[1] as if this were a bad thing. One could say the same thing of Noël Coward. My problem is that I'd rather hear the voice of Hart or Porter or Coward than the clunky, prosaic utterances of a character like Jean Valjean or the Phantom of the Opera. Steyn's critique, later extended to Stephen Sondheim, seems by implication to characterize the great gay lyricists as solipsistic. Actually, no one wanted them to write anything but Hart, Porter, or Coward lyrics. No one else could write anything so brilliant and idiosyncratic.

It is true that the lyrics of Hart, Porter, and Coward, the foci of this chapter, now exist mainly apart from the shows for which they were written. Indeed, recent revivals of their shows often rearrange scores, cutting songs from the original shows and adding more familiar songs. In this chapter, I will be reading songs out of their original context: actually recontextualizing these songs by offering gay readings closer to the lives of the writers than the shows for which they wrote songs. Looking at these songs apart from the musicals for which they were written is validated by the fact that composers in the golden age of musical theater wanted their songs to become hits out of context. Before the long-playing record, a performance of a song in a Broadway show was an effective means of song plugging. Pop singers looked to Broadway for their material. Jerry Herman notes:

Frank Sinatra, Perry Como, and all the top recording artists of the day got their material from Broadway, so they all wanted to hear the new showtunes while the shows were still being written. If you were working on a musical you would cut a demo record to get the songs out before the show went into rehearsal.[2]

Like everything else about the musical, remembering past glories is an exercise in nostalgia for the heyday of the classic American popular song. For gay aficionados, the work of Lorenz Hart, Cole Porter, and Noël Coward symbolize the best of an earlier time when camp was fun rather than grist for theorists, when effeteness and cultural literacy seemed appropriate masculine style. For now we have the records and *Frasier* episodes to offer a nineties version of that world. Porter and Coward were able composers, but gay men remember their lyrics most fondly. Now we can imagine our own scenarios for their songs, sagas of what it meant to be gay between the world wars.

GAY MUSIC?

"Play something light and sweet and gay ."
—*Noël Coward*

An historical fact of some relevance: in the 1920s, when the subjects of this chapter, Hart, Porter, and Coward, began their careers, one common code word for homosexual within the gay world was "musical." "He's musical" meant "He's gay."

Can music be gay? A number of eminent musicologists have been asking this question in various ways in recent years. Constructionists would say that one cannot even talk about homosexuality before the term was first used, supposedly in 1869, because men did not conceive of being defined by their sexual desire. So a "pre-homosexuality" composer might feel and act on his desire for other men, but he would not think of that as a defining factor in his identity as he would think of ethnicity, religion, social class, and profession. It is possible, for instance, that George Frideric Handel, the master of theater music in the early eighteenth century, acted on his desire for men, though it is far from clear that gayness affected his composition.[3] How does it matter that a composer is gay? The answer to that has more to do with the social conditions of composing and patterns of reception than the music the composer wrote. Perhaps gay musicologists write so much about Benjamin Britten because he was a more or less openly gay composer living in an era of homosexual discourse who wrote text-based music. One can see how Britten's sexual orientation affected the texts he chose to set to music and the ways in which he wrote for the idiosyncratic voice of his life partner, Peter Pears. It is much more difficult, nearly impossible, to speculate on ways in which his instrumental music is affected by his sexual orientation. Are Britten's piano and violin concerti any gayer than those of his contemporaries Bartok, Prokofiev, and Shostakovich, for instance? What can be documented are the ways in which Britten's gayness affected the reception of his music. Was it more difficult for him to get his work performed? Were there examples of homophobic critical writing that may have prejudiced the public against his work? In what ways might it have been helpful to be a homosexual composer? In America, for instance, the leading serious composers for much of this century were mostly homosexual, from the underrated Charles Tomlinson Griffes at the turn of the century to mid-century composers: Aaron Copland, Percy Grainger, David Diamond, Ned Rorem, Samuel Barber, Gian Carlo Menotti, Marc Blitzstein, Leonard Bernstein, Lou Harrison, John Cage, and Virgil Thomson, among others. According to one historian, "So many important New York musicians were gay, one wit dubbed the American Composers League the Homintern."[4] I have always wondered whether the insistence on the part of the American critical and musicological establishment on trying to force serial music on the public by denigrating tonal music at every opportunity wasn't partly an attempt to put the gay composing establishment out of business. Despite the academics and critics, it is more than possible that it was extremely helpful to be a homosexual if one wanted to get ahead as a serious composer in America. Would Aaron Copland, whose success gave him a fair amount of clout, be more interested in promoting the career of a gay composer than a straight composer? Would Gian Carlo Menotti rather have his operas conducted by a gay conductor? Would Dimitri Mitropoulos, the gay musical director of the New York Philharmonic between 1949 and 1957, rather perform new works by gay composers? These are speculations outside the scope of this book, but I want to set the scene for writing music in New York in the middle years of this century. At a time in which homosexuality was not even marginally accepted in American society, New York musical life was greatly controlled by homosexuals. The two new operas Rudolph Bing commissioned for the old Met in the fifties and early sixties were *Vanessa,* with music and libretto by Samuel Barber and his partner, Gian Carlo Menotti, and Menotti's *The Last Savage.* The new Metropolitan Opera House opened with Barber's *Antony and Cleopatra.*

The same gay dominance has not existed until recently in the world of popular music or Broadway theater music. Once an area of show business has aspirations to a mass audience, there is a pressure for its practitioners to remain closeted, so gay composers in the theater have had to be more cautious, more closeted than their colleagues in "serious music." Classical composers speak to a limited, sophisticated audience who are not supposed to care about the sexuality of its artists. Popular composers are supposed to be popular, mainstream, non-eccentric. Any sign of deviance might make one less of a profitable commodity. So gay composers moved to the safe, glamorous, though less lucrative, world of classical music and left show tunes to the straight guys. Or they were extremely cautious about their private life. Though he was known to have homosexual liaisons throughout his career, Leonard Bernstein came out only after it was fashionable to come out, but he was then more of a figure in "serious music" than a Broadway composer—he hadn't written a musical in decades. Marc Blitzstein's open gayness got him in trouble with figures like Aaron Copland, who thought him dangerously indiscreet, but Blitzstein, too, was considered a serious composer who occasionally wrote for Broadway. Supposedly Alan Jay Lerner was warned by friends not to continue his collaboration with homosexual Frederick Loewe because it would taint his own reputation. Stephen Sondheim has been extremely closeted in his life and his work and often defensive about gay readings of his songs and shows.

Race and ethnicity figure far more prominently than sexuality in discussions of American theater music. With few exceptions (Cole Porter and Stephen Flaherty the most successful), American theater music is still predominantly a Jewish field. Richard Rodgers recalls an evening he and Lorenz Hart spent at Cole Porter's palazzo in Venice. Porter had yet to have a successful musical on Broadway, but told Rodgers he had discovered

> "the secret of writing hits." As I breathlessly awaited the magic formula, he leaned over and confided, "I'll write Jewish tunes." I laughed at what I took to be a joke, but not only was Cole dead serious, he eventually did exactly that. Just hum the melody that goes with "Only you beneath the moon and under the sun" from "Night and Day," or any of "Begin the Beguine," or "Love for Sale," or "My Heart Belongs to Daddy," or "I Love Paris." These minor-key melodies are unmistakably eastern Mediterranean. It is surely one of the ironies of the musical theater that despite the abundance of Jewish composers, the one who has written the most enduring "Jewish" music should be an Episcopalian millionaire who was born on a farm in Peru, Indiana.[5]

Anti-Semitism was one of Porter's many less-than-charming characteristics (right up there with snobbery, vanity, and an excessive interest in his bowel movements); he may well have believed what he told Rodgers. His friend Noël Coward, also a good friend of Rodgers, wrote in his diary in 1955 of Americans' respect for what he called "light music":

> I suppose music is in the air more here [in the United States] and the mixture of Jewish and Negro rhythms has become part of the national consciousness because it is a goulash of all races. Very exciting and stimulating.[6]

Porter and Coward were partly right. All the great composers of popular music, which was then synonymous with Broadway theater music, were Jewish. Jerry Herman exuberantly declares: "You almost *had* to be Jewish to be a Broadway songwriter."[7] There is, however, a wide social spectrum of Jewish composers, from immigrants who grew up in the poor Lower East Side like Irving Berlin, to middle-class composers like Rodgers and Gershwin, to the affluent Jerome Kern, who moved back and forth in his youth between New York and London. These men may have had little in common. Playwright and screenwriter Leonard Spigelgass notes that "Jerome Kern disliked all of them, and they all [the composers and lyricists he knew, including Rodgers and Hart] disliked Kern . . . and everybody was right about that! They all laughed at [Sigmund] Romberg, who was a laughable man . . . and had bigger hits than any of them. Irving Berlin was beneath their contempt."[8] This is hardly ethnic or religious solidarity but demonstrates that these men were separated by social class and artistic aspiration. Romberg, Hungarian-born, was a composer of operettas, popular Broadway fare in the 1920s. His collaborator was often Oscar Hammerstein II. For writers of hip contemporary musical comedy, his work must have seemed corny and old-fashioned. Berlin, the Russian immigrant whose musical technique was rudimentary, did not emerge as a major Broadway composer until *Annie Get Your Gun* in 1946 (produced by Rodgers and Hammerstein and first assigned to Hammerstein's old partner, Kern, who died before beginning the show, and lyricist Dorothy Fields). It is likely that class consciousness and professional rivalry were stronger than religious solidarity among the Jewish men and women (Dorothy Fields was, after all, one of the great lyricists) who dominated Broadway songwriting. Yet there was over the years some sense of Jewish identity that helped these people create their work together. Historian Charles Kaiser notes that the four creators of the 1957 classic *West Side Story,* Leonard Bernstein, Stephen Sondheim, Arthur Laurents, and Jerome Robbins, were all gay men, as was the first Tony, Larry Kert. Yet Laurents would comment:

> There is one sensibility all four of us share which is much more important and really does inform the work. We're all Jews. Think about it and what it means. Creative work is undoubtedly the sum of its creators but certain elements take a bigger role than others at different times. *West Side* can be said to be informed by our political and sociological viewpoint; our Jewishness as the source of passion against prejudice; our theatrical vision, our aspiration, but not, I think, by our sexual orientation.[9]

In our post-Stonewall, AIDS generation, queer theory, gay self-consciousness era, it is difficult to imagine a relatively recent time in which gay men did not put their gayness first, did not consider that a crucial aspect of what and how they created. The background, heritage, and social consciousness of the creators of *West Side Story* stemmed from being Jewish, not from being gay. Or, perhaps, they did not know how to talk about what their sexual orientation contributed to their art. That discourse came later and is not yet totally coherent. In 1983, Laurents and two other gay Jewish artists, Jerry Herman and Harvey Fierstein, collaborated on the hit musical *La Cage aux Folles,* the first Broadway musical about a gay couple. By that time, gayness had become at least as important as Jewishness to some Broadway artists.

The 1986 musical *Rags* (composer Charles Strouse, lyricist Stephen Schwartz, and a host of book writers, from the credited veteran Joseph Stein to uncredited figures like Jay Presson Allen and Gene Saks) dramatizes vividly the moment when poor Jewish immigrants discovered on the streets of New York the sound of ragtime music and combined it with their own music to create the genre that was popular music. While the show claims to be a picture of Jewish immigrant experience, it is really about the making of American music. In that, *Rags* is a descendant of *Show Boat* and *Dreamgirls,* which dramatizes the assimilation of African-American musical styles into white popular music. *Ragtime,* the 1996[10] musical to end all musicals, follows in the same tradition. Its focal character, Coalhouse Walker, is a ragtime pianist who introduces black music into a WASP household. In the process, he implicates that household in racial politics. One can't have the music without the politics and social responsibility for the fate of those whose culture one has assimilated. Jerome Kern's graceful, elegant music has more in common with nineteenth-century American popular music and European operetta than it has with the klezmer-inflected music of Irving Berlin or George Gershwin. Porter was partially right—Jewish immigrants brought to New York the sounds of the music they knew in Eastern Europe and combined it with other popular forms, including the new jazz. But gay composers have no common ethnicity with indigenous music. Their ethnicity is separate from their sexuality. The score of *Ragtime* is by Stephen Flaherty, a gay composer of Irish-American descent. Is his music any gayer than straight Jerome Kern's?

GAY LYRICISTS AND GAY SELF-PRESENTATION

Words can be more obviously gay than music, and it is interesting that the major figures of pre-Stonewall musical theater whose homosexuality is most talked about are primarily lyricists. In this chapter, I want to focus on three of them.

With Ira Gershwin, Noël Coward, Cole Porter, and Lorenz Hart were the artists who turned the writing of Broadway lyrics into an art form during the1920s and 1930s. Their careers formed parallel trajectories during the heyday of musical comedy between the wars. Hart died the year *Oklahoma!* opened and resuscitated the genre of serious musical play Hammerstein and Kern had begun with *Show Boat.* Porter's career as a theater composer had a miraculous resurrection in the decade after World War II. Coward outlived Porter and was still writing musicals in the sixties. *Sail Away,* a wan shipboard musical enlivened by Elaine Stritch, sank in a few months. *The Girl Who Came to Supper* took even less time to flop, though that show was an interesting combination, a Coward adaptation of a play by Terence Rattigan (*The Sleeping Prince,*) another closeted gay playwright who was a bright light on the West End for decades. In his usual manner, Coward wrote the book, score, and lyrics and directed. He also directed *High Spirits,* a musical version of his *Blithe Spirit* with a score by Hugh Martin and Timothy Gray stronger than any Coward had written in recent years, which had a respectable run. But by the mid-1960s, with rock on the radio, Broadway audiences were looking for more substantial musical entertainment. Serious concept musicals *Fiddler on the Roof* and *Cabaret,* initiating the ascendance of the star director, were waiting in the wings and Jerry Herman's razzamatazzy scores for *Hello, Dolly!* and *Mame,* show music on steroids, were more au courant than Coward's faded elegance.

Coward and Porter represented the art of cleverness made stageable. Hart's greatest lyrics present a vivid picture of yearning for love and settling for sex or fantasy. In life, these men represented three approaches to being a gay public figure in the period between the world wars. Coward managed to play the witty fop but also to be seen as a figure of fashion, the ultimate in a lifestyle of the rich and famous. Porter, married but cruising waterfront bars, provided another version of the high life. Wealthy, writing for fun, never quite part of the Broadway scene, Porter was first a figure of elegance and then, after his crippling accident, an object of sympathy. His marriage helped hide his sex life from the public, but his lyrics are paradigms of camp wit. The real poet of the three, Lorenz Hart, five feet tall, prematurely balding, hating his looks, phobic about sex, presented in his lyrics a self-portrait of a person who believed real love possible only in fantasy or in art. All three men have become gay icons for show queens of the past two generations. I want to focus on these men and their work as examples of gay self-image and self-presentation in the years before Stonewall and show how their lyrics reflected that self-image. All three illustrate the flexibility and limitations of the closet. In the older sense, Coward and Porter were "out" gay men. That is, while not publicly proclaiming their sexuality, they lived to varying degrees openly as gay men among gay men. Their gayness was what it usually was for public figures then, an open secret. Hart seemed to be more closeted, if not by himself then by the people around him who denied his homosexuality. Yet all the evidence was there. Did class play into these differences? Porter lived what would be considered an aristocratic life, unfettered by financial concerns. Coward, through an image of a new social mobility possible through money and fame, perfected the image of a sophisticated aristocrat. Hart, always a New Yorker, remained stolidly middle class and parochial.

More important, the gayness of these artists was both hidden and revealed in their lyrics, echoing Philip Core's definition of camp as "the lie that tells the truth":

> There are two things essential to camp: a secret within the personality which one wishes to conceal and exploit, and a peculiar way of seeing things, affected by spiritual isolation, but strong enough to impose itself on others through acts or creations.[11]

Core's definition can serve as the theme of this chapter.

The lives of these men demonstrate that there was a gay society in the 1930s, at least for the rich and famous. Leonard Spigelgass defined the ambivalence that created and sustained gay society:

> Don't forget, homosexuality in that period had two levels: One, it was held in major contempt, and the other was that among his [Hart's] kind it was the most exclusive club in New York. That's terribly important to realize—that it was a club into which you couldn't get . . . I mean no ordinary certified public accountant could get into the Larry Hart, Cole Porter, George Cukor world. That was *the* world. That was Somerset Maugham. That was Cole Porter. That was Noël Coward. That was *it* if you were in that. And I remember those houses on Fifty-fifth Street, with the butlers and the carryings-on . . . You were king of the golden river! That was it! In spite of the attitude toward homosexuality in those days. On the one hand if you said, "They were homosexuals—oh, my, isn't that terrible," on the other hand you said, "My God, the other night I was at dinner with Cole Porter." Immediate reaction: "Jesus Christ, what did he have on? What was he wearing? What did he say? *Were* you at that party? Were you at one of those Sunday brunches?" So you had this awful ambivalence.[12]

Then, as now, there was a gay society. It was discreetly hidden from the public's view, but it evoked mixed feelings of disapproval and envy. Recent biographers of these men also demonstrate that there was a supply of sexual diversion from male brothels and procurers of "Love for Sale."

At a time in which creators of musical comedy were celebrities moving back and forth between Broadway in its heyday and Hollywood in the golden era of musicals, Porter and Hart were stars. Coward, a stage and screen star as well as composer and lyricist, had even more celebrity. Yet then, even more than now, gay celebrities were to some extent a species protected by the silence surrounding homosexuality. A companion of Lorenz Hart notes of the gay sex parties held in Hollywood in the thirties: "It was understood that what went on was confidential, and you never saw a hint of anything in Louella Parsons or any other gossip column. That was unwritten law. Everyone obeyed it!"[13] As they still do.

Coward, the only one to survive into the period of gay liberation, was horrified by the open display of gayness at Fire Island in the 1960s:

> Never in my life have I seen such concentrated, abandoned homosexuality. It is fantastic and difficult to believe. I wished really that I hadn't gone. Thousands of queer young men of all shapes and sizes camping about blatantly and carrying on—in my opinion—appallingly. Then there were all the lesbians glowering at each other . . . I have always been of the opinion that a large group of queer men was unattractive. On Fire Island, it is more than unattractive, it's macabre, sinister, irritating, and somehow tragic.[14]

This was not the "marvelous party" Coward envisioned. He was the homosexual role model of a very different age.

The closet may have been oppressive, but it also offered protection for privileged gay men to live as they pleased. Hart, Porter, and Coward took advantage of this silence. In our less silent world, their stories and their lyrics become parables of alternative expressions of one's closeted gayness.

SLEEPING IN THE CLOSET

"He was the poet laureate of masochism."
—Jerome Lawrence[15]

The scholar of the cyber era must surf the Internet. If one looks for Lorenz Hart, one finds a Lorenz Hart Web site compiled by a twenty-four-year-old Italian, Alessandro Martini. Martini's colorful page offers a useful critical discography complete with its own rating system, a catalogue of Hart's songs, links to other Web sites including those of some of Martini's friends, and an excellent essay on Hart. In the midst of all this information is a little rainbow flag signifying Martini's gayness, as his own writing on Hart—in excellent English, I might add—demonstrates that Hart for him is a romantic gay icon, a gay man who transmuted his unhappiness and loneliness into great art. Hart never thought his lyrics were great achievements and he was quickly, though temporarily, eclipsed by the enormously successful Rodgers and Hammerstein collaboration.[16] We know now that Hart's songs with Rodgers are classics, poetically complex and emotionally rich, if often disturbing. Few of his musicals will survive because we expect different things from a musical now than audiences did in the 1930s, but the songs live on, creating their own rich narrative. Hart is now known as a gay lyricist, something he would have dreaded if he understood it at all, yet as far away as Milan, a young gay man devotes his time to chronicling Hart for his generation of Web surfers. One of Martini's comments in his essay is that "Hart's lyrics are the code. His life is the key." Actually, the sentences could as easily be reversed: "His life is the code. His lyrics are the key."

More than any other major lyricist for the American theater, Lorenz Hart wrote lyrics that tell a story apart from the narratives of the musicals for which they were written. As Gerald Mast puts it:

> Hart was the most confessional of theater lyricists—the most able and willing to put his own feelings, thoughts, pains, sorrows, fears, joys, misery, into the words of songs for specific characters in musical plays. What he could never say aloud, even to his closest friends in private, he let his characters sing in public.[17]

Hart's lyrics chronicle the isolation and fantasies of a person who finds himself physically inadequate and separated from the possibility of conventional coupledom represented by the romantic fantasies of popular music. In a sense, Hart's lyrics are non-love songs. Yet they are songs of desire and unrequited love. While they are placed within the conventional heterosexual/heterosexist framework of the thirties musical, they tend to be about desire for men.

Our contemporary picture of the facts of Hart's life comes not from the lyrics but from two biographies written in the past quarter century. The first, *Rodgers and Hart: Bewitched, Bothered, and Bedeviled* (1976) was co-written by Samuel Marx, son of Groucho and author of a number of show business biographies, and Jan Clayton, the first Julie in *Carousel* and later the mother in the *Lassie* television series. While claiming to be a study of both composer and lyricist, the book focuses on Hart, partly because Rodgers's life is simply not very interesting. Marx and Clayton have based much of their work on interviews with people who knew Hart, even some who had sex with him. It is anecdotal, but very insightful about Hart and his life. Frederick Nolan's *Lorenz Hart: A Poet on Broadway* (1994) is more factual but, surprisingly for a book published in 1994, somewhat homophobic in its accounts of Hart's homosexuality, looking for causes, points of origin. Hart's life lends itself to pathos, a state balanced in his lyrics by his wit and sense of irony. Like that of playwright Joe Orton, however, Hart's life can easily be dramatized as a homosexual tragedy, a brilliantly talented man who died early because he didn't lead a "normal" life. Yet such a simplistic reading of Hart's life belies the complexity of the place of sexuality in the artist's career and work. Hart was a brilliant lyric poet who used his own inner experience to create the most heartfelt lyrics of his era. How he died and whom he had sex with are secondary to how he used his experience in his work. Clearly there were two things Hart could not accept totally: his body and his sexuality. Hart's lyrics reinforce a self-consciousness about size and ugliness. They also mourn the impossibility of the love pop lyrics are supposed to celebrate. As Gerald Mast puts it, "His refuge was the way he spied the world from inside his closet, a view he could simultaneously reveal and disguise with song lyrics."[18]

 Lorenz Hart offers one stereotypical narrative, the lonely self-hating homosexual who drinks himself to death, but in the meantime redeems his life fthrough beautiful narratives of unrequited love. If Hart had been able to express anything positive in his life, he could be seen as a romantic figure, a gay Toulouse-Lautrec, physically inadequate but celebrating a life from which he felt separate. Or Hart's life could be seen as a prototypical gay life of the period. Money allowed him the means to buy the sex he wanted. His constant companion was, from all reports, his procurer. His objects of sexual desire were tall blond men, his physical opposites. Why couldn't Hart make the adjustment to homosexuality that Porter and Coward did? Part of the answer might be his collaboration with the man he called "The Principal," the super-straight, uptight Richard Rodgers. The "normal" Richard Rodgers moved on to join another lyricist, Oscar Hammerstein, while Hart dallied with rent boys and drank himself to death. In his public statements and his memoirs Rodgers claims ignorance of Hart's sex life, part and parcel of the policed normalcy that will be reinforced later by Hammerstein's lyrics, though, in an unguarded moment, he is alleged to have said to singer Diahann Carroll: "You can't imagine how wonderful it feels to have written this score and not have to search all over the globe for that drunken little fag."[19] A sense that his collaborator would feel this way could have exacerbated Hart's drinking and self-destruction. Porter and Coward (composers and lyricists) had no collaborators to police them. However chaotic and bohemian the home Hart grew up in was, it was a closely-knit family he found difficult to leave. That connection to family made any adjustment more difficult. Then there was his sense of physical inadequacy, the converse of Porter's vanity.

 Vivienne Segal, one of Hart's close friends and his favorite leading lady, observed: "It was Larry's size that helped make him feel it was incongruous for him to be involved in romance. I think that's what started him drinking, too."[20] Hart was under five feet tall, with a large, prematurely balding head. It is not surprising that his lyrics emphasize homeliness and shortness. In "Bewitched, Bothered, and Bewildered," Vera describes Joey as a "half pint imitation." One of Hart's most beautiful lyrics, "My Funny Valentine," is to a homely man whose looks are "laughable." Homeliness is an *idée fixe* in Hart's songs. In the verse to "Glad to Be Unhappy," the singer says of herself:

> Look at yourself.
> If you had a sense of humor,
> You would laugh to beat the band.[21]

Typically, Hart's most personal lyrics were assigned to women. This cannot just be read as some sort of strategy of displacement. In traditional musical comedies, gender assignments of songs are quite specific. The women got the sensitive songs, the torch songs or songs of unrequited love. The men usually move from songs of philandering to love duets. The women's songs allowed the lyricist space for more private expression. Moreover, the women were the real singers. One wouldn't choose William Gaxton, the usual leading man of the 30s, as one's alter ego. Hart took advantage of this and voiced through the women his own sense of inadequacy, his desire, and his sense that love is impossible. Yet Hart, like every popular lyricist, had to write love songs, and he wrote some of the most complex.

What does love mean for such a person? In its most romantic form, love is only a fantasy. "Dancing on the Ceiling" verges on masturbatory fantasy as the singer, lying in bed, imagines the male object of desire hovering overhead. "Falling in Love with Love," written to one of Rodgers's most graceful waltzes, is a vision of love as fantasy. It isn't a person one loves, but love itself one falls in love with, and even that love backfires: "But love fell out with me."[22] If love does come, it is more likely to be violent than tender. Hart, the master of lyrics about love gone sour, still saw that sparring as better than loneliness:

> The furtive sigh,
> The blackened eye,
> The words "I'll love you till the day I die,"
> The self-deception that believes the lie—
> I wish I were in love again.[23]

Both the ballad "Falling in Love with Love" (*The Boys from Syracuse*) and the patter duet "I Wish I Were in Love Again" (*Babes in Arms*) focus on self-deception, on love as necessary, painful fantasy, unhappy but better than nothing. Real love is painful, but most love is unrequited, and Hart wrote most eloquently of the pleasurable anguish of unrequited love, a "bore,"

> But for someone you adore,
> It's a pleasure to be sad.[24]

Here is a perfect example of why playwright Jerome Lawrence refers to Hart as "the poet laureate of masochism." Hart's torch songs have a unique directness, a sense of emerging from experience rather than convention. Older gay audiences can hear the pleasurable pain of the love one could not admit for fear of violent rejection. Feeling such unrequited love was better than nothing.

The complexity of a song like "Glad to Be Unhappy," to my mind one of Rodgers and Hart's greatest ballads, comes from a combination of the directness of Rodgers's music combined with the pain and paradox of Hart's lyric. The lyric is witty, but sad. Rodgers gives it his usual forthright treatment. As is often the case, it seems like he has built the melody out of the rhythm of the lyrics. Compare it with another classic torch song, the Kern-Woodehouse classic "Bill" from *Show Boat*. Here the complexity comes from Kern's angular melody. The lyrics depict inarticulacy: "I guess he's—I don't know . . ." Hart's lyrics are anything but inarticulate. Emotions are directly, painfully expressed.

The realists in Hart's shows understand that "love," when it does occur, is lust, a matter of the crotch more than the heart. The dark world of *Pal Joey,* a world of hustlers and blackmailers, is the world Hart knew best, the culmination of his work. To Joey, women are "mice." He meets his match in wealthy socialite Vera Simpson, who understands what she wants from a man and what a man cannot give her:

> Useless by day,
> Handy by night.[25]

Vera understands just what a romance with Joey is, that horizontal pleasures can be bought and returned when one is tired of them:

> He's kept enough,
> He's slept enough,
> And yet where it counts
> He's adept enough—[26]

as she also understands the type of person she has invited into her bed:

> Only a wizard could reform that class of males.
> They say a lizard cannot change his scales.[27]

It was exactly that class of male Hart knew well. According to his biographers, Hart's constant companion and agent, former dentist Milton "Doc" Bender, procured for Hart. Bender is often described as Hart's corrupter. Nolan comments, "Amiable, humorous, and unashamedly homosexual, Bender would have an increasingly pernicious effect on Larry's life."[28] Leonard Spigelgass calls him "something slimy, a worm."[29] Even the more sympathetic Marx and Clayton note, "Doc Bender tied himself to Larry so closely that it was difficult to see one of them without the other."[30] It could have been that Hart tied himself to Bender, because Bender was Hart's one close gay friend, his contact with gay life as it then existed. It is interesting that no biographer wants to see Bender from Hart's point of view, as his one gay ally, protector, and link to a gay milieu. Marx and Clayton mention Bender's "Nighttime parties at which orgiastic sex and perversions were chic."[31] Nolan, who can often be disingenuous, writes of Bender: "He kept a coterie of homosexuals around him and led a life which, *for some inexplicable reason,* seemed to appeal greatly to Larry."[32] The reason seems explicable to me, but Hart's supporters have to depict Bender as the sinister prime cause of Hart's homosexual activity, his Mephistopheles. It is unjust to blame Bender for providing what Hart wanted, but it was a means of displacing disapproval of Hart's homosexuality onto another person. Such writers reflexively use the "corruption" or "recruitment" model of homosexuality: poor Hart would have been straight if Bender hadn't recruited him.

Vera's constant mention of Joey's dumbness echoes accounts of the rent boys Hart chose to be with: "He was spending a lot of time, because of Bender, with a lot of dreary, stupid people, handsome young men, but they were very stupid—tall, slender, blond young men always caught his eye. But they were very stupid . . ."[33]

> His thoughts are seldom consecutive.
> He just can't write. ("Take Him")[34]

The picture of carefree, orgiastic sex with dumb blonds (a gay parody of straight male fantasy) is muted by Hart's sexual inadequacies. One account, by a man who "dated" Hart, is almost a paradigm of the conflicted, self-hating homosexual:

> When it came to sex, he left an awful lot to be desired. Please, believe me. He had a fetish. A fetish about sleeping with anybody. Even if he had sex . . . I was one of his boys, and I know . . . you'd wake up and find him in the closet. He'd get up out of bed and go sleep in the closet. Sex frightened him. He didn't know what to do or how to do it. But he wanted to, desperately.[35]

Even sex for Hart was barely requited and intimacy was terrifying. Hollywood hoofer Dan Dailey, who had an affair with Hart, remembered: "He disliked himself before and after sex, and his partners during."[36] The only comfortable role was that of voyeur: "I can remember going to parties and seeing his eyes glittering, watching this orgy going on."[37] He confessed his homosexuality to some close straight friends, but he was terrified that his mother would find out:

> He was apparently tormented by the thought that his mother, Frieda, a stolid German woman, would learn of his sexual orientation. The director Harold Clurman, who knew Hart from *The Garrick Gaieties,* later wrote that Hart was horrified by his own homosexuality and felt thoroughly disgraced, having been brought up in a stereotypical Jewish family where such things were unheard of.[38]

He was very close to his family all his life, living at home and sharing a bedroom with his brother Teddy until Teddy got married. His sister-in-law Dorothy, who has done much over the years to keep Hart's work before the public, was also a protector of his image. Dorothy's biographical sketch of her brother-in-law focuses more on his attempts at heterosexual romance and his occasional desperate offers of marriage than his homosexuality. Like Richard Rodgers, she tries to keep Hart in the closet.[39] Hart did propose marriage at least twice: to opera singer Nanette Guilford and, toward the end of his life, to favored leading lady and dear friend Vivienne Segal:

> He was afraid that on account of his drinking "they" were going to put him away. I said, no, I couldn't do that, I'd always be a good friend of his, but marriage was out of the question. I mean, I never even *kissed* Larry. And I hated cigars![40]

One could, as Dorothy Hart did, latch onto Hart's interest in Nanette Guilford as a sign of "normalcy," or one could see it as a lonely man's attempt to "fit in." The proposal to Segal seems an act of desperation.

If only Hart could have found homosexuality an appealing possibility . . . but like many men of his era, he saw gay men as non-men. Vivienne Segal recalled that during rehearsals for the 1943 revival of *A Connecticut Yankee,* Hart asked her to keep lowering the refrain of one of her songs:

> "Larry," she protested, "if I go any lower, I'll turn into a man."
> "If you do," he retorted darkly, "you'll be the only one in the show."[41]

Hart's crack shows his own homophobia and his realization that a lot of the men in the shows he wrote were gay. There was a gay world of effeminate chorus boys from which he distanced himself. It is interesting to note how Hart, Porter, and Coward all had disdain for stereotypically effeminate gay men, the "pansy," prevalent in New York in the 1920s and travestied on the stage. It is easy to see parallels between this phenomenon and the way the buff gym boys of the nineties disdain show queens. Gay historian George Chauncey describes at length the "pansy culture" of Times Square and the theater district in the 1920s. Effeminacy was a distinct sign of gayness and sexual availability for the men who filled the tenements and the bars in this neighborhood. The display of homosexuality was ostentatious. Effeminacy, the pansy style, was also a protection for those homosexuals who did not affect it. According to Chauncey, pansies soon became a staple of musical entertainments:

> Seizing on the public's fascination with this new phenomenon, Times Square entrepreneurs began to evoke the flamboyant image of the pansy to generate business. "Pansy" acts began to appear on the stage, in the press, and in the clubs, but at this point they usually were the gay equivalent of blackface: straight actors putting on drag or stereotypical mannerisms to mimic and ridicule gay men, to the hoots and jeers of an anti-gay audience. This buffoonery became a standard feature in burlesque and high-class cabaret revues alike, which reinforced the dominant public images of homosexuals.[42]

As historian John Loughery notes, "Announce yourself as a deviant, and this travesty is what you will universally be perceived to be."[43]

Hart himself wasn't above penning a "pansy song," but reluctant to use it. "The Pipes of Pansy" was written in 1925 at the height of the pansy craze and dropped from four shows before their Broadway openings. Clearly, cigar-smoking Hart was no pansy. In joking about it, he distanced himself from it. However, with the popularity of pansy acts, and the visibility of pansies in the theater district, songwriters were bound to be asked to supply pansy songs. One of the songs in the 1930 revue *Sweet and Low,* produced by Billy Rose and with music and lyrics by Harry Warren and Ira Gershwin, was "When a Pansy Was a Flower." Hart's 1930 lyric "Ten Cents a Dance," the lament of a woman who was a "taxi dancer," contained the lines

> Pansies and rough guys,
> Tough guys who tear my gown.[44]

In the refrain, our dancer laments that, when she finds her hero, "it's a queer romance," hinting that the only love she finds is unrequited love with "queers."

Other Hart lyrics are not as overt as "The Pipes of Pansy" but invite, in their use of current gay slang, the possibility of gay readings. In "Manhattan," one of Rodgers and Hart's first hits, the lovers sing of "Greenwich [Village], /

Where modern men itch / To be free."[45] A later lyric notes, "Smart people get hot quicker / When Greek meets Greek."[46] One of the most beautiful torch songs Rodgers and Hart wrote, with a melody that sounds more like Harold Arlen than Richard Rodgers, is "He Was Too Good to Me": "I was a queen to him. / Who's goin' to make me gay now."[47] When this lovely song is sung by a gay-beloved diva like Barbara Cook, the innocent (for its time) language seems to come from the heart of a gay man.[48] Later, Hart wrote a new lyric for the Rodgers melody that did away with the queen/gay lines but created, not a torch song, but a song of praise for the appearance of a gorgeous young man: "He looks so good to me, / My arms are aching for him."[49] Were the queen/gay lines cut because they were too obviously gay even in 1930? Was the lyric that replaced it never sung on stage because it, too, was too transgressive, singing of the beauty of a man, not a woman?

One of the earliest Hart lyrics, "I'd Like to Hide It," is also easily queered:

> When I see John, reserve goes on the wing.
> Though I know I mayn't, I just want to faint.
>
> ....
>
> I'd like to hide it!
> I'd like to smother down the flame inside.[50]

Here the writer knows that his desire to "cling" has to be masked by more masculine taunts. The female singer for whom the song is written can admit her love: the closeted lyricist must hide his.

Sadly, Hart is left usually with loneliness. Even his savvy characters, like *Pal Joey*'s Vera, end up alone, "bewitched, bothered, and bewildered no more." Hart, of all lyricists, is the bard of loneliness. Haunted by feelings of guilt and physical inadequacy, the would-be lover, like Little Girl Blue, is doomed to isolation.

The saddest songs come from Hart's later years. Neither booze nor the supply of rent boys provided by Doc Bender and others could take away the emptiness. Here, too, some of the most honest utterances never reached the stage in his lifetime. Joey's final song, cut before the opening night, ends:

> I can't be sure of girls,
> I'm not at home with men—
> I'm ending up with me again.[51]

These lines occur at the end of a song that is supposed to be an assertion of self-reliance, but like many of Joey's utterances, it belies fear and vulnerability. Joey—and Hart—are trying to see the good side of being alone:

When I come home at night,
A bit too tight to see,
My wallet is all right—
I'd never steal from me.[52]

It is Hart, not Joey, who is likely to be blind drunk at night, robbed by a nameless visitor. Here, as in many of the lyrics, Hart is barely hidden by his fictional voices and personae. In his last complete set of lyrics, for *By Jupiter,* Hart writes:

Love's never sung her songs to me—
No one belongs to me.
I've never been had.[53]

The clumsy, forced rhyme is not worthy of one of our best Broadway poets, by this time a total alcoholic, but the sentiment is typical. From the lofty heights of love, we quickly descend to a double entendre that means both sexually experienced and cheated. The cynical side of Hart could always write off the love he missed as pleasant agony. The more melancholy side could provide some of Hart's most eloquent lines.

One of Hart's last lyrics was for the 1943 revival of *A Connecticut Yankee.* Some biographers think Rodgers consented to this revival, produced after *Oklahoma!,* as a means of "saving" Hart, but while Hart could still turn out good lyrics, he was so far gone that he had to be forcibly expelled from the opening night and died a few days later. In that revival, the leading man sang:

I'm no dish you ought to savor.
Feast your eye on something new.[54]

For those who felt that Hart spent his life in unrequited love for Rodgers, this is a final farewell after almost a quarter-century of artistic partnership. It is a kind of reprise, a summing up of the themes that fill all of Hart's lyrics, the self-loathing, the fear of a sexual relationship, a definition of the limits of what he had to offer. But one wonders from his life and work whether Hart ever trusted friendship.

In 1929, audiences heard a male voice sing:

Still alone, still at sea!
Still there's no one to care for me.[55]

The romantic and the cynic, the wistful yearning for love from the man who slept in the closet, combined with the rationalization that love is more trouble than it is worth. This is the narrative of the lyrics of Lorenz Hart. A gay poet who was never truly gay. Mabel Mercer is quoted as saying that Hart was the saddest man she ever knew. The self-loathing turned into high art is one response to pre-liberation gayness. Hart's work was not championed by the camp divas who would keep it before a gay public. It is only now being fully appreciated.

HOLLYWOOD

What also emerges from the candid Hart biographies is the symbol of Hollywood as a Mecca for gay artists, a place where there was not only abundant remuneration for their work, but also abundant men who would have sex for jobs or money or gifts. Some of Hart's friends felt that Hollywood was his downfall. After Hollywood, Hart could no longer control his alcoholism. Cole Porter's dangerously indiscreet gay life in Hollywood in 1937 caused his wife, Linda, to leave him and to return to their Paris home:

> Linda's main concern was with what she considered his too obvious public display of homosexual involvement. She feared that if word got out to the media of how he was carrying on, it would be terribly damaging to his reputation and career.[56]

Linda had reason to worry. There were a lot of lesbians and gay men among Hollywood actors, writers, and directors, but they were forced to keep a low profile. Actors like William Haines were fired for refusing to play the game. Others, once allowed freedom to be openly gay, like Cary Grant, were later forced to enter marriages of convenience when Hollywood's morals became objects of public scrutiny. Still, Porter stayed in Hollywood six months a year (actually a day under six months to protect his tax status), renting a house from openly gay former-actor-turned-decorator William Haines. Porter's Hollywood Sunday lunch parties were as central to the Hollywood gay social set as director George Cukor's Sunday evening parties: "the composer had become Cukor's chief rival as Hollywood's gay host. They knew better than to set themselves up in direct competition: Porter's Sunday gatherings were for lunch, Cukor's were for dinner."[57]

Hollywood conveyed a paradoxical dual image. In the days of Will Hays and self-censorship, the film studios wanted to be seen as purveyors of middle-class values, represented by Shirley Temple and the Andy Hardy films. But Hollywood was also famous as the center of conspicuous consumption, social mobility, and sexual profligacy.

What Hollywood allowed the public to see was barely contained heterosexual promiscuity. What it hid then and tries to hide now is its rampant homosexuality. Porter's and Hart's personal narratives intersect more in Hollywood than in New York. Porter reveled in Hollywood's promiscuity; Hart's response was more mixed. On one hand, he was in competition with Cole Porter. According to the biographer of Tyrone Power, one of the handsome young men who provided ornament and probably more at Hart's parties:

> Ty didn't approve of the notorious homosexual hangouts Larry Hart was known to frequent. He was too conventional and circumspect to "come out" in this way. Nor did he approve of the unspoken contest between Hart and another homosexual song writer, Cole Porter, to determine who could publicly flaunt, in the toniest gathering places, the company of the town's most handsome men.[58]

This doesn't sound like closeted behavior, but Hollywood was a walled fortress protected by the public relations machinery of the studio system. If your behavior got so indiscreet that news leaked out—as Linda Porter feared her husband's might—you got in trouble. This is still true for actors.

IN MY FASHION

More than Hart, Porter was a favorite among gay men in the thirties. George Chauncey notes that "Cole Porter's songs were mainstays in gay culture."[59] Porter's life was something of an open secret and his songs connect homosexuality with urbane and urban sophistication.

While Hollywood plays a part in Porter's narrative as the place where his homosexuality became dangerously public for the 1930s, the rest of the narrative differs considerably from Hart's. Porter was born rich and lived off of his and his wife's inheritance as well as the income from his songs. His life and work offered a mixed message. Unlike Hart, he was the songwriter as public figure, more of a celebrity than the performers who starred in his shows:

> Once he became a much-talked-about composer-lyricist of hit songs, his exciting global adventures not only were taken at their face value, but they also worked to his advantage. Cole now epitomized for the masses, too, the suave man of the world . . . [A]s much as anyone, Cole—aided, of course, by press agents and other media personnel—can take credit for promulgating the portrait of himself that the world has come to know and accept.[60]

Porter's life and work can be seen as a paradigm for the permeability of the closet for the rich and famous. While he was happily married for most of his life, the marriage was a contract that allowed Porter his sexual freedom, as long as his night life was carried on with discretion. One friend noted, "Linda became Cole's best friend and they had a mother/son arrangement,"[61] part of which was Cole's insistence that his male lovers and Linda became friends. Many of Porter's close male friends were openly, flamboyantly gay; the arranger of many of his parties was a lesbian, Elsa Maxwell. The wealth of Porter and his gay cronies allowed them more freedom of self-expression than that afforded most Americans. Porter lived much of his life in Paris, Venice, and other European capitals. His glittering, publicized social life was a stark contrast to his sex life. There were muses, young male lovers (dancers Boris Kochno and Nelson Barclift, architect Ed Tauch, sailor-turned-servant Ray Kelly, among others) who seem to have been the inspirations for some of his songs, but loving relationships were not easy for him: "most of the males he formed firm friendships with were homosexual, and he rarely seemed sure of the affection of friends who were also lovers."[62] Porter was not willing to settle for one lover when through his friends and show business connections so many men were available to him. There were also the "fucking parties" with the burly rough trade he and his friend Monty Woolley preferred and whom they picked up in waterfront bars or Harlem male bordellos. Porter the snob was sexually turned on by men he saw as his social inferiors, but he was horrified when Woolley actually fell in love with a black servant. Did Porter's colleagues know he was gay? According to British singer Elisabeth Welch, one of the original cast of *Nymph Errant* (1933), "That he was homosexual everyone in the theater knew, but it was not discussed."[63] One thing seems clear. Unlike Lorenz Hart's, Porter's sexuality was a source of pleasure and inspiration, not anguish. His life and his art are about merging the two meanings of "gay." His money and the social milieu it enabled kept the police at bay and kept him above the shame and guilt with which a more bourgeois upbringing imbued Hart.

In a recent Los Angeles tribute to Cole Porter, presented as a benefit for AIDS charities, singer Matt Zarley, dressed as a 1990s Los Angeles hustler, performed a male version of Porter's 1930 song "Love for Sale." Porter often said that this was his favorite of his songs. Sung by a man, it depicts a world Porter knew well. There is nothing gender-specific about the lyric, in which the prostitute sings of what he/she can and cannot offer:

Old love, new love,
Every love but true love.[64]

For a man known to give new cars and other lavish gifts to young men he slept with in addition to paying the fees charged by male bordellos and call boys, the world of "Love for Sale" was both familiar and tantalizing.

Love to Porter was a series of compartments. Companionship, devotion, and social life, but separate bedrooms with his wife; nocturnal sexual exploits with his gay friends; love letters to handsome young men; sex with rough trade. This compartmentalization is reinforced in "Love for Sale" by the repetition of the word "love," which has different meanings in different lines. The love the hustler knows is sex, "every love but true love." The "true love" of which poets write is "childish." Perhaps this is why Porter's lyric "True Love" from the 1956 film *High Society* is one of his wimpiest.

"Love" for Porter, if romantic love, led to vague, Hallmark-ish sentiments:

> You'd be so easy to love,
> So easy to idolize, all others above.[65]

The forced rhyme and convoluted syntax of the second line is clever, but also self-conscious, belying an emotional void sold as sophistication. Compare it to the naked emotions of Hart's lyrics. There is seldom a sense of a specific "I" and "you" in Porter. What is unique and interesting is the general nature of the lyric. Gerald Mast notes that "Porter developed the unique gift of implying everything while saying nothing."[66] Porter loved, for example, to write songs about "it" or "that thing":

> "You've Got That Thing"
> "What Is This Thing Called Love?"
> "You Do Something to Me"

That "thing" is not romantic love but sexual attraction, the necessary quantity for the "it" that birds and bees do. Sometimes the "it" is defined as something non-sexual, but Porter is always aware of the suggestive power of this indefinite, genderless pronoun. "It's Bad for Me" is from *Nymph Errant* (1933), a musical about the sexual experimentation of a young woman who gets a lot of "it." The song defines the "it," but by this time the word, repeated like a mantra, means something else. The prim Ninotchka in *Silk Stockings* understands best what "it" is: "It's a chemical reaction, that's all."[67]

This imprecision is one of the reasons so many of Porter's songs can be moved around from one musical to another, a practice Porter endorsed. As "it" had specific sexual connotations, so did "that thing": "Yes, you've got that thing, that certain thing."[68] In the comic patter songs for which Porter was celebrated, that "thing" became more specific. In 1942, Ethel Merman could celebrate her wartime service, doing "something for the boys," with such a vague but specific word. This comic song is a gloss on a lyric like:

> You've got something, darling, something
> That's driving me slowly but surely insane,
> Something tempting, something intangible,
> Something rare that I never could explain.[69]

There's something closeted about Porter's insistent vagueness, the repetition of the idea that what is most desirable cannot be spoken, much less defined. There is also the sense that the vagueness, like the cleverness, expresses a lack of desire for the opposite sex and a lack of affection for members of the sex Porter preferred.

Such purposeful imprecision allowed Porter to be naughty and nice at the same time. The audience participated in making the lyric ribald. For a contemporary audience, Porter's naughtiness can seem collegiate, but it can also be fun. "But in the Morning, No," written for Ethel Merman and Bert Lahr, becomes funnier throughout its ten verses of double entendres. In 1939, this naughtiness seemed "sophisticated," and Porter was one of the few composers who wrote songs that could not be played on the radio because of their suggestive lyrics. There are bowdlerized lyrics for Hart's "Bewitched, Bothered, and Bewildered" that allowed the song to be a commercial hit, but one cannot conceive of a G-rated version of "Love for Sale." Once in a while his entendres were barely double. This one, clearly demonstrating Porter's own predilection, slipped by the censors when MGM made the film version of *Kiss Me, Kate,* in which Bianca is willing to take

> Any Tom, Harry or Dick,
> A dicka dick,
> A dicka dick.[70]

Porter is known, too, for his "list songs," filled with specific references to people who were contemporary celebrities or his close friends. In particular, references abound to two gay actors: Monty Woolley and Clifton Webb. Woolley, an old friend from Yale who directed some of Porter's musicals before becoming a star himself with the hit comedy *The Man Who Came to Dinner,* appears so often it seems like an advertisement. Webb, a gay man who lived with his mother, Maybelle, until her death at ninety-two, was a major player in the Hollywood gay social circuit. Also mentioned often is Elsa Maxwell, that odd, decidedly unglamorous, professional social climber who was part of Porter's social circle. Porter's many references to Maxwell authorize her social significance. Maxwell was a lesbian and Woolley and Webb were rather openly gay men for their time. So these frequent references also queer Porter's lyrics.

The lyrics do contain gay slang and specific references to homosexuality. The 1929 musical *Wake Up and Dream* contains two songs that acknowledge types of homosexuals likely to be found in moneyed circles. "I'm a Gigolo" is the self-description of a paid companion to older, sometimes married women. It is clear from the song that he is hired for companionship, not sex:

> I'm a famous gigolo.
> And of lavender my nature's got just a dash in it.[71]

Also written for this show, but not used, is a song Porter liked to sing at parties, "The Extra Man," about the sort of "harmless" unattached male one invites to fill out a party.

Porter's references to homosexuality range from the suggestive to the specific. The 1941 musical *Let's Face It* had a Porter list song, "Farming," filled with specific references to contemporary celebrities. In one stanza, we find a bizarre reference to George Raft's bull: "Georgie's bull is beautiful, but he's gay."[72] In 1941, "gay"—meaning "homosexual"—was a coterie term, used only by some urban homosexuals. Porter no doubt knew it, but most of the straight people in his audience would only know the traditional (now lost) meanings of the word (happy, colorful, energetically frivolous, hedonistic). The line makes little sense without the bull being homosexual, but Porter was, in using this word, introducing its homosexual meaning to many in his audience. Porter shows gay men in the audience that he's "in the know." Others could just be baffled by the line unless something in its performance cued the audience. Since Danny Kaye, one of the singers of this song, was known for his pansy routines and would shortly go on to play one of musical theater's first gay leading characters in *Lady in the Dark,* I would not be surprised if he made clear to the audience what "gay" meant. Porter coyly puts this "gay" reference in a song in which every stanza except the one about George Raft's bull contains the word "gay" in its traditional usage: "[farming] makes 'em feel more glamorous and more gay." The lyric, then, is an interesting moment in the history of gay slang.[73] At times the word "gay" could be read either in its traditional meaning or, for those in the know, as homosexual, as in the song written for Eve Arden in 1941, but not used, "Make a Date with a Great Psychoanalyst." You should make such a date

> If you just found out that your husband has
> Ev'ry day with a gay cutie-pie a tryst.[74]

With or without the argot, homosexuality keeps cropping up in Porter's lyrics. In *Fifty Million Frenchmen,* a lady laments over her unrequited love for a croupier in a lyric that is a masterpiece of innuendo:

> I said I like John Gilbert a lot, don't you?
> He didn't answer, but when the show was through
> I realized that he liked John Gilbert too.[75]

In *Seven Lively Arts* (1944), Bert Lahr sang a drinking song that contained the line, "Drink even faster to the Astor bar." Since the bar at the Astor Hotel was a well-known meeting place for gay men during World War II, Porter's lyric has particular significance, again for those in the know.[76] Later in the song, Lahr sang:

> Drink to my brother once a boy so fine
> Who suddenly became Sweet Adeline.[77]

If serious drama was careful to avoid acknowledgments of the existence of homosexuality, Porter's lyrics are filled with in jokes. Straight auditors may have missed them, but Porter clearly felt that his more sophisticated audience would get them—and that there were gay men in the audience who would appreciate them.

In the 1919 song "My Cozy Corner of the Ritz," the singer notes that he likes his particular corner of the Ritz bar:

> 'Cause I like to see the kings
> And let the queens see me.[78]

Since later in his life Porter spoke of his fear of seeming an "old queen," we have some sense he knew the gay meaning of the term. Moreover, the Ritz bar, like the famed Astor bar in New York, had a gay side and a straight side:

> At that time [1919] the Ritz [in New York City] had two bars, a men's bar on
> the left (a frequent gathering place for homosexuals) where, as Beverly Nichols
> noted, "Cole Porter, looking like a startled leprechaun, could sip a Pernod and
> cast his dark, syrupy little eyes to the white and gold ceiling, and think out his
> devastating little rhymes," and a mixed bar on the right. Once the Cole-Linda

liaison was a fait accompli, the couple switched from the left to the right-hand one.[79]

"My Cozy Corner of the Ritz" demonstrates a crucial side of Cole Porter's work. His world was that of the Ritz. His songs were about rich, sophisticated people. As Fred Astaire developed an image of the urban sophisticate always in top hat and tails, so Porter represented the insulated world of the wealthy glitterati of his time. He was the bard of the leisure classes. It seems amazing that he dirtied his hands with Broadway at all, except that Broadway was where a songwriter had to ply his wares. Lorenz Hart could write "The Lady Is a Tramp." Porter wrote "Down in the Depths (On the Ninetieth Floor)." Porter's famous patter songs depict the rich and famous or mock social climbers. Hart's are about mismatched couples. Porter's social world offered him acceptance and discretion. It was, to some extent, above the social judgments made of Hart and Doc Bender. No one called Monty Woolley Porter's corrupter.

SIR NOËL

There will be books proving conclusively that I was a homosexual and books proving equally conclusively that I was not.[80]

There is a musical in the story of a poor young Englishman from the suburbs of London who becomes a celebrated actor, singer, composer, lyricist, playwright, director, screenwriter, film star, cabaret artist, painter, and fiction writer whose long-hoped-for knighthood is delayed for decades because he had an affair with a prince. At the very moment he was thought an anachronism, when rock groups appeared on the honors list, Noël Coward finally got his knighthood. What other show business celebrity was as friendly with the royal family? The most amazing aspect of Noël Coward's life and career are his changing images. Above all, he was an expert at self-presentation, from the elegant, effete young self-made sophisticate of the 1920s to the celebrator of "London Pride" and British values during World War II to the aging sophisticate of his 1950s Las Vegas act to Sir Noël, "the Master," in his last years. Born of lower-middle-class parents, in show business from childhood, Coward was a model of a new social mobility for England. By the 1920s he was a symbol of sophistication and chic decadence for his generation of affluent young people. Yet part of that image was a decidedly gay style. Coward, however cautious, is the most openly gay figure in our troika of songwriters.

Some recent writers have written books that compare the lives and work of Noël Coward and Cole Porter as if their experiences were synonymous and their work comparable. Both were gay and both lived the lives of wealthy world travelers. Both wrote clever, often satirical lyrics and popular tunes. Both were attacked by their detractors as merely clever and superficial, a club often used by critics to bludgeon gay writers. During Coward's lifetime, critics compared his work unfavorably to Porter's. In a review of Coward's first memoir, *Present Indicative,* Cyril Connolly wrote that the book is

> [t]he picture, carefully incomplete, of a success; probably of one of the most talented and prodigiously successful people the world has ever known—a person of infinite charm and adaptability whose very adaptability, however, makes him inferior to a more compact and worldly competitor in his own sphere, like Cole Porter; and an essentially unhappy man, a man who gives one the impression of having seldom really thought or really lived and is intelligent enough to know it.[81]

Why compare Coward, a playwright and star performer as well as composer and lyricist, to Porter? Why choose Porter for comparison among the other successful writers of popular songs at the time (the Gershwins, Rodgers and Hart, Berlin)? Because Coward and Porter were both known to be gay? Other aspects of Connolly's review are significant. His observation that Coward's memoir is "carefully incomplete" means that Coward, while not creating a heterosexual fiction about his life, does not discuss specific homosexual experiences. The book is "carefully incomplete" for good reason in an age in which homosexual acts were criminal offenses. Connolly ends this bashing with two of the most common stereotypes of gay men, superficiality and unhappiness. Unlike the other queer, Cole Porter, Coward doesn't stick to the limited craft of lyric writing but dares to claim a position as a serious writer. In 1937, comparing Coward to Porter was a way of putting the more talented and versatile Coward in his place. It makes no more sense when gay-friendly writers do it now. As much separates Coward and Porter as joins them, including their methods of dealing with their homosexuality. Coward, through all of his literary, musical, and personal performances, defined gayness for a generation of British men. As Terry Castle concisely puts it:

> Through innuendo or the well-judged, fleetingly campy aside, one might satirize hypocritical social codes obliquely without risking self-incrimination. And at this subliminal provocation Coward was eminently successful: his remarkable career as actor, singer, composer, novelist, playwright, cabaret performer, and

general arbiter of fashionable taste for more than fifty years might indeed be said to represent the single most sustained homosexual infiltration of mainstream Anglo-American culture of the century.[82]

Porter's life demonstrates how one privileged man compartmentalized various aspects of his experience, including homosexuality, and how that homosexuality sometimes spilled out into his lyrics. Coward's life and work are about gay self-presentation in a period when homosexuality was illegal. One cannot talk about Coward's performances, in musical theater or elsewhere, without talking about his centrality as a gay figure.

In his most famous musical, *Bitter Sweet* (1929), a group of young Victorian men sing of their decadent style:

> Haughty boys, naughty boys, dear, dear, dear!
> Swooning with affectation.
> Our figures sleek and willowy,
> Our lips incarnadine,
> May worry the majority a bit.
> ....
> And as we are the reason for the 'nineties' being gay,
> We all wear a green carnation.[83]

Bitter Sweet was close enough in time to the Oscar Wilde scandal for audiences to know that the green carnation worn by Wilde and his gay admirers was a sign of homosexuality as well as one of Victorian aestheticism. The Wilde trial, more than any other nineteenth-century social phenomenon, defined, however inaccurately, this new entity called a "homosexual" as "someone like Oscar Wilde": witty, effete, artistic, effeminate, giving off an air of intellectual superiority, and disdainful of patriarchy and middle-class morality. Coward's placement of this song in his hit musical acknowledges and satirizes homosexuals of the previous generation. His wearers of the green carnation may be amusingly bizarre and too camp for Coward's audiences, but the fact is that Coward by 1929 had created a new camp gay style that his generation, gay and straight, accepted as chic, if rebellious. The use of the word "gay" in the penultimate line of "The Green Carnation" is paradigmatic of Coward's ability to define a closeted new culture. "Gay," in its original meaning of high-spirited, was a common word in 1920s lyrics. Coward used the term in its original context all his life. But by 1929, within homosexual culture it already had the meaning that would later become widely used. Coward knew that line was a double entendre with a specific meaning for the gay members of his audience. As a

matter of fact, Coward's use of the word in "The Green Carnation" may have
done much to queer the word "gay." The memory of the 1890s, thanks to the
Wilde trial, was indeed gay, though actually a tragic era for British homosexuals.

Coward may have seen his made-up Victorian queens as silly, but he
gave currency to a new queenly style that had its roots in Wilde's nineties,
much as he disdained Wilde's aestheticism and what he saw as maudlin self-
pity after the trial:

> I have read the Oscar Wilde letters and have come to the reluctant conclusion
> that he was one of the silliest, most conceited and unattractive characters that
> ever existed. His love letters to Lord Alfred Douglas are humorless, affected and
> embarrassing, and his crawling letter from prison to the Home Secretary beneath
> contempt. *De Profundis* is one long wail of self pity. It is extraordinary indeed
> that such a posing, artificial old queen should have written one of the greatest
> comedies in the English language. In my opinion it was the only thing of the
> least *importance* that he did write.[84]

Coward would never publicly have "dropped the mask" as Wilde did. He was
free, as Terry Castle so vividly puts it, of "Wilde's curious, soiling streak of self-
destructiveness."[85] Like his dear friend Marlene Dietrich, Coward lived to
maintain his public image. Off stage never came on stage. The image of wit and
urbanity were always on display. Unlike Wilde, Coward was an actor from
childhood, and the act was everything. Part of the act, however unacknowledged,
was gayness. Coward always affected an innocence about setting gay fashion,
but it is difficult to believe that this master of the calculated image did not know
what he was doing:

> I took to wearing colored turtle-necked jerseys . . . more for comfort than for
> effect, and soon I was informed by my evening paper that I had started a fashion
> . . . During the ensuing months I noticed more and more of our seedier West-
> End chorus boys parading about London in them.[86]

This comment comes from Coward's memoir, *Present Indicative,* aimed at a
general audience. Here he is distancing himself from the "seedier West-End
chorus boys," known to be gay, thus distancing himself from overt
homosexuality. His dress, he claims, was practical. However, his biographer
points out that "to the homosexual enclave within the theater and without,
Noël became an icon."[87] Peter Quennell remembers, "In my raffish world, it
was never assumed that he was anything else [but homosexual]."[88] Yet he was
also a role model to straight men. As one of his contemporaries, photogra-

pher-designer Cecil Beaton, recalls: "all sorts of men suddenly wanted to look like Noël Coward—sleek and satiny, clipped and well groomed, with a cigarette, a telephone, or a cocktail at hand."[89] Alan Jenkins wrote of himself in 1930:

> I have at last seen *Bitter Sweet,* whose tunes I have been playing on the piano for months. I am also trying to write songs, and I realize that they are all imitation Noël Coward. In my private fantasy, I *am* Noël Coward: brilliant, witty, adored by women. I do not yet know that he is homosexual: when I find out, the shock lasts for two days.[90]

Jenkins's comment is vivid evidence for Coward's crossing of gay and straight styles. He could be a role model to straight men until they found out his open secret. Then masculine anxiety set in with a vengeance.

Present Indicative is a kind of performance. In it, as biographer Philip Hoare notes, one could read Coward's homosexuality "between the lines."[91] He spends pages on Jack Wilson, but only as friend and business manager; no woman takes pride of place and there is no pretense of heterosexual romance. Coward could offer no more openness in England's post-Wilde age of Draconian legal treatment of homosexuals. Coward had seen colleagues go to jail and he was terrified that might happen to him:

> What stuck in his craw was the Oscar Wilde trial. . . . He told me once "I'm not going to court." He was absolutely petrified about that sort of thing. . . . That ate into his soul.[92]

Yet if one got into the right circles, if one were discreet enough, one might be able to lead a gay life. One of the most telling stories about Coward is his lecture to Cecil Beaton about sartorial style:

> It is important not to let the public have a loophole to lampoon you . . . I take ruthless stock of myself in a mirror before going out. A polo jumper or unfortunate tie exposes one to danger.[93]

The "dangers" were exposé, potential arrest, and limit of one's mass appeal and marketability. Coward as a performer would have to be more conscious of that than would a designer like Beaton.

Yet Coward seemed to have a very matter-of-fact attitude toward his homosexuality. In a late short story, "Me and the Girls," a memoir of a gay performer, the central character says:

I never was one to go off into a great production about being queer and work myself up into a state like some people I know. I can't think why they waste their time. I mean it just doesn't make sense, does it? You're born either hetero, bi or homo and whichever way it goes there you are stuck with it. Mind you people are getting a good deal more hep about it than they used to be but the laws still exist that make it a crime and poor bastards still get hauled off to the clink just for doing what comes naturally as the song says. Of course this is what upsets some of the old magistrates more than anything, the fact that it *is* as natural as any other way of having sex. . . . [94]

However natural Coward felt homosexuality was, he always was conscious of the sensibilities of his public. When Sheridan Morley wrote the draft of his 1969 biography of Coward, Coward wanted mention of his homosexuality removed. He knew his audience was as old as he and not as tolerant as the younger generation, who were not interested in him: "I can't afford to offend their prejudice nor do I really want to disturb them this late in their lives."[95] When Cole Lesley and others wrote their more candid biographies of Coward after his death, there was an openly gay readership interested in figures like Coward.

Two publicity photos of Coward epitomize the mixed signals he sent to his public in his heyday. The first was on the cover of *The Sketch* magazine (April 1925), during the run of his sensational drama of mother fixation and drug abuse, *The Vortex*. The caption is "Noël the Fortunate: The Young Playwright, Actor, and Composer Mr. Noël Coward, Busy at Breakfast." Coward is sitting up in bed, wearing a fancy dressing gown, much like the one he wore on stage in *The Vortex*. His breakfast tray is laid out before him, and he is talking on the telephone. The headboard of the bed is upholstered, the bed itself lavishly appointed. A curtained screen stands behind, and there are fancy fabrics laid out on the bed. There is a decanter and cigarettes on the bed table. Coward carefully staged this portrait of elegant indolence with hints of decadence as his image of a 1920s version of Oscar Wilde hedonism. Its transgression against norms of masculinity and the work ethic could be seen as an early corollary to the gender-bending, rebellious image of 1970s rockers like David Bowie. And one must remember that part of Coward's image was of rebellious youth:

> Let's lead moralists the devil of a dance,
> Let's succumb
> Completely to temptation,
> Probe and plumb
> To find a new sensation.[96]

Unlike rock stars, Coward wanted to portray a man of the utmost world-weary sophistication, not screaming working-class rebellion. Yet his image screamed "effeminate" and "degenerate" to more conservative men, whose harsh voices could do considerable damage in 1925.

Two years before Coward's photo, Gertrude Lawrence's photo had been on the cover of *The Sketch;* in it, she was sitting on an ornate bed talking on the phone. The picture was actually a shot taken from Coward's sketch "Early Morning." A small proscenium frames Lawrence and her elaborate bed. In Coward's later photo described above, his life, or at least his public persona, seems to imitate his art as he takes over Lawrence's role. Coward almost mimicked Lawrence's pose in another 1927 publicity photo in which he sits on a bed, legs crossed, and talks on the phone. Coward was creating for conservative England a Hollywood image of sexual availability. The public is, in essence, invited to see this star in his bedroom. Of course, who received in their bedrooms? Royalty. Class is always paramount in understanding Coward's image. What we take as queer, he meant as aristocratic, elegant, sophisticated. Like Wilde's, his image blurred sophistication and gayness.

The second picture is the famous publicity photo for Coward's 1932 Broadway play, *Design for Living.* Here pajama-clad Coward and Alfred Lunt are entangled with nightgown-clad Lynn Fontanne in what is obviously a ménage à trois. Coward's head is cradled in Lunt's arm as he lies in Lunt's lap, and Fontanne is holding hands with both of the men. It would take a good deal of naivete or denial to avoid the clear sexual relationship depicted in this photo. The more one knows, the more is shown. It purports to dramatize the final moment of the play in which Otto, Leo, and Gilda laughingly accept their fate to be together as a threesome and mock the conventional values of Gilda's husband, aptly named Ernest. Since Lunt was bisexual, the picture also suggests the free sexuality of the play's stars.

In both pictures, Coward is clad in sleepwear and lying down, signs of indolence and sexual availability. Terry Castle emphasizes another, more private photograph that first appears in the volume of memoirs and photos assembled by Coward's literary executors after his death. Lying face down in the sand, probably at Coward's Jamaica home, are five naked figures: Nancy Hamilton, the lover of actress Katharine Cornell; Cornell; Cornell's gay husband, Guthrie McClintic; Coward; and Coward's lover Graham Payn—it is an "exquisite, if risible, emblem of gay and lesbian solidarity."[97] This is Coward's private life, shared with lesbian and gay friends. Coward may have preferred the public to see him in full dress at lunch with his pal the Queen Mother. His later image is a fascinating, contradictory mix of the icon and the queen.

The danger was that too overt signs of gayness could lead to public exposure, which would have ruined Coward's career. Like current closeted Hollywood stars, Coward wanted universal acclaim *and* a gay sex life. Unlike Hollywood stars, however, he never pretended to have romances with women, though many of his best friends were women, often lesbians or bisexuals. In his diaries he notes a dinner he spent with gay fifties singing star Johnnie Ray. Coward was friends with Ray: if one reads between the lines of the diary, he seems smitten with Ray, but he found the act Ray had to play to maintain his heterosexual image silly:

> On Monday, Johnnie Ray's first night [at the London Palladium]. Squealing teenagers and mass hysteria, quite nauseating, but he gave a remarkable performance both on stage and later at supper at the Embassy, where he fondled Terry Moore for the cameras. Poor boy.[98]

The final note of condescending sympathy was from a man who would never do something so unseemly as to pretend to heterosexuality.[99] In some ways, however, Coward was naive and careless about exposing his homosexuality. He was the only one of our triumvirate to have long-term romantic liaisons. Moreover, he always, often foolishly, made his lovers part of his professional world. American financier Jack Wilson was Coward's lover in the 1920s and 1930s, but Coward "covered" for Jack's domestic position by making him his business manager. Even after Coward and Wilson broke up romantically and Wilson married, Coward maintained him to handle his American business dealings, which Wilson did terribly. Typically, Coward remained friends with Wilson and his wife even after it was clear that Wilson had botched Coward's finances. Wilson later was director of *Kiss Me, Kate* and, supposedly, Cole Porter's lover for a while. Wilson later drank himself to death. His cruelty toward Coward's next lover, Graham Payn, which amounted to attempts to sabotage Payn's career, as well as his rampant alcoholism suggest that he never got over his love for Coward.

In the late 1940s, Coward wrote songs and shows for handsome Graham Payn, with whom he had a romance that turned into lifelong friendship. Coward wanted to make Payn a star, his romantic leading man when Coward could no longer play that role himself, but Payn had neither the charisma nor the determination. Moreover, he was undermined by the rumors surrounding his casting as Coward's leading man. However indiscreet Coward may have been about Payn, he thought he maintained discretion. Even in his dairies Coward never mentions a romantic relationship. Eventually Payn came on Coward's payroll as "understudy" to Cole Lesley, Coward's servant, secretary, traveling companion, friend, and, later, biographer:

> I have decided once and for all that he must do the job as Coley's "understudy." It doesn't matter that he can't type. He has a loving and loyal heart and no future anywhere but with me. He will do all he can to help and now, having made this decision, I feel happier than I have felt for a long time. . . . Graham's stage career is non-existent. It has worried me for years thinking of him struggling to get work and failing. He will be forty-nine next birthday and the jig is up.[100]

Coward's relationship with Wilson and Payn demonstrate Coward's sometimes blind loyalty to the men he loved and befriended. Or did he naively think that keeping them in key positions in his professional life justified their position, in the public's eye, in his personal life? He was willing to risk exposure to find a place for them in his professional and personal worlds. He left the bulk of his estate to Lesley and Payn, who were, in most ways, his family.

Coward claimed that he was a failure at romantic love: "To me, passionate love has always been like a tight shoe rubbing blisters on my Achilles heel . . . I resent it and love it and wallow and recover . . . and I wish to God I could handle it, but I never have and know I never will."[101] How could someone with Coward's fear of exposure and his primary need for mass adulation give himself to another person? Payn and Cole Lesley were willing to play the role Coward could deal with, loving satellites.

The image Coward cultivated—sophisticated man of the world—was much like his friend Cole Porter's. Unlike Porter, he did not have aristocratic status, a degree from a prestigious university, or infinite amounts of money. Coward's finances were often precarious, as he lived on what he earned. He couldn't be as cavalier about his work as Porter was. Moreover, much of the success of Coward's work depended on his own performances of his plays, musicals, and songs, thus the need for caution in his self-presentation. At the same time, Coward's homosexuality was at best an open secret, and some of his romances, such as that with Prince George, Duke of Kent, the brother to the heir to the throne, may have been the cause of the long delay of his knighthood. Cecil Beaton, coming down from Cambridge to begin a career in London as a designer, was advised to attach himself to Coward and his set, but he worried because he didn't want to become a "terrible homosexualist" and thus thought it "dangerous for me to get in with the Ivor-Noël crowd."[102] The very state of British musical theater at the time is encapsulated in Beaton's diary entry. The most celebrated figures as composers and stars were Ivor Novello and Coward, both pop icons for the 1920s and both known by people in and around the theater to be gay, stars in a society in which homosexuality was frowned on and homosexual behavior policed and viciously punished. The world of musical theater floated somehow above middle-class sexual morality.

Coward wanted more than stardom in musical theater, or even in theater more generally. He wanted social stardom. Like gay American writer Truman Capote, Coward craved celebrity and social status. It was not enough to have audiences cheering. He wanted friendships with royalty as well as show business celebrities. He wanted to be, and was, a British institution, but only when he became an older reminder of a lost pre-depression, pre–World War II era, only when time had defanged him and he was no longer a rebellious youth. Careful to the end, he attended his knighthood investiture not with his lifelong companions Payn and Lesley, but with novelist Joyce Cary and designer (and lesbian) Gladys Calthrop. But who didn't know by then? Coward was even writing about gay characters in his plays and stories and playing old queens in films like *Bunny Lake Is Missing* ("I play an elderly, drunk, queer masochist, and I am in no mood for any wisecracks about typecasting . . ."[103]), and *Boom!,* a disastrous film version of Tennessee Williams's disastrous play *The Milk Train Doesn't Stop Here Anymore.* In *Boom!,* Coward played the bitchy socialite, "The Witch of Capri," written originally as a woman's role, presaging openly gay actor Rupert Everett's essaying on stage the central character in *Milk Train,* Flora Goforth, in 1997. Coward liked his work in both films and had no comments for his diary about being typecast as old queens. The *Boom!* role seems a perverse homage to Coward's image in the 1960s as a queer anachronism.

In the twenties and thirties, lyricist Coward, like Porter, was a chronicler of the high life, including its gayness. One of his songs, "I Went to a Marvelous Party," has been central to Coward's image among gay men. It was scripture, known by heart by many of my friends thirty years ago. The song was supposedly inspired by one of lesbian socialite Elsa Maxwell's grand soirees:

> Everyone's here and frightfully gay,
> Nobody cares what people say,
> Though the Riviera
> Seems really much queerer
> Than Rome at its height . . .[104]

This song was written for Beatrice Lillie to sing in a New York revue, *Set to Music.* It probably would not have passed the Lord Chamberlain's blue pencil in Coward's native land. The song sends Coward's typical mixed signals. It is a satiric catalogue of decadence among the rich, made safely silly by Bea Lillie's hilarious delivery, but it also acknowledged that gays and lesbians were very much a part of that fascinatingly decadent set out there on the Riviera (though not of course in Belgravia or New York). The song is set on Cap Ferrat, the setting for F. Scott Fitzgerald's best novel, *Tender Is the Night* (1934), in which homosexuality and lesbianism are signs of the decadence of the rich that destroys American innocent Dick Diver. Gay men in the audience—and Lillie had a large gay following—would know that this was Coward's world. Moreover, in 1938 when any mention of homosexuality was a kind of affirmation, Coward was offering the gay men and the lesbians in his audience acknowledgment of their existence in the most fashionable social world.

"Mad About the Boy" was also in *Set to Music*. Coward had used it in the British revue *Words and Music,* where it was the hit of the show. In that production, a group of women from different walks of life are looking at a poster of a matinee idol outside a movie theater. The poster lights up from behind to reveal the star in a less glamorous pose: he is wearing a dressing gown, his feet are in a mustard bath, he wears glasses, and he is having his nails manicured. There is an air of effeminacy surrounding this matinee idol who is the center of the women's fantasies. In its original British form, there were hints of gayness throughout the song, from the appearance of the star to innuendoes in the lyrics:

> He has a gay appeal
> That makes me feel
> There's maybe something sad about the boy.[105]

For its New York appearance, Coward wanted to add a businessman who would sing:

> And even Dr. Freud cannot explain
> Those vexing dreams
> I've had about the boy.[106]

The management wisely banned this verse. New York was not ready for such unabashed, uncritical acknowledgment of homosexual desire on the stage in 1938. Yet, like Tennessee Williams a decade later, Coward pushed the envelope. He wanted to protect himself and the currency of his work, but he was insistent in raising the specter of homosexuality in his plays and musicals.

For anyone with an historical imagination as well as a love for musical theater, Hart, Porter, and Coward represent more than ghosts of closets past. They were as open—sometimes more open—than their public would allow. If anything, they pushed the envelope of acceptance of homosexuality a bit more in our direction. To some of us, they also represent a lost style that is in great part a gay style.

"YOU'VE GOT TO BE CAREFULLY TAUGHT": HETEROSEXUALITY AND US

In order to examine the ways in which musical theater—its writing and performance—allowed space for transgressions from normative heterosexuality, we need to look at the queer ways in which musical theater depicted the norms—gender-appropriate behavior and heterosexual romance. A show queen was and is able to see that gender and heterosexuality are seldom as "normal" as they seem in musicals, which is one reason some of us are show queens. Then there is Rodgers and Hammerstein.

I begin with three musicals from 1955 because as a thirteen-year-old kid I went to a lot of musicals that year. Adolescence and my emergence as a show queen hit simultaneously. Though only somewhat aware of my sexual orientation at the time, I was attracted to these spectacles in much the same way I am attracted to them as a gay adult. Since I was attracted to some of the men on stage, I placed myself in the position of the leading lady. The musicals were offering their automatic message of heterosexual love and marriage, but I found a space within that to experience enormous exhilaration.

"Without love, what is a woman?" So sang Ninotchka in Cole Porter's *Silk Stockings,* clearly a pre-feminism, pre–gender studies view of women. Women exist to be loved by men; without that love they are parodies of masculinity. Ninotchka's intellectual, overly-rational Soviet woman was expressed through a sexless baritone voice that gave her a stereotypical hint of lesbianism. She could be "saved" by becoming feminized, brought into the paradigm of what poet and essayist Adrienne Rich calls "compulsory heterosexuality." *Silk Stockings* was the epitome of the 1950s view of gender—the same view that had television moms Barbara Billingsley, Jane Wyatt, and Donna Reed at home in high heels and skirts buoyed up by crinoline petticoats teaching their children, with the help of wise, manly fathers, to be proper men and women. *Silk Stockings* was a musical about male representatives of the "evil empire" converted by good old hedonism and the Soviet career woman made feminine by an American man. The threat of the evil empire was that its women were intelligent, educated, and devoted to their careers, but it took only one night in bed with an American man to change that. This is how American men ruled their world, their country, and their homes in 1956:

> I'd like to gain complete control of you.
> And handle even the heart and soul of you.[1]

Ninotchka had to learn that once one crosses to our side of the Iron Curtain, particularly to Cole Porter's Paris, what she thinks is only a "chemical reaction" gives American males supreme power. What irony that the songs to this capitalist, sexist, heterosexist sexual fantasy were written by a representative of one of the groups considered to be the greatest threat to the hegemonic rule of the straight, white, potent, American male in the fifties, a homosexual! But the history of the musical is full of such queer ironies. Porter seemed aware that he could get away with less queerness in the fifties, an era in which straight lyricists ruled the musical theater.

Who is the representative of American femininity in *Silk Stockings?* A dumb, brassy, blonde, Esther Williams–type swimming star whose head seems to be filled with chlorinated water—a cartoon woman who belts the show's up tunes, filling the old Ethel Merman role in a Porter musical, but with a parody of sexiness that wasn't part of Merman's repertoire. *Silk Stockings* showed the double bind for women in musicals in the fifties. You were either an undersexed non-woman or an oversexed mock woman. In musicals, women who weren't domestic were bound to be parodic.

Plain and Fancy, another hit from the same season, shows the double bind even more clearly. A glamorous, brassy, bleach-blonde baritone belter Elaine Stritch manqué and her stolid but rich boyfriend go to Pennsylvania Dutch country, essentially a foreign land with none of those machines essential to life in the 1950s, not even zippers. She proves her total ineptitude at domestic duties, to the amusement and horror of the Amish women. But the young Amish women are imprisoned by the horrible fact that they cannot choose whom they will marry. The Amish ingenue lead, Katie Yoder, loves the wrong man, but since her choice is the best-looking man who gets the show's hit ballads, you know everything will end up all right. The comic ingenue, Hilda (Barbara Cook), runs off to a carnival to live the life of a wicked woman, but the carnival offers only tawdry strippers and violence. She goes back home disillusioned and the romantic leads are properly joined at the end. The Amish are an extreme of repression, but more on the right track than the brassy blonde city girl who can't cook or sew but who at least realizes that the dull, sexless, but reliable lug she is going with is the right man for her. She may be right in singing "Our love has all of the thrill of shredded wheat," but marriage is domestication, and the values of community are more important than city sophistication. The problem with the Amish, according to fifties Broadway, is not that the women spend most of their time in the kitchen; it is that the women don't choose their men on the basis of romantic love. "Follow your heart," sings the handsome young man to the woman he loves. The Amish don't agree.

The showstopper in the 1955 hit *Damn Yankees* is the witch-temptress Lola's attempted seduction of baseball hero Joe Hardy, "Whatever Lola Wants." Donning a Latina accent and attire, Lola comes into the locker room and performs a grand mock striptease while singing her temptress's credo, "Whatever Lola wants, Lola gets." The song is false advertising. Temptresses in American musicals are quite safe. Middle-aged Joe Hardy sells his soul to become a baseball star and save his beloved Washington Senators, a boy's dream. He may be turned into handsome Stephen Douglass (a bit old to play a twenty-three-year-old), but he doesn't give up his mature, manly fidelity to his wife, which is why "Whatever Lola Wants" is a grand comic number, a camp strip act, more Carmen Miranda drag than strip. In the hands of Gwen Verdon, a great dancer and a great comedienne, it became a showstopper. It was funny and sexy. Fifties gay boys like myself could read ourselves into Lola. If one suffered the unrequited crush on the gorgeous jock, if one saw the locker room as an erotically charged space in which one could fantasize winning the bodies, if not the hearts, of the hunks, one could read into Lola's funny, futile seduction. There were a few hunks in my gym class I dreamed of seducing in the locker room ("Come on, Joe, it's me, Lola"), but my attempts at seduction would more likely have led to physical harm than a gentle rebuff. In the film version, our only record of one of Gwen Verdon's classic performances, the number takes on an added irony in hindsight as we watch gay Tab Hunter easily resist Gwen Verdon's blandishments. In the London cast of the recent revival, Lola was played by a charmless, technically proficient singer/dancer with no comedic skills, and the question became not will Lola get her clothes off, which she does too soon in the number to be funny, but will she get Joe's clothes off.

Though she doesn't make her entrance until well into the first act, Lola, the cartoon woman, a four-hundred-year-old witch, is the star of *Damn Yankees*.

She has the star turns. Lola is the typical fifties naughty girl. Supposedly she tempts men and destroys them, but what we see is a sweet, inept girl who falls in love with the men she is supposed to tempt. There's no danger here. Men, after all, are irresistible. Lola also is moral enough to help Joe win his series and go back to his wife. What more can you expect from the eternal Other Woman?

Lola is brought in by the devil, Mr. Applegate, to keep Joe from his wife. In the original production and the film, Mr. Applegate was, in Ray Walston's hands, more than a bit camp, swanning across his suspiciously colorful boudoir in magenta robes, tempting Joe in the red bow tie that in the twenties was part of the gay uniform. Applegate seemed to see Lola more as rival than as object of attraction—his very lack of interest in her was suspicious. Victor Garber's Applegate in the 1995 New York cast could be positively bitchy.

Here, in a nutshell, is the sexual politics of the musical of the Cold War era. The star turn may be performed by a character who is a threat to marriage, but the threat is benign. Men are boys at heart, but like good boys, they want to stick with Mom. The problem for the woman is to lure the boy away from his games (baseball, craps) long enough to marry her. The threat to American home and hearth is diabolical, wears Communist red, and like those Commies, just might be homosexual as well. Lola is a sister to Lorelei Lee in *Gentlemen Prefer Blondes* and Adelaide in *Guys and Dolls* as Joe is the brother to Sky Masterson and Nathan Detroit. In musicals of this era marriage is the essential finale, even if the boys would rather play with the boys (non-sexually, of course).

Heterosexuality may have been a necessity in these musicals, but it was hardly something to be taken seriously. Is the wedding of Nathan and Adelaide in *Guys and Dolls* really necessary and inevitable? Heterosexuality is the hanger on which we place the glitzy attire of the musical. What other option did musical comedy have? Comedy, after all, traditionally ends in marriage, though some of the greatest comedies, like Molière's *Le Misanthrope,* don't, and some comic masterpieces, like Etherege's *The Man of Mode,* end in less conventional male-female alliances. Often Shakespeare's comedies demonstrate the arbitrariness of the marriage they seem to affirm. In the case of *Twelfth Night,* even the gender of the beloved seems arbitrary. Musical comedy was as much comedy as musical, peopled with great comics and created by superb comic writers, so the boy-girl plot was going to be central, but not necessarily convincing. Given that the comedy was musical, the boy-girl plot also afforded opportunities for the meat and potatoes of popular song, love ballads.

In musical comedy in the twenties and thirties, the plot was purely functional, grout to hold the songs and jokes together. Somewhere along the line boy and girl got together, feuded, and got together again. Why else would you have love songs, feuding songs, and torch songs? To allow for more musical variety, there were usually two couples; one serious romantic couple played by singers who could do justice to the ballads, complemented by a comic couple who did the patter songs and possibly the dance numbers. Often there was a climactic wedding scene, though not always treated reverently:

> It's never too late to Mendelssohn;
> It doesn't matter how long you have tarried.
> Two hearts are at journey's Endelssohn—
> And we're invited here to see them married.[2]

Ira Gershwin's 1926 lyric for *Oh, Kay!,* later recycled in *Lady in the Dark,* is typically irreverent for musical comedy of the period. The object of the show was fun, and the lyricist was more interested in playing with the names of the composers associated with wedding music than he was with the emotional reality of the moment. The wedding doesn't take place anyway. If anything, irreverence was a significant component of musical comedy. Nothing was to be taken too seriously, not even love and marriage. Ira Gershwin's best collaborations with his brother, George, are brilliant spoofs, a combination of their idols, Gilbert and Sullivan, and their contemporaries the Marx brothers. In some of their best shows, the original version of *Strike Up the Band* and *Of Thee I Sing,* the romance is as silly as the satire.

Such a premium on irreverence made it easy for composers temperamentally unsuited to the serious treatment of heterosexual relationships to thrive in musical theater. Cole Porter's great shows seldom contain songs describing or celebrating love relationships.

> Most gentlemen don't like love,
> They just like to kick it around,
> Most gentlemen don't like love,
> 'Cause most gentlemen can't be profound.[3]

One senses here that Cole was most interested in the play on words of "don't like love" and the characteristic clash of dictions in "kick it around" and "profound." Meaning came second to cleverness, but the song rejects the very notion of true love for a man. Even *Kiss Me, Kate,* his later "integrated" musical, doesn't contain a serious love duet for either set of lovers. "Wunderbar" is a spoof of operetta waltzes. The leading lady gets one of the most masochistic ballads ever written, more suited to wimpy Julie Jordan in *Carousel* than the tempestuous Lilli Vanessi:

> So taunt me and hurt me
> Deceive me, desert me.[4]

The song's "over the top" extremity however is fitting for Lilli's hypertheatricality. It's Cole Porter—we're not to take it too seriously, and, as we know, *Kiss Me, Kate* is a classic example of gay men creating a straight romance that is only heterosexual "in its fashion."

As we saw, Lorenz Hart's lyrics were better at unrequited love or requited sex than full-fledged romance, but who cared as long as the songs were fun or beautiful? Composers were prized for their wit, shows for their humor. The busiest leading man of musicals of the twenties and thirties, William Gaxton (*A Connecticut Yankee, Anything Goes, Fifty Million Frenchmen, Leave It to Me!, Louisiana Purchase, Of Thee I Sing*), wasn't known as a romantic or sexy figure, but as a hyperkinetic con man who could sing.

In the late thirties, Porter and Rodgers and Hart controlled the Broadway musical, competing for fun shows (Gershwin died in 1937). Rodgers and Hart were the innovators, moving from a show ending in a big ballet (*On Your Toes,* 1936), to a Shakespeare show zany enough to rival the Gershwin brother's earlier hits (*The Boys from Syracuse,* 1938), to their classic, the seamy, steamy *Pal Joey* (1940), much more about the crotch than the heart. If *Pal Joey* went too far for critics and some audiences of 1940, it was the culmination of a decade of musicals built on naughtiness and cynicism.

Operetta, with its romance in exotic places, its sentimental duets for soprano and baritone, had died on Broadway in the twenties and moved to Hollywood, where flouncy Jeanette MacDonald and stalwart Nelson Eddy, vying for who could wear the most makeup, still warbled "Indian Love Call" in those camp operetta extravaganzas trimmed of much of their music. Operetta had been where boy-girl romance was taken seriously. Oscar Hammerstein II, the musical's bard of heterosexual normality, made his name in operetta. Hammerstein wrote the books and lyrics for three of the most popular operettas of the 1920s, *Rose-Marie* (1924), *The Desert Song* (1926), and *The New Moon* (1928), all a decade later turned into MacDonald-Eddy film extravaganzas. Oscar Hammerstein was responsible for taking the romance from the operetta and grafting it onto the musical. He did this in that grand hybrid, *Show Boat* (1927), but really had his heyday in the 1940s and 1950s with his collaboration with Richard Rodgers. *Show Boat,* though one of the longest running hits of its decade, was not influential at first. *Oh, Kay!* (1926), with its zany heroine and madcap bootleggers and breezy Gershwin score, or the rousing college musical, *Good News* (1927), were more typical and more in the spirit of the age. *Show Boat* was a success precisely because it was sui generis. Hammerstein would wield enormous influence over the future of the musical in a less giddy time than the jazz age. He would be the controlling voice of the World War II and Cold War musical. For Hammerstein, romance was serious business, the province of melodrama, not comedy. Hammerstein could be witty, but unlike his peers he was more interested in characters who weren't, and Hammerstein's great contribution to musical theater, particularly in his collaborations with Richard Rodgers, is appropriateness of diction. Ninety-nine percent of the time the diction of the songs perfectly fits the vocabulary his characters would have. "I Cain't Say No," Ado Annie's song of promiscuity in *Oklahoma!,* is a far cry from the wit and innuendo of Vera Simpson's "Bewitched, Bothered, and Bewildered." Vera is the living embodiment of jaded sophistication. In Hammerstein's hands, a song about sexual promiscuity is sung by an innocent farm girl with healthy, unjaded impulses. He took a lot of the old-fashioned sexual double entendres out of musicals. He also wrote of a world in which homosexuality, if it existed at all, was not mentioned, much less sung about. Gay may be the nickname of one of his heroes, but not, in our sense of the word, a character description. Julie Jordan may be "a queer one," but she's definitely heterosexual. Yet between Hammerstein's *Show Boat* and the last of his collaborations with Richard Rodgers, *The Sound of Music,* there were some fascinating, popular musical depictions of heterosexual romance that also acknowledged the existence of homosexuality. In fact, in some cases, as has been true in so much American popular culture, it is only the potential of homosexuality that maintains the appearance of conventional heterosexuality.

CHEEK TO CHEEK

In 1933, the same year as Busby Berkeley's first hit Gold Diggers film and Fred and Ginger's first film duet in *Flying Down to Rio,* there's a classic moment in a lesser film called *International House,* one of those filmed variety shows that were popular in the decade. Ironically, the film is about the invention of television, which would destroy this sort of musical. The setting is Wu Hu, China. Oh, don't ask why. W. C. Fields, three sheets to the wind, lands his helicopter on the roof of a building and asks, "Where am I?" In his classic queenly manner, Franklin Pangborn, lips pursed and hands akimbo, answers in a soprano voice, "Wu Hu." Fields removes the large trademark flower from his lapel and snarls, "Don't let the posy fool ya." When I first saw that film at a college film society in the mid-sixties—we worshiped Fields back then—we who saw something of ourselves in Pangborn, the monster we were hiding inside that might, like the alien inside John Hurt, pop out at any moment and actually had already made itself visible—howled at this cinematic fag joke. A nonviolent, funny exchange had taken place between heterosexual (asexual?) and fairy. But what we inner Pangborns loved about Fields was that his humor was kind of gay. In his snarly way, he was the master of the queenly putdown. Fields was more what we aspired to be than Pangborn. This moment in *International House* is typical of a number of films in the thirties in its assertion of heterosexuality by denying its negative, the fairy. Perhaps, as contemporary queer theorists maintain, heterosexuality can only be defined in opposition to homosexuality.

Most of us would rather be Fred Astaire than Eric Blore or Erik Rhodes (actually I've always aspired to Helen Broderick), but Astaire's masculinity/heterosexuality was also defined by its opposite. The nine enormously popular films Fred Astaire and Ginger Rogers made together in the 1930s are considered the epitome of film romance for the period. Dick Powell sang to the squawking Ruby Keeler in his Broadway tenor voice in the Busby Berkeley extravaganzas; Nelson Eddy bellowed to the warbling Jeanette McDonald in their MGM operettas. Neither pair was particularly sexy. The sexiness in the Busby Berkeley films came from all those crotch shots of the robotic chorines. I've never been able to figure out what was sexy about Nelson and Jeanette, whose operettas seem to define kitsch. Fred and Ginger's big numbers were romantic and their films had stronger books than many Broadway musicals of the period. Their films had a rigid musical formula: courtship duet, novelty solo for Fred, grand final duet with Ginger spectacularly gowned. The scores were as strong as Broadway scores of the period, written by Berlin, Kern, Porter, and Gershwin, a great improvement on Al Dubin and Harry Warren, who provided the scores for the Berkeley epics (catchy simple tunes, idiotic or incoherent lyrics). The books for Astaire-Rogers musicals were formulaic, variations on the same story, but often more coherent than the patchwork Broadway musical books of the period. More than those Broadway musicals, the Astaire-Rogers films were star vehicles for an ingenious piece of casting: the match of Fred and Ginger.

Ginger Rogers had been the second lead in Broadway musicals and the sassy sidekick in Berkeley's *Gold Diggers of 1933,* singing "We're in the Money" in pig Latin at the top of the film. She aspired to being a serious actress and won the 1940 Academy Award for Best Actress as Kitty Foyle. After the nine Astaire-Rogers films, she had a long career, nowhere near the enduring stardom of Astaire, but continuing to work. She replaced Carol Channing in *Hello, Dolly!* and played Mame in London. I saw her in the early 1970s in a summer-stock version of the Katharine Hepburn vehicle *Coco.* In her incarnation of the chic Parisian designer Coco Chanel, Rogers opened her front-slit skirt to show her still-shapely legs and whirled around the stage as if expecting Astaire to materialize!

Fred Astaire managed to remain a star in musical films without Rogers. Rather than being eclipsed by Gene Kelly at MGM, Astaire found his own niche in *Easter Parade* and *The Band Wagon.* Like female divas, he became a symbol of longevity, proving that grace and elegance were still possible in one's middle age. Like Cary Grant, he endured to be a middle-aged representative of a past suavity that probably only existed in Hollywood films. Fred Astaire was an odd leading man: skinny, not particularly handsome, and a dancer, which was hardly a model of masculinity. However, Astaire made film dancing masculine and thus marketable. Though dancing in tails might be considered effete, Astaire was a tap dancer, with its emphasis on rhythm and athletic prowess, more "manly" and democratic than ballet or the newly emerging modern dance. Sissies did ballet, but real men tapped. There is, after all, something aggressively macho about making all that noise, and tap is as much rhythmic noise as it is graceful movement. Tap stars could be leading men, from Astaire on. Gene Kelly, the original Pal Joey, built his film dancing style somewhat in opposition to Astaire, loafers and white socks instead of top hat and tails (as if one could really tap in loafers. Hollywood sound technology was one of Kelly's dance partners). More recently Gregory Hines on stage and screen made tapping sexy. Now Savion Glover presents tap as an expression of African-American manhood.

Astaire also popularized ballroom dancing. It is difficult for people younger than I to realize that the final Astaire-Rogers number in each film was an elaborate version of popular dancing of the period, though ballroom dancing seems to be coming back, thank God! "Cheek to Cheek" and "Let's Face the Music and Dance" are grand fox-trots. In the thirties, couples went to Fred Astaire Dance Studios to learn to dance like Fred and Ginger. There are still Fred Astaire Dance Studios across America. In *Swing Time,* Ginger teaches at a ballroom dance studio, albeit one presided over by queeny Eric Blore, but we never see Blore dance. Straight Astaire turns a two-step into an athletic event with Kern's bouncy "Pick Yourself Up." *Swing Time* ends with a Kern waltz that combines the traditional nineteenth-century romantic dance form with energetic contemporary swing, thus Americanizing and energizing a past European form. In top hat and tails, Astaire made elegance democratic and masculine.

Equally important was Astaire's singing, which was more naturalistic than audiences were used to from film leading men and would influence popular singing for decades. Astaire was a crucial chapter in the transformation in popular singing wrought by the technology of the microphone. His light voice was a far cry from the loud whiskey tenor of Dick Powell or stalwart baritone of Nelson Eddy, both traditional pre-microphone Broadway leading man vocal types. Astaire, however, represented a new kind of singer, light-voiced (perfect for the microphone) and with both a dancer's sense of emphasizing the rhythm of his songs and a true respect for the lyrics. George Gershwin, Cole Porter, and Irving Berlin thought him the best singer of their music. Astaire was closer to pop stars like Bing Crosby and Frank Sinatra than he was to Broadway singers.

He had less voice than either, but surer technique. Unlike film, theater depended on big legit voices until the advent of the body mike in the 1960s, thus maintaining for decades an anachronistic style of singing. You can hear the stylistic change technology wrought on the stage in the singing of Jerry Orbach, Broadway's leading man in the 1960s. In *Carnival* (1961), Orbach's first Broadway musical, he sings like every Broadway baritone of the past thirty years. He could be John Raitt or Stephen Douglass or Ray Middleton. For *Promises, Promises* (1968) a few years later, he's clearly singing to a microphone closer to him, making more of the words and bringing natural speech inflections into his singing. He's got more voice than Broadway singers do now, but his singing is more relaxed, more like that of pop singers. Astaire's great talent was making singing seem effortless. Hollywood and recording technology were necessary for him to become a singing star.

Astaire had come up through vaudeville in an act with his sister Adele. Since they had to be paired for the musical numbers in their shows, song and dance didn't mean romance. It often meant novelty numbers showing off their dancing skills to Astaire's choreography. At the end of musicals like the Gershwins' *Lady Be Good,* Fred and Adele were paired up with spouses, but the pairings were plot conveniences, not dramatic inevitabilities.

In the RKO musicals with Astaire, Ginger Rogers had to move from tough, perky, slightly naughty second lead to romantic, elegant leading lady. Astaire moved from half a brother-sister act to romantic lead, but he kept his old part as well. In their movies, rather than a conventional romantic couple who sing ballads and a comic couple who do novelty numbers, Fred and Ginger do both. The brilliance of their musicals is that the comic numbers were also romantic: "Start All Over Again," "Let's Call the Whole Thing Off." As long as there were no conventional masculine figures around Astaire, he could be a credible romantic leading man, singing charmingly, dancing brilliantly, but always seeming nonchalant. It's his relaxed quality that makes him successful as a leading man. As Arlene Croce puts it: "The miraculously casual low-key delivery, the elegance of his handling of props, tells us that he's omnipotent."[5]

Fred Astaire was surrounded by effeminate men in many of his films, from Eric Blore's (*Gay Divorcee, Top Hat, Swing Time, Shall We Dance?*) patented prissy butler with the royal or marital "we" to Erik Rhodes's epicene Italian (*Top Hat, Swing Time*) to Edward Everett Horton's fey sidekick (*Gay Divorcee, Top Hat, Shall We Dance?*). These men were cast as foils to Astaire's lean androgyny. Next to them, his slim elegance looked macho. But the gender coding of the Astaire-Rogers musicals is a bit odd. Arlene Croce writes of the Horton-Blore-Rhodes supporting cast in *The Gay Divorcee* (1934):

> A male star was supported by a comic, and it's surprising in how many musical
> comedies and operettas of the Twenties effeminacy was a comic's stock-in-trade.
> In *The Gay Divorcee,* which had a retrogressive book, all the male comics seem
> queer. The title was changed (from the Broadway show, *The Gay Divorce*) to
> take the edge off that hard word divorce. Perhaps something should have been
> done about the adjective.[6]

The same could be said of *Top Hat* (1935), in which Astaire is again surrounded
by Edward Everett Horton, Eric Blore, and Erik Rhodes, grand comic actors
who project different versions of effeteness. When a conventionally "masculine"
leading man appears in the Astaire-Rogers films, it is the non-singing, non-
dancing, stalwart Randolph Scott (*Roberta, Follow the Fleet*). Given what
contemporary viewers now know of Scott's homosexuality (in the thirties he
was Cary Grant's "roommate"), his presence as stalwart macho hero only adds
another layer of irony and queerness.

Astaire plays a version of himself in *Top Hat,* Jerry Travers, a musical
comedy star appearing in London. Horton plays Jerry's producer and buddy,
Horace Hardwick, who seems to spend little time with Madge, his wisecracking wife, played by deadpan Helen Broderick. Broderick was often the comic
female in the Astaire-Rogers films, wry and butch next to Rogers. Horace
seems to spend far more time in Astaire's bedroom than he does in the one he
shares with his wife. His closest, though most turbulent, relationship is with
his butler, Bates, played by one of Hollywood's grandest sissy actors of the
thirties, Eric Blore. At the beginning of the film, Jerry discovers that Horace
and Bates aren't speaking, the result of a feud about the appropriate shape for
a necktie. Horton's hateful glances at Blore and Blore's eyeball-rolling and
grand camp enunciation take innuendo about as far as it can go. When Horace
and Jerry get to Venice, they share the bridal suite. When asked to vacate the
suite, Jerry jokingly says to Horace, "We've hardly settled in yet, have we,
angel?" Here, as throughout the film, there are hints of potential homosexuality acknowledged by Jerry, though his heterosexuality is demonstrated
through his romance with Dale Tremont (Rogers), which is the only
conventional heterosexual relationship in the film. When, through confusion,
Dale thinks she is being courted by Horace, Madge doesn't take it at all
seriously. She knows Horace wouldn't put the moves on any woman, and that
if by some miracle he did, it would spice up their marriage.

Thinking that Jerry is Horace, Dale settles for the Erik Rhodes character,
the Italian fashion designer Alberto Beddini for whom Dale models. Up to this
point, clearly Dale and Beddini have had a sexless business relationship, though
they have traveled together, for hints of homosexuality are attached to Beddini,

most in his own fractured English. When angry at Dale, he shouts, "Never again will I allow women to wear my dresses." Later he cries, "I am no man. I am Beddini." One could accept this as the sort of poor English jokes later epitomized by Desi Arnaz and Charo, but the homosexual innuendos are consistent. At one point, thrilled at something Horace has said, Beddini kisses him, to which Madge responds, "Go right ahead, boys. Don't mind me." These queer innuendos are possible because sexual behavior between the men in the film was unthinkable, impossible. As the historian John Loughery notes:

> The key was that the sex drives of these characters had to remain obscured, even neutered, and no man was allowed to hint at his passion for another. In this reading, as far as the censors were concerned, a sissified man was *not* necessarily a pervert . . . but simply an amusing fugitive from virility.[7]

Gay men in the audience may have been less naive. After all, according to gay historian George Chauncey, the pansy was a mode of gay self-fashioning in the twenties and early thirties, particularly around the theater district in New York. In *The Celluloid Closet,* Vito Russo recalls that in 1975, Arthur Bell wrote an essay for *The New York Times* equating the comic sissies of Eric Blore and his contemporaries Grady Sutton and Franklin Pangborn with the black stereotypes of Stepin Fetchit and Butterfly McQueen. Russo goes on to claim that "to the public, these characters were homosexual. To gays, these characters represented a pattern of oppression similar to the one suffered by blacks."[8] It is equally possible that homosexual men in the thirties were grateful for any sign of their existence in the mass media. The only such recognition of potential gayness was from sissy comics from Eric Blore to Jack Benny who offered a healthier stereotype than the potentially gay gangsters like Edward G. Robinson's *Little Caesar,* enamored of his dancing buddy, or the dour victimized gays of postwar Hollywood melodrama like Sal Mineo's Plato in *Rebel Without a Cause.*

Within this atmosphere of potential homosexuality, perhaps because of it, Astaire defined conventional masculinity and heterosexuality. While Horace shows more interest in Bates than Madge, and Beddini seems relieved to lose Dale, Jerry has eyes only for Dale from the moment he sees her. Astaire and Rogers also represent traditional American morality set in the moral ambiguity of American expatriates and their retainers. *Top Hat* hardly offers the serious treatment of this subject found in Henry James or in F. Scott Fitzgerald's 1934 novel, *Tender Is the Night,* but Dale, a person of moral rectitude, is appalled at Jerry's seemingly cavalier attitude toward his supposed marriage. Jerry thinks of nothing but Dale from the time that he meets her. Since she and Madge seem to be the only women in Europe, that isn't surprising. *Top Hat* combines sophistication with conservatism.

As Jerry's masculinity is supported by tap dance, so dance defines his romance. His first number in the film, "No Strings," celebrating Jerry's disinclination to be married, leads to a noisy tap number that wakes Dale up (she is sleeping in the hotel room underneath his). She comes up to complain and it is love at first sight. To sooth her to sleep, he converts to a quieter soft shoe. His novelty number, "Top Hat, White Tie and Tails," defining Astaire's costume and image, combines elegance with masculine aggression as his cane is turned into a gun with which he shoots the men in the chorus. Tap is manly—it can kill! The first courtship duet is the famous "Isn't This a Lovely Day (to Be Caught in the Rain)?" Ginger is wearing butch riding clothes (plus a crop!) and must be courted and made more conventionally feminine by Astaire's dance with her, which begins as a walk and turns into an elaborate routine. The finale is "Cheek to Cheek," with Rogers in that wonderful feathered dress on that outlandish Venice set. Though the dances represent perfect romantic harmony, Astaire leads, most strongly through choreographing the dance routines. He worked them out with his assistant, Hermes Pan, who later taught them to Rogers. It would have been interesting to see these sessions with the routines danced by two men! Indeed, it may be the fact that the dances were worked out by two men that led to the equality of male and female roles in the dances. In performance Ginger seems an equal partner.

The paradigm of dance as romance followed through the best of the Gene Kelly films, Vincente Minnelli's *An American in Paris* (1951) and the Kelly–Stanley Donen *Singin' in the Rain* (1952). The beautiful dance Kelly and Leslie Caron do to Gershwin's "Our Love Is Here to Stay" along a stylized version of the Seine has been one of my favorite movie moments since I first saw it at nine years old. It was a defining moment of difference, as I was conscious that I would have loved to be Kelly's dancing partner. Then there is the lovely Kelly–Debbie Reynolds dance to "You Were Meant for Me" in *Singin' in the Rain.* In the 1998 film *The Object of My Affection,* that dance number becomes the central image of the impossible illusion of heterosexual love for gay George and straight Nina. When George tells Nina that he had a girlfriend in high school (a piece of information that gives her false hope), she says he liked her because she was a great dancer. Dancing is George's strongest connection to heterosexuality as it is the most romantic connection he and Nina have, pretending they are Gene Kelly and Debbie Reynolds. Just before they end the fantasy of being partners, George and Nina dance spectacularly at his brother's wedding. Screenwriters Stephen McCauley (who wrote the novel on which the movie is based) and Wendy Wasserstein and director Nicholas Hytner have tapped into the strong attraction many gay men feel to these sublime moments of film dance. For me, too, movie dancing provides a romantic ideal that I can queer as I watch. I am surprised that I rather unconsciously put references to my favorite dance moments in my plays.

The norm for heterosexual romance in a film musical was Fred and Ginger, even when Kelly's style, partly a reaction to Astaire's, seemed to dominate and Astaire and Rogers only existed in memory. Now, in the eternal present of videotape, Astaire and Kelly are contemporaneous. Kelly is better looking, but he works too hard, a better clown than a romantic lead. His partners are never quite a match: perky Debbie Reynolds, siren Cyd Charisse. His most famous numbers are solos, for Kelly seems to be a loner. Slim, sleek Astaire in black formal wear is almost a phallic image, coupled with Rogers in one of those grand gowns that seem to have a life of their own. In their films, as Arlene Croce comments, "dancing was transformed into a vehicle of serious emotion between a man and a woman. It never happened in movies again."[9]

SINGING FREUD

Just before the appearance of the Rodgers and Hammerstein "normative" heterosexual musical play, spelling out appropriate gender relationships and marriage as the appropriate goal, there were two works that slightly queered the musical while policing heterosexuality. *Pal Joey* (1940), with book by novelist John O'Hara and music and lyrics by Rodgers and Hart, begins with an acknowledgment of the potential of homosexuality in the sleazy nightclub world in which Joey Evans works. Joey is being interviewed by Mike, the proprietor, for a job as emcee at the nightclub:

> MIKE: Umm—so you don't drink. How about nose candy?
> JOEY: Not that, either. Oh, I have my vices.
> MIKE: I know that. Well, we have a band here. The drummer is just a boy.
> JOEY: Hey, wait a minute.
> MIKE: Okay. We got that straight.[10]

This oblique dialogue is as blatant about homosexuality as this musical, considered very naughty for its time, gets. Joey is declared straight, though Joey is more than willing to be a kept man, hardly a model of masculinity. Surely opportunistic Joey would be willing to be "trade" for a wealthy gentleman, but like Richard Gere's Julian in *American Gigolo,* Joey has to make clear that he doesn't do fags. In the sleazy world of *Pal Joey,* our hero's heterosexuality has to be established against the possibility of homosexuality.

The original production of *Pal Joey* starring Gene Kelly had a respectable run of almost a year. The 1952 revival starring Harold Lang did even better. Boyish, pouty-faced Lang, formerly a ballet dancer, was, from Gore Vidal's report, typecast as Joey and the perfect Lorenz Hart–Cole Porter leading man (he had played Bill in *Kiss Me, Kate*): "I did not in the least mind that Harold was, simultaneously, having affairs with the author [of *Look Ma, I'm Dancing*] and its star, Nancy Walker, not to mention as much of the British navy as he could take aboard when we were in Bermuda for a week" (he was taking Vidal aboard as well).[11] Leonard Bernstein, another Lang "admirer," said, "Harold's ass is one of the seven—or whatever number it is—wonders of our time." The revival of *Pal Joey* also made a Broadway star out of another androgyne, tall, loud, over-the-top Elaine Stritch, one of those postwar Broadway cartoons of femininity who would remain a favorite of gay men.

Less than a month after the opening of the original *Pal Joey,* with its Lorenz Hart cynical view of sexual mores, the Moss Hart–Kurt Weill–Ira Gershwin musical, *Lady in the Dark,* opened five blocks north. *Lady in the Dark* was a unique hybrid, a serious "musical play" interspersed with musical episodes representing the fantasy life of the central character, fashion magazine editor Liza Elliott. Hart had been through psychoanalysis, very fashionable at the time (he battled depression all of his life) and, after making his name with his madcap comic collaborations with George S. Kaufman, was eager to find a means to dramatize his conversion to Freud and to establish himself as an individual playwright rather than a collaborator. Eugene O'Neill had already had commercial and critical success in the thirties with his turgid Freudian plays, but during that enlightened decade Freud would have been the object of spoofing in musicals, not serious consideration.

Like O'Neill, Hart and his colleagues focused their quasi-Freudian sights on a woman who needs to learn her proper role in society. There's a lot of similarity between *Lady in the Dark* and Eugene O'Neill's *Strange Interlude.* In both, a sexually confused woman must choose among a group of men who represent symbolic aspects of masculinity. Through psychoanalysis and finding the right man, Liza becomes "well adjusted" by the end of the play. Hart may have felt that a man's coming to terms with his fulfillment as a man was not the appropriate subject for a musical. Musical stars, after all, were women. Who would care about the adjustment problems of William Gaxton or Victor Moore? Moreover, from Freud's early cases, psychoanalysis seemed a masculine-feminine relationship. A woman, lying down, would recount her inner life to a man, who would interpret it in a way to aid the woman in adjusting to her role as a woman. Was it appropriate to dramatize a man lying on his back, opening his secrets to another man? How unmasculine!

Moss Hart himself in the thirties was a prolific writer and director of comedies and book musicals as well as a prolific womanizer who did not settle down until his mid-forties. Legend has it that he used to tell women who wanted a commitment that he was still mourning the loss of his first love, a schoolteacher who had died:

> He delivered this fiction so emotionally that almost everyone believed it. George Kaufman summed up its effect one evening when he saw his partner coming into a restaurant with his latest conquest. "Take note," he said. "Here comes Moss Hart with the future Miss Smith." [12]

According to Porter biographer Charles Schwartz, some of Hart's friends and colleagues were sure his ambivalence about commitment to a woman was a sign he was gay. Critic Martin Gottfried notes that at the time of the writing of *Lady in the Dark,* "there were whispers that the thirty-five-year-old and still-unmarried Hart might be a homosexual": "In Hart's case, [the rumors of homosexuality] were inevitable, given his affectations of speech and manner, his slender fashionableness, his advanced stage of bachelorhood, and his friendships with Cole Porter, Monty Woolley, and Noël Coward." [13] Charles Schwartz claims that Cole Porter and Monty Woolley tried to convince Hart that he should switch to men. Hart never did, however. Eventually he settled down into a celebrated marriage with opera and musical star Kitty Carlisle.

When *Lady in the Dark* begins, in a psychiatrist's office, Liza is austerely dressed and wearing no make-up. Why is the editor of a magazine called *Allure* so unfashionable, so unfeminine? Of course, in 1941, being a career woman was considered by many to be unfeminine. During the course of her analysis, Liza rejects two men: the older married man who has been supporting her professional activities and offering her a comfortable relationship without the commitment of marriage, and a handsome young movie star who is looking for a mother figure. She ends up with Charley, her wisecracking assistant editor, the man who demands that she be a "woman." We are to believe that Charley hits the nail on the head when he accuses Liza of not being a woman: ". . . if we ever need a good man over there I'll make you an offer." [14] Liza responds violently to Charley's challenges to her femininity—they hit home. She goes to the psychiatrist because she has lost control and thrown a glass paperweight at him. But Charley knows the Universal Truth that women are created to be subservient:

> Would you come out into the open where *I'm* the boss, Miss Elliott? Just once? Dinner, cocktails—name it yourself. Any place away from that Goddamned desk! I'll even make it my office and my desk. How about it? [15]

What Liza discovers through reliving her dreams—the musical sections of *Lady in the Dark*—is that she never thought she was physically attractive. Her glamorous mother thought her an ugly duckling and Liza accepted that harsh judgment. Her entire life has been compensating for her own inadequacy as a normal woman:

> I think, then, that you withdrew as a woman. That you would no longer risk being hurt as a woman competing with other women. But the longing remained—and so did the rage and that deep sense of injustice. And what you are facing now is rebellion—rebellion at your unfulfillment as a woman.[16]

After hearing her life interpreted by a man, her psychiatrist, Liza is ready to assume her proper, subservient position with a man, which will lead to her fulfillment as a woman. At the end, she makes her assistant editor her co-editor, but at the final curtain he is dictating the future format of the magazine. Clearly, even in the world of women's fashion, the strong heterosexual male knows best. Liza is normalized. She dresses better, wears make-up, and knows who is supposed to be boss. She has rid herself of weak men who let her have her way and grown up to "real men" who pinch female workers' behinds and assert their testosterone. Viva Freud! The psychiatrist explains to Liza that she has felt unfulfilled as a woman. Clearly the only fulfillment is in the arms of a strong man.

The introduction to the published edition of *Lady in the Dark* is an essay by "Dr. Brooks," Liza's psychoanalyst, which justifies Liza's final acceptance of Charley. Actually, the essay was written by Hart's psychiatrist, Dr. Lawrence S. Kubie:

> The ultimate man is the one who refuses to play the role either of the subservient parent or of the submissive child, and who, by his outrageous mockery and overt erotic foolery, challenges her right to live in her no-man's land between the sexes.[17]

As a successful unmarried woman who will not submit power to a domineering male, Liza is neither masculine nor feminine. Ironically, she was played by the charismatic Gertrude Lawrence, one performer who would never be considered in a "no-man's land between the sexes." Lawrence was hardly typecast as an austere businesswoman who was sexually timid. She was an image of the elegance and sophistication and sexual daring of the previous two decades. Yet Liza Elliott was one of her most successful roles. The show ran through three seasons.

Appropriate feminine behavior is spelled out in *Lady in the Dark*. So is appropriate masculine behavior. Men should not be weak with the women they love, so the older, doting Kendall must be rejected. They should not display their insecurities, like the sensitive Hollywood hunk, Randy Curtis, who wants the managing Liza to take care of him:

> I need someone like you, Liza—someone with your strength and courage—to lean on—to always be there. I guess the truth is, I'm pretty frightened inside.[18]

No chance for a sensitive man. Men need to be tough and strong like Charley, strong enough to tame the shrew. Yet the script makes clear that womanizing, wisecracking Charley needs to grow up. Maggie, the inevitable, plain-speaking pal-of-the-heroine tells Charley, "Oh, stop being a pixie Charley—you're getting a little too old for it."[19] Charley later admits to Maggie that underneath the macho exterior is a sensitive man: "I'm kinda sick of being cute—even to myself. Yep. Here's a big secret—inside I'm romantic as hell."[20]

There's another possibility of masculine behavior offered in *Lady in the Dark,* the homosexual Russell. *Lady in the Dark* may be the first Broadway book musical with a homosexual as a major character. In this "serious" musical, the flamboyant queen is the major comic character. Russell is the stereotypical homosexual: effeminate, emotional, bitchy, flamboyantly funny—the pansy as clown. Russell is more one of the girls than a real man. Danny Kaye's performance as Russell catapulted the clown into stardom and to Hollywood (though not in the movie version of *Lady in the Dark).*[21] Partly as result of the writing of Kaye's wife and creator of his nightclub and revue material, Sylvia Fine, Kaye had already done a number of routines in which he was a stereotypical pansy. One of the routines Hart saw Kaye perform in his nightclub act, when he thought of Kaye for Russell, was "Anatole of Paris," about a pansy designer:

> . . . with it, Sylvia was once again creating effeminate material for Danny. It was, after all, a song about a fey fashion designer who "shrieks with chic." Once more, [Sylvia] was either responding to an androgynous quality in his manner or inspiring it.[22]

What is flamboyantly queeny Russell doing in this gallery of symbolic masculine types? Probably Hart and his colleagues knew that even this daring serious musical needed a clown—you could only be so innovative. How do you work a clown into a musical about a fashion magazine editor? A pansy employee, of course. There are two kinds of men who work in the woman's world of *Allure:*

heterosexual men who avail themselves of the sexual playground this world of glamorous models allows (Charley) and the pansy who finds a safe space in this female society. Did Hart base Russell on Kaye's pansy numbers or did they merely show Hart Kaye's appropriateness for the part of Russell? In either case, they, and the one number added for Kaye, "Tchaikovsky," based on a lyric Gershwin had actually written in 1924, made Kaye a star so in demand he left the show after six months to appear in a Cole Porter musical, *Let's Face It*.

For all its political incorrectness, here is a musical that sets out what a conventional woman is supposed to be like in 1941 as well as a gallery of positive and negative masculine role models and one of the first pansies in a book musical. Moreover, *Lady in the Dark* was a groundbreaking musical, a true musical play in which the dream world of the music and that of the realistic drama were separate. There was no overture; after a brief introduction of "My Ship," the dialogue begins. There's no music until almost the end of each act when the dream sequences begin. *Lady in the Dark* was not the first musical to be so book heavy. Many thirties musicals seem to be plays with a few songs thrown in (for example, *You Never Know*). However, the quasi-operatic nature of Liza's dreams, the only place music is used, allowed Weill to work with more elaborate musical structures than the thirty-two-bar song. These dream sequences are the kind of elaborate musical scenes that Sondheim would later develop. With *Lady in the Dark,* elaborate operetta finales become the tool for serious musical sequences. Compare, for instance, the dream sequences with Sondheim's groundbreaking work in *Anyone Can Whistle*, in which each act ends with an extended musical scene.

The weak link in *Lady in the Dark* is Ira Gershwin's lyrics. Gershwin is writing zany, as if this were *Strike Up the Band*. *Lady in the Dark* needed a different, eerier approach, more fitting the character's anxieties and fear of rejection. It needed Lorenz Hart. Gershwin uses the dream sequences to be clever. Perhaps the show needed that to be a commercial success, but here is a case in which the music deserves far more dramatically probing lyrics, and who could write them in 1940?

Among the show's many qualities was its success as a star vehicle for one of the stage's great divas. Gertrude Lawrence stayed with *Lady in the Dark* through two and a half seasons (typically for its time, the show closed for the summer) and was the show's principal drawing card. A recording of a condensed radio broadcast gives some sense of what she was like. The British accent was there and the characteristic singing around the notes, but clearly Lawrence tailored Liza to her stage persona. Here was a part that allowed her to be in a serious drama and a musical comedy simultaneously. A film version was made in 1942, though not released until two years later. Ginger Rogers, talented, of course, but miscast and a far cry from the stage charisma of Gertrude Lawrence, stars. Neurosis isn't the first thing that comes to mind with Ginger Rogers. Lawrence, whose personal life was always a shambles, could empathize more with Liza. The film score is shorn of almost all the music except snippets of a few choruses and "The Saga of Jenny." Even the most important number, "My Ship," was cut on orders from the producer, Buddy de Sylva. Hollywood was obviously nervous about mixing a serious story with music and perhaps more nervous at Weill's complex score. (A few years later, MGM took most of Leonard Bernstein's music out of *On the Town* and replaced it with hackwork.) It's too bad, because under the direction of Mitchell Leisen (one of the few openly gay directors of the period) and with the designs of Hans Dreier, the dream sequences are visually stunning. Russell is played by Mischa Auer, not as the blond madcap of the script, but as a middle-aged sissy of the Eric Blore–Edward Everett Horton school. Russell still snaps at the women, provides the only witty banter in a solemn script, and moons over matinee idol Randy Curtis:

> Girls, he's God-like! I've taken pictures of beautiful men, but this one is the end—the *end!* He's got a face that would melt in your mouth . . .[23]

However, Russell's age makes him less of a sexual threat. He's just another Hollywood eunuch.

In 1997, it was possible to revive *Lady in the Dark* as a period piece, an innovative musical to be admired as an historical document, but not to be analyzed for its sexual politics. The charismatic Maria Friedman made a lovely, sympathetic Liza at London's Royal National Theatre, and the modernist staging by the enfant terrible of contemporary opera directors, Francesca Zambello, was less elaborate than the original production with its four revolving stages, but appropriate and clever. Russell was camped up to an extreme of the stereotype by James Dreyfus, who makes Danny Kaye seem downright sedate. The talkiness and the sexual politics all now seem quaint, but in 1941, *Lady in the Dark* was revolutionary in being an attempt at an exploration of character in the musical theater. As such, it tells us much about gender assumptions on the eve of America's entrance into World War II. *Lady in the Dark* didn't leave much room for its heroine's happiness apart from a masterful man, but it did allow the possibility of male homosexuality and a single, perhaps not-so straight woman, the inevitable wisecracking female sidekick, Maggie.

Lady in the Dark was the beginning of musical theater experiments of the early forties: *On the Town* (1944), with its adventurous, sometimes discordant score, a weird blend of Stravinsky, Copland, and big band, and its emphasis on dance to tell its story, and, of course, Rodgers and Hammerstein's early works. *Lady in the Dark,* with its urban sophistication and emphasis on the worlds of fashion and publishing, and *On the Town* are very much New York shows.

On the Town starts from the most heterosexual of premises—three sailors looking for girls on their twenty-four-hour leave, but opens up space for fantasizing less conventional desire. The score's most beautiful song, *Lonely Town,* could be any urban male's search for love in an alienating urban environment. It is interesting that the brassy female lead, Hildy (short for Brunhilde), has been played by gay-friendly divas (Nancy Walker, Bernadette Peters, Tyne Daly) and in 1997 by an openly lesbian comic, Lea DeLaria. When listening to the various albums of *On the Town,* I've always found it easy to give a gay spin to Ozzie's passivity with Hildy or to Claire's fiancé, Judge Bridgework. The joy of cast albums can be that of revising the plot—folding the songs into your own musical—queering the show. The 1998 revival, directed by George C. Wolfe, offered us sailors who didn't seem likely to be very interested in women.

"YOU'VE GOT TO BE CAREFULLY TAUGHT"

It's virtually impossible to queer Rodgers and Hammerstein. Clearly Hammerstein's vision dominates the Rodgers and Hammerstein musical, as one finds musicals that define and celebrate "proper" gender roles. How easily Rodgers moved from the always unconventional Lorenz Hart to the poet laureate of gender conventionality in the musical! Oddly enough, like medieval marriage fables (Patient Griselda) and Jacobean drama (*All's Well That Ends Well, Measure for Measure*) that gender conventionality has its share of built-in sadomasochism.

In *Me and Juliet* (1953), a woman sings to her beau:

I am a difficult girl.
You're an impossible character—
Why don't we give it a whirl?[24]

These lines encapsulate the essence of a Hammerstein libretto: an independent-seeming, headstrong young woman meets and falls in love with a dysfunctional man to whom she remains devoted regardless of his behavior. Often the issue becomes issue—the woman's role as mother when the man is incapable of being a proper father.

I find it hard to discuss Rodgers and Hammerstein's supposedly revolutionary works, *Oklahoma!* (1943) and *Carousel* (1945), separately from Oscar Hammerstein's earlier groundbreaking American musical, *Show Boat* (1927), which set the formula for his later works. *Show Boat* is a "serious" musical. Unlike most American musicals before it, it takes its characters and relationships seriously and does not give them the generic, predictable twists of plot and the easy reconciliation of conventional musicals of its time, though one could say the reconciliation of Gaylord and Magnolia thirty years after he leaves her is, well, easy. *Show Boat* is interesting because all the romances and marriages in its narrative span are problematic. Captain Andy is saddled with stern Parthenia, Ravenal and Magnolia break up, Frank and Ellie fight, and Julie loses Steve somehow. Even Joe and Queenie are still feuding together forty years later. *Show Boat* is based on a best-selling novel and was expected to be more or less faithful to its source, even though such adaptations were rare in the twenties and there were no hard-and-fast rules. Hammerstein was always at his best with adapting and finding musical opportunities for other people's material.

Every problematic relationship in *Show Boat* is judged within a paradigm of an ideal marriage that fails because of innate gender differences. It is typical of Hammerstein that all the marriages demonstrate his vision of the natural battle of the sexes (feckless, immature men versus tough women), but love endures. Men may leave their wives, but they still love them. The romantic version of this paradigm is the love and marriage of Gaylord Ravenal and Magnolia. He is dashing, romantic, more sensitive than other men, but feckless because he is unable to fit into the capitalist system. Gaylord is a riverboat gambler, in trouble with the law. His "profession" keeps him outside the work routine most men must endure, but it also bans him from the happiness of "normal" domestic-romantic relations. When we first see him, he is torn between his freedom and a sense that something is missing, specifically "a mate." Gaylord's musings are accompanied by the bad piano playing of his future mate, Magnolia, a nice way to introduce their discordant romance. At the end of Gaylord's solo, Magnolia appears and she and Gaylord sing a typical Hammerstein courtship duet, "Make Believe." In Hammerstein's musicals, the lovers fall in love at first song. There is no leading up to their romance. It happens within the first twenty minutes of the show. As usual in Hammerstein's major works, the plot complications ensue after they fall in love. In one sense, "Make Believe" is a clever beginning of a romance. The free-spirited but experienced Gaylord and the innocent but curious Magnolia can safely court each other in the subjunctive. However, the song also suggests that their romance will always be "make believe," that feckless Gaylord is incapable of being the mate the heroine deserves. The very free-spiritedness that makes him attractive also makes him incapable of fitting into the economy and being a proper husband. On the riverboat Gaylord gets a job as an actor when Steve and Julie have to leave, allowing the marriage-finale of Act I, a far more serious marriage than Ira Gershwin envisioned in *Oh, Kay!* Hammerstein has presented this marriage celebration in Victorian-sounding language appropriate to the setting (1885). Yet Hammerstein is always aware that there is a great difference between romance and marriage. Gaylord and Magnolia have some of the most beautiful love duets in musical theater. The grand waltz, "You Are Love," is pure operetta, but ravishing. It is the appropriate idiom for these nineteenth-century characters and one of Kern's great melodies, though it stops the narrative dead in its tracks. Yet we know from the beginning that marriage between these two people will be a disaster because of Gaylord's lack of economic stability. Marriage in Hammerstein's world is about social and economic compatibility. Women are willing to risk everything for love, but men fail them because of their social or economic position. Once off the show boat and thrust into the economic jungle of Chicago, that favorite setting of turn-of-the-century American naturalism, Gaylord fails as a husband, not because he isn't loving, but because he has no stable place in the economy. He disappears from the show, returning mysteriously and incredibly for the final curtain (thirty years later!). Where has he been? Who cares?

Show Boat poses an interesting dramatic problem for the musical. It is about music as economy, but earning a living through singing is a feminine occupation. Magnolia learns songs from her black friends, Julie and Queenie. Eventually, when forced to make her own living, she learns to support herself by combining the black music she learned as a girl with popular white music. Magnolia and Gaylord's daughter, Kim, becomes a singing star. In one sense, *Show Boat* is a musical about music and performing, like *A Chorus Line, Dreamgirls, Side Show,* and the greatest of them all, *Follies,* yet performing in *Show Boat* is feminine. Gaylord sings his feelings to the audience, but we are to believe that Gaylord is not a singer. Real men don't sing, though sensitive men worthy of our heroines sing to themselves and their more romantic, worthy feelings can be heard as songs. In *Show Boat,* white men talk and women and black men sing—even if we hear white men singing—and what women sing about is their dependence on inadequate men they "can't help lovin'."

Music may offer women economic freedom and mobility, but they sing about men. Only Kim, the next generation, a flapper star in the more liberated 1920s, sings about something else, but that final song kept changing depending on the talents of the Kim. In Hal Prince's recent spectacular production, Kim sings a Charleston reprise of "Why Do I Love You," which makes little sense since she is the one unattached character in the show.[25] Kim seems to be a woman who doesn't need a man, thus strangely out of place in the domestic fantasy Hammerstein celebrates.

The Magnolia-Gaylord thwarted marriage is reflected in the narrative of Julie and Steve. Steve may heroically claim black blood to stay with Julie, but when we see her in Chicago she is a lonely alcoholic. Steve has left her and she sings about another inadequate man, to whom she is devoted, "Bill." There's also the married song-and-dance team, Ellie and Frank, who, in the original script (their dialogue is severely cut in Hal Prince's production and they don't return for the finale) become parodies of bourgeois aspiration. At the end, they have substituted their razzamatazzy numbers for social grandeur.

Of the women, only Captain Andy's termagant wife, Parthenia, doesn't sing (except in the Hal Prince production, where she sings "Why Do I Love You" to her granddaughter). Parthenia represents the repressive values of a Puritan time and place and she constantly resists the freedom, liberality, and liberalism of the show boat. For Hammerstein, the show boat represents the best of theater. It embraces into its economy and community all who are willing to live by its rules of family feeling. It is a version of the best of American values. Its adversaries are representatives of a repressive and noninclusive legalism. It is governed by a benevolent patriarch, Captain Andy, who must resist the encroachments of agents of the law and the dour authoritarianism of his wife. Captain Andy and his wife are parodies of typical male-female qualities in Hammerstein's work. He is the boy-man who manages to create an environment of play and freedom that also makes money. She is steadfast and principled, but adversarial to the culture that supports her. Parthenia looks back to an older America; Andy is the transition to the twentieth century. Neither really sings. Only Magnolia seems to be able to thrive off of the show boat. The other characters fall prey to the social ills of the land—rampant capitalism, prejudice, cruelty. For the most part, the ills are masculine ills. Women help each other, as Julie, even in her cups, helps Magnolia establish her career in Chicago. Joe may think the continuity of nature is represented by a masculine "Ole Man River," but Hammerstein and Ferber's vision is of benevolent nature as feminine.

There's nothing gay about *Show Boat* (except, of course, some of the cast and other creative personnel and the male lead's nickname). Like most of Hammerstein's work, it represents the most rigid example of the heterosexist fantasy that became the center of the serious musical. It is, at its best, a radical (for 1927) show about race relations and the changing place of African Americans in popular music. It is an open acknowledgment of the score's debt to black music: ragtime and blues. Magnolia becomes a success singing a supposedly black song (actually a genre of song known then as a "coon song," a white imitation of black music of the sort made famous by blackface performers) she learned from Julie. Yet Julie's walking out so Magnolia can sing at the Trocadero suggests that Hammerstein believed that blacks, and half-blacks, are to step aside to allow the white person the spotlight. Limited racial inclusion is allowed, but the only appropriate relationship is heterosexual marriage, and mixed-race couples are never allowed the lasting, if fraught, marriages white people have.

Hammerstein's gender formulation remained the same when he merged with Richard Rodgers for *Oklahoma!* Women are tough and independent (financially independent in the case of the heroine, Laurey). The three leading women in *Oklahoma!*, Laurey, Aunt Eller, and Ado Annie, all know their minds. Aunt Eller seems happy to live as a single person—we don't know whether she is spinster or widow. Laurey seems to be heiress to a farm (we know nothing of her parents). Ado Annie wants to settle down with a husband but doesn't want to stop enjoying male admirers. Though the young women seem smarter than the men, the plot hinges on the necessary choice of a mate. As Ado Annie cannot choose between Will Parker and Ali Hakim, Laurey can't decide, in Act I, between two strong-willed but limited men, cheery cowboy Curly and dour farmhand Jud Fry. The key scene is an auction in which Curly and Jud bid for Laurey's box supper. Both end up bidding everything they have—Curly's saddle and gun, necessary for his work, and Jud's life savings—foolish gestures of love and/or possession, but the prize is not only pretty, smart Laurey, but a share in her farm. Yet, despite the elaborate auction scene, which puts a high price on Laurey's head, Hammerstein plays down the material reward of securing Laurey's love. The auction is about the men's impractical use of money. Will Parker has to have $50 to win Ado Annie, but he wastes the $50 on gifts for her. Laurey has the power not only to reject Jud, but also to fire him and banish him from her land. In this mythical *Oklahoma!*, as in mediaeval romance, the fair lady is won by the most honorable man, and won in combat. Chivalry is a crucial part of this American dream. However honorable and strong Curly is (and drop-dead gorgeous in the recent London revival), we know Laurey is smarter.

Oklahoma! doesn't sound western at all. Curly's opening song is a typical Rodgers waltz, very similar to his "Falling in Love with Love," written a few years before for *The Boys from Syracuse*. Hammerstein's lyrics set a scene, but it could be anywhere in agrarian Middle America. "The corn is as high as an elephant's eye" could as easily describe Kansas in August. But how authentically western is the ersatz country-and-western music gay men line dance to?

Is there a space for gay men in *Oklahoma!?* Male sexuality itself is closeted. Jud lives alone in the smokehouse, an appropriate setting for a man who has a picture of a naked woman on the wall and who lusts after chilly Laurey.

The Persian trader, Ali Hakim, who pursues "easy" Ado Annie is the one ethnic Other. He is another voice of male promiscuity. Ado Annie will settle down with unthreatening Will Parker. It is interesting that Jud's choice of weapon to kill Curly, sold to him by Ali Hakim, is a phallic peep-show telescope that hides a switchblade knife. Lust and violence are connected in this weapon as they are in Laurey's dream. Jud is uncontrolled sexuality, a walking, brooding libido, totally out of place in the box-social world of *Oklahoma!* If he fails to control his sexual impulses, if he can't be civilized into a woman-dominated society, if he can't fight fairly, poor Jud must die. Yet Jud gets the most interesting song in the show, "Lonely Room,"[26] which has one of Hammerstein's darkest, most poetic lyrics. "Lonely Room" is a song of unhappiness in a show in which everyone is supposed to be happy, but it gives Jud a brain and a specificity none of the other happy cardboard characters has. Gay author and show queen extraordinaire Ethan Mordden refers to "Lonely Room" as "obscure."[27] To me it is a welcome, jarring note in *Oklahoma!,* but what makes that and other Hammerstein shows particularly interesting are their discordances: the tension between farmer and cowboy, Laurey's fear of sex, the undercurrents of violence policed by Aunt Eller. Jud is frightening because he is aggressively sexual, and *Oklahoma!*'s subtext is sexual anxiety. Jud has dirty pictures in his lonely room, suggesting he masturbates there. In Laurey's "dream ballet," Jud, the force of male sexuality, wins over sweet, Dream Curly. What could be more frightening? But that was supposed to be an act-closing nightmare. In the 1998 London revival (directed by Trevor Nunn, choreography by Susan Stroman), the dream ballet was danced by the leads, not dancing replacements, which made the dream less pretty and abstract, more frightening.

If straight Jud was the outsider, the queer, in *Oklahoma!,* what would a gay man be? Invisible, of course! Or the object of the chorus, "It's a scandal, It's an outrage." There are a couple of jokes about the possibility of a man kissing another man, but they are easy laughs at something inconceivable in that world.

Carousel is less epic than *Show Boat* (though it does get to heaven and back), but the romance of Julie Jordan and Billy Bigelow is a more problematic version of that of Magnolia and Gaylord. The independent Julie is attracted to a man from outside her closed New England society. Billy is a Rodgers and Hammerstein version of Joey Evans, a man who lives by his sexual attractiveness. Given Hammerstein's anxieties, that also makes Billy something of a Jud, a man who cannot control his more violent impulses. Nor is he a proper heterosexual male. Jud was a masturbator; Billy is a kept man, though it is never made clear why being kept by a woman is bad in a society in which the women seem to own most of the property. Being attracted to someone so sexual makes Julie "queer." Julie and Billy, in that masterful extended musical scene, sing of their independence and eventually hypothesize on what their love would be like. "If I Loved You" is a brilliant duet of a doomed love, far from "You Are Love." The two characters never sing together, and the lyric is of failure to connect—"I'd let my golden chances pass me by"—and a presage of Billy and Julie's unhappy, abusive marriage. In Hammerstein's universe, a marriage based on sexual attraction is bound to be a disaster. During the scene, both Billy and Julie lose their jobs: Billy because he defies the woman who employs him and loves him; Julie because she rebels against the dour discipline of the mill and mill boarding house. Julie finds shelter from the good-hearted Nettie Fowler. Here, as in *Oklahoma!*, women form a strong supportive community while men compete, fight, and cheat and ultimately depend on women for support. Billy rails against the discipline of marriage and the expectation of work and listens longingly to the sound of the carousel where he was matinee idol. When he finds out Julie is pregnant, he wants to be a good father—Hammerstein men are sentimental about fatherhood though they are failures with women—but doesn't know how to fit into the economy of marriage. He is the opposite of the forthright, responsible Enoch Snow, who lives for buying more fishing boats to support his fleet of children. Boats and children are comparable industries to this ambitious member of the bourgeoisie. Carrie Pipperidge and the ambitious if odiferous Mr. Snow come to represent the respectable world to which Billy and his daughter, Louise, can never adapt. After all, Billy got and kept his job on the carousel by servicing his female employer—his marketable commodity is his sexual attractiveness.

Oddly, the musical celebrates Julie's choice of Billy. He may be an economic failure, a thief, a womanizer, and a brute, but he is more complex and sensitive than the other men. For all Hammerstein's anxieties about sex, fortunately he fears conservative "respectability" more. He is a liberal who was born and bred in show business. He's not going to side with Parthenia or Carrie Pipperidge Snow, with her debased taste in theater. Julie is outside conventional notions of respectability. She refuses to abide by the warnings of her employer and the policeman to avoid Billy, who has a reputation of cheating women out of their money. She doesn't obey orders to go back to the mill boarding house before curfew. Billy's unconventionality, his rough kindness, and his sexual profligacy intrigue her, though those traits will doom the marriage. Herein lies the problem of *Carousel*. It supports the role of loving wife as loyal and long suffering:

> He's your feller and you love him—
> There's nothing more to say.[28]

In the script's most grotesque moment, after Billy, returned from heaven to redeem himself by doing a good deed for his daughter, slaps her in his typical dysfunctional style, Louise asks her mother:

LOUISE: But is it possible, Mother, fer someone to hit you hard like that—real loud and hard—and not hurt you at all?

JULIE: It is possible, dear—fer someone to hit you—hit you hard—and not hurt at all.[29]

The emphatic repetition of the line makes it eerier for contemporary audiences. Hammerstein was celebrating the love and steadfastness of an idealized woman, a love all the more beautiful for being expended on an unworthy object. But what man in Hammerstein's world can live up to a strong woman's goodness? Now, when we are aware of the damage caused by domestic abuse, it is difficult not to wince at Julie's all-encompassing love.[30]

The London and New York revival of *Carousel* highlighted the problems of reviving a musical "classic" from the past. Like many British directors, Hytner opted for actors rather than singers in the leading roles, either operating under the misconception that the kind of quasi-operatic singers *Carousel* requires never can act or that a Billy Bigelow who could sing well wouldn't be realistic enough, as if Hammerstein's clammy Maine and kindly Starkeeper were realistic! Since Hytner's Billy Bigelow couldn't meet the part's musical demands (and above all one expects a Billy Bigelow to be able to make something of his great musical scenes), the focus moved from the music to the words. With the dated "method" interpretation of Michael Hayden, Billy became a troubled, James Dean–like creature out of a fifties movie rather than the singing hero of a musical. His brutality became shocking rather than a sign of his frustration at his inability to articulate. Since America is full of good, legitimate singers who are also good actors, Hytner's casting choice destroyed the balance of music and words that makes *Carousel* work. We accept Billy Bigelow because he can sing, because his music redeems his actions. If he can't sing, if the end of the soliloquy doesn't thrill us, he's a lout. We get mad at the character for being a brute, at Julie for being a wimp, and at the production for cheating us of the singing that justifies the revival. We notice all the more the problematic aspects of Hammerstein's sentimentality; its insistence that marriage depends on women enduring whatever abuse comes their way. Women are superior to men but must lovingly and loyally suffer whatever men do to them.

It is interesting to compare Billy to the Joey Evans of Rodgers and Hart and John O'Hara. Joey is a braggart and a womanizer, but no bully. Like Billy, he is supported by an older woman who keeps him around for his looks and his sexual prowess. However, in the world of *Pal Joey,* women dump men who become inconvenient and call the police on men who try to tyrannize them. Joey meets his Julie Jordan, sweet Linda English, but Joey knows better than to get involved with a nice girl. There's no profit in it. To my mind, O'Hara and Hart's cynical view of human relations is less dangerous than Hammerstein's sentimental view. When, in *Carousel,* the Starkeeper asks Billy if he's sorry he hit Julie, Billy responds, "Ain't sorry for anythin'."[31]

For Hammerstein, marriage was both a norm and a test of real manhood, but the woman had to do most of the work. A song in *Allegro* (1947) tells us that a fellow needs a girl who will "agree with the things he'll say."[32] In this duet, the woman echoes the man's lines. There is no verse or refrain in which she sings of what *she* needs. Does it matter whether and/or why a woman needs a man? Hammerstein assumes a woman "naturally" sees that her primary function is to love a man—regardless. She is the superior creature who makes "marriage-type love" possible. A good man will quit roaming and settle down, but there is no question in an Oscar Hammerstein musical of the love and steadfastness of the woman. A character in *Me and Juliet* (1953) sings: "I'm the girl you own."[33] Own?

Though the women are strong, the suspense in Rodgers and Hammerstein's musicals is built on what will happen to the man. Will Curly beat Jud? Will Billy steal the money? Will John go back to middle America? Will Emile and Joe Cable be killed by the Japanese? Will the king beat Tuptim? Will the Captain ditch the Baroness? This plot focus on the vagaries of the male was one of the defining features of Hammerstein musicals and one of the reasons they seldom fit within the customary casting policy of Broadway musicals of their time. Hit musicals starred a funny belter like Merman, an edgy comic leading man like William Gaxton, and a bunch of star comics like Victor Moore, Bob Hope, Bert Lahr, or Jimmy Durante. The ingenues got love songs, but they weren't the stars. Ethan Mordden, who has written the best book on Rodgers and Hammerstein's formal innovations, though he shies away from discussing their sexual politics, states: "The central performance in most musical comedies is that of the star, while the central performance in the musical play is that of the authors, and in this matter Rodgers and Hammerstein were authors of musical plays."[34] Rodgers and Hammerstein avoided star casting in their first three shows, but had their greatest successes from 1949 to 1959 with their version of diva musicals starring Gertrude Lawrence and Mary Martin.

Hammerstein preferred variations on the operetta format of a serious romantic couple and a comic romantic couple. It is not surprising that the secondary comic lead in *Oklahoma!,* Ado Annie, became the star-making role for Celeste Holm and, later, in a New York City Center revival, Barbara Cook. Ado Annie's star turns, "I Cain't Say No" and "All er Nothin'," are variations on the comic belt song. In the New York cast of the recent revival of *Carousel,* the radiant Carrie, played by Audra McDonald, not the limp dishrag of a Julie, was noticed. There were plenty of good ingenues who could sing Julie and Laurey, and act them competently, but they weren't made stars through those roles. To the pair of women, ingenue and soubrette, Rodgers and Hammerstein added the contralto maternal figure, nurturing but usually comic as well, a mixture of Parthenia and Queenie in *Show Boat:* Aunt Eller, Nettie Fowler, Bloody Mary. From *Carousel* on, these cheery souls also got the show's anthem: "You'll Never Walk Alone," "Bali Ha'i," "Climb Ev'ry Mountain." In *The King and I,* in which the two leads have all the comedy, the contralto, Lady Thiang, became more solemn but still got the anthem, "Something Wonderful."

YOU CAN'T GET A MAN WITH A GUN

Annie Get Your Gun (1946) was the first big post–World War II musical hit and, not surprisingly, represented the changing role of women during and after the war. The show represented firsts for its composer and star. Irving Berlin had never written an integrated book musical, and, in the post–*Oklahoma!* and *Carousel* climate, this was a real challenge. Songs could not be stuck in shows without a purpose. They had to define character and/or advance the narrative. This narrative was written by old pros Herbert and Dorothy Fields. Herbert had concocted some of the better books of musicals of the thirties and Dorothy was in her own right one of the theater's finest lyricists. Ethel Merman had never appeared in an integrated musical, though by this time, integrated or not, every Merman musical was a vehicle for her voice and brash presence. Whatever role she played, Merman was a New York girl, accent and all, but Hammerstein had moved the musical into a mythical past heartland. *Annie Get Your Gun* was produced by Rodgers and Hammerstein, who as producers already had a hit with another mythical view of a non–New York American past, *I Remember Mama* by John van Druten. Merman would have to move out to this mythic landscape. Or, rather, the landscape would have to be adapted to her. Merman was as unchangeable as the Empire State Building.

    Annie Get Your Gun is about famous sharpshooter Annie Oakley and her fictional rivalry with her husband, Frank Butler. In the show, he is a successful shooter but also an ace womanizer; "I'm a Bad, Bad Man," he boasts to his women admirers. The question implicit in the narrative is one of the most insidious ones in male-female relations: how successful can a woman be and still be attractive to men? Frank is attracted by Annie's talent and her refusal to play a subordinate role, but he is not up to rivalry with a woman and runs to another show. At their best, Annie and Frank are drawn together because they are both good and enjoy their rivalry. The eleven o'clock song is the competitive duet "Anything You Can Do." But Annie also wants to be a woman, which, as we know from *Lady in the Dark,* means being professionally subordinate to your man. Many of her songs are about her awareness of sex and romance: "Doin' What Comes Natur'lly," "They Say It's Wonderful." When Frank leaves for another show, Annie closes Act I singing a mournful reprise of "You Can't Get a Man with a Gun." Actually, Annie does get her man with a gun. She realigns the sights so that she misses the target in her final competition with Frank, allowing him the manly role of victor. To win Frank, she has to lose. Yet, you could say that, despite Annie's compromise to get her man, who remembers who played Frank? (Ray Middleton.) We remember Ethel Merman's Annie. Frank wins the plot, but Merman wins the show. In a touring production I've seen a fine Frank (Brent Barrett) totally steal the show from Annie (Cathy Rigby), but it didn't improve the show.

Annie Get Your Gun opened the year after the end of World War II, at the moment when women who had worked during the war and experienced a fair amount of autonomy found themselves back in the kitchen while their husbands took back the jobs that had been theirs. The show may be set in the past, but like *Lady in the Dark* it has a specific message for women who don't know their place, while offering a woman performer her most successful starring role. *Annie Get Your Gun* may be a Berlin-Fields show, but it is also very much an Oscar Hammerstein show about gender roles in an idealized America, and, as in *Show Boat,* the business in this mythical America is show business.

NORMAL AS BLUEBERRY PIE

After the success of *Annie Get Your Gun,* and the failure of their *Allegro,* Rodgers and Hammerstein combined their musical play formula with that of the star-vehicle musical comedy and created two of their greatest shows, *South Pacific* and *The King and I,* their most revived work. After a string of minor successes (*Flower Drum Song, Me and Juliet*) and major flops (*Pipe Dream*), their last collaboration was also a star vehicle, *The Sound of Music.* With Mary Martin, Hammerstein found his ideal heroine, a performer who could play both sides of the postwar split female personality, and with the barely singing Yul Brynner, his most successful male star. (Remember—real men don't sing!) Their careers are the most identified with Rodgers and Hammerstein and most represent the paradigmatic Rodgers and Hammerstein woman and man.

No female star more epitomized the possible changes in image and acted as a kind of bellwether for mainstream attitudes about women than Mary Martin. Unlike the cartoon women of fifties musicals, Martin seemed credible even in the most outlandish circumstances. Martin's career spanned four decades and her roles, particularly her roles in the fifties, defined conventional notions of femininity and domesticity just as those terms were beginning to be seriously and passionately questioned. What is interesting about Martin's career is how it was built on the kind of roles that defined femininity for their time: bimbo, glamour girl, tomboy, submissive wife and mother. She offered up versions of the norm.

The irony was that these conventional versions of femininity were played by a woman whose alleged private bisexuality was hardly conventional outside of show business. An essay on Martin in a collection of essays on gays and lesbians in the American theater[35] (surprisingly short on gay men) paints Martin as something of a lesbian icon because of the iconography of her roles, not her private life. She had a close, somewhat dependent relationship on her supposedly bisexual husband—manager Richard Halliday—but also intense friendships with women, particularly film star Janet Gaynor, with whom Martin was rumored to be romantically involved. In the years after *South Pacific,* Martin and Halliday lived in a remote corner of the Brazilian rainforest, which couldn't have allowed for much philandering, though the ranch was supposedly close to that of Janet Gaynor and her husband. Unless one has access to a person's innermost thoughts and desires, it is inaccurate to define a person who has had sexual relationships with men and women as lesbian or gay. Such rigid, inaccurate categorization is a vestige of a time of a rigid straight/gay binary opposition that was both wrong and stultifying. Whichever she was, her ambiguous sexual desire and identity, which, if known, would have destroyed her career, may have enabled the androgyny that makes her performances so appealing and complex. Needless to say, it also created a typical irony for musical theater; what seems most straight may not be straight at all.

Martin began as a sex kitten. Her career took off in 1938 when she appeared in the Cole Porter musical *Leave It to Me,* with a book by Sam and Bella Spewack who, a decade later, would write *Kiss Me, Kate* with Porter. Like Porter's *Silk Stockings* seventeen years later, *Leave It to Me* is a comic parody of U.S.–Soviet relations. It starred an odd mix of personalities: meek comic Victor Moore (Fred Astaire's sidekick in *Swing Time*); the legendary, brassy Sophie Tucker, whom one doesn't associate with book musicals; and perennial leading man of thirties musicals William Gaxton. The trio of Moore, Tucker, and Gaxton were not going to give a musical much in the way of sexual allure. *Leave It to Me* did contain three Porter classics: "Get Out of Town," "Most Gentlemen Don't Like Love," and a ditty sung and demurely stripped at a remote Siberian railroad station. Mary Martin's mock-sexy rendition of "My Heart Belongs to Daddy" stole the show the way Gwen Verdon's "Garden of Eden" number stole Porter's *Can-Can* fifteen years later. "My Heart Belongs to Daddy" is one of Porter's greatest lyrics. The tune is one of Porter's sinuous mock-klezmer melodies set to a Latin beat. The lyrics are ingenious, full of witty rhymes and naughty double entendres (which Martin claims she never understood). The singer of this song, to paraphrase a great Lanford Wilson line, knows which side she is buttered on. She may philander, but she remains loyal to the sugar daddy who pays the bills. Diamonds are her best friend. Martin's first role, then, is as the embodiment of gay Cole Porter's wit and world. As is often the case in Porter's songs, sex is a commodity and "heart" in any sentimental sense is a contested term. Since Porter and Hart were the dominant lyricists of the late 1930s, the Broadway stage allowed for a transgressive, commodity view of sexual relations. Martin, married to a sometimes abusive man who controlled her career, her commodification, may not have understood the implications of the lyrics she sang, as she claimed not to understand their sexual subtext, but the song made her famous.

Unlike most Broadway divas, Martin was both pretty and, in a conventional sense, feminine. Next to larger-than-life co-star Sophie Tucker, she must have seemed like the perfect sex kitten. The famous publicity photo of Martin singing her first hit could be a Hollywood starlet pose. She is sitting on a suitcase, wrapped in furs that, of course, don't cover her shapely, coyly crossed legs. It's not surprising that her performance of "My Heart Belongs to Daddy" turned her into a Paramount starlet. Unfortunately, Paramount wasn't the place to be to become a Hollywood musical star in the late thirties, and Martin, like most Broadway divas, languished in Hollywood.

For the rest of her career, Martin was to build her career on playing conventional, straight-male visions of women. Her next Broadway hit was a glamour part, the title role in the Kurt Weill–Ogden Nash–S. J. Perelman musical *One Touch of Venus* (1943). With a series of gorgeous Mainbocher gowns, Martin got to look more beautiful and glamorous than Hollywood had allowed her to be. She was also given four gorgeous Kurt Weill songs. Mary Martin might not yet have been a Broadway star, but Venus was a star role and, by all accounts, she was superb in it. Venus had originally been written for Marlene Dietrich, who thought it too naughty for a mother of a young daughter to play. When Martin was cast, the script was rewritten to make Venus more down to earth, less naughty, more "American." This Venus is a very safe sexual fantasy, though her songs, particularly the classic "Speak Low," suggest something less conventional. Martin considered herself a belter, even asked Rodgers and Hammerstein why they wanted "two baritones" in *South Pacific,* but on her recording of songs from *One Touch of Venus* Martin's voice is a well-produced, mellow, smoky mezzo soprano more akin to great forties band and radio singers like Dinah Shore and Jo Stafford than to the brassy Ethel Merman or the Broadway lyric sopranos who played Laurie and Julie Jordan. She could sound vulnerable in a ballad and forceful in a patter song without losing the sweet quality of her voice. When the album was made of the show (now available on CD), it was not made as an "original cast" album, but as a showcase for Martin. She and whiskey tenor Kenny Baker, her leading man, sang all the songs. Unfortunately, either Martin's personality does not come through in the recording studio or she decided to produce a pleasant, bland "radio" sound. Compared to recent recordings of the big songs from *One Touch of Venus* (no complete recording has been made) by a variety of singers from cabaret artist Ute Lemper to opera mezzo Anne Sofie von Otter, Martin is blah. Surprisingly, she makes little of the words. Unfortunately, we have no visual record of her Venus. As is typical for the treatment of Broadway divas, Hollywood cast someone else for the film (Ava Gardner). So did television (the reliable but wooden Janet Blair, a staple "girl singer" on fifties variety shows who played Nellie Forbush in the road company of *South Pacific*).

Martin then achieved acclaim for playing a loyal, wronged Chinese wife in a strange faux-oriental concoction, *Lute Song,* which had a few songs written for her by Raymond Scott, a forties composer-conductor whose offbeat originality started to be fully appreciated in the 1990s, long after his death.

Her first forties musicals showed the "feminine" side of Mary Martin: the sacrificing Chinese wife and the unearthly Venus out of place in New York City and mismatched to a sweet barber. Few other stars succeeded so well as both wife and siren. Then came Annie Oakley in the national tour of *Annie Get Your Gun,* an important transition for Martin, who proved that she could combine the tomboy with her femininity to develop a character that would be seen as an ideal American woman: not too bright, kind-hearted, practical, slightly goofy, but devoted to the man she chooses to love—the prototype of the fifties television sitcom heroine, but with more androgyny. It is hard to believe that Merman would let a man win a shooting contest. Martin would, but she'd turn it into a triumph for proper womanhood. Martin had to make Annie Oakley her own, tenderer in the ballads, goofier in the comic numbers. She got the chance to reprise her Annie on national television after her success in *South Pacific.*

Nellie Forbush in *South Pacific* became the perfect Mary Martin part and created the Martin persona that lasted the rest of her career. She was at least a decade too old to play the young Navy nurse on a Pacific island during World War II, but eternal youth, easier to maintain on stage than on screen, became part of Martin's persona. Though she was far from suburbia, Nellie defined many aspects of the contemporary image of American women. From Little Rock, Arkansas, like Lorelei Lee in *Gentlemen Prefer Blondes,* she was "a cockeyed optimist," a combination of romantic and practical. She was nurturing by nature and by profession. She was vulnerable yet something of a tomboy. Nellie is a combination of the traits usually split between the two leading ladies of musicals of the period, so there's no second female lead. Nellie is both romantic and clown, leading lady and tomboy. Liat, the ingenue, is a cipher who is sung to. Nellie gets most of the songs. Her leading man, Emile, gets endless reprises of "Some Enchanted Evening" and a second-act ballad, "This Nearly Was Mine." Most of the songs Nellie, the all-American girl, sings are, in a quintessentially American way, "I" songs of self-description or self-assertion:

> "I'm only a cockeyed optimist"
> "I'm gonna wash that man right out of my hair"
> "I'm as corny as Kansas in August"

Emile and Joe Cable sing "you"; Nellie is all "I," but it is her self-consciousness that allows her to change. Joe can lament his crippling prejudices in "Carefully Taught," but Nellie exorcises hers.

Mary from Weatherford, Texas, and Nellie were a perfect match. Martin wore very short hair for the part, partly because she had to wash it on stage every night, setting a fashion in modified crew cuts for women. (How butch!) In one of her big numbers, she sang and danced in a drag duo, she as a male sailor, Luther Billis as the sexy "Honeybun." But, ultimately, typical of Rodgers and Hammerstein's version of Mary Martin, Nellie's heart belongs to Daddy. She falls in love with a man much older than she with two children by a previous marriage. She also learns, through loving Emile's racially mixed children, the evil and folly of racism (against Eurasians, not blacks. This was 1949!). She had the values and prejudices of Middle America, but she was enough of a "woman" to sacrifice her prejudices for the love of family and because it is the right thing to do:

> I know what counts now. You. All those other things—the woman you had before—her color. . . . (*She laughs bitterly*) What piffle! What a pinhead I was![36]

Ezio Pinza's age made Martin look younger than she was, but Nellie made Martin an embodiment of eternal youth, innocence, and general good will. She could clown around, but she was always a lady. She was the archetypal "American girl," a far cry from the bimbo at the Irtusk railway station or Venus. Of course, Mary got the guy, but the guy was Daddy, an older, more sophisticated, European man with a ready-made set of children.

South Pacific came at a crucial period in the history of mass culture in America. *South Pacific* was one of the first original cast albums to appear in the new long-playing record format, and it was a best seller. The original cast recording of *South Pacific* gives us a better sense of Martin as a singer than the recording of *One Touch of Venus* does. Her big numbers are truly exuberant. She connects with a simple Rodgers waltz better than she did with the sinuous line of a Kurt Weill ballad. The interesting number is "Twin Soliloquies." Rodgers has written an operatic vocal line for Nellie, but Martin sings it with a pop voice. She keeps in character, which provides a contrast to Pinza's vocal style.

Television was burgeoning, and television in 1949 was based in New York and aspired to Broadway. Shows, all live, often came from Broadway theaters that had been converted to television studios. For a brief period, before television moved to Hollywood and dumbed down in the mid-1950s, Broadway stars were the elite of television personalities. So Mary Martin washed her hair and sang of her corniness on live television on shows like Ed Sullivan's (then named *Toast of the Town*). Martin became the diva of television specials in the fifties, making grand joint appearances with Noël Coward and Ethel Merman and appearing in tributes to Rodgers and Hammerstein. As Ethan Mordden points out, in the fifties, "Martin becomes something like the essential R & H performer, not only because she was the only star to open two of their shows on Broadway but because after *South Pacific* she was constantly associated with them."[37]

Mary Martin and her successors as Nellie, Martha Wright (who also replaced Martin as Maria in *The Sound of Music*) and Janet Blair, were the sort of female singing stars television courted. Martin's next success was more a television phenomenon than a Broadway one. At age forty-one, Martin essayed the role of Peter Pan in a new musical version that was performed live on NBC right after its short run on Broadway. Here was middle-aged Martin flying on national television in double drag, male and eternally young. Having a woman play Peter Pan takes much of the danger out of the myth. The eternal boy evading responsibility and refusing to grow up isn't a boy at all. In the Eisenhower era, this piece of barely disguised male drag seemed to underscore that this version of Peter Pan was really about the danger of women, what would happen to children if Mother ruled the roost instead of Father. We all know what Freud thought would happen! And in this *Peter Pan,* in which Cyril Ritchard plays a queeny Captain Hook camping around his young captives like a British pantomime dame, Freud's myth about how gays are made by Mother, taken as gospel in the fifties, seems very present. Martin claimed that Peter was her favorite part. It was certainly the part in which she was seen by the most people. *Peter Pan* only lasted a few months at the Winter Garden, but millions saw it on NBC. Martin clearly is more comfortable playing the tomboy than she was playing Venus. Jule Styne's "Neverland" sounds like any Mary Martin rendition, but the big songs have such exuberance that one forgets who's singing. Moose Charlap's "I've Gotta Crow" and "I'm Flying" are not great songs, but Martin sings them like she believes them. Martin is more identified with Peter Pan than any other role. It and a television version of *Annie Get Your Gun* made her a television star and got her signed up to do classy two-person shows with Noël Coward and Ethel Merman. Martin, after all, was wholesome, thus perfect for television. And, despite her Peter Pan drag, she could look more conventionally feminine than the other Broadway divas. She was a good foil for the urbane, English Coward and for the brassy Merman, and much more telegenic than either of them.

In her mid-forties, Martin played the young nun, Maria, in Rodgers and Hammerstein's *The Sound of Music* (1959), a smash hit despite almost universal critical disdain. Like *Peter Pan, The Sound of Music* is what one would call a "family musical," appealing to children as well as their parents. It is no surprise it was one of the last hit Hollywood musicals (1965). Appropriately, its 1998 Broadway revival was funded by Hallmark greeting cards. *The Sound of Music* was created as a Mary Martin vehicle and co-produced (with Rodgers and Hammerstein) by her husband-manager, Richard Halliday. Broadway hacks Howard Lindsay and Russel Crouse wrote the book; Hammerstein merely wrote the lyrics. To some extent, the musical played on Mary Martin's persona the way the film played on Julie Andrews's. Nellie Forbush and Peter Pan are out of place in a monastery. Martin's character goes out into the world, meets and falls in love with an older man with children, and helps save the family from the Nazis. Maria is a wonderful caregiver to the Trapp kids because she is a kid. She yodels, she does puppet shows, she sings inane children's songs in one of the most nauseatingly mawkish scores ever written. No other Broadway star could have made *The Sound of Music* work (though I would love to see it with Elaine Stritch!). No one else could have taken it seriously! In casting that must have had Hitler spinning in his grave, the Austrian aristocrat Captain von Trapp was played by Austrian-born folk singer and actor Theodore Bikel, a Holocaust survivor. It wasn't enough to get across the alps with anti-Nazi Austrians. Mary got across with an Austrian Jewish husband. Even at this stage, Martin is playing a kind of child-woman mated with an older man and a ready-made family of singing children.

It is ironic that treacly *The Sound of Music* won the Tony for Best Musical in 1960 instead of the tough masterpiece *Gypsy,* and that Mary Martin won as Best Actress in a Musical over Ethel Merman. Both shows are about mother figures creating showbiz acts for their kids. But while Rose is a steamroller, flattening everything and everyone in her path, Maria is one of the kids. She gives up her nun's habit and finds a daddy. It certainly offers a more palatable view of motherhood for its time. Rose, after all, is a single mother, which was not very fashionable in 1959, and a bad one at that. *Gypsy* is the classic, but *The Sound of Music* was the beginning of a new genre, the "family musical," that would eventually smother Broadway. Who is more appropriate to launch the first smash-hit version of this genre than wholesome Mary Martin, pushing fifty, but always the child-woman?

We have minimal film records of Martin's heyday in the 1950s. There are kinescopes of some of her television appearances, but the films of *South Pacific* and *The Sound of Music* were made without her. Mitzi Gaynor is characteristically perky amidst the acid-trip-colored filters of Joshua Logan's film of *South Pacific,* but the film is like most films of Rodgers and Hammerstein "classics," heavy-handed and joyless, bereft of the energy a good performance can have on stage. Robert Wise's highly scenic film version of *The Sound of Music* benefited from a performance by Julie Andrews very different from Martin's, but perfect in its own crisp way. Rodgers gave Andrews new songs that are far better than the originals, but he reduced Maria's rival, the Baroness, and the aristocratic impresario, Max, to speaking roles. On stage, Kurt Kaszner was clowny as Max. On screen, Richard Haydn played him as a stereotypical upper-class queen, a gay hanger-on who hasn't the courage to resist the Nazis. At least, for once, there is a gay presence in a Rodgers and Hammerstein musical, even if he is a relic of the thirties. Not much had changed in gay representations between Eric Blore and Max.

I will never understand the success of *The Sound of Music.* To my ears, the score is virtually tuneless, and experiencing the show on stage or screen is like drowning in a sea of ginger ale. Obviously I have a heart of stone.[38] Maria, however, is the capstone to Rodgers and Hammerstein's idealized depictions of women: a nun who becomes the ideal mother and devoted wife and who is able to humanize her emotionally crippled man; a woman who is Mother but also childlike; feminine, but tomboy. The perfect Mary Martin role.

Martin gamely went on into the sixties with a flop vehicle, *Jennie,* the two-character history of a happy marriage, *I Do! I Do!,* and as Dolly Levi on tour and in London. Despite this variety of roles, she was most identified with Rodgers and Hammerstein.

REAL MEN DON'T SING

Rodgers and Hammerstein had a problem with male leads. Curly and Billy are supposed to be romantic, masculine characters played by men who can act and sing very well. To the extent that romantic singers can be stars on Broadway, Alfred Drake and John Raitt were made stars by *Oklahoma!* and *Carousel.* Neither appeared in many more Broadway shows (Drake in *Kiss Me, Kate* and *Kismet,* then the ill-fated *Kean* and *Gigi;* Raitt in the hit *The Pajama Game* and a succession of flops like *Three Wishes for Jamie*), but both were considered name-over-the-title Broadway stars. Basically they were strong-voiced baritones who could project personal charm. Curly doesn't take a lot of acting—there's very little character there—and Billy's sympathetic moments come through song. These were the days before microphones when subtlety was as much an impossibility in the musical theater as it was in an opera house. Voice mattered and no one expected naturalistic acting in a musical. Neither Drake nor Raitt remained associated with Rodgers and Hammerstein the way Mary Martin did. For one thing, popular singing styles had changed with the advent of radio and recording technology. Crooners like Crosby and Sinatra represented popular singing style. The quasi-operatic singing of Broadway baritones was an anachronism. Yet the Broadway baritone survived through the fifties until miking made him unnecessary.

In the fifties there was an army of handsome young male singers who appeared and mysteriously disappeared after a show or two. William Tabbert played Lieutenant Joe Cable for the entire run of *South Pacific,* then stayed in the Majestic Theater to play Marius in *Fanny.* Tabbert had the kind of strong tenor voice needed to make something out of a ballad like "Younger than Springtime" or "Fanny" in the cavernous Majestic in the days before microphones. I remember seeing *Fanny* from the back row of the balcony under a very noisy light booth and hearing only Tabbert. (Did I have ears only for him?) The *Fanny* cast album shows him to be a bit off-pitch at times, but always passionate, a contrast to the staid, older male voices of Pinza and Walter Slezak. Stephen Douglass (Billy Bigelow on the national tour) was Ulysses in the wonderful 1954 Jerome Moross–John Latouche show, *The Golden Apple,* then moved on to play Joe Hardy opposite Gwen Verdon in *Damn Yankees.* He had good looks and a real operatic baritone, but Joe Hardy is a thankless role—the guy is supposed to feel no sexual chemistry for the sexy leading lady and to sing love songs and duets to a middle-aged woman. Joe is a total square, but so were most of the roles for handsome leading men. You didn't reach stardom playing these guys even if you got to sing the hit songs. People like Eddie Fisher or Johnny Mathis would make the hit singles. After *Damn Yankees,* Douglass disappeared, or morphed into George Wallace, who had the ballads in Gwen Verdon's next vehicle, *New Girl in Town.* Handsome young David Daniels, also strong of voice, had the hit ballads "Young and Foolish" and "Follow Your Heart" in *Plain and Fancy,* but the glory went to Barbara Cook. Cook had a better version of the voice of the fifties ingenue (Doretta Morrow, Florence Henderson) but was a much more characterful singer and a performer of immense personal charm. I remember *Plain and Fancy* fondly, mainly because winning young performers played kids not much older than I was. In the Eisenhower era there was an erotic charge to seeing a Broadway show that focused on young people, particularly a show with a good-looking young man like Daniels (Douglass seemed a bit mature for young Joe Hardy), whose character went through the kind of adolescent rebellion one saw in movies of the time. His character, Peter, is considered "different" by the members of the conformist Amish society and is shunned by all of them at the end of the first act, a ritual version of what every fifteen-year-old most fears. Even then, long before I ever heard the word "gay," though I had heard the word "homosexual" and knew it applied to me and feared the shunning I thought would inevitably come, I was eroticizing and queering the show. Daniels, too, disappeared from view, to appear later in the second cast of *The Boys in the Band.*

Then there were Larry Kert and Michael Callen and all those boys in *West Side Story.* Kert was not a stalwart baritone. His voice was higher, more adolescent-sounding, sexier to this sixteen-year-old. Ethan Mordden notes how one can see the primary love triangle in *West Side Story* as Riff loves Tony who loves Maria.[39] I'm not sure I was conscious of that at the time, only that the show had an erotic charge unusual for Broadway in the fifties. Whatever we saw in musicals of the period, whatever flamboyant alternative universe we came to love, it may have been magic, fabulous, but it seldom was sexy. Kert disappeared from view until he understudied and replaced Dean Jones in *Company* in 1970. In the years in between, he was selling dogs in California, living proof that young male singers didn't become stars. Carol Lawrence and Chita Rivera were launched by *West Side Story.*

These handsome young singers didn't become lasting stars, though they provided some of us with fodder for fantasy. Meanwhile, the big male stars of postwar musicals were older men who had established careers in other fields: singers who could sort of act, like Ezio Pinza and Robert Weede from opera, and actors who could sort of sing, like Rex Harrison and Robert Preston from the movies, appearing in shows that followed *The King and I*'s example and turned the comic older man into the romantic lead. They were seen by an aging Broadway audience as sex symbols of sorts.

The lasting musical star of the period, and the one male performer who was totally identified with a Rodgers and Hammerstein show, was Yul Brynner, who built his stage career until his death on one part, the King of Siam. I would assert that it wasn't so much Brynner, though he was ideal for the part, but the part itself. The King is both the ideal Rodgers and Hammerstein leading male role and the most typical of Hammerstein's gender politics and the gender politics of the postwar musical. Moreover, the King is one of the few truly sexy male roles in the American musical canon. Well, yes, Brynner was sexy, which most Broadway musical leading men aren't, in great part because their roles don't allow them to be. But there's something about the role of the King that captivates audiences. Curly is cute but dull and Billy is a bully. Emile and Captain von Trapp are cardboard characters, fantasy romantic leads. But the King is the quintessence of the Oscar Hammerstein male.

The King and I has been Rodgers and Hammerstein's longest-running Broadway musical play, if one counts the Yul Brynner revivals that toured the country and came into New York. There is the 1956 film, directed by Charles Lang, less impersonal than most film versions of Rodgers and Hammerstein and enlivened by Deborah Kerr's Anna (with Marni Nixon's voice) and, of course, Brynner, in his most successful film role. There also were revivals in the 1960s at the New York City Center (Farley Granger with the radiant Barbara Cook) and at Lincoln Center (Darren McGavin, surprisingly good in a clunky production), and tours with Rudolf Nureyev (weird) and Stacy Keach (wooden). The score boasts a number of albums, though none is complete (only the least satisfactory, with retired Met star Rise Stevens wobbling her way through the score, has the terrific ballet "The Small House of Uncle Thomas"). The 1996 Broadway revival with movie star Lou Diamond Phillips (followed by Kevin Gray) was also a hit.

Though the musical was written at the behest of Gertrude Lawrence (who supposedly wanted Cole Porter to write the score!), it is the King, who has only a couple of patter songs and half of "Shall We Dance?," who is the star role from Brynner to Phillips. It's hard to believe that Rodgers and Hammerstein originally thought of Noël Coward for the King. He had been closely identified with Gertrude Lawrence, and British actor Rex Harrison had played the King in the hit 1946 film on which the musical is based (despite the credit to Margaret Landon's 1944 novel). Obviously the Coward-Lawrence team over the title would have been great box office for the few months Coward would have been in it, but disastrous casting. The King needed someone who was exotic, not louche. Yul Brynner, supposedly suggested by Mary Martin who had worked with him in *Lute Song,* was the ideal choice. Brynner became the only male star to "sell" a Rodgers and Hammerstein musical. In his many tours of the show, it was the King, not Anna, audiences went to see. Brynner's Annas for many years on tour and in New York, the reliable Constance Towers and Mary Beth Peil, were clearly second bananas.

Strangely enough, a great part of the King's sexiness is that he doesn't (or usually can't) sing. Before *The King and I,* the comics couldn't really sing and they did the patter songs. The leading men were baritones who could sing "Oh, What a Beautiful Mornin'" or the "Soliloquy" from *Carousel.* But, however macho their characters, singing reduced them. Real cowboys don't sing about surreys with fringe. However, Rodgers and Hammerstein believed that making the ballad singer the hero created the combination of sensitive masculinity they prized. Curly and Billy are rough around the edges but can appreciate a beautiful morning or starry sky. Their love of nature makes them better men than their more focused, less musical alter egos, Jud and Jigger.

Ironically, all the things that shouldn't have worked for the King did. He was written as a comic lead with a couple of patter songs. He didn't get any of the show's many hit tunes. He was racially "Other." Like Billy Bigelow, he could be seen as a brute, though his treatment of his recalcitrant Burmese wife (one of many) Tuptim and her lover, Lun Tha, is toned down in the musical from *Anna and the King of Siam.* His opulent clothing, which could be seen as feminizing, was also more revealing and sexier than chaps. Yul Brynner, who had been a stage manager and director at CBS television, was turned into a sex symbol by playing the King, but he couldn't parlay that into other roles (his greatest film triumph other than the film of *The King and I* was as a robot in Michael Crichton's *Westworld*). It was the part, not the player, though player and part became inextricably entwined during Brynner's lifetime. Lou Diamond Phillips, a more versatile actor (and, though he tries to hide it, a better singer), recently made the part his, something no actor in Brynner's lifetime could manage. But making the King one's own means having that *je ne sais quoi*—sexiness—and it seems to be easier for a man to be sexy if he doesn't have to sing. (Though few of us will forget Phillips lying on the floor singing "A Puzzlement." I thought one friend of mine was going to faint.) Lun Tha was stunningly gorgeous in the recent revival and sang his two beautiful ballads well, but it was Phillips's King everyone was mesmerized by. Remember that the next sex symbol in a musical was Rex Harrison, talking his way through the songs in *My Fair Lady.* Do you remember who sang "On the Street Where You Live"? (John Michael King.) One year after that, Robert Preston made a grand comeback as Harold Hill in *The Music Man,* another role defined by patter songs (Barbara Cook got all the ballads). In other words, if you want to be a star in a musical, don't sing the ballads. That's sissy stuff. Jerry Orbach, the reigning Broadway leading man in the sixties, had his biggest hit in *Promises, Promises,* in which he got most of the Bacharach novelty numbers and the driving, rhythmic title tune. The villain got the ballad, "Wanting Things."

The King and I still plays in the late nineties, particularly with a great comic singing actress like Faith Prince as Anna, because we have no doubt that she could rule Siam. The issue is not cultural superiority but shrewdness. *The King and I* is acceptable where as *Carousel* is not, because Anna is tougher than the King. Now, more than in 1950, this is a matter of gender, not of culture. Clearly the Siamese men and women are better dressed than their Western counterparts. The court of Siam is ravishingly beautiful in this megamusical treatment. The King's wives are proud, not submissive. And most recently the

King is Lou Diamond Phillips, a proud representative of American multiculturalism, in 1990s style more cuddly teddy bear than sexy tyrant.

Though highly erotic if cast correctly, *The King and I* is the most blatant
of Rodgers and Hammerstein's stories of gender education. Anna Leonowens
is brought to the court of Siam to educate the sixty-plus children of the King in
Western ways. Ultimately, however, she must also educate the King in proper
Western behavior, which means proper masculine behavior. He must learn to
keep promises (and to give her the house stipulated in her letter of appointment),
to treat a lady with respect, and not to be brutal to women. His behavior to men
is never an issue in the play. He is seen in a society of women and children.

Without irony *The King and I* takes the colonialist's side. There are good
things about the King, but he is both an untamed man and a child to be taught
by the Western woman. There is never a moment when Anna is made to think
that she may be acting disrespectfully to a king or insensitively toward another
culture as old and as valid as hers. When his mores differ from hers, when he
wants to punish Tuptim for dishonoring a king by committing adultery and
desertion, Anna calls him a barbarian, which stops him in his tracks and seems
to lead to his death: "You have destroyed him," the Prime Minister cries. Anna
has certainly embarrassed him in front of his subjects. Why doesn't the King
punish her? Because he is redeemed by realizing that she is "right." In the five
years since *Carousel,* Hammerstein has changed his tune on hitting women.

The matching soliloquies in Act I define the King and Anna and
demarcate their gendered behavior. "A Puzzlement" places the King at a
crucial intellectual moment, deciding how much to give up his country's
traditional isolationism without losing its culture and security. He knows that
alliances with colonizers could lead to betrayal and colonization. (China is to
his East and India to his West, after all; he knows what the British are capable
of, though the 1951 musical omits the more barbaric side of our allies the
English.) The King is full of questions. He needs Anna's knowledge of the
West and her decisiveness. Anna's angry soliloquy is about how spoiled the
King is. She is not interested in The King, the revered public figure, but in the
private man who dares to see this employee as a subject. There are greater
stakes here than in Hammerstein's other scripts, and he comes closer to rising
to the occasion. He can't resist falling into his usual gender formulations, but
for postwar America they look more enlightened. The King suffers from
masculine weakness—vanity, stubbornness, sureness of his privilege, a touch
of brutality. Other men would betray him, but good women are loyal, no matter
how he treats them. A well-connected British woman can help him make the
proper diplomatic alliances and the proper impression to Western eyes. The
price is reassessing his behavior toward Anna and offering the Western woman

the respect due her. Anna can counsel the King, but she must pretend to be guessing what he has decided for himself. At the end of the first act, Anna gets her house, but the King gets her to place her head below his. The subtext of *The King and I* is Rodgers and Hammerstein's usual domestic romance. Women must understand men's blind spots and defer to them, knowing all the while that they are the morally superior beings. Men are children, incomplete adults, but must be allowed to rule. Anna Leonowens is a Victorian woman, but also a post–World War II creation.

Shortly after we meet the King, he is defended by his senior wife in the obligatory contralto aria, "Something Wonderful," a sister song to "You'll Never Walk Alone" and "Climb Ev'ry Mountain," but much more specific to the characters and situation. Like all of Rodgers and Hammerstein's heroes, the King is redeemed by his "thousand dreams." It is dreams, aspirations, that redeem a man. Like Miller's Willy Loman in *Death of a Salesman,* which opened on Broadway two seasons earlier, those dreams may be wrong or unrealized, but they save a man from mediocrity or cruelty. They are the qualities a woman can understand. Anna's own cultural baggage prevents her from at first seeing the good in the King.

The love ballads "We Kiss in a Shadow" and "I Have Dreamed," two of the most beautiful ballads Rodgers and Hammerstein ever wrote, are given to the young lovers, Lun Tha and Tuptim. "I Have Dreamed" is cut from the film. In *South Pacific* and *The King and I,* the handsome young man who sings the ballads dies as part of a quasi-Oedipal narrative. He's not the uncivilized man of *Oklahoma!* and *Carousel,* but a father figure has been introduced (Emile, the King) and the surrogate son cannot survive. Cable is not as strong as Emile; he cannot let go of his white supremacy and marry the girl he loves, nor can he survive the Japanese snipers on Marie-Louise island. The father figure comes back alive; the surrogate son dies. Lun Tha tries to take Daddy's wife away. He's not strong enough to survive such usurpation of phallic power. The King's real son wisely sticks to political pronouncements.

Anna and the King can never acknowledge their love in song, only their gender and cultural difference. Toward the end of the show, they are given two duets, one of which is the eleven o'clock song, "Shall We Dance?," which is as close to a Fred and Ginger number as Rodgers and Hammerstein ever wrote. As in a Fred and Ginger movie, dancing is the most clear sign of sexual attraction and courtship. In the 1996 production, particularly as played in 1997 by Faith Prince (who replaced Donna Murphy), the sexual subtext of the dance becomes text. When the King approaches Anna to dance the encore, he is too aware of his attraction to her to continue the dance. It turns instead, almost, to a kiss, interrupted by the Prime Minister. The night I saw the production, the audience audibly groaned when the Prime Minister walked in on the couple about to kiss. In 1951, *The King and I* was about friendship, then considered a rare quality between men and women. In 1996, the musical was also about unrequited passion.

The fight between Anna and the King is based more on gender difference than cultural difference. In acting like a king, the King is acting like a man. The 1996 production makes Anna a feminist in the King's court, both proud and sexually attracted to the King. And the other wives know that he is not only fascinated and irritated by this outspoken woman, but turned on by her. The King's belief in his right to promiscuity is every man's fantasy. His belief in his dominance over inferior women is every man's, as is his sense of authority over his own domain. "A man's home is his palace," the old saying goes, but what does that make the woman? What justifies this king are his doubts, his love of his children, and his sexiness.

For this reason, there's more space for fantasy for gay men in *The King and I* than in any other Rodgers and Hammerstein musical. *The King and I* came just a few years after Tennessee Williams's groundbreaking play, *A Streetcar Named Desire,* in which, for the first time on the American stage, a man is the object of the erotic gaze. Brynner's bare-chested King was the logical successor to Marlon Brando's bare-chested Stanley Kowalski, another sexy barbarian, created in part as one gay man's erotic fantasy. For once, we get to enjoy looking at a sexy man onstage. The King is all the more attractive because his love for Anna isn't requited. This isn't the typical heterosexual romance. There's hope for all of us!

"HERE SHE IS, BOYS!": ON DIVAS, DRAG, AND IMMORTALITY

A drag queen is exactly what every man watching a musical is led to want to be.
—*D. A. Miller,* Place for Us: Essay on the Broadway Musical

AGE CANNOT WITHER

In 1998, Stephen Sondheim's musical *Follies* finally received a much longed for revival, the first fully staged, New York–area revival since its original production. The cast is filled with figures from musical theater's past—Kaye Ballard, Phyllis Newman, Liliane Montevecchi—and from Hollywood, Ann Miller playing the survivor, Carlotta Campion (how intentional was that appropriate last name?). Miller was the tap dancer with the metallic black hair that never moved, the steely smile, and the legs who was second lead in dozens of MGM film musicals. Miller was something of an odd girl out in her films. She was usually worked into the plot to do the novelty tap numbers, a one-woman Rockette show. She knew how to dance, but she didn't stand still very well. She never was required to act much. She danced on top of things, displaying her legs. She was also a bit forbidding. Was there a human being behind that smile or was this some form of android? She is an eternal symbol of the silliness of the MGM Freed Unit musicals rather than their occasional sublimity. For many of us looking at her films in the late sixties when we were all taking Hollywood seriously and bandying words like auteur, Miller was camp, right up there with Esther Williams and Sonja Henie. In *Follies* she was a different kind of camp, an old lady performing "Ann Miller," but was either more real?

In *Follies,* Miller is the star attraction for us show queens in the audience and for the *Times* critic, Ben Brantley, who dubbed her "the very essence of this emotionally rich, exquisite-looking production."[1] We did not see the same performance Brantley saw. He writes of Miller's "heartbreaking sincerity" in "I'm Still Here," Carlotta's classic autobiography and one of the most popular numbers in the show queen's hymnal. Sometime between Ben Brantley's visit to *Follies* and ours, Ann Miller decided to take the easy route and, instead of giving a "heartbreaking" account of the drama in "I'm Still Here," she did the song as an Ann Miller routine: tough, swaggering, over-rhythmic, a fierce act of will. It had its own drama. A seventy-five-year-old woman was playing "Ann Miller." From row Q of the Paper Mill Playhouse,[2] the imitation was quite convincing. The black wig looked just right. The make-up created a middle-aged "Ann Miller," but "Ann Miller" always seemed middle-aged to me. She wore a blue sequined gown with the trademark slit skirt, showing a shapely leg, but the leg was encased in what looked like a white surgical stocking. The gestures seemed right, the attitude was there, but the Queen of Tap walked with difficulty. This was elderly Ann Miller playing "Ann Miller," a kind of drag routine that is central to one aspect of the diva: the performance of a fierce, Pyrrhic victory over mortality, like Carol Channing playing Dolly in her seventies or Chita Rivera in her sixties vamping as the Spider Woman. On stage, these women are forms of Norma Desmond, frozen in time. Unlike Norma, they have their triumphant comebacks. Miller is not the chameleon survivor that Sondheim's Carlotta Campion is. She was never a "sloe-eyed vamp," never "careered from career to career," and she did finish two volumes of her memoirs. The act of survival for Ann Miller was getting through the song and basking in the wild adulation of the large gaggle of show queens in the audience who cheered her every move. On this night, Ann Miller was the diva, and the show queens were cheering the survival of a star of fifty years ago and the survival of camp. In his definitive essay on camp and gay sensibility, Jack Babuscio notes that:

> Camp, by focusing on the outward appearances of role, implies that roles, and,
> in particular, sex roles, are superficial—a matter of style. Indeed, life itself is
> role and theater, appearance and impersonation.[3]

Ann Miller in *Follies* epitomized this element of camp. She intermittently tried to act Carlotta Campion, but "Ann Miller" was as much a role. The noticeable physical effort with which she played "Ann Miller" made the role-playing all the more dramatically powerful. One of Philip Core's "Camp Rules" in his marvelous book, *Camp: The Lie That Tells the Truth,* is "Camp is a disguise that fails."[4] On this night "Ann Miller" was such a disguise; it worked until she moved. Scott Long writes: "Camp does not consist merely in a disproportion between form and content, but also in the creation of an attitude by which the whole relationship between form and content can be seen with new eyes. This point exists in the *spectator.*"[5] The spectator who can most appreciate and rethink the relationship between form and content is the gay man, particularly the gay man who was reared in the time of the closet.

The original Carlotta was B-movie actress Yvonne De Carlo, fresh from her stint on television's "The Munsters," a living version of "I'm Still Here." De Carlo was never a big enough star to steal focus from the original stars of *Follies.* For many in the audience of this revival, Ann Miller was *the* star. Her presence had a positive effect, making Carlotta's ruthless survival, her focus on maintaining her career, her willingness to settle for a decades-long string of flings with younger men a foil to the unhappiness of the married ex-chorines, never stars, who tried to live with and through the men they loved. She tells Ben Stone, who had an affair with her thirty years ago:

> We had some fun once; it was just a thing. That's all you meant to me, Ben: just
> a thing. The guy I'm living with, he's just a thing, too, but he's twenty-six. I like
> him. I liked you. Next year, I'll like some other guy.[6]

That's divadom. Take what you need from men, but live for The Career and the eternal spotlight. That's the weakness of Andrew Lloyd Webber's *Sunset Boulevard:* Norma needs Joe more than she needs her career. A real diva would have ordered her priorities differently. She wouldn't have shot Joe Gillis. Like Vera Simpson in *Pal Joey,* she would have dumped him and bought a new one.

The definitive "I'm Still Here" was performed by the diminutive comedienne Nancy Walker in a 1973 Sondheim gala. Walker, another survivor who would be even more miscast as Carlotta than Ann Miller, relished every word in the musical minidrama. She understood that Carlotta lived through will and through irony, a queen's diva. Ann Miller doing Ann Miller doing "I'm Still Here" had little to do with any words in the song except the title, but that was enough for her and the show queens. She gleefully accepted the wild ovation as if it had been proffered without any irony. For five minutes this elderly lady and

"Ann Miller" almost intersected. It seemed clear that in her mind they did intersect. That is what we saw and what we cheered.

There were gay men of all ages in the Paper Mill Playhouse audience for *Follies,* but middle-aged show queens predominated, men like me who were baffled by Ann Miller in their youth before they laughed at her in their thirties; men who, like me, may have seen the original production of *Follies;* men who, like me, now find their own resonance in "I'm Still Here." For us, diva worship was part of being gay. For us, camp was the gay way of relishing theater and life. There is a camp element to much diva worship as there is a drag element to most divas. It is these aspects of a past gay culture that I will focus on in this chapter.

"I THINK THEY'RE MADE OF STEEL"

In the 1977 Canadian film *Outrageous!,* written and directed by Richard Benner, Craig Russell portrays Robin Turner, a Toronto drag queen who, in Hollywood showbiz style, gets the gumption to give up his hairdressing job and move to the Big Apple to become a star. On the drag circuit, becoming a star means moving from sleazy lower Tenth Avenue joints to posh Upper West Side gay clubs, from thrift-shop outfits to gorgeous glitter (run up, we are supposed to believe, on a second-hand sewing machine). Along the bumpy road of Benner's confused narrative of Robin's relationship with his schizophrenic roommate, filled with seventies platitudes about the sanity of madness and the dreariness of sanity (*Equus* redux), Robin gets to do his act, or, rather, Craig Russell gets to do *his* act, which progresses from Tallulah Bankhead to singing divas: Barbra Streisand, Mae West, Carol Channing, Marlene Dietrich, Ethel Merman, Bette Midler, and, of course, Judy Garland. Unlike many drag performers, Russell does his own singing. *Outrageous!* doesn't have the sheer camp joy of the later classic drag epic, *Priscilla, Queen of the Desert,* or the more authentic *Paris Is Burning,* but it shows us a drag queen's repertoire twenty-plus years ago when drag queens "did" divas. Now, like RuPaul and the queens in *Priscilla,* drag queens are usually self-styled divas who may be ignorant of camp icons of the past.[7]

Why does Robin become a drag performer? "Those gals are tough! I think they're made of steel. But they're dazzling! Alive! They've got guts. And they're fun."[8] In other words, Robin displaces onto women characteristics usually reserved for men: guts, toughness, steeliness (Superman in chiffon).

Daniel Harris observed the masculine side of pre-Stonewall drag queens and gay diva worship:

> Diva worship provided effeminate men with a paradoxical way of getting in
> touch with their masculinity, much as football provides a vicarious way for
> sedentary straight men to get in touch with their masculinity. Despite
> appearances to the contrary, diva worship is in every respect as unfeminine as
> football. It is a bone-crushing spectator sport in which one watches the triumph
> of feminine wiles over masculine wills. . . .[9]

There is, after all, a great similarity between the kind of pandemonium gay males create at the opera house or theater in their shows of adulation of a diva and the pandemonium at a sporting event. The major difference is the gender of the object of the cheering. Opera and show queens talk statistics just the ways male sports fans do. What is being worshiped, however, is strength of a very different kind from the strength of a Michael Jordan. Athletics are about physical prowess and winning against other men in a competitive sport separate from the real world. Divas conquer men in more personal arenas. Feminine assertiveness and survival are the hallmarks of a diva. The drag queen is the male intercessor between gay fan and diva, emphasizing the gender politics involved in diva worship. The tough, brassy broad, the bitch, or the vamp get their way over the enemy, the straight man.[10] In musical divas, the toughness comes out in performance, which is often a triumph over personal limitations or disaster.

In my youth, diva worship was more a part of operatic culture than that of musical theater. The old Metropolitan Opera house would shake from the wild cheering of Tebaldi, Milanov, Callas, Price, Nilsson, Sutherland, and Rysanek fans. The last hysterical display of diva worship I saw was at a performance of *Jenufa* at the Metropolitan Opera featuring veteran diva Leonie Rysanek. In her sixties, the great Viennese singer-actress gave a vocally and dramatically riveting performance. The hysterical ovation was in part a response to the performance, but more an adoring response to the last of the divas. Rysanek, who began at the Met in 1959, was still going strong thirty-five years later, giving a kind of all-stops-out, honestly intense performance that the younger generation of sopranos simply cannot give. Ethan Mordden titles his tribute to opera divas *Demented,* and Rysanek was always the most demented of divas. The prolonged wild cheering she received that night was equally demented. Thirty years before, when opera queens were fierce in their partisanship in the gladiatorial competition of divas, worshipers of another diva, Renata Tebaldi, issued death threats against Rysanek for daring to sing one of Tebaldi's roles, Desdemona, in a Met broadcast matinee. Ah, *those* were the good old days!

The most apt critique of operatic diva worship is not in print, but on stage in the performances of the drag opera troupe La Gran Scena di NewYork. The first time I saw them perform, the audience was filled with opera queens and Met singers. Ira Siff (on stage Madame Vera Galupe-Borszkh) and his colleagues understand both the gender politics of the great diva roles and the mannerisms and excesses of the divas themselves. What Siff captures brilliantly about operatic divas and diva roles is toughness playing vulnerability, homeliness playing glamour. In other words, the drag of all opera. Is there much of a difference between the show queens and the operatic divas they adore? The diva who is beatified by many opera queens, most of whom never heard her live, is Maria Callas because her artistic limitations (a voice less beautiful than her rivals, and with unreliable top notes) and personal life (the temper tantrums, the marriage to a father figure, the romance with and betrayal by Onassis, the lonely death) make her a model for the diva mythology of performance as a fierce act of will in the face of physical limitations and personal unhappiness. Most of Callas's contemporaries were women who put their art and divadom first and whose private lives seemed not to exist. Now the private lives tend to overwhelm the public accomplishments of artists. So Broadway diva Patti LuPone, fresh from her highly publicized betrayal by and lawsuit against Andrew Lloyd Webber,[11] appears as Callas in a daytime television talk show version of the diva in Terrence McNally's *Master Class.*

For Robin in *Outrageous!,* the women he imitates are "dazzling," which men seldom are. Men may be attractive, but in *Outrageous!* they are homophobic, nasty, or uninterested in an effeminate man. Robin encapsulates the gender politics of the seventies drag queen: a sexual attraction to straight-acting men combined with an idealization of stars who have personae of tough, unconventional women. Drag artist Craig Hurst says of his attraction to playing divas like Mae West and Marlene Dietrich: "The sensuality of these women is mostly reminiscent. . . . But I also show the tremendous strength that replaces youth, sex appeal, flesh appeal. When that goes, their personality comes in, their sense of showmanship."[12] The drag queen substitutes the toughness of the diva for masculine strength and attractiveness. There may have been old-fashioned gay self-hatred under the glitter of some drag queens of yore, as there may be a lack of a self-image under the inflated body of the 1990s gym boy, itself a form of drag, but there was also fabulousness. Craig Russell's Robin is a pudgy, pouty wimp before his drag transformation, which is the gay version of the sort of manly transformation body-building courses used to offer: "They used to kick sand on me at the beach." The models for the transformation are the tough broads of showbiz. But those broads were themselves creations, playing rigidly prescribed roles that barely changed from film to film and eventually, as in the case of Bette Davis and Joan Crawford in their late Gothic period, turned into camp self-parody. When the New York drag diva Lypsinka (John Epperson), appeared in a play as opposed to his lip-synching performance, it was in an outlandish stage version of the Joan Crawford epic, *Lypsinka Is Harriet Craig!* His singing sidekick was played by a drag performer with the wonderful name Varla Jean Merman. "Varla Jean" echoes Marilyn Monroe's real name, Norma Jean. "Merman" can only echo one thing for a drag queen.

In a review of *Harriet Craig, New York Times* reviewer Ben Brantley noted, "Drag artists at their best make us see how much of what we think of as womanly is only a mask."[13] What Brantley does not say is that by showing the arbitrariness and artifice of women's personae, the drag artist is also showing the arbitrariness and artifice of masculine personae—of any gender identity.[14] Is Humphrey Bogart's or John Wayne's persona any less calculated than Bette Davis's? It has become something of a truism to say that lesbians and gay men are more aware than heterosexuals of the fact that gender is a performance— sometime in our lives, we felt the need to "play straight," thus learning that masculinity is an act, not an essence. Writer Paul Rudnick dramatizes this hilariously in the scene in *In and Out* in which Howard tries to follow the self-help tape on acting masculine. Performing masculinity is a series of negatives— real men don't dance! A sense of gender as performativity is the core of drag performances and the core of show queens' love of musical divas.[15]

The best-known drag queens of the sixties and seventies did impersonations of female stars. Jim Bailey and Craig Russell played Las Vegas and daytime talk shows. Straight audiences could accept them better than they could a drag queen who lip-synched to a record. In an era in which television variety shows were still full of male impressionists like Rich Little, a Jim Bailey was a recognizable commodity (though there is something odd in doing a drag imitation of Phyllis Diller. Phyllis Diller *is* a drag imitation). Jim Bailey's video, *The Jim Bailey Experience,* is filled with clips of his seventies television appearances on sitcoms and talk shows like Joan Rivers's. Like Russell, Bailey does Judy Garland (of course), Phyllis Diller, and Barbra Streisand. Unlike Russell, Bailey tries to separate his drag act from any discussion of gayness. He is a serious artist "acting" his female roles. This way he doesn't scare off the potential customers in Las Vegas. It is not surprising that both Craig Russell and Jim Bailey are most convincing doing women who themselves were self-parodies.

What do drag artists like Craig Russell and Jim Bailey have to do with a discussion of musical divas? I believe that you can't talk about these divas in the context of gay culture without talking about drag queens and show queens. The great musical divas of this century either begin or end their careers consciously in the world of the show queen, playing for predominantly gay audiences. The great stage divas are often imitated by drag queens because their personae have much in common with drag queens. More important, the great roles of the Broadway divas are themselves, like drag queens' personae, distillations and exaggerations of certain feminine traits.

This is not to say that musical divas were only of interest to drag queens. They were central to the experience of urban gay men before gay liberation. The dwindling body of show queens still maintains and creates divas. Adulation of Ethel, Judy, Marlene, Barbra, Bette, and their sister divas was a means of asserting commonality through shared cultural icons. The same could be said of the adulation of Maria Callas, Renata Tebaldi, Zinka Milanov, Leonie Rysanek, and other Met divas of the period. The current Broadway musical seldom allows for diva performances, but cults are still built around performers like Bernadette Peters and Betty Buckley.

FROM DRAG TO DIVA—AND BACK

A discussion of the relationship between the musical diva and drag has to begin with Mae West, a stage star in the twenties before her move to Hollywood. In the 1920s West represented all forms of sexual transgression. She was both writer and star of her stage vehicles, which focused on her persona as a comic siren who always got her men, a figure of promiscuity.

In her fascinating book, *"When I'm Bad, I'm Better": Mae West, Sex, and American Entertainment,* Marybeth Hamilton points out that that favorite of old-time drag queens, Mae West, got her persona and her act from New York drag queens in the 1920s: "West had borrowed heavily from 1920s camp to create her suggestively swaggering temptress. . . . Like gay men, she impersonated a flamboyant woman with sly, tongue-in-cheek extravagance."[16] Pamela Robertson has a more complex reading:

> West did not simply copy gay style; she also linked certain aspects of gay culture
> to aspects of a female sensibility. West modeled herself on a camp gay style
> because she believed [as did many at the time] that gay men were like women,
> not only because she adhered to inversion models of homosexuality, but also
> because she believed that gay men and women were similarly oppressed by
> straight men. . . . West impersonates gay men and female impersonators not to
> expose the gay style, but to exaggerate, burlesque, and expose stereotypical
> female styles as impersonation.[17]

No one, male or female, really talks like Mae West, no one's body is connected to her words quite the way West's is. Her dialogue—she wrote her own best material—is filled with obvious double entendres that are underscored by a slight undulation of the hips and elevation of an eyebrow. Her figure was that of a nineteenth-century star, all curves at a time when the flat look was in fashion. West looked more like a drag queen's idea of a woman than a woman of her period. Like Sophie Tucker, she sang the kind of raunchy songs black women performers sang in the twenties, about men servicing her on demand or else, but her candid, ironic insinuations and propositions could be those of a twenties New York queen.

West got herself in trouble with the powers that be with her 1927 play with music, *The Drag,* a presentation on stage of twenties gay life replete with current gay slang[18] and a drag ball. The gay characters were played by gay performers and much of the dialogue came from the conversation of the actors during early rehearsals. The play was banned from New York performance. Late in her career, when West became a camp icon, she pointed to *The Drag* as evidence of her lifelong struggle for gay rights. It also presents the source of her persona. *The Drag* never made it to Broadway, but it is a crucial part of understanding Mae West and her cultural position.

In the thirties, West went to Hollywood, but she returned to the stage later in her career as even more of a self-parody. In her seventies and eighties, West appeared as a cartoon of herself, cavorting in nightclubs with a beefcake chorus of body builders, and in films like *Myra Breckenridge* and *Sextette.* She was as much a product of makeup as any drag queen. Her audience was, to a great extent, gay men. West epitomizes the complex relationship between drag and gay diva worship.

West's legitimate post-Stonewall successor was Bette Midler camping it up at the Continental Baths in the early seventies, accompanied by Barry Manilow. (Talk about camp!) A supporting player in *Fiddler on the Roof,* Midler began her solo career as a performer for gay audiences, then went mainstream. Midler never got her Broadway vehicle—she came along after the mid-sixties diva musicals—so she created her own vehicles and took them on the road. Her concert tours, really more musical extravaganza than concert, played to predominantly gay audiences around the country but crossed over into the mainstream when one was taped for Home Box Office and another filmed and shown in theaters as *Divine Madness.* In her days as a gay diva, Midler acknowledged Sophie Tucker (another favorite of past drag artists) more than West. She liked Tucker's tough Mama act, her raunchiness, and her Jewishness, but, like West, Bette (note the camp spelling, like a drag queen) knew her roots were in gay culture. Writer Boze Hadleigh rightly calls her "a cartoonish woman imitating a gay man imitating a woman."[19] A drag queen could try to "do" Bette Midler, but, like Mae West, Midler "did" drag queens! In fact, in her early concerts, she outdid the drag queens by outflouncing the most flamboyant queen, outdoing their drag, and outtrashing their repartee. Craig Russell may have appeared as Ethel Merman, but never as a mermaid in a motorized wheelchair! Midler strutted around the stage like a female Mick Jagger, spouting gross jokes. Her musical numbers were a drag queen's version of the Ziegfeld Follies—glitz with irony. In the concert tour that was filmed as *Divine Madness,* Midler makes her first appearance carried in on a giant platter of food. Her backup team, the Harlettes, were foils to her outrageousness: "These girls don't know shit about Euripides but they know plenty about Trojans." Throughout the show, Midler is a perpetual motion machine, strutting about the stage during her X-rated patter and her musical numbers. In one, "Chapel of Love," she is dressed in an outrageous costume as both the male and female figures on top of a wedding cake. Unlike Garland and Streisand, Midler used a rock band and sang rock tunes as well as forties swing tunes. Show tunes were too passé for her and her audiences. Above all, Midler played to a gay audience at a time when audiences could be openly gay and demand to be acknowledged by their divas, and she made her name performing in one of those pre-AIDS palaces of pleasure, not a conventional nightclub.

Her film debut was as a rock diva in *The Rose* (1979). Rose is a strange morphing of a Janis Joplin–type rock star with Midler herself. Rose's patter on her concert appearances is Midler without the camp, but Midler does acknowledge her core audience when Rose goes into a drag bar and sings with a gaggle of drag queens, including one done up as Midler/Rose! It's an extended homage to the drag queens from whom Midler got crucial parts of her persona. Moreover, the joy Rose feels at singing a number with a drag queen "doing" her suggests that the ultimate validation for this diva is becoming part of a drag queen's repertoire.[20] At the end of the number, Rose is carried around in triumph on the shoulders of the drag queens. It is her happiest moment in the film. But *The Rose* was made at a time in which gay men were more into construction-worker drag than sequins and feathers. Midler's raunchy drag queen quickly became passé in the age of the clone look, then the age of AIDS. Midler's 1998 album, *Bathhouse Betty,* is an attempt to retain her raunchy queer image by harking back to her early pre-Disney years as diva of the Continental Baths. The album ends with a song from the gay revue *When Pigs Fly.* Midler's album is part of a phase of nostalgia for the institutions of post-Stonewall, pre-AIDS seventies culture. Does it play for the gay men born since 1972?

If Midler represents the period just before AIDS, Barbra Streisand was the New York gay icon of the pre-Stonewall sixties. Streisand and Midler share the trajectory of divas of their generation: beginnings in gay clubs as performers who acknowledge that their audience is primarily gay, then mainstreaming, then

Hollywood. Streisand made her name performing in a Greenwich Village gay restaurant. From all accounts, she won her first audiences through sheer ineptitude:

> She was hostile and terribly nervous. She had no contact with the audience and was hunched over the microphone and made something that was supposed to be patter, but was so convoluted and interior that all you felt was this hostility and terrible resentment from this ugly girl.[21]

She could sing, but she was a homely, ill-dressed creature who acted like she had no idea what to do on stage and wished the audience weren't there. She sang old show tunes and songs that could be considered camp. It is not surprising that it was gay writer-director Arthur Laurents who discovered her and fought with producer David Merrick to get Streisand in her first Broadway show. Streisand was enough of an oddball in the early sixties to be invited onto New York–based talk shows. She was personally unpredictable and strange looking, but she could sing up a storm. Her comic turn in *I Can Get It for You Wholesale* kept the flawed show running. Columbia signed her and by the time *Funny Girl* opened at the Winter Garden in 1964 she had made two successful albums. Streisand didn't need Broadway. She already had television and records and a film contract. After the hit film of *Funny Girl,* she was miscast in the film of *Hello, Dolly!* (1969). She was too young for the part and its camp was not hers, but by 1969 Hollywood was not going to cast a middle-aged Broadway star in an expensive musical.

In the 1997 film *In and Out,* Howard's love for Streisand is his primary sign of gayness. Why Streisand? In a way, Streisand is a transitional figure, coming at the end of the era when a song like Jule Styne's "People" could be a hit tune (*Funny Girl* [1964] was Styne's last hit score). She could sing standards without seeming nostalgic or ironic, though her take on the standards in her early albums is highly idiosyncratic. Her early persona was that of a homely oddball who gets her man. *Funny Girl* was the perfect vehicle for her, a backstage Cinderella musical. But Streisand was also a diva. Her first song in *Funny Girl* was "I'm the Greatest Star," and she meant it. From the very beginning, stories abounded about her temperament, her toughness. This ugly duckling became a major player in Hollywood: performer, director, producer. Streisand has the toughness drag queens aspire to, and the breach between her glamorous image and the crossed eyes, big nose, and Brooklyn accent gave her image irony, however unintentional. It is interesting to see how defensively Columbia photographed Streisand on her first solo album cover in 1963. She is shot at an angle that makes her nose look smaller. Everything above the eyebrows is in shadow and the eyes are heavily made up à la Elizabeth Taylor in *Cleopatra* though she's dressed like a Smith undergraduate of the period. Yet before long, on screen this girl would win the hearts and bodies of Omar Sharif (in one of the weirdest castings of the period—an Egyptian as a New York Jewish gangster!) and Robert Redford. Drag queens can also respond to the mannered delivery of the early Streisand, overwrought in the ballads, manic in up tunes like Cole Porter's "Come to the Supermarket (in Old Peking)." Even the choice of such a dated novelty song for a 1963 album is camp. And what could be more camp than a young singer choosing to sing show tunes in the era of The Beatles?

Three decades later, there was the much-touted, videotaped concert tour, hyped as one of the concerts of the century, which offered Streisand in her grand diva role. She needed TelePrompTers for the lyrics—Hollywood superstars don't need to remember lyrics. Here we saw the current Streisand: star and mother (gay son Jason was seated up front with his father, Elliott Gould), an echo of Judy's performances with daughter Liza. Streisand in her nineties Hollywood-goddess getup—blond hair, fancy gowns—is the role she always dreamed of playing. Like Judy Garland on her television show and in her later concerts, Streisand was trying to prove she could do it, that she was a survivor. Streisand was the Queen of Show Business holding court. She may have lost the irony to see that the queen of show business is as much a form of drag as her *Yentl* getup, but her show queen fans haven't. Drag queens have an easier time with the early Barbra. It's more idiosyncratic, an odd combination of ugly duckling and diva.

Streisand made a version of *A Star Is Born*. The film was something of a giant ego trip, but it was also a way of placing herself as the new Judy Garland, the Great Hollywood Singing Star. The film moves her away from the kind of show tune material she had been identified with into the world of the rock star as a way of avoiding nostalgic identification with the Garland film, but redoing *A Star Is Born* is placing yourself on a pedestal with Judy—or trying to knock Judy off of that pedestal. The film backfired on Streisand, painting her as arrogant and self-indulgent rather than heroic. Garland's film is a heroic comeback and a summation of a career in film of a person who, more than any other, defined Hollywood musicals. One can understand Streisand trying to move away from period backstage musicals into a contemporary backstage musical, but too much symbolism is attached to *A Star Is Born,* particularly for gay men.

BARBRA, JUDY, AND ETHEL

There's a famous episode of Judy Garland's television show (1963-64) that features Garland with Ethel Merman and Barbra Streisand.[22] Here are three of the drag performer's favorite subjects singing together. Garland and Streisand do a series of solos and duets before Ethel Merman struts out of the audience— she claims to have just stopped by from a taping in the next studio—and, at Judy's insistence, belts "There's No Business Like Show Business." Judy and Barbra join in. It's a grand moment, a show queen's wet dream. Three eras of singing—past, ever-present, and future—going at it. A friend told me about a 1998 screening of this sequence at a benefit for the Museum of Television and Radio in New York. After a screening of Great Moments in Televised Sports, which the straight men in the room cheered, on came the tape of Barbra, Judy, and Ethel: "The gay men in the room went wild"—many of whom weren't alive when the show originally aired. There on one small screen were three versions of the toughness that makes divas. Merman is the old-style Broadway Star, always facing center and belting her sassy lines with the same gusto with which she belts her songs. Made of steel, all brashness and belt, she sings like microphones needn't have been invented. There's a businesslike quality to her singing—it's no wonder "There's No Business Like Show Business" became her theme song. Merman very rarely missed a performance and gave the same performance every time: "Call me Miss Bird's Eye—the show's frozen," she would tell writers and directors trying to make changes during the final weeks of rehearsals. Merman had her personal disappointments and tragedies, but they never affected "the performance." Above all, Merman was a performer, not a singing actress. Stephen Sondheim, an artist who believes in complex characterization in musicals, called Merman "the talking dog," a mindless freak, a remnant of vaudeville.

On the video, Merman does her characteristic rhythmic pumping of her arms like a zealous aerobics nut. Like Streisand, Merman's a bit of an ugly duckling. She can move energetically in rhythm, but the gestures are meant to work from a distance, not close up. As I said, my show queen students can do Merman, though they have never seen her and probably only have heard one of her records. Her vocal mannerisms are easy to imitate—that slight grace note on a high note, that emphatic sense of rhythm. Drag queens who do Merman usually only need a minute or two. Once you get the voice and that rhythmic movement, there isn't anywhere to go. What was best about Merman is irrelevant with modern technology. She had a voice that could fill a 1500-seat theater and she had perfect diction. Not only the sound but the words reached the balcony. We have microphones for that now. Merman's imitators forget how important she was to the history of musical-comedy singing. She's the queen of belt singers.

Merman was always the brassy broad. She could play the tomboy in *Annie Get Your Gun* or the pushy socialite in *Call Me Madam* or the monster mother in *Gypsy.* She couldn't play sensitive. She could sing a ballad, but it had to be a rare tender moment for a tough character. There was nothing vulnerable about Merman. She never felt stage fright, and she was a total diva backstage, insisting that the company refer to her as "Miss Merman." She would have people she didn't like or found threatening fired. She did the same thing with her marriages—Ernest Borgnine rates a blank page in her autobiography. There's always something butch about Merman. Her idea of a gay couple was her buddies J. Edgar Hoover and Clyde Tolson.

Merman usually got the guy in her musicals, but a romantic finish wasn't convincing, particularly in the sexist conclusion of *Annie Get Your Gun.* She screamed toughness and independence. In her early Gershwin shows, she was brought on to sing the big numbers but had little to do with the plot. In the late thirties Porter shows, she was paired up with clowns—Jimmy Durante, Bert Lahr, or Bob Hope. The post-*Oklahoma!* Irving Berlin shows had more character (Rodgers and Hammerstein produced *Annie Get Your Gun*), but they were parts tailored to Merman's persona.

Merman did make some films in the thirties, but she never became a film star. Paramount, her studio in the 1930s, didn't hype her as a star, and Merman didn't like making movies:

> I preferred delivering my performance in person. I liked to be in control. You couldn't be in films. And I already learned it was cold down there as the face on the cutting room floor.[23]

Gay comic Paul Lynde once remarked: "She was too big for them [the movies] and put the men off."[24] Not surprisingly, she seldom got to do the film version of her great roles. There is a film of *Call Me Madam,* but Betty Hutton got to play Annie Oakley after Judy Garland was pulled off the film, and Rosalind Russell (with Lisa Kirk's singing voice) got to do Mama Rose. But close-ups weren't Merman's métier. She was great at blasting to the balcony. You get to see the strengths and weaknesses of Merman on screen when she co-starred with Donald O'Connor, Mitzi Gaynor, Marilyn Monroe, veteran Hollywood trouper Dan Dailey, and gay fifties heartthrob Johnnie Ray in *There's No Business Like Show Business* (1954). The film offers one of the weirdest smorgasbords of performing styles of any fifties musical and, for audiences now, a gay subtext. Merman plays a sassy vaudevillian and stage mother to O'Connor, Gaynor, and Ray. Husband and father is played by hoofer Dan Dailey who, unlike most Hollywood performers, eventually was somewhat open about his gay life in Hollywood. Given the fact that Ray's sexuality was something of an open secret, it is amusing to see Merman worry about her son's sensitivity: "He seems far away, like a poet or somethin'." When Ray announces that he is going to become a priest, his parents lament that he'll never have a wife and children. He explains to his father, played by Dailey: "Some people are meant to be one thing, some another." This is as close to having a gay husband and son as a movie musical would give a mother. Merman and Dailey's other son takes up with Marilyn Monroe, another fifties caricature of femininity. (Who thought up the idea of a romance between Monroe and Donald O'Connor?) It seems hilariously apt that Merman and Dailey would sire Johnnie Ray and get Marilyn Monroe as a daughter-in-law!

There's No Business Like Show Business ties a lot of Irving Berlin songs together with a rather flimsy plot. Merman is best in the "onstage" musical numbers. The camera avoids close-ups—this is a CinemaScope movie—which benefits Merman. She can perform as if she were on stage. The dialogue scenes are another matter. Merman has a veteran stage performer's habit of looking straight ahead when listening or talking to another character. Watching the film is like watching a group of drugged actors. With Merman's indifferent but loud line delivery, Monroe's offbeat delivery with her eyes moving back and forth as if she thought someone would pull a gun on her, and Johnnie Ray's spacy, smiley acting (where did he get those teeth?), combined with the chronic perkiness of O'Connor and Gaynor, this is a camp classic.

There's an interesting moment when Mitzi Gaynor tries to imitate Merman doing a number Merman performs at the opening of the film ("When The Midnight Choo Choo Leaves for Alabam'"). She just doesn't get it right, even though it sounds like they've mixed a little Merman into the voice. Gaynor moves too well and is perky rather than brassy. Merman and Gaynor do a male drag act as two sailors singing about their tattoos—one of Berlin's worst songs. Merman, oddly enough, is not good at male drag. Her forte was female drag, a pumped-up version of a sassy, tough woman. Gaynor is in training for "Honeybun."

According to Dennis McGovern and Deborah Grace Winer, "In her later years, Merman limited herself to concerts. While retaining her older fans, she also attracted a large and loyal gay following."[25] She always had that following! In the late seventies, Merman made one of her most bizarre albums—her greatest hits belted to a disco beat. Merman, of course, sings every song the same way she always sang them—the producers may have been using old tracks of Merman—and her style simply does not fit the Bee Gees type of accompaniment. It sounds like two different records are being played simultaneously. Show queens played Disco Merman at parties for laughs. Who else did it appeal to? As Streisand, West, and Midler began their careers with gay audiences, Merman ended hers. Merman was a relic of a different era, another facet of camp:

Camp aficionados prized the garish, the tasteless, the tacky and artificial. Above all, they prized the outmoded—relics of popular culture that had become obsolete.[26]

On *The Judy Garland Show,* Merman's singing style doesn't quite fit in with Garland's and Streisand's. Her idea of a duet is a competitive song like "Anything You Can Do" or "You're Just in Love." The latter, from *Call Me Madam,* is a wonderful queer moment. Wimpy Russell Nype (oddly, one of Merman's favorite co-stars), with his horn-rimmed glasses and crew cut looking like a fifties geek, moons over his love: "I hear singing and there's no one there"; then in comes Merman, tough and pragmatic, in the most parodied of Merman's songs, "You don't need analyzin' . . ." The duet does not move to unison singing, but counterpoint, Nype's sweetness and Merman's sass, an interesting gender-role reversal for the fifties. This sort of counterpoint became the backbone of medleys of Garland's television show, a style Carol Burnett picked up with her guests in the seventies. When megabelter Elaine Stritch had her first starring role in *Goldilocks,* who should be cast as her wimpy fiancé but Nype.

On the show with Merman, Garland and Streisand combine their "happy" songs. Streisand's famous torch version of "Happy Days Are Here Again" was her first defining number. She worked against the intention of this up tune, filling it with foreboding. The end is more a manic willing of happiness than an expression of it. It was perfect for Streisand's early image of a neurotic who was going to triumph by sheer force of will—and a terrific voice. Garland's happy song, "Get Happy," defined the new adult Judy in *Summer Stock* (1950). Instead of the proper dresses of Dorothy or Esther, Judy wore a fedora, tails, and a short skirt that showed off her legs, a kind of take-off on Dietrich's drag of the thirties that according to critic Marjorie Garber, was based on lesbian styles of the twenties.[27] However, "Forget your troubles, come on, get happy" had to have an ironic edge when Judy sang it.

Garland's screen image was nurtured by gay men. She was the diva of the Freed Unit at MGM, known in the business as "Freed's Fairies" for the large number of gay men on the creative team.[28] Charles Walters, who danced with Judy in *Girl Crazy,* staged the musical numbers in *Meet Me in St. Louis,* and directed *Easter Parade* and *Summer Stock,* was one of those "fairies." Garland's husband and director, Vincente Minnelli (*Meet Me in St. Louis, Summer Stock*), was bisexual. *A Star Is Born* was directed by George Cukor.

On the Garland show, Streisand seems socially inept, incapable of carrying on television banter with Garland, who hangs on to her for dear life. Garland is trying to treat Streisand as a pal, the way she and Merman are pals, but Streisand can't be friendly. Garland offers her tea; Streisand refuses. Garland tries to engage in banter; Streisand, when she does respond, talks so quietly the microphones barely pick her up. When Streisand sings on the show, first a painfully slow version of "Bewitched, Bothered, and Bewildered"—in those days, Streisand's trick was to switch the usual tempo of a song—there's an eerie inwardness, like a lonely little girl singing to herself. Garland tries to flatter Streisand by placing her in the pantheon with her and Merman: "You really belt a song. There are very few of us left." Barbra doesn't seem interested in being linked with these two past greats.

In 1963, Garland, a haunted, spectral version of the wide-eyed innocent of the MGM years, sings as if singing brings her her only happiness. But that's the Garland image that many gay men loved: Judy the emotional wreck, a vision of substance abuse, paralyzed by stage fright, but once pushed on stage, singing up a storm and basking in the adulation of her audiences. Culture critic Camille Paglia catches one crucial aspect of this Garland image:

> Bloated or anorexic, Garland never felt at home in her skin. Onstage, as her petite frame literally throbbed with her huge voice, she seemed at war with her own body, something that many gay men deeply understood. Her romantic cravings and serial humiliations were theirs. It was as if she sang "The Man That Got Away" just for them.[29]

Part of Garland's attraction for gay men was her own bisexuality: "Garland loved men—and women—of all persuasions. She had five husbands, three children, and frequent lesbian affairs; she also got a special kick out of seducing gay and bisexual men."[30] The transgressive Garland, like the emotional wreck, gave an irony to the wide-eyed heroine of her MGM musicals. For drag queens and their audiences, doing Dorothy was funny—doing Vicki Lester or the Judy of the concert tours was doing the ravaged but heroic Judy, but even the best drag performers don't quite get Judy right. When Craig Russell and Jim Bailey do Garland, they don't do Dorothy or Esther Smith in *Meet Me in St. Louis,* they do the Garland of *A Star Is Born, The Pirate,* or the concerts. Garland's mannerisms are easy to parody. She holds the microphone in the right hand. The left hand seems to have a life of its own, touching her hair or her face, raising itself above her head, holding herself. But you can't parody Garland the way you can parody Merman. She's too good, too versatile a singer. She had vocal mannerisms—all singers do—the swelling on certain notes, the trouble on top in later years, but she's a pure singer. You can only imitate the physical mannerisms, but not as the sort of parody one does with Merman or Channing. Drag queens do Garland as an homage.

Charles Kaiser calls Garland an "icon of camp culture."[31] This isn't totally accurate. Film critic Richard Dyer puts it more specifically: "She is not a star turned into camp, but a star who expresses camp attitudes."[32] We don't read Garland as camp; she performs camp and also, according to Dyer, performs on "the knife edge between camp and hurt, a key register of gay culture."[33] Dyer uses camp not in the sense of ironic worship of kitsch, but as communicating ideas shared particularly by gay men of an earlier time: "Looking at, listening to Garland may get us inside how gay men have lived their experience and situation, and made sense of them."[34] Garland is not camp in the sense that Merman or Mae West is. She happens to be a great singer who was showcased in a series of good to great musicals. She may have been asked to play the juvenile, the girl next door, too long, but in *Meet Me in St. Louis,* directed by her husband Vincente Minnelli in 1944, she gets to sing three of her classics and she does them brilliantly. I have always been most struck by her performance of "The Trolley Song." It's the one silly solo Garland has (we'll ignore her duet with Margaret O'Brien, "Under the Bamboo Tree"). In the film, "The Trolley Song" is sung while Garland is waiting for her beau, the boy next door, played by Tom Drake. As she sings lyrics that have virtually nothing to do with what she is feeling, we watch her anguish as she searches in vain for him on the trolley and her sheer delight when she sees him chasing after it and finally jumping on board. Garland acts out a real drama of adolescent love while she sings the inane lyric. It's that belief in what she's doing that makes Garland captivating—that and the brilliant singing. The performance is refreshingly honest, more honest sometimes than the parts call for. Given the extreme of the anxiety she is projecting while singing an inane song, "The Trolley Song" becomes a classic camp moment. In his defining essay "Camp and the Gay Sensibility," Jack Babuscio discusses the sense in which Garland can be called camp:

> Camp as a response to performance springs from the gay sensibility's preference for the *intensities* of character, as opposed to its content: what the character conveys tends to be less important than *how* or *why* it is conveyed. Camp is individualistic; as such, it relishes the uniqueness and force with which personality is imbued. This theatricalisation of experience derives both from the passing experience (wherein, paradoxically, we learn the value of the self while at the same time rejecting it) and from a heightened sensitivity to aspects of a performance which others are likely to regard as routine or uncalculated. It is this awareness of the double aspects of a performance that goes a long way to explain why gays form a disproportionately large and enthusiastic part of the audience of such stars as, most notably, Judy Garland.

> In part, at least, Garland's popularity owes much to the fact that she is always and most intensely herself. Allied to this is the fact that many of us seem able to equate our own strongly-felt sense of oppression (past or present), with the suffering/loneliness/misfortunes of the star both on and off the screen.[35]

Nowadays, we would argue with Babuscio's essentialist, universalizing assumption of a "gay sensibility," but in the days of Garland worship, such terms were more common.

What makes Garland most allied to camp is not the moments when she both justified and overwhelmed essentially silly material but the real-life psychodrama: Dorothy breaking down, the awareness that the Girl Next Door is a mask. Perhaps it is hindsight, but this is what makes *Meet Me in St. Louis* so fascinating. On the surface it is one of those celebrations of a mythical past Middle America central to our culture during World War II, a more sophisticated *Oklahoma!*, but there is a darkness to the film. It keeps skirting into scary, neurotic territory. As Jud is part of the idyllic world of *Oklahoma!*, so childhood and adolescent terrors are always there in Minnelli's film. Esther seems the stable center of the film, but her songs are of longing, of willing happiness. "Have Yourself a Merry Little Christmas" is not altogether a happy song. Supposedly Garland thought its initial lyrics were too depressing and got Martin and Blaine to raise its spirits a bit. (The song leads to that weird moment when Tootie, forever symbolically killing father figures, runs out and destroys the family of snowmen.) Perhaps, though, I am reading back from the late Garland, which gives greater complexity to the film than it has. While my young, pre-Stonewall self never bought into the Garland myth—my camp self focused on Zinka Milanov and Leonie Rysanek—I certainly was aware of it. Ethan Mordden, the best writer on Garland, cogently sums up her cultural position for her devotees in the sixties:

> For a generation, Garland fitted into the musical's rigid belief that show-biz glory is self-realization. For the next generation, Garland appears to prove that this glory is dissolution, a loss of nerve. After all, stardom in America is based not on one's gifts, but on one's image. . . . She is losing control while she takes control, one ship passing itself in the night.[36]

It wasn't totally sadism to adore Garland for her weakness. To some extent it was identification for gay men at a time when they had nothing but silence or negative comments from any corner of the culture and often had internalized their society's hatred. Garland was the Wreck Who Went On—brilliantly.

The television shows tried at first to capture the excitement of the personal appearances. There are constant shots of the audience, but they are far too polite. These eerily placid creatures aren't her worshipers. In fact, it looks as if Garland's usually hysterical fans were replaced by pod people from *Invasion of the Body Snatchers*. In her solo numbers, played before the orchestra, Garland has a maddening habit of not looking at the camera, of trying to pretend it isn't there and that only the live audience matters. She only relaxes when someone else is sharing the screen with her. These are pale replicas of her live appearances. If Garland was a film star in the thirties and forties, her stage appearances at the Palace, London Palladium, and Carnegie Hall in New York in the fifties and early sixties were major performances for show queens, a magical example of the bond between us and our divas. Her New York concerts were Events—all the glitterati attended, plus the adoring queens. The response to Garland's performance was a wild demonstration of mass adulation:

> It was absolute pandemonium. The entire audience ran to the footlights with their hands in the air, screaming "Judy! Judy!" And she touched all the hands she could. Then Rock Hudson lifted Lorna and little Joey on stage, and she hugged them and leaned down to kiss Liza, who was in the front row, and the audience screamed for more.[37]

Writer William Goldman has a vivid, if characteristically homophobic, description of Garland's closing night at the Palace:

> And now, through the eleven minutes of curtain calls, more and more people press toward her. People sitting in the front rows who wanted to leave were trapped there. Curtain down and up. Curtain down and up. The clapping and the crying never die. And a young boy, maybe twenty-one, maybe less, is staring up at her and wringing his hands. He cannot and will not stop with his hands, even though his constant wringing pressure has forced the skin to burst. He holds a handkerchief as he continues to stare up at her and wring his hands and bleed.[38]

The recordings prove that, until the last few years of her life, Garland was brilliant in her concerts. There's a video of a London Palladium appearance that shows that even the staid British went wild for her. She loved the adulation, the interchange with the audience. She had the gift of being intimate with a crowd in a large theater.

One couldn't approach Garland with camp condescension. It was pure diva worship, which is something else. Daniel Harris may be correct in assuming that diva worship, particularly the wild shows of adoration for Garland, were more about the audience than the performer in that they allowed gay men a communal presence forbidden elsewhere: "Fandom, in other words, was an emphatic political assertion of ethnic cameraderie."[39] The downside of the adulation was that gay men in the sixties preferred their divas to be flawed geniuses. Tebaldi had the voice, but Callas was a case of fierce will working with inferior equipment. Garland had the talent but fought a battle of attrition against her demons. Would Streisand have been so adored if she had been beautiful and well adjusted?

The Wizard of Oz has been discussed many times as an allegory of gay experience. In its own bizarre way, I Could Go On Singing, Garland's last musical film, represented another that is appropriate to the decade of The Boys in the Band. In this film, Judy plays a singing star who has an illegitimate son she has never acknowledged. Mother is reunited with her son when she goes to see him play the ingenue in a boys' boarding school production of a Gilbert and Sullivan operetta. What a mother-son reunion that is! Mom immediately takes to her son, who is in full make-up and drag. Son (who does not know she's Mom) skips school to sit adoringly at Judy Garland concerts. What would a son of Judy Garland be like? Daddy, by the way, is Dirk Bogarde, fresh from making one of the first major films about the perils of the British homosexual, Victim (1961).

Was there a causal relationship between Garland's death and the Stonewall riot, which began the day her funeral was held farther uptown in New York? Historians disagree.[40] If there was no causality, the death of the most important icon to gay men in the pre-liberation period was one more cultural marker of a major change in gay culture. The success of Mart Crowley's play The Boys in the Band (1968) gave urban gay men a new visibility. The self-hatred the play demonstrates was bound to turn into anger at a moment when other groups were also reaching the boiling point. The self-image Judy symbolized had to be buried with her and she had to move into the camp past. But she is part of our history and still comes alive via drag performances. In 1998, Timothy Gray and Hugh Martin put together a Judy Garland musical, I Will Come Back, in which Judy was played by drag performer Tommy Femia. Gray was co-writer (with Ralph Blane) of the original songs for Meet Me in St. Louis.[41] It is interesting that for these older writers, thirty years after Garland's death, a tribute to Garland would have to be a drag performance rather than a star turn from a female singer. Can we imagine anyone but a drag artist doing Garland? Does her connection to gay culture have to be mediated through drag? What do younger gay men make of this connection? Actually, the contemporary singer who seems to have modeled his style on Garland's is the young gay singer-composer Rufus Wainwright. Compare Garland's singing of the Irving Berlin classic "What'll I Do?" with Wainwright's on The McGarrigle Hour CD. When

I watched the video of Garland singing that song, I understood Wainwright's slurred words, his ability to be simultaneously simple and overwrought.[42]

THE HEIRESS APPARENT

In the early sixties, Judy Garland tried to establish her teenage daughter, Liza Minnelli, as her successor with her fans. The Palladium videotape is a mother-daughter act. Adoring Mom sits at the edge of the stage and watches her daughter sing and dance. Mother and daughter do duets together, embracing with each ovation. Again, on videos of Garland's television show, Liza is there as crown princess. Clearly on these videos, Liza is a talented singer who has also been extremely well trained. She's homely and gawky, but she can dance. One could say that she has inherited her mother's talent. A look into her desperate eyes as she performs and you can see she has also inherited that insatiable hunger for mass adulation.

From the beginning, there has been something of an obligation placed on Judy's fans to love Liza, particularly since Liza was going to work so hard to earn her audience's approval. She starred in a 1963 Off-Broadway revival of the old college musical *Best Foot Forward*. Mother Judy didn't go until the second night so that the opening-night focus would be on Liza. Two years later, Kander and Ebb wrote *Flora, the Red Menace* as Liza's first Broadway vehicle. The show was not a smash, but Liza earned rave reviews and was off to Hollywood for an excellent performance as a lovable neurotic wreck in the non-musical *The Sterile Cuckoo*. Liza didn't go the faux glamorous route Streisand chose. She was the ugly duckling who worked harder than anyone else—sang harder, danced harder, acted harder—to earn an audience's love.

Of all the divas, only Liza Minnelli is so closely associated with one songwriting team. Two of her mother's greatest films had Harold Arlen scores, but all of Minnelli's major work has been with the songwriting team of John Kander and Fred Ebb. They rewrote their Broadway score of *Cabaret* for the film so that Sally Bowles's numbers were tailored to Liza's talents. They wrote the original songs for her television special, *Liza with a Z,* for the movie, *New York, New York,* that gave her her most famous song, and they wrote the scores to all her Broadway shows: *Flora, the Red Menace, The Act,* and *The Rink.* When Gwen Verdon became ill, Liza replaced her for six weeks in Kander and Ebb's *Chicago.* Kander and Ebb are masters of the old-fashioned show tune. They know how to build a song on a vamp—as they do in the classic "New York, New York"—and to create a song that builds in a crescendo of a simple phrase repeated over and over, like "New York, New York," or the title song from

Cabaret. They know how to exploit the dynamic range of Minnelli's voice, from sweet to belt within the same song.

Minnelli's defining role is Sally Bowles in Bob Fosse's film of *Cabaret*. Sally is a bit of a sham, claiming a sophistication she doesn't have and posing as a decadent in an environment far more decadent than she realizes. Her lover, Brian, says to her in a moment of anger and honesty, "You're about as *fatale* as an after-dinner mint." On stage Sally was played by British actress Jill Haworth. Haworth wasn't very good, but that seemed appropriate for Sally. Her singing was flat and awkward. Minnelli's musical numbers—more of them than Haworth had—are terrific. Her voice is less individual than her mother's, but she's a fine, unmannered singer. Minnelli's Sally is doomed by her looks, not her talent, never to be the star she dreams of being. Minnelli also captures Sally's neediness and confusion. Sally is always over-the-top, always "on."

While the Broadway version of *Cabaret* falsely revised the experiences and stories of Christopher Isherwood on which they are based, Americanizing and heterosexualizing the young writer, thus turning his relationship with Sally into a conventional musical narrative with stolid straight hero and transgressive woman, Jay Presson Allen's screenplay tiptoes into forbidden territory. Before meeting Sally, British doctoral student Brian (Michael York) has had three disastrous sexual experiences with women. His early reticence with Sally leads her to the assumption that he's gay. He doesn't deny that he might be gay—he merely tells her he has failed with women before. Is Brian's relationship with the bizarre, needy Sally (it begins as consolation the night her father has stood her up for a dinner engagement) an escape from the ramifications of his lack of interest in women? Minnelli's Sally, after all, for all her sexual bravado, is more a fag hag than a sexually promiscuous woman. In the film's most famous moment Sally and Brian confess that they have been sleeping with the same man:

> BRIAN: Screw Maximilian.
> SALLY: I do.
> BRIAN (*after a pause*): So do I.

When Sally aborts the child that might be Brian's, she hints that he might someday leave her for a man. Brian goes back to England and Sally goes back to the Kit Kat Club, the scene of a decadence the Nazis will soon purge. If the film of *Cabaret* looks safe now, a bisexual musical was very daring in 1972. If anything, the film showed a possibility of a serious, daring film musical seldom seen since. It suggested that Hollywood could be far more daring with material than Broadway—that it could go beyond standard musical conventions. The kind of George Grosz grotesquerie the film uses so well would become Fosse's style for everything on film and stage after *Cabaret,* but it's perfect for *Cabaret.* Homosexuality and bisexuality become the paradigm for the "divine decadence" Sally seeks in the Weimar Republic Berlin of *Cabaret* rather than an option for many people in 1972. In hindsight, though, the film suggests that those who resist the encroachment of such decadence are Nazi types.

Sally Bowles became Liza's image, carefully orchestrated by her artistic advisers, particularly Fred Ebb—the innocent who is fascinated with but untouched by decadence.

In a prescient moment, Sally says to Brian: "I'm going to be a great film star—that is, if booze and sex don't get me first." Minnelli peaked in her twenties, then settled for being a celebrity, appearing regularly at Studio 54, that nightly performance of seventies chic decadence, whose most visible owner was a gay man. Like her mother, she went through a series of bad marriages, the first to a gay singer-songwriter, the late Peter Allen, then, among others, the son of the actor who played the Tin Man. Minnelli has outlived her mother, but like her she is a combination of a survivor and a self-destructive personality. She left *The Rink* early to enter the Betty Ford Clinic, but she makes public statements of denial of any drug problem. She depends on a gay audience but has been homophobic in interviews.[43] She didn't show up for rehearsals of *Victor/Victoria* when she replaced Julie Andrews. In her fifties, with hip problems that make dancing painful and vocal surgery that has left her with the remnant of a voice, she continues to perform in concert. Liza took on her mother's image as the doom-ridden star as she inherited many of her mother's gay fans. When her half-sister, Lorna Luft, wrote her family saga exposing Liza's drug problem, Liza refused to appear on stage with her at a tribute to their mother.

Minnelli's career was greatly built on her gay following, which was ensured by her mother's blessing on her right to the Garland royal line. Her brilliantly constructed 1992 Radio City Music Hall show, later presented on television, was more feminist than camp, with Minnelli performing with an ensemble of women of various sizes, shapes, and ages, a living critique of the uniformly svelte, high-kicking Rockettes who usually appear on the Radio City Music Hall stage.

Minnelli is no longer a figure on Broadway, in part because there are no more star vehicles, in part because of her own indifference to the long run necessary to make a vehicle pay off and her awareness that there is more money to be made in a few shows a week on the concert circuit, and in part because of her lack of discipline. As I write this, her now-giant face is on the cover of two supermarket tabloids, under headlines like "Liza Is Eating Herself To Death!!!" Still, for some show queens she remains a musical diva, the daughter of the greatest pre-Stonewall gay icon who, to some extent, allowed history to repeat itself.

THE QUEEN OF FLOPS

Only one contemporary of Minnelli's, Bernadette Peters, has as loyal a New York gay following and is as connected to gay culture. Like Bette Midler and Barbra Streisand, Peters began in gay venues, but unlike her peers, she has remained devoted to musical theater. Peters made a sensation in a camp little Off-Broadway musical, *Dames at Sea,* in the 1960s. *Dames at Sea* was a product of that decade's discovery and worship of old movies, including the rediscovery of the Busby Berkeley musicals. The show began in 1966 as a one-act quasi spoof that was performed in the legendary Caffè Cino, a Greenwich Village coffeehouse that holds legitimate claim to being the birthplace of gay drama in the United States. Gay playwrights like Robert Patrick, William Hoffman, and Lanford Wilson got their start there. *Dames at Sea* was lighter than much of what was done at Caffe Cino but appropriate to this pioneering, alternative gay theater. An expanded version had a hit commercial run Off-Broadway in 1968. *Dames at Sea* was, in its own way, as much an expression of where New York gays were in 1968 as *The Boys in the Band,* which opened the same year. In one sense *Dames at Sea* is a perfect example of sixties camp, recreating with minimum resources the extravagance of the Berkeley musicals while both spoofing and celebrating their cardboard characters and silly plots.

Gay men were rediscovering Busby Berkeley musicals in the mid-sixties at urban revival houses and university film societies. I remember that a couple of gay men got control of one of the film societies at my university at this time, alternating nights of thirties films with "experimental" films by Kenneth Anger and Jack Smith. My friends and I were thrilled to discover *Gold Diggers of 1933* and *Shanghai Express* the same week. "E'reway in the Oneymay" and "It took more than one man to change my name to Shanghai Lily" became staples of our repertoire. I'm not sure I knew the word "camp" then, but I experienced that mixture of love and superiority that define a camp perspective.

Dames at Sea is an amalgam of Berkeley plots. Understudy becomes a star, sailor falls in love with showgirl, and when the theater is destroyed, the show moves onto a battleship for the finale. What wasn't camp was the witty, tuneful score that was actually less silly than the songs it imitates. Between its 1966 performance at the Caffe Cino and its 1968 opening at the Bouwerie Lane Theater in Greenwich Village, the show had been expanded to a full-length musical. The show doesn't work anymore because the Busby Berkeley craze is long over and that form of camp seems only to appeal to the older generation of gay men. I remember seeing a short-lived revival of *Dames at Sea* in London in 1996 featuring Kim Criswell, an American performer with a gay following in London, and the terrific song-and-dance man Jon Peterson. The show was very well done and as charming as ever, but there may have been forty people in the audience, all gay men. In 1966 *Dames at Sea* could launch a career. Most of Peters's later shows that ran at all were cult shows, seen and loved by a small group of people. "Cult" show usually translates to a show that only show queens really enthuse over.

This particular cult show made a star out of Peters who had been "discovered" at the Caffè Cino presentation of *Dames at Sea* and had gone into another, less successful thirties spoof, *Curley McDimple,* which sent up Shirley Temple films, and into a supporting role on Broadway in the Joel Grey vehicle *George M!* But the expanded 1968 Off-Broadway production of *Dames at Sea* really launched her career.

Peters had the perfect qualities for this sort of camp musical. While she didn't at all resemble Ruby Keeler (among other things, she can carry a tune), she could convincingly evoke a wide-eyed innocence and she sounded a bit like another thirties film icon, Betty Boop. Peters has a "stage face"—its features read to the back row of a theater—big eyes, a cupid bow mouth. She also has an inimitable voice. It may not be to everyone's taste, it may not be beautiful, but it is distinctive. It is big enough to belt out a torch song but can also narrow to a sweet, touching, more lyric sound. While Peters can play a serious scene beautifully, she has the face of a comedienne.

Peters's career began at the tail end of diva musicals. In 1968, when *Dames at Sea* opened Off-Broadway, *Hello, Dolly!* had been running for four years with Carol Channing followed by Ginger Rogers, Pearl Bailey, Betty Grable, Phyllis Diller, Martha Raye, and Ethel Merman in New York and Mary Martin and others in London and around the country. *Mame* was running with one of Angela Lansbury's replacements (Jane Morgan, Janis Paige, Celeste Holm). The same month (December 1968), the heavily miked Burt Bacharach musical, *Promises, Promises,* opened uptown at the Shubert and changed forever how musicals and their stars would sound.

While Peters is as close to a diva as the New York theater has produced in the past thirty years—only Patti LuPone and Betty Buckley rival her—her Broadway career has not been a string of successes. *La Strada* (1969) was one of those flops that earns a prominent position in the wall of posters of disasters at Joe Allen's. A revival of *On the Town* (1971—Peters had the Nancy Walker part) foundered on poor choreography and weak leading men. Moreover, in the midst of the Vietnam War, no one cared about a musical about loveable sailors on leave in a mythical, innocent New York City. A bad idea. Then Peters landed in one of the great cult flops, Jerry Herman's *Mack and Mabel.* The cast album was a collector's item for years for Herman's best score and Peters's performance. Now it's widely available on CD. Despite the great score, *Mack and Mabel* was plagued by a lot of bad ideas. Many of the big songs go to secondary characters the audience doesn't care about because there's no dramatic reason for the songs. The book is a bummer, inventing a death for Mabel that is neither historically accurate nor theatrically effective. Audiences for a Jerry Herman musical did not want the leading lady to die. Jerry Herman musicals are supposed to be about survivors. Peters was praised for her performance, but *Mack and Mabel* was not a hit. By this time in her career, Peters was typecast. If one was going to do a musical about a waiflike character from old movies—Shirley Temple, Ruby Keeler, Giulietta Masina, or Mabel Normand—Bernadette Peters got the call. Still in her twenties, she was identified with a kind of nostalgia. Even her role in the ill-fated *La Strada,* based on the classic Fellini film, was a kind of arty nostalgia for a past type of performer.

Ten years later, Peters had her best role as George Seurat's mistress, Dot, and Dot's daughter, Marie (at age ninety-eight), in Sondheim's *Sunday in the Park with George* (1984). The show was a succès d'estime, loved by critics and aficionados but not a long-running hit. The hit of the 1983-84 season was Jerry Herman's *La Cage aux Folles,* in which the diva role goes to a man, underscoring the drag potential in all Broadway divas. Peters then played the witch in Sondheim's *Into the Woods* to great acclaim. The show was a moderate success, but the witch is hardly a diva turn. Her role in the Lloyd Webber song cycle *Song and Dance* should have been a diva turn—the first half is essentially a one-woman concert—but its narrative of a British girl in New York didn't create a sensation. It isn't a diva role—just a bunch of good songs for an ingenue. In the 1990s, Peters got her name above the title in a starring role in a musical comedy, *The Goodbye Girl,* which died the death of many conventional musical comedies in the 1990s. In 1999, Peters returned to Broadway in *Annie Get Your Gun.* If you can't find decent new material, make a classic your own.

Peters has the qualities that make a Broadway musical star. She is something of an exaggeration of certain stereotypically feminine qualities. The childlike voice makes her perfect for waiflike characters. The offbeat personality works in the right comic situations. But something didn't click for Peters.

First, she never had a defining role. Peters has been superb in a number of roles, but there never was the sense that she was essential to a part. No one has played Lola as well as Gwen Verdon, Nellie Forbush as well as Mary

Martin, Lorelei Lee as well as Carol Channing. I have seen equally good Dots, Rubys, and Mabels. That isn't Peters's fault. She made her mark on those parts and we have both the CD and video of her brilliant Dot, but you don't build a career on one of Sondheim's songs from *Sunday in the Park with George.* Of course, the problem is that there are no defining roles as there were in the forties or fifties. Peters came along too late. With a couple of exceptions (Lloyd Webber in *Evita* and *Sunset Boulevard*), no one is writing diva roles. How can one be a star in *Beauty and the Beast, The Lion King,* or *Titanic?* There are enormously talented people in these shows, but the shows aren't showcases for them in the way *Hello, Dolly!* or *Mame* were showcases. Folks aren't writing or producing diva musicals anymore.

Nor did she ever have a defining song. Broadway divas were identified by a particular song. In his book *Broadway Babies,* Ethan Mordden talks about "numbos." In one sense, numbos are hit tunes that make a show a hit. They also can be songs that define a star's persona. Mordden talks about Gertrude Lawrence singing "Someone to Watch Over Me" in Gershwin's *Oh Kay!* as such a defining song, perfect for Lawrence's voice and persona. The same could be said for "I Got Rhythm," Ethel Merman's defining song in *Girl Crazy.* When one thinks of Merman, one thinks of big razzmatazzy songs like her first hit. "My Heart Belongs to Daddy" defined the glamorous, naughty Mary Martin of the thirties and forties as "A Cockeyed Optimist" defined her fifties androgynous persona. The defining song depended on a universal popularity of show tunes that allowed a singer to establish herself beyond the parameters of a particular song. You don't need to know the context of the song to appreciate "I Got Rhythm" or Merman's belting of the song. Carol Channing built her career on "Diamonds Are a Girl's Best Friend" in the fallow years between *Gentlemen Prefer Blondes* (1949) and *Hello, Dolly!* (1964).

Peters never had that kind of identification with a song. The great songs in her best score, *Mack and Mabel,* can be sung by any good ballad singer, and 1974 was well past the time one could have a hit with a torch song. By the seventies, Broadway tunes were seldom pop hits, and producers who had to think about long runs and cast replacements didn't want songs too identified with one performer.

In 1997 Peters performed an AIDS charity benefit at Carnegie Hall. She was magnificent, making a grand star turn. On stage and in the audience were hundreds of gay men for whom Peters is one of the last Broadway divas. The adulation you hear on that Carnegie Hall album and the recording of the Gay Men's Health Crisis 1995 benefit performance of *Anyone Can Whistle* attest to her continued popularity with show queens.

BLONDE VENUS

At the same time Judy Garland was doing her concert appearances at the Palace, Carnegie Hall, the London Palladium, and other major venues, another favorite of drag artists was having a second career making concert appearances as chanteuse and camp icon. Marlene Dietrich was rediscovered by film buffs and show queens in the sixties when it became chic to watch thirties films. After a brilliant performance as Lola Lola, the third-rate cabaret performer and sexual magnet in Josef von Sternberg's *The Blue Angel,* Dietrich was an international star. To 1960s eyes, the film is a camp delight. Dietrich lures men in her quasi-male drag and Emil Jannings overacts. Dietrich moved to Hollywood and became a sex symbol in a series of films tailored to make her alluring. She was neither a good singer nor a versatile actress, but she became sex personified, the Blonde Venus. The songs written for her—"Falling in Love Again" and "See What the Boys in the Back Room Will Have"—became part of a camp vocabulary. By the time Orson Welles made *Touch of Evil* in 1958, a camp film if ever there was one, Dietrich was playing a kind of self-parody, a border-town madam with a bad make-up job to make her look Latina (admittedly more convincing than Charlton Heston's Latino make-up) and a German accent: "He vass some kind of mann." After her film career was over she took to the stage, singing the songs she sang in her films. This Dietrich was easy for a drag queen to do. Like Mae West, here was an older woman trying to look glamorous, sexy. Dietrich would appear in her special spotlight in a silver gown and barely move. She had an odd Elmer Fudd accent and two or three notes in her voice. To older fans, she was the last fading ember of thirties sophistication and glamour. To lesbians, she was a heroine, a woman who kissed another woman on screen and was bisexual off screen. To gay men, she was camp itself. Moreover, she was a bit of an oddball, mopping the stage like a charwoman before performances, cleaning her hotel room herself, and being notoriously cheap.

In 1997, Pam Gems's play with music, *Marlene,* played in London starring Sian Phillips. Set in a Paris theater in the 1970s, it chronicles Dietrich preparing for and giving one of her performances. Dietrich is a showman, but a cheap one. She is careful about reusing the flowers that will be presented to her, as she is careful about keeping the performance going "till the hotel room door is shut." In the second half, Phillips does a Dietrich show, thirty minutes of the songs she made famous, interspersed with the patter she delivered between songs. The event is an exercise in nostalgia, in trying to recreate a past glamour and sexiness. The famous Dietrich face is painted on an elderly woman's face. The low-cut gown has a flesh-colored top that goes to the jewels that cover Dietrich's neck so as not to show signs of age. When another actress plays Dietrich, one is even more aware of how the old Dietrich of the stage appearances was a type of drag act. For older people in the audience, it was nostalgia. For gay men it was the survival of another icon, another femme fatale turned into a survivor. The theater at the performance we saw was divided between elderly women and middle-aged gay men. For us the nostalgia was not so much for the thirties, but for the time when divas like Dietrich were part of our gay culture.

Dietrich never appeared in a scripted stage show in the United States. She was probably aware that she didn't have the skill for that kind of performance. Like Garland, she "played the Palace," in a kind of nostalgic tribute to vaudeville. Hollywood divas who are central to gay culture needn't be in musicals. Their personae become more important than scripted performance, particularly in an era in which star vehicles aren't being written. If such a diva wants to do a star turn, she has to turn to the concert stage. Garland proved to be a great concert artist apart from her film work. Dietrich was a grand ghost. Gay men who cheered their performances at the Palace or Palladium in the sixties knew them from their movies. Where else could gay adolescents and young men escape before television? When these men came to the city to find a supportive community, that community was built on camp culture. These women were the goddesses of that culture. Once in New York, men discovered other goddesses, icons of a lost Broadway filled with divas like Merman. By the sixties, these divas were best known as concert artists.

In the London cast of the 1997 revival of Kander and Ebb's *Chicago,* German singer Ute Lemper, who bears an uncanny resemblance to Dietrich, played Velma Kelly. When she and Ruthie Henshall, in her costume reminiscent of Judy Garland's "Get Happy" outfit, perform their duets, the performance has a camp nostalgia that offers a new dimension to the prevailing Calvin Klein–ad look of the production.

INGENUE TO DIVA

Barbara Cook is an interesting instance of a performer who became an icon for show queens after she stopped performing in musicals. Cook starred in a number of shows of varying quality in the fifties and early sixties. While her biggest hit was as Marian the Librarian in *The Music Man,* fans remember most her appearance in cult musicals like *Flahooley, Candide,* and *She Loves Me.* Cook was wonderful in all her shows. She had an old-fashioned lyric soprano voice, but she used it like a great song interpreter. Her idol was jazz great Marian Mercer, who had a very different kind of voice. She was an excellent comedienne, but in the artificial world of fifties musicals, she earned cheers by seeming to be nakedly honest on stage, absolutely committed to her characters. Her last major role was in the cult favorite *She Loves Me* in 1963. After that, cartoon women took over musicals—*Hello, Dolly!* opened the next year. Soon there were no musicals for a singer like Barbara Cook, but Cook never loved her life in musicals anyway. I heard her say to one audience: "People tell me I was part of the Golden Age of the Musical. I wish they had told me back then. I might have enjoyed it more." So, under the expert tutelage of conductor Wally Harper, and with the help of arranger Bill Brohn (who would go on to orchestrate *Les Misérables, Miss Saigon,* and *Ragtime*), Cook moved from musicals to concerts. Along the way, she also gave up the anorexic-thin body and became a happy, chubby woman. Cook and Harper knew their first core audience would be show queens. Cook's legendary 1975 Carnegie Hall concert[44] and her appearances at other venues became the kind of love feasts gay diva worshipers reveled in. Twenty years later (Cook is now in her seventies, born in 1927) she is a survivor. The voice is a bit worn, but she still is a great interpreter. It is interesting to note that Cook's albums tend to be tributes to lyricists rather than composers (Dorothy Fields, Oscar Hammerstein). Every song becomes a drama. There is nothing overwrought in Cook's performance, but the words are both simply and deeply felt. Listen to her sing John Bucchino's lovely song "Sweet Dreams" *(Live from London),* a sad tale of a gay boy and an unhappy girl who run away to Hollywood. There's a heartache in the refrain other singers miss or overdo and a specificity to every nuance of the song's narrative. Or compare her singing of the Jule Style–Bob Merrill "Who Are You Now?" from *Funny Girl* on the Carnegie Hall album with Streisand's performance on the cast album. Streisand distends the line and distorts the lyric with extra vowel sounds. Cook sings simply. The words come across, but so does the heartbreak.

I recently attended a Cook concert at the Theatre Royal, Drury Lane, London. The concert was an AIDS benefit, the audience mostly gay men, many in musical theater. It was fascinating to see these young men so enthralled with Cook's performance. For me, it was one kind of nostalgia—I saw Cook in *Plain and Fancy* and *She Loves Me.* For many of these young men working in the chorus or backstage at current musicals, it was a tribute to the kind of great singer and great singing no longer required in contemporary musical theater. Cook is also careful to acknowledge her gay audience. Her London performances include Michael Callen's gay anthem, "Love Don't Need a Reason."

It is easy to understand Barbara Cook's diva status among show queens. There are camp aspects to Cook's persona, but she doesn't exploit them. There are rumors of an unhappy life during her Broadway years, of eating disorders, but Cook is a trouper. Yet there is the transgressive body. When Cook moved from playing ingenues to playing herself, she took on the corpulent body of a diva. Like the once-skinny Rosemary Clooney or Peggy Lee, she moved from the fifties to the post-Stonewall world by changing her body, or allowing her body to change. Did this have any part in her success as a diva for gay men? Michael Moon has written:

> One happy story of my own and many other gay men's formations of our adolescent and adult body images is that the fat, beaming figure of the diva has never been entirely absent from our *imaginaire* or our fantasies of ideal bodies; besides whatever version of the male "power-body" of the seventies and eighties we may have cathected, fantasized about, developed or not developed, and, in our time, pursued down countless city streets, the diva's body has never lost its representational magnetism for many of us as an alternative body-identity fantasy, resolutely embodying as it does the otherwise almost entirely anachronistic ideal, formed in early nineteenth-century Europe, of the social dignity of corpulence, particularly that of the fat bourgeois matron.[45]

In defying body type, the overweight diva is defying appropriate gender appearance and identification, thus becoming, in a sense, queer. Callas, through sheer force of will, changed from fat to glamorous, but myth has it that the voice went with the fat, another part of the paradoxical myth of Callas as tough victim. Cook's image as a woman who happily shed an artificial skinniness was part of her mystique. At a time when coming out was a crucial part of gay culture, Cook "came out" as a fat woman and was "liberated" from the strictures of a painfully maintained ingenue drag she had aged out of anyway. She was free to be herself and sing whatever she wanted to. Her history, her liberation from ingenue roles, and her appearance resonated with show queens.

This is not to say that Barbara Cook is merely a camp icon. Like Garland, Cook is a great singer: one cannot condescend to her. The front rows of her London concerts tend to be filled with other singers. She mixes past and present songs, so she does not deal in pure nostalgia. Like Garland, she can turn a great theater into an intimate room. And, like Merman and Garland, she represents the power of a past musical theater for some gay men. And the power of the old-fashioned popular song. Cook now plays posh venues like the Café Carlyle, alternating with another sort of diva, Bobby Short. But she still has a special meaning for show queens.

Why do I end this chapter with someone who, except for a brief lapse into the megadisaster *Carrie,* got out of musicals decades ago? Barbara Cook is one diva who didn't fight time and nature and reinvented herself as a concert performer. She is not just a vestige of the past.

There is still an adoring audience for the remaining Broadway divas— Bernadette, Patti, Betty, Julie, Chita—the performers still capable of a star turn, but no one is writing shows for them. They are stuck in a time warp of revivals of shows written for earlier divas. Bernadette Peters in her fifties as Annie Oakley? Timelessness is now part of the diva mystique: "Age cannot wither her, nor custom stale . . ."

THE DIVA MUSICAL

Barbara Cook's last great musical, *She Loves Me,* opened in 1963. *The Judy Garland Show* ran during the 1963–64 season. Barbra Streisand's *Funny Girl* opened on Broadway in 1964; less than two weeks later Angela Lansbury made her brief debut as a Broadway musical star in the Stephen Sondheim–Arthur Laurents musical *Anyone Can Whistle.* The then-unknown Bette Midler joined the umpteenth cast of her only Broadway show, *Fiddler on the Roof,* in 1968. I mention all this because it is important to note that the mid-1960's were the last gasp of the diva musical. There were theatrical reasons for this. The director-driven concept musicals like *Fiddler on the Roof* and *Cabaret* were starting to replace musical comedy. Musical comedies were becoming outmoded as their style of pop music was being replaced by rock and roll. Producers were becoming leery of shows built on stars who will only perform for a year or less when musicals could take years to recoup their investment.

However, my interest is in the intersection of musical theater and gay culture. The decade in which the musical is changing is also the decade in which gay culture is changing, leading to that conjunction in the death of Judy Garland and the symbolic beginnings of gay liberation with the Stonewall riots in June of 1969. The diva musicals that were central to Broadway, from *Gypsy* in 1959 to *Follies* in 1971, were the grand final death throes of one sort of musical theater and the pinnacle of gay musical theater. The central figures of this dozen years of diva musicals were not only the women the shows glorified but two gay composer-lyricists, Jerry Herman and Stephen Sondheim, who represented the tension between two points of view toward musical theater that reflected two different expressions of being gay in the sixties. The diva musical continued into the nineties in the work of the songwriting team of John Kander and Fred Ebb, whose first Broadway musical, *Flora, the Red Menace,* a vehicle for Judy Garland's daughter and heir apparent, Liza Minnelli, opened in 1965.

As the drag queen sees becoming the diva as an escape from an oppressive life into magic, the diva musical is about a woman's escape from the humdrum. Whether it's Dorothy being whirled from Kansas to Oz, from black-and-white to color, a metamorphosis symbolized by glittering red shoes, or Rose (*Gypsy*) getting out of a dismal trap in Seattle through show business, or Eva Peron sleeping her way from the hinterlands to the Big Apple, the diva fights for liberation from stasis in a grim, everyday world. To closeted gay men, the diva heroine was a figure of identification. Where does one find magic if one is different and must try to hide one's difference? The ideal is escape from the provincial, where one is hated, and fabulousness, an antidote to grayness and the strong sense of entrapment. In the process the diva gains glamour and power.

Rose's first song in *Gypsy* is the archetypal battle cry of the diva:

> Some people can get a thrill
> Knitting sweaters and sitting still—
> That's okay for some people who don't know they're alive.[1]

As gay men responded to the divas who sang these battle cries, they cheered the musicals that contained them.

FOR ME!

Why is *Gypsy* more of a diva musical than Ethel Merman's previous vehicles, *Call Me Madam* or the dismal *Happy Hunting?* The earlier shows are vehicles for a star who had held the stage for over two decades and are aimed at an aging audience who had enjoyed Merman through those years. They use the persona and skills Ethel Merman honed throughout her career. It's a tribute to Merman's showmanship and her ability to hold a loyal public that a nothing like *Happy Hunting* could make it through a season. Through a fascinating constellation of creators, *Gypsy* becomes more than a star vehicle. It's a dark love song to the musical theater, nostalgia tinged with irony. Gay artists Arthur Laurents and Stephen Sondheim were able to turn Jule Styne's pleasant Broadway tunes into something darker and more complex. The mordant Sondheim and pop tunesmith Styne are an odd combination. Styne's scores are usually filled with excerptable hit tunes: "Just in Time," "Make Someone Happy," "People." Sondheim tailors lyrics to the character and dramatic situation. His most ironic songs are the ones that sound happy. In the context of the show, every typically cheerful Styne tune becomes ironic. Merman's voice becomes not merely a familiar institution of the history of the musical, but something fierce and frightening. This isn't cheerful belt. Merman's powerful sound is the perfect expression of Rose's character: loud, forceful, unyielding. Even the comic "Mr. Goldstone, I Love You" becomes a vocal exercise in force-feeding. "Everything's Coming Up Roses," out of context a great up tune, is in the show a chilling end to Act I, as Rose decides to force shy Louise into the role Baby June fled from. The show closed with that "Brunhilde's Immolation" of musical comedy numbers, "Rose's Turn," a display of anger, disappointment, and ego, ending with that fierce "For ME!!!" *Gypsy* is one of the half-dozen truly great musicals. It's a saga of the history of show business from vaudeville to burlesque, a troubled picture of an American family, and a lament for the power of the hunger for recognition and success that drives show business. The Laurents-Sondheim Rose is a grand monster, one of the greatest characters in an American musical, more three-dimensional than most. She's one of the pantheon of monster mothers in American theater, right up there with Mary Tyrone, Craig's Wife, Amanda Wingfield, and Albee's Martha (thank God that son is imaginary!). As do they, three of which were created by gay playwrights, Rose inspires a love-hate relationship from everyone on stage and the audience. Above all, Rose loves an old-fashioned notion of show business, a world that's tawdry, but an escape from dreary routine and domestic entrapment. Merman, the former secretary who became a stage star, the epitome of professionalism, was the living embodiment of the world Rose loved.

      Gypsy has had three hit runs in New York in the forty years since it opened. First the combination/clash of that force of nature, Ethel Merman, with a role that used her voice and stamina for dramatic effect; then, in the seventies, Angela Lansbury bringing more light and shade to the part in London and New York; and, finally, in 1989 with Tyne Daly, the most vocally tentative but fiercest of Roses in the best production of the classic musical. On film, Rosalind Russell made Rose more of an eccentric than a monster, a bit too much Auntie Mame, and Natalie Wood as Louise/Gypsy is never the ugly duckling. In the mid-nineties, Bette Midler played Rose on television, often coy rather than cunning, working too hard to please her audience, but television isn't the medium for the grand *Gypsy* or its anti-heroine. *Gypsy* is a celebration of the stage. It doesn't fit any other medium.

      What is gay about *Gypsy* (except for its lyricist Stephen Sondheim, its librettist Arthur Laurents, and its director Jerome Robbins)? Everything one might say comes out sounding like stereotype. But there was a time when gay men proudly, if secretly, played to their stereotypes, the time of the diva musicals. There was a lot a gay young man in 1959, used to reading his fantasies through women characters, could read into *Gypsy*. Even Howard in *In and Out* (who has Debbie Reynolds for a mother!) has the Merman *Gypsy* cast album playing in his home. *Gypsy* is about a monster mother who turns her withdrawn, ugly duckling child into a diva of the debased, sexually transgressive world of burlesque, but a diva nonetheless. Some of us can see ourselves in the transformation of shy Louise, forced to dress as a boy, into sultry star Gypsy Rose Lee. Gypsy rises above the damage her mother has caused to become a diva herself, impervious to her mother's commands and guilt trips. *Gypsy* becomes a parable for all the gay men with powerful mothers. Part of our fabulousness may come from the sacred monsters who reared us and from whom our Herbie fathers could not protect us, but if we're lucky, we become divas who are no longer vulnerable to the wounds those mothers can cause. If we're lucky we, like Gypsy, discover that we're not ugly ducklings, neither male nor female, but powerful and sexy. It is not surprising that lines from *Gypsy,* particularly Rose's entrance line, "Sing out, Louise," became part of camp vocabulary. It recognizes the ubiquity of a domineering mother, but also the verbal transvestitism older gay men mastered. We could enjoy Rose and identify with Louise.

Most important, the score of *Gypsy* is the apotheosis of a great old-fashioned musical score, a hymn of praise to the brashness and hypertheatricality of the classic musical. From the fanfare opening of the rousing overture—the best of all Broadway overtures—right to the end of "Rose's Turn," the score captures what is captivating about the musical. Each song is superb and dramatically forceful. "Some People," in which Rose tells her father how she despises people who settle for the ordinary, establishes Rose's determination through both the lyrics and the relentless quality of the tune.

The later incarnations of *Gypsy* were Events for show queens. A younger generation was introduced to the show through a television version starring, appropriately, a diva of post-Stonewall gay culture, Bette Midler. Perhaps this is why there were so many young gay men at the 1998 revival of *Gypsy* at the Paper Mill Playhouse with another diva, Betty Buckley. Perhaps Buckley herself, raising those cute sons on *Eight Is Enough,* was a childhood memory for some of the men in the audience.

By this time, in the dark ages of musical theater, *Gypsy* has become the *Norma* of musicals, the ultimate diva challenge. Some of the audience at the Paper Mill are there for a pleasant suburban evening out, but a sizeable proportion of the Saturday night audience are gay men of all ages, many from New York, who have come for a Diva Event blessed by *The New York Times.* In the lobbies and on the promenades outside this beautiful suburban theater in Republican North Jersey, I see our uneasy assimilation. This sizeable, vocal gay presence is impossible to ignore, but there is no socializing of gay and straight groups. The gay men go outside at the intermission, the heterosexuals stay inside. Do they know that *Gypsy*'s words are by gay men? Would it in any way matter to them?

I have not experienced an audience response like the one at Betty Buckley's *Gypsy* since the grand diva nights at the Met. Buckley is cheered wildly at her entrance, which stops the show for almost a minute. Every song is cheered wildly, and "Rose's Turn" gets a standing ovation. At Buckley's curtain call, the roar goes on and on. This is truly an evening of diva worship.

The history of Mama Rose is the history of musical divas from Merman to Lansbury to Tyne Daly, a television star who found the perfect role for establishing herself as a leading lady. Betty Buckley moved from Broadway musicals to a hit television series, after which she went back to New York and replaced Gretchen Cryer in the Off-Broadway hit *I'm Getting My Act Together and Taking It on the Road.* She has had to endure horrors like *The Mystery of Edwin Drood, Carrie,* and *Triumph of Love* and sing "Memories" for a year in *Cats.* Buckley returned to the musical stage in its post–*Sweeney Todd* Gothic period and had to specialize in the deranged characters this genre spawns, culminating in two years as Norma Desmond. Compared to Carrie's mother and Norma Desmond, Mama Rose is normality itself, a chance for Buckley to show she can play a three-dimensional character.

A masterpiece cries out for fresh interpretation, and Buckley who, unlike her predecessors, has specialized in vulnerability more than indomitability gives this to *Gypsy*'s Mama Rose. Buckley sings the part better than her predecessors, but this isn't enough, any more than it is for a great *Norma.* Rose is one of the great acting roles in the American theater, and every song gives us a different aspect of Rose's personality. More than any of her predecessors, Buckley has found a way to create a dynamic Mama Rose who begins as a determined, eccentric, but funny stage mother and grows before our eyes into something terrifying. At first, this Rose can be loveable, but the dream of stardom is her Moby Dick. She can't help pursuing it. Every time domestic normalcy and happiness come into view, she literally freezes. Having been abandoned by her mother as a child, this is not a dream she trusts. Showbiz is the only reality. When her beloved Baby June abandons her, she relives that earlier betrayal. Determined not to feel the hurt or to be daunted, she turns to her shy, untalented Louise to recapture the dream. As she sings "Everything's Coming Up Roses," she grabs hold of poor little Louise as if she is trying by some mystical power to transfer her dream and determination to her. Ben Brantley calls this the scariest song in musicals. Buckley makes it that:

When at one point she scratches the air frantically with her hands, you feel you've witnessed something you shouldn't have been allowed to see. You knew that this Rose was a hungry, determined woman, but you had no idea that she was this sick.[2]

Often at the end of "Everything's Coming Up Roses," I have wondered why Louise and Herbie don't run for the hills. I was convinced Buckley's Rose had them mesmerized. When she stutters over "M—m—m—m—ama" during "Rose's Turn," you realize that it is a cry for the mother who deserted her. During this greatest of all eleven o'clock numbers, whereas most Roses stay relatively still and let the words and music do the work, Buckley roams the entire stage, as if her hurt and rage and unfulfilled longing make simple human gestures impossible. Before Rose begins singing her great number, she cries,

What I got in me—what I been holding down inside of me—if I ever let it out there wouldn't be signs big enough! There wouldn't be lights bright enough![3]

With Buckley seeming to expand and fill the vast, empty stage with all that has been held down, the audience watches her "let it out." Betty Buckley not only matched the great divas of the past, she surpassed her predecessors. For us old show queens at this great performance, for three hours musical theater was not nostalgia but a living art form, the communal worship of a woman with magical powers. Buckley never became a cartoon woman, a drag distillation. There was always both indomitability and vulnerability, terror and allure, fierceness and love.

At the end of this great performance, I heard many in the audience ask, "What will she do next?" Nothing new is being written for great divas like Buckley. Nothing in American musical theater even matches Mama Rose. Callas and Sutherland could go on and on doing their Toscas and Normas around the world. Our goddesses may only get to be worshiped in Millburn, New Jersey, but they do endure, as *Gypsy* will endure.

IS IT REAL, OR IS IT . . . ?

David Merrick, the producer of *Gypsy* and many of the fifties musicals, wanted Ethel Merman to play Dolly in his musical adaptation of Thornton Wilder's *The Matchmaker.* Merrick had produced the play in 1955 with Ruth Gordon as Dolly Levi. Gordon's performance was a bizarre, fussy, mannered sort of acting that would look extremely odd now. Every word had extra syllables, every sound was accompanied by some sort of twitch or flouncing of the wrists. Gordon's

Dolly Levi was a cartoon figure. One never sensed that she felt anything, but the script didn't require that anyone feel much, not even the lust usually essential to farce as lust was a subject the closeted, bookish Thornton Wilder steered away from. *The Matchmaker* was a period farce, the sort of innocent comedy that high schools could produce in the fifties (mine did). I remember my friend Stephen and I thought it would make a terrific musical. We were going to take it on as soon as we finished our musical of *The Catcher in the Rye,* a bad idea whose time still hasn't come. Too bad Merrick and Jerry Herman got there first.

When Ethel Merman decided she didn't want another Broadway show, the role of Dolly went to Carol Channing, the first in a succession of Dollys: Ginger Rogers, Betty Grable, Martha Raye, Phyllis Diller, Pearl Bailey (her understudy, Thelma Oliver, went on a lot!), Bibi Osterwald, and finally Merman in New York; Mary Martin and Dora Bryan in London; Barbra Streisand in the lumbering film. There were always rumors that David Merrick wanted Liberace to play Dolly, though Liberace's drag was of a different, if more flamboyant, sort. In 1984 in London, the inevitable finally happened when drag performer Danny LaRue played Dolly. In his book on drag Roger Baker notes of this failed production:

> The central flaw to the production was that one character, Danny LaRue, was playing another, Dolly Levi, and the battle for supremacy between these two overblown creations—allied to LaRue's inability to create a character—totally destroyed the internal dynamics of the show. Broadway musical heroines have been traditionally played by larger-than-life women who have themselves proved role models for drag queens and inspiration for drag acts and it is ironic, but somehow appropriate, that when a drag performer took on a role that had by then become identified with drag queens, the confusion it caused broke the back of the show.[4]

Ethan Mordden describes *Hello, Dolly!* perfectly:

> It's easy to enjoy, very funny and dancy; but it's also a grand, gorgeous excuse for a large cartoon of a woman to come pushing in and out with the bass of a Chaliapin, the warmth of Fort Ticonderoga, and enough wigs to outfit a drag ball.[5]

Who better to fit this description, and who better to succeed—and exceed—the bizarre mannered performance of Ruth Gordon than Carol Channing?

Flashback to a black-and-white video of a 1959 *Ed Sullivan Show.* Carol Channing performs "Diamonds Are a Girl's Best Friend" from the 1949 musical

Gentlemen Prefer Blondes. Did Channing make that song famous or did the song make Channing famous? In these pre-Dolly days, the two seem synonymous. Channing is dressed in a bejeweled modified flapper dress with a glittering cloche on her head. On television she is a tall, flat-chested string bean who is all eyes and mouth, more clown than sex symbol. "Diamonds Are a Girl's Best Friend" is a song about a gold digger, a woman who is "companion" to rich men. She is not likely to become the wife of a millionaire, but she will exact a high price—diamonds—for her company and her services. The song is the testament of a blonde who may not be educated, but who is shrewd. It is a naughty song for 1950s television, but with Channing, is anyone really listening to the lyrics? Unlike Marilyn Monroe, who cooed the song in the 1953 film, Channing isn't sexy. She's playing a clown version of a gold digger. Though she is on television, she is obviously playing to the balcony of a Broadway theater. Her giant dark eyes are everywhere, taking in the gallery and the downstairs audience. Her large mouth drawls the words in that characteristic Channing way. Her voice is more baritone than soprano. There's something almost Brechtian about Channing's performance, a distance from the lyrics or meaning of the song, even a distance from the character she is playing. Indeed, the only character she is playing is Carol Channing doing her signature tune. No one could do it the way she does. At the instrumental bridge, Channing starts throwing jewelry into the audience, then goes down into the aisle of the Broadway theater from which the *Ed Sullivan Show* is broadcast and throws more jewelry into the well-dressed audience (people wore suits and fancy dresses to the *Ed Sullivan Show* in 1959). Channing's performance is characteristically bizarre.

Between *Gentlemen Prefer Blondes* in 1949 and *Hello, Dolly!* in 1964, Carol Channing had no Broadway hits. She replaced Rosalind Russell in *Wonderful Town* for a while and she starred in a flop about a silent movie star, *The Vamp*. She had a one-woman show, *Show Girl,* that played Broadway briefly and toured the country. She played nightclubs and made appearances on variety shows. She loved to tour and had that uncanny trouper's ability to do exactly the same performance every time and make it look fresh.

As the strippers sing in *Gypsy,* "You Gotta Have a Gimmick," and Channing's gimmick was "Diamonds Are a Girl's Best Friend." During her fallow years between 1949 and 1964, that song was Channing's stock-in-trade. She was a somewhat endearing but not particularly versatile performer. She did, however, represent one aspect of the Broadway diva. The diva's persona is likely to be outside conventional notions of femininity that are replicated repeatedly in musicals from the Bolton-Wodenhouse-Kern Princess Theater shows to the hits of the eighties and nineties. Women are naughty, brassy, or ultrafeminine. The ballad singer gets the leading man. The comedienne gets the comic, after much feuding. Diva roles, however, either transgress these conventional notions of femininity or expand them almost to the breaking point. Carol Channing is the paradigm of this sort of Broadway diva. The hair is obviously a wig. Like a clown's face, her face looks painted on. The delivery is extremely stylized. The diva is both imitable—it's easy to parody Merman or Channing—and inimitable—you can't build a career on sounding like these performers. Divas—or at least the personae divas choose—are cartoon women. They express in an exaggerated way parts of women, which become separate from an entire personality. They need to find roles that express that part of them. Carol Channing, for instance, moved from the young gold digger in *Gentlemen Prefer Blondes* to the middle-aged scheming matchmaker in *Hello, Dolly!* In *Hello, Dolly!*'s stylized version of late 1890s America, Channing's flamboyant getup was a form of drag, totally unrealistic. She was always a cartoon woman. She didn't inhabit a part—a part expressed her.

I spent a few hours in Channing's company in the early sixties when she appeared in my university town, and, well, Carol Channing was Carol Channing, always "on," with that wide-eyed "golly gosh" look and perfectly timed quips. There was a sense that nothing was spontaneous, yet she was totally likeable. Most of all, there was an odd androgyny about Channing. This was a zany performance of femininity, but somehow it didn't seem to be real, partly because I couldn't find a real face under that make-up, even when within a few feet of her. I had to accompany Channing to a local department store where she made an appearance in order to stir up lagging ticket sales for her performance. Placing Channing in a setting filled with average housewives was . . . odd, emphasizing her calculated but good-hearted caricature of femininity. Recently a student of mine decided to shake up the dress rehearsal of a play I was directing by appearing backstage as Carol Channing. He had a semblance of the Dolly gown, the blond wig, and via about three tubes of lipstick, the mouth. He also had the tipsy-sounding drawl. The straight men in the cast stared as if they were watching a traffic accident—you don't see drag often at Duke. The gay men played along with the act, as "Carol" wished the cast luck. If you're a novice drag performer, Channing is a good place to begin.

After 1964, Channing's new signature tune was the title song from *Hello, Dolly!,* her grand entrance to the Harmonia Gardens. Channing descended the staircase in an ornate red gown that is a drag queen's dream. From the waist down, the gown seems to be a giant valentine. No real human being ever wore such an outfit. It's pure Broadway. Dolly/Carol was serenaded enthusiastically by an army of singing and dancing waiters who underscored her camp appearance with another brand of gayness. Dolly then promenaded on a passarelle in front of the orchestra pit. It was a grand, gay moment.

After *Hello, Dolly!,* Channing went backward, into a sequel to *Gentlemen Prefer Blondes, Lorelei,* which dashed up on the rocks shortly after it opened. She was too old for Lorelei and no one wanted a wan reprise of Channing's 1949 performance. They'd seen it on Ed Sullivan. So Channing was doomed to a lifetime of trotting out revivals of *Hello, Dolly!,* the fate of a performer who is always a caricature and who was willing to spend a lifetime doing a self-parody. Until. . . .

In May 1998, Carol Channing held a news conference in New York City to announce her divorce from her husband and manager, Charles Lowe, to whom she had been married for forty-one years. For the first time, the woman under the make-up made a public appearance. Grayed and wrinkled, Channing appeared as a striking older lady (she is well into her seventies). The only hints of "Carol Channing" were the collagen-filled lips. There were no giant eyelashes, no oversized blond wig, just a vulnerable older woman alleging that her husband had only had sex with her twice in her marriage, had abused her, and, the crux of the divorce, had cheated her out of much of the money she had earned. Channing's story was a sad but typical one. Poor Doris Day was robbed blind by her husband-manager. Rumors abound about Mary Martin's husband's treatment of her, though she never acknowledged them. A number of these divas were managed by their husbands: the women performed, the men took the money. Channing's image, however, was of the woman who seemed dumb but always demanded, "Show me the money!" She was the woman who knew to get the diamonds, the woman who "arranges things." More than the other divas, she was the make-up, not the face under the make-up. She was bizarre, larger than life, but not a victim. This was a new image of Channing as victim, tailor-made for daytime talk shows. Oprah and Sally Jessy will commiserate, Kathie Lee will find her a new lawyer, and perhaps Judge Judy can officiate at her divorce hearing. Women viewers will be delighted to find that Carol is just another ordinary victim in the grand narrative of female victimhood that is daytime television.

Diva worshipers, however, will not be amused. Callas, the most legendary diva, was best known for three operas: in one she stabs the man who tries to seduce her, in another she kills her husband on his wedding night, and in the third she talks her faithless lover into burning to death with her. Maria didn't go on Oprah and lament about Aristotle Onassis leaving her for that wimp Jackie. She went into grand seclusion in Paris. Even victim-divas like Judy Garland were adored for singing their hearts out before an adoring audience despite backstage agony. For our time, the ultimate diva is Madonna, who takes what she wants from men and moves on, a creature both exhibitionistic and deeply private. Carol Channing has a new act, but the drag is off, and the audience is women. The old act lasted her fifty years. This one will only last until the next victim has a press conference. Seeing Channing give this performance was like hearing news of her death. She has shed her diva indomitability and become human.

Carol Channing is—was—the most extreme form of the musical diva. It is not surprising that she introduced the camp diva musical of the sixties and seventies. The genre demanded cartoon women who were survivors. And *Hello, Dolly!* is a revved-up version of a fifties musical. These shows were built for cartoon women.

DOLLY AND THE DIVA MUSICAL FORMULA

In writing his score for *Hello, Dolly!,* Jerry Herman developed his ironclad progression of songs for his version of the diva musical. Act I begins with a song establishing character and ends with a song re-establishing the character's resolve at a turning point in the plot. Somewhere near the beginning of Act II, the chorus sings a rousing, show-stopping hymn to the leading lady who also gets an eleven o'clock song. You can see this formula when it works in *Hello, Dolly!* and *Mame.* Dolly's "I Put My Hand In" establishes Dolly's character— all of it. "Before the Parade Passes By" shows Dolly's resolve to enjoy the remaining years of her life. (Parade songs were *de rigueur* in 1963 and 1964. Add to Dolly's song Cora's "A Parade in Town" in *Anyone Can Whistle* and Fanny's "Don't Rain on My Parade" from *Funny Girl.*) Dolly's eleven o'clock song, "So Long Dearie," a razzmatazzy cakewalk, is a rousing comic number. The ballads in *Hello, Dolly!* went to the ingenues. Ballads aren't Channing's forte. They depict tender emotions that don't fit her cartoon persona. When Ethel Merman went into the show, the ballads that had been written for her and cut when Channing was cast were reinstated.

Mame fits into the same musical formula. "It's Today" establishes Mame Dennis's desire to live each moment to the fullest. "We Need a Little Christmas" shows that even in poverty, Mame wants a celebration. The title song is the big hymn to the diva. Since Mame was written for a performer of considerably more versatility than Carol Channing, the big number in the second act is one of Herman's best ballads, "If He Walked into My Life." In later shows, like *Mack and Mabel,* the formula doesn't work as well. The hymn to the diva, "When Mabel Comes in the Room," is a better song than the title songs of the earlier Herman musicals, but it is so dramatically unnecessary as to make no impression. It is sung by a minor character and the chorus, and it's there because Herman always puts a song like that in the second act, not because it is necessary, like the extraneous "The Best of Times" from *La Cage aux Folles*. "Time Heals Everything" is a great ballad, but we don't care enough about Mabel at that point to be moved dramatically by the song.

Herman's problem with *Hello, Dolly!* and *Mack and Mabel* was in great part his book writer, Michael Stewart, who simply wasn't very imaginative. When given a simple adaptation like *Hello, Dolly!*, he could write a functional script. *Mack and Mabel* is a mess. The 1995 London revival, which Herman inaccurately calls a hit in his memoirs, still didn't fix the problems (a Broadway revival with more book revisions is scheduled for Spring 2001). *Mame,* tailored by Jerome Lawrence and Robert E. Lee from their hit play, and *La Cage aux Folles* with a book by Harvey Fierstein, fare better.

The best of the Herman musicals is *Mame,* an interesting bridge between the drag queen potential of Dolly Levi and the actual drag of Zaza in *La Cage aux Folles.* In a way, Mame is the gayest of the Herman shows. In the gay world of the 1950s, at least, Patrick Dennis's Auntie Mame always had a gay subtext and a drag potential. Mame was the older gay man introducing the younger gay man into "the life." The horror is when Patrick decides to marry into the camp of the ultimate enemy, suburban straights, whom Mame demolishes in the greatest scene of the play, film, and musical. Patrick may remain straight, but he sires a son who will be Mame's next convert at the end of the play. The world of Mame is the bohemian world of New York in the twenties and thirties when a wealthy gay man would likely be a real queen.

Rosalind Russell was the perfect choice for the play and film of *Mame.* Russell can be grand, elegant, but also a bit butch. *Auntie Mame* played on her androgyny perfectly. In the New York production of the play, Russell was replaced by Greer Garson, who was too grandly feminine, then, in one of Broadway's most bizarre casting moves, by Beatrice Lillie, who was doing something absolutely hilarious, but it wasn't exactly Auntie Mame.

The casting for the title role in *Mame* was inspired. The previous season, Angela Lansbury made her Broadway musical debut as the villainess Mayor Cora Hoover Hooper in the Sondheim–Arthur Laurents flop *Anyone Can Whistle.* While the show ran only a week, Lansbury proved herself a musical star worthy of Mame Dennis. Here was a woman who had been on the screen as a character actress for twenty years, often playing mothers of men her own age. She's the monster mother in the classic *The Manchurian Candidate,* and Elvis's mother in the non-classic *Blue Hawaii.* Lansbury never became a screen star because she came on too strong. She actually had a perfect stage face—big eyes, strong angles. For the next fifteen years, Lansbury was a Broadway diva, moving from *Anyone Can Whistle,* to *Mame,* to the revival of *Gypsy* in London and New York, to the Jerry Herman disaster *Dear World,* to Mrs. Lovett in

Sweeney Todd. She couldn't keep a bad show running—by this time, no one could; there would be no more *Happy Huntings*—but she always rose above the disaster around her. Though *Mame* ran long past Lansbury's participation in the show, no one else was as good. Celeste Holm was charming. Jane Morgan could sing the music. (Ironically, Morgan got involved in a very publicized affair with an underage young man during her run in *Mame,* which was a bit too close to the show's subtext.) Then there was the film with Lucille Ball on the other side of the Vaselined lens looking blurry and brave but all wrong. Mame isn't Lucy, a very different sort of clown woman, and Lucille Ball was never much of a singer. Mame must be grand, a diva.

Who but the queens in the audience could really appreciate Angela Lansbury and baritone Bea Arthur playing Mame's sidekick Vera, singing the bitchy "Bosom Buddies," or Bea Arthur archly singing "The Man in the Moon Is a Lady," both songs filled with gay argot. Arthur's butch Vera was the perfect foil for Lansbury's Mame. Lansbury could be elegant with her short, chicly androgynous haircut and great clothes. She could be funny and sing Herman's score brilliantly. No one minded that there really isn't any romance in *Mame.* The straight men in the show are all cartoons. Mame gets a big torch song in the second act, "If He Walked into My Life," but it is a song of loss for young Patrick. What did Mame do wrong as a surrogate mother figure? Why is she lamenting? Because surrogate son is straight and interested in another woman. Mame wouldn't have needed a torch song if Patrick had been the gay man she raised him to be. Mame herself couldn't bear a son of her own—she'd have to be a woman to do that instead of a stand-in for a drag queen. D. A. Miller claims, "the Broadway musical is the unique genre of mass culture to be elaborated in the name of the mother."[6] With the exception of Mama Rose, the ultimate monster mother, Broadway diva roles are quite sterile, androgynous actually, either inheriting children from others or not having them at all. Their maternal instincts tend to go toward flamboyant surrogate sons (Cornelius and Barnaby, Patrick, Molina). It's no wonder *La Cage aux Folles* looked so familiar. The anomaly is not that the women aren't actually mothers, but that the surrogate sons so rarely turn out to be really gay. The most outrageous, flamboyant queen I ever knew used to call himself Mother. Then again, my best friend from high school thought my mother was like Auntie Mame (Rose was closer to the truth).

Gay subtext came closer to text with the 1970 musical *Applause,* adapted from the camp classic *All About Eve.* In this year after Stonewall, the creators of *Applause* acknowledged the relationship between diva and gay men and played to the gays in the audience. In the musical, Margo Channing is a Broadway star and the award in question is the Tony, not the Oscar. Her sidekick in the show is not a Vera Charles, a drag queen's idea of a woman, but Duane, a gay hairdresser. Her first number, "But Alive," takes her to a gay bar where she is adored by all the queens. Margo might have been the perfect Angela Lansbury role, glamorous but tough when played by a great actress who can sing. Instead it was a Grand Musical Debut for a camp figure, forties film siren Lauren Bacall. Bacall, another Broadway baritone, can't carry a tune, and her voice sounds lower than that of her leading man, Len Cariou. She can't really dance. She is a Presence, which means most of the musical work goes to the supporting cast. Bacall begins a number, but the ensemble quickly takes over. Her one ballad, "Hurry Back," is a dull, two-note affair for a singer with two notes. But Bacall is a celebrity, a star at a time in which there is a dire shortage of musical stars. And she represents those two essential aspects of the Broadway diva. She is a figure of nostalgia and she is a survivor in a show about survival. Ethan Mordden calls shows like *Applause* Big Lady Musicals:

> The Big Lady aesthetic doesn't rely on talent as much as on guts, on a self-willing celebrity—*famous* guts—that virtually forces the public to applaud one's entrance, one's numbers, even one's lines; and, of course a standing ovation at the close is now formal ceremony. It's good show biz, but bad musical comedy, to build an evening around the glamor of guts.[7]

Here was a diva musical with a schizoid notion of the diva. Margo, the good diva, renounces show business at the final curtain and walks off into the sunset with her dull boyfriend. Eve, the bad diva, earns the curse of divadom, which she won by tricks and bitchery. The folks in from Jersey can rest content that stardom isn't worth it, after all. It's much better to run off with a nice man than be a star and have nothing better to do than dance all night with a bunch of queens. Some of us in the audience would rather do all of the above.

After Bacall's contract ran out, the producers went even more camp. Anne Baxter, who played Eve Harrington in *All About Eve,* came in as Margo. She had no credentials for starring in a Broadway musical but actually was a better performer than Bacall. Still, the reason for her being there had nothing to do with talent. It showed that the producers knew that camp value was the essential quality needed for this musical of a camp movie. After all, queens already knew the film by heart, and drag performers had been doing Bette Davis's Margo for eons. Anne Baxter's debut in *Applause* was a major gay event in New York. Baxter was replaced by B-movie actress Arlene Dahl. Who would be next, Rhonda Fleming? Ruth Roman? The bus-and-truck Margo was Patrice Munsel, a former Met soubrette and veteran trouper. She actually could sing the music, which made the score seem paltry. But *Applause* without a real diva wasn't a diva musical. The part didn't call for a Musetta: it called for a

Tosca. Actually, it called for what it originally got—an aging forties camp film star: "You know how to whistle, don't you, Steve? You just put your lips together . . . and blow."

In the mid-1990s, some mad producers got the idea of reviving *Applause* with Stefanie Powers. The show died somewhere on the road. The former star of television's *Hart to Hart* wasn't camp enough and *All About Eve* means nothing to the younger generation of gay men, for whom disco is camp. For the preceding generation of show queens, Bette Davis's classic line "Fasten your seat belts. It's going to be a bumpy night" was right up there with "Toto, I have a feeling we're not in Kansas anymore." If turning the famous line into a mediocre song didn't add anything to its force in gay culture, the show recognized the importance of its camp elements. More important than the appearance of Bacall, *Applause* recognized that show queens existed on both sides of the Broadway musical footlights.

Some years later, producers adapted another forties film, the Katharine Hepburn–Spencer Tracy comedy *Woman of the Year,* for Lauren Bacall. When Bacall left the show, Raquel Welch replaced her. Casting diva musicals no longer had anything to do with talent. There was an audience who would pay to see a celebrity on stage. In the sixties the Palace Theater, home of vaudeville, housed legendary appearances by aging stars who had a legitimate claim to be singing for money. A decade later it is aging film stars "appearing in," as opposed to performing in, musicals that are odd exercises in nostalgia.

FROM CRYPTO TO GAY

Diva musicals are both restrictive and liberating. While they are limited to heterosexist narratives, they open space for gender transgression. The drag potential of the diva musical shows its potential to question, if not deconstruct, conventional notions of gender. What conventional definition of femininity contains Carol Channing? She can only explode the stereotypes she spoofs. In celebrating feminine strength, the diva musical also is built on masculine weakness. Diva musicals are seldom love stories (*Funny Girl* is an exception to this). They celebrate women's independence and survival:

> Good times and bum times,
> I've seen them all, And my dear,
> I'm still here.[8]

If diva musicals occasionally take account of gay diva worship or are tacitly built on the diva worship of gay creators, they still must be created for a mass audience that isn't interested in and doesn't want to know about that dimension of the show.

What happens when the diva musical comes out of the closet? The two most successful examples show both the power and the compromises in creating a gay musical hit.

To see the similarity of *La Cage aux Folles* (1983) to Jerry Herman's earlier blockbuster hit, *Hello, Dolly!,* one only has to look at photographs of Carol Channing and George Hearn singing their big numbers. Who isn't in drag? Where *La Cage* is different from Jerry Herman's earlier musical hits is not in the presentation of the diva as a drag artist, but in the domestication of the leading lady. In becoming gay, Herman's heroine becomes more domesticated. *La Cage aux Folles* was hyped as a great leap forward for gay men in musical theater. It really wasn't. It was the product of a gay creative team (composer Jerry Herman, book writer Harvey Fierstein, and director Arthur Laurents), but so are many musicals. What is unique about *La Cage aux Folles* is that it was a long-running musical hit about a gay couple—sort of. The French film *La Cage aux Folles,* based on a hit Paris stage farce, was for its time the most successful foreign-language film release in the United States, so successful that it spawned two sequels. The film was so outlandishly farcical that its gayness was far from dangerous. When retrograde Hollywood finally got around to producing an Americanized version of the French films, *The Birdcage,* in 1996, it was a blockbuster hit. Georges and his "wife" Albin are a gay couple Middle America can understand. Even in 1983, turning *La Cage* into a musical was sure fire—and not just in New York.

I saw the original production of *La Cage* in New York and San Francisco. At the ascent of the AIDS epidemic, it was a fantasy version of gay life for tourists, playing the Palace, where Garland and Dietrich held forth a generation before. In the 1990s, a performance by the Dundalk Community Players says a lot about where we are now. We traveled to the Dundalk Community College on a spring Sunday afternoon in 1995 to see this incarnation of *La Cage.* This is duty. A neighbor, a gay undertaker, is in the cast and is an officer of the Players. Dundalk is a working-class area on the outskirts of Baltimore, Maryland. Right on the harbor, Dundalk used to be a major port community. For Baltimore, it is relatively white and verging on suburban. When we pull up outside the auditorium, we see families, dressed in their Sunday best, going into the building. Have we come to the wrong place? *La Cage aux Folles* is hardly my idea of Dundalk Sunday family entertainment. Or is it? The thousand-seat auditorium is sold out, as it has been for every performance. It turns out the Dundalk Community Theater is a big deal here. Though Dundalk is just a mile or two from Baltimore's professional theaters, this audience feels more comfortable here. And the audience gets its money's worth. The two leads are played by former professional actors. The lavish production tries to recreate the Broadway sets and costumes. The Dundalk audience loves this musical about the trials and tribulations of a gay couple. They may not give the rousing cheer to "I Am What I Am" that gays in the Broadway audience gave the Gay National Anthem of the eighties, but they clearly love the show. And we worried about driving through Dundalk with a rainbow sticker on our car!

Though the romantic leads in *La Cage aux Folles* are a gay couple and the chorus is made up mostly of drag queens, the show is less transgressive than many diva musicals. *La Cage* is about a middle-aged couple who have been together for twenty years who are worried about their son's marriage and his rejection of his parents. It is more universal than parochial. Yes, gay men may find the drag acts funnier (if they aren't uptight about drag) than the straights in the audience, but there has always been a straight audience for drag performers, and the original "Cagelles" were so convincing you forgot about the drag (in Dundalk about half of them were women). Yes, Albin sings the out and proud "I Am What I Am," but what he is doesn't include sex. Yes, straights are the butts of the jokes, but they're rich, powerful straights. The show bombed in London. Roger Baker notes:

> One of the complaints about the brief West End run was that Albin, the drag cabaret star "wife" to club owner Georges, was simply another version of Dolly Levi or the eponymous Mame and that *La Cage* was basically a show about family life. . . . [Broadway audiences] could see that *La Cage* was an essentially *heterosexual* show, the latter [London audiences] stayed away in droves from the London Palladium, home of "family entertainment," because they misinterpreted the musical as being about drag and about queers.[9]

Harvey Fierstein had already proved with the success of his *Torch Song Trilogy* that a large New York audience will come see a show about a gay man if his experience can be placed within a heterosexual, family paradigm. When Jean-Michel, who has been raised by his father, Georges, and George's lover, Albin, becomes ashamed of his flamboyant, drag queen "mother," George admonishes him with a song:

> So count all the loves who will love you
> From now to the end of your life
> And when you have added the loves who have loved you before
> Look over there
> Look over there
> Somebody loves you more.[10]

Albin has been a loving, doting mother. His "son" commits the worst sorts of betrayals: he falls in love with a young woman whose parents are right-wing crusaders, and he is willing to sacrifice Albin to please these future in-laws. Albin makes his figurative relationship to Jean-Michel literal when he appears in drag as his mother at the dreaded meeting of the parents. The situation in *La Cage* is the same as that in *Mame*—a son becomes ashamed of his non-biological mother and has to learn that her world is better than the uptight straight world he wants to marry into. In his memoirs, Jerry Herman presents *La Cage* as a daring political statement:

> The hero of the show is a gay man who finds his pride by challenging his son's bigotry towards homosexuals. The moral of the piece is actually very wholesome, because it is about standing up for yourself and fighting bigotry.[11]

Actually, the son isn't bigoted against homosexuals. He's an adolescent ashamed of his parents—a common trait many young people experience and grow out of. It was a typical Broadway formula (and the formula of the eighties television sitcom *Family Ties*) that the curse of liberal, eccentric parents would be a straight, conservative son, the reverse of what parents went through in the sixties.[12] A sophisticated New York audience, desiring a liberal reputation if not true liberal politics, would find right-wing conservatives funny—even in the Reagan era. It's the universality of the heterosexual narrative placed on homosexual characters that made *La Cage* a hit. Herman and his collaborators knew what they were doing:

> If we *had* written a stronger, tougher political message into the material, the New York *Times* might have loved us more. But that would have given our show too narrow an appeal and it never would have found the huge universal audience that it did.[13]

Gay men were going to go anyway, and they did appreciate a show in which a gay couple walk hand in hand into the sunset at the end, as we appreciated the glitzy, camp Cagelles numbers and, of course, "I Am What I Am."

La Cage operates on a very old-fashioned notion of homosexuality, but one that is clear to straights. Here is a classic butch-femme couple. It's clear who is on top, particularly when Albin identifies himself as a woman. The lovers get a love song, but it couldn't be more cautious, a song about any middle-aged couple reminiscing, not this particular gay couple. It's about the comfortable marriage of a middle-aged couple. What could be more appropriate for the audience of a Broadway musical?

At least in the first act, *La Cage aux Folles* follows the formula of a Jerry Herman musical. After an elaborate opening chorus for the Cagelles, Albin has his character song, "A Little More Mascara." It's a theatrical tour de force in which the actor, with the help of hidden dressers, is transformed quickly, before the audience's eyes, into a drag queen. Drag is magic, liberation, the romance of femininity. Albin is an average-looking middle-aged man. When he is in drag, he becomes what Craig Russell's Robin and all the other drag queens want to become—dazzling:

> Cause everything's ravishing,
> Sensual,
> Fabulous,
> When Albin is tucked away and Zaza is here![14]

The first act ends with the heroine's song of resolve, here "I Am What I Am." Albin will not be hidden or closeted. He will not be ashamed of his flamboyant gayness or his effeminacy. In the original production, the song ended with Albin marching up the center aisle of the Palace Theater and, figuratively at least, out into the street. It was the one political moment in the show. But would the middle-aged straight folks in the audience have been as comfortable with the song if Albin were not in drag, if he did not carry the stereotypical signs of homosexuality? The straights in the audience are not likely to encounter an Albin—not in costume, at least. They are likely to encounter gay men who look and act like they do. This is a case in which drag is a safe, comforting choice of gay representation. It was not the standard costume of a New York gay man in 1983, or of the gay sons of the 1995 Dundalk audience. At the turn of the twenty-first century, Georges and Albin would probably be happy bears.

La Cage aux Folles worked in Dundalk. The audience cheered the cast and the show at the end. Its politics looked very different than they did on a Saturday in 1983 when I saw the show in New York with a mostly gay audience. A lot has happened to gay men since 1983, and gayness is an historical inevitability the folks of Dundalk will accept—on stage, if not in their neighborhood—under the right circumstances. Do they know that much of the cast is gay? They don't want to know, which means that for them *La Cage aux Folles* is as much fantasy as, say, *The Wizard of Oz*. For all the show's faults, we know better. In the years since the 1995 Dundalk production the right wing has become virulent against even *La Cage aux Folles*. Recent planned productions in Greensboro and Raleigh, North Carolina, right around me in Helms country, were scrapped because of feared backlash from the Christian right. Raleigh replaced *La Cage* with *Annie*. Perhaps the debate about gay marriage has made

La Cage seem more dangerous. More likely, the Christian right's desperate, losing battle against the mainstreaming of homosexuality is just getting sillier. And, alas, musicals are increasingly seen as "family entertainment," which is the deathblow to a form historically naughty and safely transgressive.

DRESSING UP

In the musical version of Manuel Puig's great novel *Kiss of the Spider Woman,* an effeminate gay window dresser, taken prisoner for soliciting sex from a minor, keeps his sanity by remembering the films of a glamorous star, Aurora, who has all the glamour and all the power his life lacks. And, unlike lonely Molina, Aurora always gets her man:

> Her name is Aurora
> And she is so beautiful
> No man who has met her can ever forget her.[15]

Aurora is a floating signifier in the musical. She represents the escape into fantasy that is the allure of movies and that allows Molina to keep his sanity in prison:

> You've got to learn how not to be
> Where you are
> The more you face reality, the more you scar.[16]

But Aurora also plays the Spider Woman and the kiss of the Spider Woman is the kiss of death, which is bound to come once one meets the love of one's life in a world in which love between men is forbidden.

The only glamour Molina has known comes from his elegant dressing of the mannequins in his store window. Aurora is to him what the divas of the past were to drag artist Craig Russell in *Outrageous!* Molina's love arrives in his cell in the person of straight revolutionary Valentin. Enlisted by the police to wheedle information out of Valentin, Molina turns instead into his protector. On Molina's last night in prison, Valentin has sex with him, not out of love, but to make sure Molina will deliver a message for him when he leaves prison:

> If we touch before he goes
> He'll make that call.
> He'll do anything for me.
> Anything at all.[17]

However, when Molina is killed to save him, a real-life version of the movies he loves, Valentin realizes the extent of his heroism, which is much greater than his own.

When I first saw *Kiss of the Spider Woman* in London, where it wasn't a success but was kept on till the Livent people thought the show was ready for New York, I thought of the musical-within-a-movie, "Springtime for Hitler," in Mel Brooks's *The Producers.* Who would like a prison musical, set in South America, in which the two leading men have sex because one of them—the straight one—wants to recruit the gay one into his revolutionary political conspiracy? Would straight people buy a musical about sex between a queen and a straight man? Would gay people buy the offensive changes made to the novel to make it palatable to straight audiences? In the novel and the movie, the sex is something of an act of love, if not desire, on the part of the straight man. Would women buy the notion that the only women on stage are a fantasy film siren in chic male drag and a gay man's over-doting mother? Would straight men want to see a show in which the only skin is displayed by an all-male chorus? I was sure that the answers to all these questions would be a resounding No. Boy, was I wrong! On Broadway, *Kiss of the Spider Woman* wasn't a long-running megahit à la *Phantom of the Opera* or *Les Misérables,* but it got rave reviews, Tonys, and had a respectable, profitable run.

So I was wrong. The producers and the writers had gauged their audience well. My show queen friends were not as offended by the musical as I initially was. After all, *Kiss of the Spider Woman* is basically a musical about gay diva worship. The unifying principle of the musical is not the gay/straight cellmate couple, but the diva Aurora, the Spider Woman, who has most of the big songs. The gay hero is obsessed with this character out of old movie musicals. He introduces the revolutionary to her films. So the basically all-male show focuses on the woman of the gay man's dreams. In the novel, the queen told his cellmate the plots of films that were Nazi-produced romances. Molina didn't see or care about the political assumptions of these romances, the same assumptions that drive the police state that has imprisoned him. They are romances of a noble, suffering woman. In the musical, the Spider Woman appears in—what else—musicals.

In removing the politics from a great political novel, the creators of *Kiss of the Spider Woman* are akin to their hairdresser hero. The glitz and fantasy are everything. The Spider Woman offers escape, but only through death. In her various musical numbers, Aurora appears in a number of elaborate fantasy diva disguises: silk and satin bath and boudoir attire, men's white formal dress with matching fedora hat, feathered Follies-type outfit, and, of course, Spider Woman outfit. These are figments of Molina's memory and imagination. He may not be a drag performer but, like Robin in *Outrageous!,* he longs to be a woman, for the only glamour is in such fantasy women:

> She's lucky
> So lucky
> She's a woman.[18]

Kiss of the Spider Woman shows what gay writers and straight producers think Broadway audiences will accept ten years after *La Cage aux Folles.* The men are no longer a middle-aged couple, one of whom is a "wife." But one still bears the stereotypical signs of gayness—a stereotypical job, effeminacy, and devotion to his mother. In the novel, these were tied to a critique of the conventional stereotype and self-image of gay men in macho Latino culture. For a Broadway audience, there is no such localization and critique of the stereotype, merely direct presentation. A straight man might have sex with a gay man in a South American prison.

To their credit, McNally, Kander, and Ebb do tread into more dangerous territory after Molina and Valentin have their night in bed. The next morning, as Molina prepares to leave, Valentin challenges his pride and his masculinity:

> VALENTIN: Molina, I want you to promise me something. I want you to promise me you'll never let anyone humiliate you ever again.
> (VALENTIN *takes* MOLINA's *face in his hands and kisses him on the mouth*)[19]

When Molina leaves, Valentin says: "Come on, Molina. I'm counting on you. Be a man. Be a man."[20] Manhood doesn't necessarily mean heterosexuality, but it does mean pride and courage, both of which Molina demonstrates to save his beloved at the end of the musical. The writers carefully lead their audience to that most dreaded of moments, a male-male kiss. Anyone who has seen audiences' reactions to gay works knows the idea of sex is not as horrifying as the reality of a kiss, which mixes erotic attraction with affection.[21] Optimistic gay members of the audience can read the show as a mutual conversion: initially homophobic Valentin stops Molina from being too nelly and Molina cures Valentin of his homophobia and opens Valentin to the possibility of loving another man. After all, Valentin's girlfriend, Marta, is as much a fantasy as Molina's Aurora:

> But it's never ever her
> It's just a dream of her.[22]

Molina's final kiss is with the leading lady, the diva with whom Molina has identified, the Kiss of the Spider Woman. But Valentin remembers and dreams of Molina with the same music with which Molina dreamt of Aurora.

In the original cast, Aurora was played by Chita Rivera, the Latina veteran of forty years of musicals from *West Side Story* on and two previous Kander and Ebb musicals—*The Rink,* in which she played Liza Minnelli's mother, and the original *Chicago.* Rivera is the ultimate Broadway diva, an aging survivor who sings in male drag and basically in young drag. Here is another of those performers in their sixties who masquerade successfully as their young selves. She still can sound like she did as Anita in 1957 and still move fairly well with the troupe of male dancers. From the balcony, she looks like she used to look. Her voice is more baritone than it used to be, but baritone voices are part of the gender transgressiveness of the Broadway diva. Once again, the subtext of the diva show is survival and the worship of survival of glamorous women. Men age; female stars go on forever.

For those who believe, as D. A. Miller does, that the diva roles are all mother figures, *Kiss of the Spider Woman* complicates the issue. Molina is dedicated to his beloved mother, an usher at a movie theater, thus literally his guide to the movies he loves. Going to the movie theater for him is not the homoeroticized space it is in Tennessee Williams's short stories, but an Oedipal space. Mother shows you to your seat where you watch Aurora, played by a sixty-something woman, another mother figure, though a glamorous diva mother who is both sex symbol, role model, and bringer of oblivion.

When Rivera left the show, young black siren Vanessa Williams took over. The camp element went and the show did even better business, but the diva symbolism vanished. Valentin, the revolutionary, was played by Brian Stokes Mitchell, a far more charismatic performer than the original Anthony Crivello. The queen, Molina, was taken by another white performer, Howard McGillin, so as not to make the targeted black audience think that there are black queens. I'm told that some audiences who went to see Vanessa Williams were audibly hostile when the Valentin–Molina relationship moved from homophobia to homoeroticism. Ironically, the show foundered when Vanessa Williams left and the producers decided to target the show to Latino audiences by casting Maria Conchita Alonso as Aurora. Latinos stayed away in droves and the show closed.

Whatever its limitations, *Kiss of the Spider Woman* is the last diva musical of the twentieth century, a show that allows space for a series of star turns for a female star who is a reminder of the history of the last four decades of Broadway, whose age allows for the myth of agelessness that is part of the diva mystique— dancing up a storm in her sixties—whose very eternally young looks are itself a form of drag. Vanessa Williams had a triumph in *Kiss of the Spider Woman,* but for show queens, themselves remnants of another era, it's Chita Rivera's role, and the most vivid image is of her looking glamorous in that white male drag singing those catchy Kander and Ebb faux sambas—a true diva in a gay-created musical about the role of divas in the life of an unliberated queen.

THE POST SONDHEIM DIVA

In the late nineties, the only diva shows were Kander and Ebb revivals creating new divas: *Chicago* with Bebe Neuwirth or the divine Ute Lemper and Ruthie Henshall, *Cabaret* with Natasha Richardson. These revivals offered the audience a major thrill of musical theater, a great performance from a grande dame. Lord knows you don't get that from *The Lion King* (unless you count Tom Hewitt's grande dame performance as Scar)!

Why is *Chicago* such a hit? Like *Rent,* it says something about a contemporary audience's expectations of a musical. The spectacle associated with the quasi-operatic Cameron Mackintosh megamusicals of the eighties has split in two directions. One is the Disney spectacle in which performers are reduced to playing teacups and giraffes. However brilliant and enjoyable the spectacle, the performer is secondary to the effect, akin to Gordon Craig's dream of replacing the actor with übermarionettes to remove the too realistic human body (which can be nothing but itself) and the variability of the actor. Julie Taymor's designs for *The Lion King* keep the human body and head in view, but that does not allow the performer any humanity. But long before Taymor did her clever work, the megamusical had robbed the performer of individuality. The quite different presentational styles of *Rent* and *Chicago* emphasize the performer over the role.

Fosse's version of *Chicago* was over-the-top-glitz, an LSD vision of the flapper era. Fosse had ambivalent feelings about the diva musical. On one hand, he literally loved his leading lady, Gwen Verdon, and created brilliant vehicles for her. On the other hand, by the 1970s style was everything for Fosse and, like other choreographer-directors, he wanted to be seen as the star of his shows. The 1996 revival doesn't have the Fosse glitz. It looks like an ad out of a chic magazine. A gold false proscenium frames the action. A bandstand is given a shiny frame that reflects whatever colored light shines on it. The performers wear scanty black costumes that display their bodies without looking like gaudy burlesque outfits. Like Levi's and Calvin Klein ads, they highlight the perfectly shaped bodies of the dancers. One chorus boy wears only a vest and pants cut to begin just above the pubic hair, emphasizing his washboard stomach. All the boys have tight T-shirts—or only vests, which show off well-developed biceps and pecs. Fedora hats make the chorus boys look tall. These dancers aren't built like dancers, but like buff gym queens. The women are statuesque and in perfect shape, a far cry from anorexic-looking ballerinas or the petite gamines of yore. The production is meant to be a celebration of Bob Fosse's style of choreography, but it is more a celebration of the nineties ideal of male and female bodies as created, not by God, but by the StairMaster and Nautilus. The dancers are terrific, though the choreography—Ann Reinking's homage to Bob Fosse—is less quirky than Fosse's original. The night before I saw the London production of *Chicago* with the dream cast of Ruthie Henshall, Ute Lemper, and Clarke Peters, I saw a revival of *Sweet Charity* in which the Fosse choreography had been much more accurately recreated and which was brilliantly danced by the ensemble (less so by the lead, Bonnie Langford). This group of dancers looked much more like human beings who spent more time in the dance studio than the gym. They were cute, lithe, and well built, but not "buff." Actually, they radiated much more individuality than the *Chicago* ensemble, who, in nineties manner, give off more attitude than personality. The dances in *Sweet Charity* are charmingly dated. "Rich Man's Frug," a six-minute satire of sixties dance crazes, is followed by "The Rhythm of Life," a hippie celebration. *Sweet Charity,* however well-performed, is dying because it is dated—a sixties book musical with a great score and superb choreography tied to a story we no longer care about and to the conventions of the book musical, which audiences no longer accept. It's not that the book musical is not realistic enough. It's too realistic. Or inappropriately realistic. The Oscar Hammerstein vision of characters singing in a "musical play" has been supplanted by a more abstract sense of the musical: pure spectacle or a concert with the band on stage and the story told through the musical numbers. Half a mile away from the Adelphi Theatre, the Hal Prince megaproduction of the first great book musical, *Show Boat,* lost money, as did the faithful revival of *Sweet Charity. Chicago* is one of the biggest hits in London.

Chicago was originally subtitled "A Musical Vaudeville." Nowadays, people have only the vaguest sense of what vaudeville is. This *Chicago* is as abstract and presentational as vaudeville, but in a totally different style. It is closer to what audiences want than faithful revivals of book musicals.

I saw the touring company of *Chicago* in Washington, D.C., on a day on which both leads were played by understudies; then I saw it in London with Ruthie Henshall and Ute Lemper. The London production showed how much the show needs stars doing star turns. It was, after all, written for two divas, Gwen Verdon and Chita Rivera. When the competent understudy played Roxie Hart in Washington, I still heard Gwen Verdon, as I did when I heard Ann Reinking on the first recording of the revival. When Ruthie Henshall did her big number, "Roxie," memories of Verdon on the first cast recording were supplanted, though not erased. I can't help but be faithful to the divas I grew up with. Henshall made the part her own, as did Lemper with Velma. Like Chita Rivera, Ute Lemper is a distinctive, idiosyncratic performer. She is larger than life and a bit freakish. A large head with a face like Dietrich's sits on a skinny body with long, long, pencil-thin legs. Henshall is unusual for a musical star. I have seen her in *Crazy for You* and *She Loves Me* as well as *Chicago,* and she's totally different in each one. She doesn't even look the same. There's no trademark—she's a chameleon. Henshall and Lemper did what past divas did— they imposed their own styles on their numbers and made you believe for two- and-a-half hours that there was no other way to perform them. What made the London production of *Chicago* special was the exhilarating sense of watching stars do star turns, something lost in the anonymous megamusicals of the present. The *Sweet Charity* revival was presented as a vehicle for Bonnie Langford, who can only offer a generic perkiness. She can't dance as well as Gwen Verdon—she can't dance as well as the rest of her cast! And she can't project a fascinating stage persona as Henshall and Lemper can. Mama Rose sings "You either got it, or you ain't." Henshall and Lemper got it, yet the New Diva isn't camp. She's too high style for that. Rather than having any hint of drag, Henshall and Lemper are set in contrast to a drag performer who plays the gossip columnist, Mary Sunshine, and the male drag of the butch prison matron, Mama Morton. Mary Sunshine is pure androgyny, falsetto voice (the only person singing in a legit soprano voice complete with operatic cadenzas), long hair, and chic black pants suit, which is a contrast to the scanty outfits of the leading ladies. Butch Mama has short hair in a man's haircut, but so does Roxie Hart. She wears a tuxedo that she opens to reveal a low-cut black bodice. Is this drag or high fashion? The lesbian stereotype of the prison warden is deconstructed, except when lesbian comic Lea DeLaria played Mama on the national tour. The chorus boys look butch, but where do men wear outfits like theirs? Right—gay clubs. The show is less a memento of a great seventies musical than a celebration of nineties high style androgyny and gay chic. At the curtain call, as they descend on their stage elevator, Henshall and Lemper kiss each other on the lips.

Is *Chicago* nineties camp? Fosse's *Chicago* was a period piece about Chicago in the twenties as well as a Bob Fosse hymn to glitz. This revival is commentary on the age of the O.J. trial, Monica Lewinsky, and fifteen-year-olds having their fifteen minutes of celebrity by killing their schoolmates. You can get away with murder, and the public will love watching every minute of it. When the trial's over, there's always another murder or celebrity car crash or presidential fellatio to steal the spotlight. It's timely, something one doesn't expect a revival to be, and a great diva event for our time. Like the greatest of diva musicals, *Gypsy,* it ironically is about women who don't make it to the top of show business. We're supposed to believe that Roxie Hart and Velma Kelly are better murderers than performers. It's hard to believe that when Lemper and Henshall do their final number in front of that tinsel curtain. It is sheer magic.

The one grand *new* diva show, actually the first great postmodern diva musical, is the rock musical *Hedwig and the Angry Inch,* with a brilliant book by John Cameron Mitchell and terrific songs by Stephen Trask. Instead of the cautious, closeted composers and lyricists of recent decades, we have openly gay collaborators creating a grand drag act that reminds us how retro *La Cage aux Folles* was. This drag artist doesn't lip-synch; she wails a dozen or so rock tunes and tells her life story, a tale of cultural and sexual confusion. In good postmodern style, *Hedwig and the Angry Inch* is about identity, particularly gender identity, but it is also about diva survival, though in the language and iconography of rock and roll.

Hedwig was born Hans, the child of an American G.I. and an East German mother who had some kind of liaison in East Berlin before the wall was torn down. From childhood this gay boy born in a divided city thought of himself as incomplete, half of a person, and dreamed of finding his other half:

> What does this person look like? Identical to me? Or somehow complementary? Does my other half have what I don't? Did he get the looks, the luck, the love? Were we really separated forcibly or did he just run off with the good stuff? Or did I? . . . And what about sex? Is that how we put ourselves back together again?[23]

We're told in the Playbill that *Hedwig and the Angry Inch* is loosely based on Plato's *Symposium,* which contains the legend of divided individuals eternally searching for their other half, presented in the show as the song "The Origin of Love." Is Hans's other half a black G.I. named Luther? Luther offers marriage and U.S. citizenship, but Hans has to pass the physical. The transgender surgery is botched and Hans, now Mrs. Hedwig Robinson, is neither male nor female; a man without genitalia, a woman with an "angry inch":

> A one inch mound of flesh—
> Where my penis used to be—
> Where my vagina never was.[24]

Mr. Robinson has abandoned Hedwig, who is still hoping to find his/her other half, in a trailer park in Junction City, Kansas. With some Korean sergeants' wives, "she" has formed a rock-and-roll band called "The Angry Inch." In true

Mrs. Robinson style, he/she finds his/her completion, "the words to complete the sentence 'I am'," in a teenage boy, the son of an army general. Out of pimply faced Tommy Speck, Hedwig fashions rock star Tommy Gnosis, a merger of her creativity with his. She gives him his name, the trademark silver cross on his forehead, and his hit songs. When he discovers the angry inch, her sexual incompleteness, he leaves her. Her only fame comes from being the "mystery woman" Tommy was with when his limousine crashed into a busload of deaf schoolchildren.

Hedwig performs in the shabby ballroom of a tacky flophouse hotel on the Hudson River (where the performances actually take place). Through the door, she can hear Tommy's amplified voice—he is performing across the river in Giants Stadium—and she waits to hear some acknowledgment of her part in his life and career. Repeating her own history, she has married a Jewish Croatian drag queen so that he could have U.S. citizenship. As she had to pay the price with her male genitalia, husband Yitzhak must leave his wigs behind and, unhappily, be a man, Hedwig's roadie, and the husband of a creature he finds repulsive.

The acknowledgment from Tommy does come, in a mystical but theatrically riveting way, and Hedwig realizes from her music, not her history, that she is complete:

> Know in your soul
> Like your blood knows the way
> From your heart to your brain
> Know that you're whole.[25]

Is it really Hedwig up there? Is Tommy Gnosis a creation of Hedwig, or is Hedwig a creation of Tommy Gnosis? At the end we're not sure who is on stage, Hedwig or Tommy or some mystical combination of both suggested by the quote from Plato printed in the *Playbill:*

> Hephaestus came with his tools and stood over the pair. "What do you humans want from each other? I can melt you together, to fuse you into one person so that you share a single life and a single death. Will this make you happy?"

Has such a fusion really taken place, or is it a creation of Hedwig's or Tommy's imagination?

We have known all along that Hedwig is played by a male actor, originally by her creator, John Cameron Mitchell. At the curtain call, the performer playing Yitzhak, her husband, appears in full drag. No, wait! Yitzhak was the drag act, played by an actress out of drag for the curtain call. *Hedwig and the Angry Inch* gender bends until the very end.

In one sense, *Hedwig and the Angry Inch* is the archetypal diva act, a ninety-minute rock version of "I'm Still Here." In her first number, Hedwig roars, "Try and tear me down," which amounts to her credo. She is like the Berlin Wall she watched razed on television from her Kansas trailer, "standing before you in the divide between East and West, slavery and freedom, man and woman, top and bottom."[26] Hedwig discovers she is neither one nor the other of these things but both, thus whole, "more than a woman or a man." Hedwig begins like something out of *Passion,* obsessively looking for a connection that will subsume her or her partner's ego, a search all humans seem doomed to make. Love is not imprinting another individual, but allowing them to be free, as you can be free—letting go, as Hedwig lets Yitzhak go. Yet love exists as a mystical connection, a blurring of identities. At the climactic moment in the musical, we in the audience are not sure whether we're watching Hedwig or Tommy or both merged into one body.

In the tradition of much contemporary theater, Hedwig is basically a solo act, asserting through its form that the performer's body is his/her principal medium and that identity and love are forged from within the individual, not in dialogue with others. This may remove some of the glitz and glamour of traditional musicals, but *Hedwig and the Angry Inch* does offer the best book musical, the best combination of dialogue and song, written in years. Hedwig, in postmodern style, eschews the traditional divas of gay culture—Judy, Barbra, Bette, Liza, Bernadette, Betty—for the divas of rock and roll: "Patti and Tina and Yoko, Aretha and Nona and Nico and me." And we in the audience have no doubt of Hedwig's diva status.

Hedwig and the Angry Inch is a hit, with a cast album and impending film version. As if to confirm Hedwig's diva status, *The New Yorker* ran a one-and-a-half-page Richard Avedon color portrait of "her" at her grandest as embodied by her creator, John Cameron Mitchell, though other performers have played and will play Hedwig. Yet *Hedwig* raises questions about the continual questioning of the relationship of gay identity to gender identity. Mitchell, the son of a distinguished army general (Tommy Speck/Gnosis is also the son of a general), must be aware of the masculinist culture in America and the difficult path gay men take through that culture. Young gay men are willing to assert their homosexuality but are still frightened of being considered "limp wristed," as if limp wrists are a side effect of coming out. Fear of effeminacy is still strong in our culture. Rock and roll, traditionally testosterone music, has been stirring up the gender issue for years from chic bisexuality (Mick Jagger, David Bowie, Michael Stipe), to glitzy homosexuality (Peter Allen, Elton John, now sanctified by Disney), to various forms of drag. More than Broadway, which has religiously maintained the trappings and traps of heterosexual romance even to tell gay stories, rock has offered liberation from the notion of natural formulations of gender and sexuality. By merging the traditions of musical theater with those of rock-and-roll performance, *Hedwig and the Angry Inch* has found a more liberating stance in which gender and sexuality remain mysteries both poignant and comic.

3. A diva for our time: John Cameron Mitchell as the transsexual Hedwig in *Hedwig and the Angry Inch*. Photo by Carol Rosegg.

4. (Next page) A queer chorus line. The swans in Matthew Bourne's *Swan Lake*. Photo by Joan Marcus.

CHORUS *BOYS*

A couple of days before I saw *Kiss of the Spider Woman* in London I made my first visit to a West End Cares Monday-night cabaret, where each week the cast of a London musical puts on an hour-long cabaret as a benefit for AIDS charities. The audience is mostly theater folk who have just gotten off work. The performances usually give the gypsies, the talented folk in the chorus, the chance to strut their stuff in front of their peers. It is also a space in which the gayness of a number of the performers is acknowledged and celebrated. On this particular Monday, the cabaret featured the company of *Kiss of the Spider Woman*. Chita did not perform—she was sitting in the audience a few feet from me looking, thanks to a lot of make-up, much like Chita. Nor did Brent Carver, who played gay Molina, appear, but there was enough real gay presence to make up for it. The two gypsies who emceed the show were almost stereotypes of chorus boys; good looking, well built, competent singers and terrific dancers, and unabashedly gay.

Two days later I sat in the Shaftesbury Theatre watching these men play shirtless macho prisoners in this musical extravaganza set in a South American prison, singing of longing for their women "Over the Wall." That afternoon, *Kiss of the Spider Woman* failed to work its magic on me. What bothered me? That I knew that some of these guys were gay? You can tell the ones who aren't now because they list wives and girlfriends in the program so you'll know they're straight (or bisexual). Somehow the entire tension on which the musical depends, the somewhat parodic display of the illusion of heterosexuality in the face of innumerable, unacknowledged signs of homosexuality, collapsed, because in *Kiss of the Spider Woman* the old-fashioned, stereotypical representation of queerness overwhelms everything else, making the puny signs of straightness seem mean-spirited. Having seen those macho men camp around a couple of nights before toppled an always uneasy balance. The show just seemed dumb.

The chorus boys (there are no chorus girls) play two roles in *Kiss of the Spider Woman*. On one hand they are the heterosexual male prison community against which we see Molina's flamboyant homosexuality. The musical follows the typical fantasy of popular-culture depictions of gay men, that there is only one gay man and the only objects of desire that man could have would be straight. I know that in the culture Puig describes and critiques in the novel on which this musical is based and which it travesties, a gay man like Molina, trained by his culture to see himself as not fully male, would be attracted to straight men rather than half-men like himself, but the musical doesn't even pretend to explain its social environment. What we get is stereotype. *But* Molina gets to have sex with a straight man—his life's fantasy. If one of these men is sexually available (it is prison after all), perhaps they all are in the right circumstances—after one of Molina's good dinners and tales of Aurora—even though the show maintains that this is a prison in which homosexual activity does not usually take place. How can this sort of fantasy hold up for those who know that for most of the performers, heterosexuality is only a role, like playing a South American, that heterosexuality is no more substantial than the projections used to create the settings? "And what I am is merely illusion." Had I gone to see these chorus boys, whom I now knew to be gay, in, say, *Oklahoma!* or *Miss Saigon* would I have been as bothered? Actually, the Engineer in *Miss Saigon* only made sense to me as a character when I saw him played by a performer I know is a drag queen. He makes no sense to me as a straight man. *Kiss of the Spider Woman* actually closets the gay chorus through its insistence that only Molina is gay, which makes the show's politics incoherent.

Yet it may be that the illusion of heterosexuality created by the chorus boys is the musical's most tenuous fantasy. Perhaps this is why the "tired businessman" is actually less interested in musicals than his wife or gay son. Or why Stephen Sondheim, so eager to closet his gay not-so-subtexts, so often dispenses with the chorus.

In *Top Hat,* as part of his London stage show, Jerry Travers (Fred Astaire) performs Irving Berlin's "Top Hat, White Tie and Tails." He is backed by a chorus of men dressed in the same formal outfit. At the end of his novelty tap routine, Travers/Astaire raises his cane and, pretending it is a gun, shoots each of the chorus boys. Straight Jerry/Fred understands the phallic potential of his noisy, rhythmic tapping and his long, sleek cane. The chorus boys, who have him outnumbered, never think of firing back. They're as ineffectual as the supporting cast of sissies who surround Astaire in the dialogue scenes. A real man turns dancing into violence. The chorus boys, being only partial men, can only fall limp.

Real men don't sing, but if they do, they had better sing of their sexual interest in women. How often is the chorus the voice of conventional heterosexuality in the musical? Yet rather than the voice of sexual experience it is often the voice of frustration or disinterest. The men in that South American prison can't get at the "big-busted women over the wall." The men on the Polynesian island in *South Pacific* sing that "There Is Nothin' Like a Dame" but never seem to do more than whistle at the "dames" around them. One could think that they enjoy each other's company more than the women's and that the song represents a performance of heterosexuality necessary to stave off the specter of homosexuality from the male military society ("Don't ask, don't tell") and from the chorus who sings the song. The Washington Senators in *Damn Yankees* seem to get a lot of sex but are lousy ballplayers. They should have "thought about the game." These are "normal" guys, but too much sex has kept them from professional excellence. Their one champion player, Joe Hardy, is totally domesticated and monogamous. The gamblers in *Guys and Dolls* are much more interested in their vocation than in women. The chorus in these shows represents heterosexual boys not yet matured to the professional or domestic responsibilities of manhood. The leads usually grow up and marry by the final curtain.

The chorus may be made up of boys but the traditional sound of the chorus was the voice of testosterone. Listen to the original cast album cuts of male choruses like "Blow High, Blow Low," "There Is Nothin' Like a Dame," "I'm on My Way" from *Paint Your Wagon,* or the opening chorus of *Damn Yankees.* A beefy sound with lots of bass. Real men! In the pre-sixties musicals, there was a singing chorus and a dancing chorus. Opera stars like Cornell MacNeil began their careers in Broadway choruses. The changeovers in the big numbers were anything but realistic. The leads would sing, the singing chorus would march on and sing, then clear for the dancers, then return with the leads to sing the final chorus. When the dancers took over the singing—both an economy measure and an artistic decision to raise the coherence level of the musical—the sound became lighter. Compare the sound of the chorus in *Kiss of the Spider Woman* with that of earlier shows. These guys sound like—chorus boys. The imported quasi-operatic megamusicals don't have much in the way of dancing—the scenery moves more than the performers. It also dispenses with that sexually suspect dancing boy.

Why is it that chorus folk, particularly dancers, are called "boys" and "girls?" In an age in which a lot of women, particularly women who were the objects of the male gaze, were called girls ("Here they come, / Those beautiful girls"), it is not surprising that the chorus girls got their appellation. But chorus boys? It brands them as male, but not quite men. How often do straight people refer to their gay friends, regardless of age, as the "boys?"

Like chorus girls, chorus boys exist to be looked at. The sailors singing "There Is Nothin' Like a Dame" are shirtless, flaunting their bare chests. In the locker-room scenes in the 1995 revival of *Damn Yankees,* there is always the unrealized possibility of full exposure of the bodies of the team members. There are showers at the back with doors that tease that they might become transparent, but never do. The only man who is exposed is the fattest, least-attractive member of the team. There is a flirtation with the possibility of visual pleasure for the gay men in the audience, partially realized by cute guys in towels. The boys in *Kiss of the Spider Woman* spend a lot of time bare-chested. For whom is this spectacle of male flesh being played?

Howard Crabtree thought the place for him, a high school sissy, was as a Broadway dancer, one of the guys who substitute for the real men in the dream ballets, a "Dream Curly." Dance was a separate world linked to the musical, sexually suspect, but acceptable as divertissement. When a dancer took a lead role, his heterosexual credentials, like Joey Evans's in *Pal Joey,* had to be established early in the show. Ray Bolger may have played a ballet dancer in *On Your Toes,* but the audience knew he wanted to get to that "small hotel" with the girl before he started doing the fancy stuff. The dances were safely about heterosexual desire, but not the dancers, those cute ageless chorus boys we gay boys wondered and fantasized about and even wanted to be, had we been cute enough, lithe enough, or short enough. As far as I know, no one has ever taken a survey of chorus boys past and present but, as D. A. Miller puts it, there is a "widely suspected fact that, where the chorus of a Broadway musical is concerned, gay men do not form a minority."[1] I know a lot of people in musical theater and my impression is that the "widely suspected fact" is indeed fact.

So what? Well, for this gay young man, the chorus was like the chorus of Athenian drama, an intercessor between the goddess who ruled the musical theater and us in the audience. The leading men were often too stolid, too old and unattractive, for a teenage incipient queen. But there was something about those boys we show queen cocoons could relate to. When the chorus boys became the principals, as they did in *West Side Story,* the show was to die for: "You got brothers around."

In *Kiss of the Spider Woman,* the chorus boys play both the macho prisoners and the fantasy dancing boys who surround Molina's dream diva, Aurora. Here they play the primary role of the chorus boy in the diva musical, acolyte to the goddess: welcoming Dolly back to the Harmonia Gardens, singing Mame's praises, paying homage to Mayor Cora Hoover Hooper, cheering and jeering Evita, dancing up a storm around Aurora or Julie's Victoria. The chorus boys are the jewels in the diva's crown, offering the tangible worship of song and dance while we in the audience can only cheer. What a spectacle! A middle-aged or older woman playing a gay man's ideal, an indomitable, flamboyant monster surrounded by adorable young dervishes singing and dancing her praises. At the end of the first act, the prison transforms into a tropical landscape. Aurora sings "Let's Make Love." The chorus, dancing wildly around her, sings "Gimme love, gimme kisses; gimme love." To whom are they singing? Aurora or us? Both, silly!

The queerness of the chorus boy only became confused when it became acknowledged, for acknowledging the queerness of the chorus, which in a strange way also acknowledged the queerness of some of the audience, led to odd, futile attempts to keep the musical itself closeted so as not to scare the straights away. There is also a subversiveness in those chorus boys not present in the principal narrative. The chorus is protean. The "boys" in *Kiss of the Spider Woman* are macho prisoners and flamboyant dancers who sing of the power of fantasy. A decade before, the Cagelles sang: "What we are is an illusion." An illusion of femininity, of course, but visually a very convincing, alluring illusion. The same chorus boys who play the Cagelles are the macho men who do the dance break in "Masculinity." The chorus can play masculine or feminine, gay or straight, unlike the drag diva, Zaza, who is convincing as neither masculine nor feminine, who can only be gay. The chorus boys offer the possibility of liberation through imagination and theatrical pose. They can be anything. The minute they become leading characters, they become trapped into a singular identity and stereotype.

Lauren Bacall's star vehicle, *Applause* (1970), gave her a gay sidekick, "hairdresser, buddy, and confidante"[2] Duane (played by Lee Roy Reams), who, in the first big production number, "But Alive," takes Margo Channing into a gay bar to receive the adulation of her gay fans. In this moment, the show acknowledges the gay diva worship that makes an extravaganza like *Applause* possible. At the same time, it places a gay bar on stage, a first for a Broadway musical. The chorus boys get to "play" gay men, just as they played baseball players and cowboys. They play us safely by overplaying us. Nowhere in the script does it actually say that this is a gay bar, merely that the customers are all men "dressed in varied flamboyant attire."[3] The giveaway is that the script refers to the men in the bar as "boys." Margo refers to them as "silly boys." The boys, of course, offer their diva near-bacchanalian worship. She is a goddess who has descended into their mortal world. It's Margo's happiest moment in the script, far happier than her lugubrious moments with her boyfriend that inspire some of Charles Strouse's weakest music.

During the rest of the show the chorus boys play themselves, gypsies. Like the men in so many other choruses they are defined and redeemed by their devotion to their profession, which, we are told, is rewarded with very little money but does offer "the sound that says love," the audience's applause, which is also their approval—from a distance. These gypsies the chorus plays aren't as flamboyantly gay as the "boys" in the bar, but one can't help associate the two. Throughout *Applause,* there is a tacit acknowledgment that there are gay men on stage and "out there in the dark." Why else include a bare male posterior in one production number?

Seesaw (1973), based on William Gibson's hit two-character play, *Two for the Seesaw,* depicts the romance of a Midwestern WASP with a New York Jewish girl, Gittel Mosca. In the style of the best and worst Cy Coleman musicals (*Sweet Charity, The Life*), *Seesaw* turns into a celebration of Manhattan multiculturalism. There's a big Puerto Rican number ("Spanglish"), a black number ("Ride Out the Storm"), and that favorite staple of Broadway comedy in the late seventies, the gay neighbor, who gets the most camp production number. Each of the picturesque New York groups—blacks, Latinos, show queens—is presented as an amiable stereotype, part of the New York experience. All the numbers are pleasant, though the Latin number doesn't sound very Latin and the black number doesn't sound very black. Does the gay number sound gay? There's nothing specifically gay about the lyrics and I'm not sure what gay music sounds like (Aaron Copland? disco? Elton John? Tchaikovsky?). The show assumes that gay music sounds like Broadway razzmatazz. Tommy Tune plays David, the gay neighbor and a choreographer (a gay choreographer! Mercy!); the number is his dream number. The power was in the political symbolism. Tune, who choreographed his character's Big Number, remembers:

> I believe I'm historically accurate in saying that I was playing the first openly gay, major role in a mainstream musical comedy on Broadway, and I was the first long-haired, character juvenile to dance across the hallowed hetero stage boards in "sunny openness" as John Simon wrote . . . I know it was a first that had no cringe factor, like you would have if a homosexual character had been dropped into Walt Disney's *Bambi,* if you can imagine such an inconsistency.[4]

Tune *isn't* historically accurate. Lee Roy Reams got there first in *Applause,* but Reams, an excellent singer and dancer, had no solo number. Bonnie Franklin, the girl gypsy, walked away with the accolades and the sitcom contract. Reams was last seen as Jerry Herman's sidekick in his ill-fated attempt to move from composer of diva musicals to diva. In *Seesaw* Tune got the eleven o'clock number and won the 1974 Tony for best supporting or featured actor in a musical because he was terrific, not because he was playing a gay character, but the event was symbolic. Unlike Danny Kaye thirty-some years before in *Lady in the Dark,* Tune played a gay man who was not a comic caricature. His character was part of New York and part of musical theater. David's number, "It's Not Where You Start," was outrageous, but childlike and totally sexless. The chorus was covered in balloons. It was the showstopper that established Tommy Tune as performer and choreographer-director.

My father, a man of few words, said to me as Tune took his curtain call, "He's very courageous." As I have pondered over the years the mysteries my father presented, I often think of that assessment, but that's another book. For my father, what was courageous was doing what an older generation most feared, publicly proclaiming one's difference. Tune was, after all, not just appearing in *Seesaw:* he pretty much created his numbers. His character, David, was seen to be Tune's creation. There was safety, though, in the specificity of Tune's character; he played a Broadway dancer-choreographer, a safe distance from bourgeois respectability. Who didn't think that sort of character was likely to be gay? It would have been another matter if he had played a dentist. Yet Tune was playing a "generic gay" for a straight audience, a young man who lived in a New York City neighborhood where "unconventional" people lived and worked in show business. Finally, a chorus boy was outed and made a star, but in the process became a theatrical stereotype, the gay neighbor. Meanwhile, the real gender blurring was going on behind him where all those balloons became flamboyant unisex costumes blurring the gender differences of the chorus boys and girls.

Where David's gayness in *Seesaw* had been a matter of flamboyant pride, Paul's in the enormously successful *A Chorus Line,* produced a couple of years later, was a matter of shame. *A Chorus Line* was a theatrically unique presentation of the hopes and dreams and reality of a group of young people who opt for the unconventional life of the dancer. Their individuality was explored in first-person monologues, their commonality in song and dance. At the end, through talent, discipline, and the survival instinct so often celebrated in musicals, the kids become a collective entity, a gold-clad chorus line. Their move from individual to group through ruthless competition (here an audition) is the experience of middle-class adolescents who loved the show. Poor gay Paul is the only character in this hit musical to be an object of pity and condescension. In the longest monologue in the show, Paul tells the story of his experience in a drag revue and his embarrassment the night his parents came to see the show. To his surprise, his father doesn't reject him but tells the director, "Take good care of my son," a gesture of acceptance that we all know is just what happens when fathers discover their sons in dresses. Larry Kramer is more on target in *The Destiny of Me* when the father almost castrates his dress-wearing show queen son. After Paul has tearfully told of this moment of embarrassment and parental tolerance, Zack, the director, who spends most of the show giving orders from the back of the house, comes on stage and, in a grand gesture of tolerance, puts his arm around the sobbing Paul. Paul's speech often got an ovation from the audience, as if the audience was offering him its sympathy and approval. It's the kind of ovation sports audiences give an injured athlete as he hobbles or is carried off the field. Poor kid, maimed but he keeps trying. To complete the metaphor, Paul gets injured and has to be taken to the hospital, thus losing all chance of winning at the audition. This gay chorus boy is ethnic other (Paul is Puerto Rican), effeminate (a drag performer), and physically too weak to complete the audition (a sissy), but he's courageous enough to tell us he's gay and respectable enough to be ashamed of it. The poor guy doesn't even get a song, as if gay people aren't musical. Paul's tragedy isn't that he's gay—there is one other openly gay man auditioning—but that he's effeminate, a sissy. Gregg also admits to being homosexual and he, too, is eliminated from the line. The lie of *A Chorus Line* is its assumption that there may be gay dancers out there, but chorus boys who get cast are heterosexual, a myth maintained by the film *Fame,* in which there is one homosexual at the High School for the Performing Arts, and he's the one lonely, pitiable character in the film. Given the sexuality of *A Chorus Line*'s creators, their treatment of Paul is an example of gay men keeping themselves and their fellow artists in the closet. The show also allows its audience to toy with liberalism and tolerance without having to include a gay in the group the show celebrates. It's actually a harbinger of AIDS dramas in which audiences are allowed to feel tolerance and pity for a dying character they will not have to accept into their world (ironically, the creators of *A Chorus Line* died of AIDS). *A Chorus Line* is a classic example of how a musical can simultaneously acknowledge the existence of homosexuality and deny that there are any homosexuals on the stage.

Ironically, these prosaic depictions of gay performers were considered groundbreaking at the moment glitter rock, which performed the notion that gender and sexuality were theatrical poses to be chosen and performed, was popular with young people. While sad, shamefaced Paul was carried off, David Bowie and Lou Reed were proudly proclaiming bisexuality and wearing more glitter than the Cagelles would. Todd Haynes's brilliant film *Velvet Goldmine* (1998) explores this age of sexual fluidity and gender-fuck, an age in which teenage boys wore platform shoes and make-up, in which the only people who seemed lost and confused were those fixed in conventional notions of gender and sexuality, whether gay or straight. For Haynes, these flamboyant creatures were the true descendants of Oscar Wilde and the true sexual revolutionaries. The bisexual Brian can reinvent himself while the gay men and straight woman who love him seem lost in the shadows. Mad rocker Curt Wild, whom our glitter star Brian idolizes and sleeps with, may expose his penis and ass to the audience as sexual provocation and invitation, as sign of their power and availability, but, unlike the body, costumes can be changed and Brian can reinvent himself. Haynes says: "We live in a society that insists on prescribing our identities. I think the glam era posed some of the strongest dangers to that by encouraging a refusal of any fixed category for sexual orientation or identity in general."[5] While our contemporary theater may seem liberal in presenting homosexuality, it is conservative in maintaining rigid distinctions of gay/straight, masculine/feminine, only broken successfully by the chorus.

EVERYTHING IS BEAUTIFUL AT THE BALLET

Dance is a crucial part of the musical precisely because it is erotic and dangerous. It is dangerous precisely because its eroticism is not easily controlled or channeled. Kenneth MacMillan's pas de deux for the revival of *Carousel* is so sexy it almost throws the chaste sentimentality of the show out of kilter. Suddenly, particularly in the New York cast, there is a sexually magnetic man on stage who makes Billy look like a wimp joining with Louise in a dance that makes the singing of "If I Loved You" as sexless as a nursery jingle. This must have been a threatening moment for straight men. Yes, the sex displayed was ostensibly heterosexual, but the choreography ensured that the man was the focus of the gaze. A generation earlier Jerome Robbins's choreography for *West Side Story* eroticized the boys. Even in a number like "America," the women's skirts twirling and kicks, though exuberant, weren't as sexy as those Sharks twisting and leaping in those black pants. Rob Marshall's use of chorus boys in *Kiss of the Spider Woman* and *Victor/Victoria* makes their quick turns and Fosse-like extensions steal focus from the diva. Even straight Fosse made the boys sexy by making the dancing unisex.

A few nights ago I turned on the television to find my screen filled with men in red loincloths that displayed their buns dancing around a high orange tower. I had found my way into the Metropolitan Opera telecast of *Samson et Dalila* at the beginning of the famous *bacchanale*. I'm sure it's hard for a contemporary choreographer to know what to do with this music. At times it cries out for tutus and toe dancing, then swings into its faux orientalism. I am sure that the opera's first audiences expected any indecorous display of skin to be offered by the ladies of the ballet, not the gentlemen. In this Met production, the ladies were covered in body stockings; the flesh was male flesh. There wasn't a lot of male coupling, but it was clear that the women were of secondary importance at this *bacchanale*. When Samson made his way to the phallic column and pushed it over, it seemed an act of homophobia rather than justice against the Philistine oppressor. This ballet wasn't quite as blatantly homoerotic as the wrestling match between scantily clad white and black hunks that was offered as the triumphal ballet in the Met's 1974 production of *Aida,* directed by John Dexter, but audiences at the opera are straighter these days, I am told. On television, which is so prudish about the display of male flesh, it was a refreshing change to have so many male derrieres aimed at the camera (the choreography called for the men to spend a lot of time with their asses toward the audience). It seemed clear that someone thought that part of the spectatorial pleasure of this *Samson et Dalila* would be male skin. It was. The *bacchanale* was enthusiastically cheered.

Some years ago, PBS aired a San Francisco *Aida* with enough male skin to satisfy most of the opera queens in the audience, thus, like the *bacchanale,* placing a gay spin on an event with a sizeable gay audience. Opera may be about transcending bodies through beauty of voice, of being transported to a world in which the overweight diva and divo bodies no longer matter, but no one said the rest of it can't offer visual pleasure. As the young men of the Jockey Club demanded the visual pleasure of the Paris Opéra ballerinas in the nineteenth century, so the men in at least one club are happy with the sight of some of the men in the corps de ballet.

We see the gypsies, the male chorus of the musical, as the bridge between the heterosexist fantasy the musical offered us gay men in the audience and our fantasies. Not all gypsies are gay, but a lot are, God bless 'em, and their participation in the event helps make it ours. They may be singing Dolly Levi's praises, or dancing shirtless around Chita Rivera's Spider Woman, or baring their buns in *Applause.* Sometimes the choreography (Rob Marshall's comes to mind) shows the men off in ways that are particularly gay-friendly. The gypsies are usually the best-looking men on stage in a musical and the most likely to be exposed in a way that offers gays some spectatorial pleasure.

Thirteen blocks down Broadway from the Met, where the gypsies' buns were bared to Saint-Saëns, Matthew Bourne's production of *Swan Lake* was being performed at the Neil Simon Theater after successful runs in London and Los Angeles and on British television. In this production, the swans are not ballerinas in tutus and toe shoes, but bare-chested, barefoot men wearing low-cut feathered pantaloons. The prince's duets with the swan are magnificent, homoerotic dances. The "black swan" appears at the party garbed in black leather. An even more homoerotic duet ensues. The final scene takes place on and around the prince's bed. Bourne's *Swan Lake* is not the first queering of a classic ballet. We've already had gems like Mark Morris's witty revision of *The Nutcracker, The Hard Nut,* in the theater and on television, and modern dance and ballet here and abroad have been giving us gay dance for decades. The difference and excitement in Bourne's queering of a classic are its hot eroticism and its commercial success outside of the usual venues of ballet. This isn't the first time ballet or dance has been presented in a Broadway theater, but here and in London megamusical producer Cameron Mackintosh has produced and sold this event to the audiences that would usually go to West End and Broadway musicals. This *Swan Lake* is aimed at show queens as much as balletomanes. It may even work for "straight-looking and -acting" gay men. A woman friend of mine thought it the "hottest" thing she had ever seen on stage.

The prince in this *Swan Lake* is a sissy. We can understand why. No father figure, a mother cold to him and anything but to the young men around the court. The prince has, to put it mildly, an unnatural attachment to his mother. He drinks too much, is not attracted to the floozy the minister tries to arrange for him, and he has erotic dreams about swans. When his sexual frustration and loss of self-control reach crisis point, the prince goes to the park to drown himself. There he encounters the swans and finds himself enthralled by their masculine power. These swans are anything but dainty. They could be members of a large punk rock band. They are, despite the feathers, very butch. They can knock a man down. They're both attractive and menacing. The lead swan has to protect the prince from his fellow swans. Eventually, a tender relationship is established between the prince and the swan, and the prince decides to live if only to savor the memory of this strange nocturnal encounter between two creatures who cannot ever really be joined. In their duets, unlike the original choreography, the swan picks up the prince and cradles him in his wings. The prince takes the traditional feminine role. The swan seems to offer the only affection he has experienced.

The prince appears at a royal ball visited by a beautiful man in black leather who bears a resemblance to the swan. Wait a minute! How can a person resemble a swan? Here is the fascinating confusion of all versions of *Swan Lake*. We see a dancer play a swan, but *Swan Lake* is always about repressed eroticism. In the original, the swans were maidens transformed into animals by an evil magician, so the prince fell in love with swan and woman simultaneously. Could the woman be freed from the spell? What was the spell anyway, but turning human into animal? In Matthew Bourne's version, the villain, the evil minister, seems to be able to turn animals into humans. Is this beautiful young man in black leather a human transformation of the loving swan of the previous scene? The confusion of swan and human is more complex here than in the original.[6] This black swan is the Oedipal prince's worst nightmare. In a moment of fantasy the two connect in an erotic pas de deux, but reality soon intrudes. This sexy man in black is classic rough trade, a combination flirt and bully, encouraging the prince's desire then taunting him for it. He's interested in the queen, not the prince. The prince cracks up, takes out a gun to shoot his mother, but accidentally shoots the girl he has been dating. In the final scene, another reversal of the original, the good "white" swan comes to save the dying prince but is viciously attacked by his fellow swans for taking up with this alien being. The butch swans don't like the sissy prince much. There's no place for him in their fraternity. At the end, prince and swan are dead, but they appear transfigured, the swan cradling the boy prince in his wings as the grown prince lies dead. This is a gay fairy tale a tortured soul like Tchaikovsky could appreciate, a contemporary queer spin on a nineteenth-century classic. Part of the pleasure of the ballet is watching these beautiful men in their feathered pantaloons, cut almost to the crotch, perform these dances which celebrate the male body.

In the first act of this *Swan Lake* the queen, prince, and prince's girlfriend go to the ballet. What they see is a witty travesty of nineteenth-century ballet, complete with "manly" hero, wilting ballerina, and evil sorcerer, the very formula this production revises. What this *Swan Lake* has given us, though, is wilting hero and manly swan. Supposedly Matthew Bourne was taken aback when some Los Angeles gays saw the prince as a gay victim.[7] He's gay and he's a victim, but what probably shocked Bourne is that American gays tend to read everything through the lens of gay politics. Bourne wants us to read his *Swan Lake* through the lens of the original and what we now know about Tchaikovsky. The prince is now more like the tortured heroes of Tchaikovsky's operas than his ballets. Bourne's *Swan Lake* asks whether a late nineteenth-century homosexual sensibility and a late twentieth-century gay sensibility can be merged. When gorgeous Adam Cooper and his army of swans are on stage, one doesn't quibble about such matters. The dancing manages to be sexy and dangerous, something a Broadway chorus seldom accomplishes.

John Lahr, whose writing on gay theater represents a "liberal" straight point of view, says the duets in this *Swan Lake* are "not really about gay sex but about sexuality itself."[8] I'm not sure how a love duet with two men dancing is not about gay sex. Would the pas de deux of male dancer and ballerina be "not about straight sex"? Lahr's comment shows that straight critics' attempts at erasure of gayness continue. He is trying to universalize (i.e., straighten) Bourne's *Swan Lake* but in the process denies a crucial part of it. Bourne's *Swan Lake* is not *only* gay, but it is gay. What Lahr is doing isn't very different from what the musical has always done—denied its own gayness, closeted itself to make itself palatable to straight critics and audiences, even when it seemed to be gay. Bourne himself plays down the homoerotic element: "When the two men dance together in *Swan Lake,* it's not with a man, it's with a swan. It's a piece that should shock people, but doesn't."[9] At the same time, Bourne admits, "I find the male form a sexual thing and I like working with that."[10] Homoeroticism infuses the work even if one can believe the work isn't about homoeroticism.

The commentary circulating around Bourne's *Swan Lake* reflects the continuation of the open secret about dancers and chorus boys, a knowledge of the prevalence of homosexuality or bisexuality among dancers and homoeroticism in choreography combined with erasure in the name of "universality." Yet implicit in this sad tale in which both principals die (though in the mythology of Broadway immortality, they rise behind the scrim at the final curtain) is the potential for liberation from the stereotypes. The sexy lead swan is protean. He can transform his body and his desire. The prince is fixed in his identity and his sexuality. His dancing partner offers the freedom of theatricality we've always had in the chorus boys, who manage to escape the rigid narratives being enacted by the principals.

SONDHEIM AND I

In the spring of 1999 my play *Randy's House* was produced by Theater on the Square in Indianapolis, Indiana. What followed my play into that theater? *Sweeney Todd.* I'm sure this information is of no interest to Stephen Sondheim, but I was thrilled. My play was about how a gay couple dealt with the homophobia in their southern town. *Sweeney Todd* is about a heterosexual serial killer and has no gay characters. Is it gay theater? For many gay men, the answer is yes. Being part of a theater season that included Sondheim for a brief moment authorized me as a gay playwright.

Ten years ago, some of my colleagues at Duke wrote about reader response, the notion that the text is in the eye of the beholder. Gay men have always been experts at reading our own texts into musicals (and everything else). Indeed, the gay musical cult is built on such readings and identifications. Sondheim is a gay icon because his work seems highly susceptible to such readings, even though he doesn't acknowledge them. Though gay piano bars may favor the songs of Jerry Herman and Kander and Ebb, Sondheim's songs resonate powerfully with show queens. How does one talk about something so personal as that resonance without being personal? Autobiography seems unavoidable in this chapter, for my problem in writing on Sondheim is that I connect Sondheim musicals, particularly the early ones, to very important moments in my own life as a gay man.

For me, understanding the often discussed gay or closeted dimension of Sondheim's work is understanding where a lot of gay men were at the time his songs were written. Not that either Stephen Sondheim or I am "typical," if anyone outside of medieval drama or television commercials is "typical," but his work resonated with me, as it did with many individual gay men, because it spoke to something in our own experience. Sondheim is a dozen or so years older than I, which places him even further back in the history of gay identity and self-definition. Eve Kosofsky Sedgwick has written, "The closet is the defining structure for gay oppression in this century," and what is the closet but a system of proscriptions on language? In the fifties and sixties, the closet meant "Thou shalt not say 'I am gay' unless the other person says it first." If one did find a group of congenial gay friends in the pre-liberation days, one's conversation was often a less pitying version of Mart Crowley's *The Boys in the Band* (1968), a play that, however exasperating, was a revelation to us. Sondheim called it "the shot heard 'round the world."[1] Yes, Virginia, people did talk like that. Being gay meant being witty in a deconstructive way and/ or being camp. *The Boys in the Band* may have presented its characters as sometimes tedious victims of self-pity, but it also presented what language sounded like inside the closet. Where had people heard that language before? In Edward Albee's *Who's Afraid of Virginia Woolf* (1962) and in the camp extravaganza *Anyone Can Whistle* (1964), a show doomed on Broadway but a bellwether for the intersection of gay and mainstream theater that would happen elsewhere temporally and geographically.

Stephen Sondheim is not just a composer-lyricist of a score of musicals written over the past forty-plus years. He has become a paradoxical phenomenon: a composer who has had few songs that can count as pop hits and few shows that made money for their producers and investors, yet who is considered the leading composer of Broadway shows of the past generation. Revivals of Sondheim musicals are major events in New York and London. No other Broadway composer has as many cast recordings of his shows. Every revival gets a new recording including some new or revised songs Sondheim has added. At this writing, there are four major recordings of *Company,* five of *Follies,* five of *A Little Night Music,* even multiple recordings of the commercial flops *Anyone Can Whistle* (3), *Merrily We Roll Along* (3), *Passion* (2) and *Pacific Overtures* (2), as well as recordings of every major Sondheim gala and necessary albums like the Bernadette Peters Carnegie Hall Sondheim concert. Sondheim devotees, like me, have them all. He is the subject of a variety of books: a comprehensive biography, critical studies of his works, histories of the productions of his musicals, doctoral dissertations, chapters in other books from the laudatory to the scurrilous, and a raft of newspaper, magazine, and journal articles. I almost shudder to add more words to the Sondheim critical canon. My interest here is in Sondheim the gay icon, in itself a paradox. Sondheim galas are often sponsored by gay charities and are attended by a large number of gay men. There is a large proportion of gay men in the audience at performances of

Sondheim musicals and gay men are considered his core audience. I remember going to a performance of *Passion* in London a few years ago. The theater was less than half full, but it was like a reunion. I saw gay acquaintances from Maryland, Florida, and New York in that audience.

Sondheim's great following, his core audience, is the dwindling army of show queens who care about musical theater. Indeed, an excessive love of Sondheim musicals is another gay stereotype. In Terrence McNally's *The Lisbon Traviata,* a gay character plays *Sweeney Todd* to impress a date. There is truth to the stereotype, though it is a stereotype of one kind of gay man, urban and of a certain age. To us, Sondheim is something of an icon, a composer-lyricist who speaks to us. There is a Sondheim cult and most of its members are gay. Gay men I know who don't like Sondheim feel they have to express their dislike defensively, as if they know it's a failing, a deficiency in the gay gene, what Billy in *Billy's Hollywood Screen Kiss* calls "the show tune gene." Yet Sondheim has never written a gay character or a song about gay desire and has tended to argue against gay readings of a character like Bobby in *Company,* who for many of us has to be a gay character. There's only one song about a gay person, the hilarious, oft performed cabaret number "The Boy From . . ." (music by Mary Rodgers) that he wrote for *The Mad Show* (1966). The song, a parody of the sixties Antonio Carlos Jobim hit "The Girl from Ipanema," is a woman's lament over the fact that a beautiful Spaniard who comes from an unpronounceable, multisyllabic town, doesn't return her affection. The humor of the song is in the woman's inability to read the Spaniard's obvious and stereotypical signs of gayness:

> Why are his trousers vermilion?
> Why does he claim he'th Cathtilian?
> Why do his friends call him Lillian?[2]

The punch line of the song is not that "The Boy From . . ." is gay, but that he moves from an unpronounceable Spanish town to an unpronounceable Welsh one. The song is an extended fag joke, but an extremely witty one that has become a cabaret repertory staple. That's it. Sondheim's gay lyric.

His most ostensibly autobiographical show, *Sunday in the Park with George,* is about an artist who places his art above his private (heterosexual) life. What muse George Seurat has is definitely heterosexual. At the end, Seurat's grandson, a conceptual artist also named George, is cured of his emotional problems by his professional vocation. *Sunday in the Park with George* is a boon to those who mythologize Sondheim as an uncompromising artist savaged by ignorant critics. Actually, Sondheim has been championed by *The New York Times* drama critics. His three shows with James Lapine (*Sunday in the Park with George, Into the Woods,* and *Passion*) contain gorgeous music but beg all sorts of questions. The former sees art as impersonal and unerotic and never resolves the story of its contemporary character, George. Instead it gives us a reprise of the magnificent finale to Act I, as if that had anything to do with Act II. I don't believe Sondheim is so able to keep his libido at bay when he creates, though he may want us to think he does. *Into the Woods* is best when it's dark, worst when it tries for talk of community and cooperation instead of Sondheim's strongest themes of isolation and alienation. It's no wonder that "No One Is Alone" sounds like Sammy Davis, Jr.'s gooey hit, "Candy Man." *Into the Woods* is best read as a coming-out allegory—the traps that wait when you face your sexuality and admit to it. It has also been interpreted as a response to the AIDS epidemic.

It is only recently that Sondheim has to any extent come out publicly, yet I have often wondered if the antipathy some straight folks have toward Sondheim's work isn't connected to an unsettling sense that heterosexuality is being seen from the outside, an awareness that some straights in the audience are being criticized, even mocked, by someone with a superior attitude toward them. However, as with Oscar Wilde, beneath Sondheim's sharp wit there is an enormous amount of compassion and empathy for his characters. Often in his musicals of the 1970s there is a tension between the facile, bitchy wit of the books by the likes of George Furth and Hugh Wheeler and the richness and compassion of Sondheim's lyrics, as there is between the intimacy of his narratives and the grandiose productions they often received.

Meryle Secrest's conscientious biography of Sondheim is candid about the fact that Sondheim is gay, but not clear about what that means. A queer theorist like Judith Butler would ask, "What are you telling me when you tell me Sondheim is gay?" There is no monolithic "gay" any more than there is a monolithic "heterosexual": different strokes for different folks. The key question is: What does Sondheim's sexuality have to do with his work? The answer to that is determined in part by the age in which he grew up. Sondheim told his biographer about his attitude to his sexuality as a young man: "I was never easy with being a homosexual, which complicates things. I don't think I knew more than four homosexuals in the fifties and sixties who were openly so. . . . Everybody knew the theater was full of homosexuals but nobody admitted to being so."[3] Sondheim was born in 1930 and began work in the theater in the repressive fifties. Though his collaborators were often gay, this was not something you admitted. The Tony Award ceremonies in the fifties were not the grand coming-out ceremonies they became in the nineties (though, ironically, the Tonys have become less openly gay since Rosie O'Donnell, a personality whose own sexual orientation has been the subject of gossip and speculation, has become their star). Writing musicals was working within the world of popular entertainment built on heterosexual fantasy. Sondheim recalls, "I had the idealistic notion, when I was twenty, that I was going into the theater. I wasn't; I was going into show business, and I was a fool to think otherwise."[4] In show business, you give the public the fantasies they want, including the fantasy of compulsory heterosexuality. Like most of his colleagues in musical theater, Sondheim was Jewish, and Jewish people in the entertainment industry had for decades closeted their Jewishness in their work to appeal to a mass audience. It isn't surprising that a group of men closeted about their Jewishness in their work would also be closeted about their gayness. Leonard Bernstein once proclaimed, "To be a successful composer of musicals, you either have to be Jewish or gay. And I'm both."[5] Bernstein was right, but success also depended on not being openly gay.

Through therapy, Sondheim came to realize homosexuality was not his primary problem: "It was about not being open to let someone else into my life. I had thought it was all about homosexuality, but when homosexuality became the lingua franca [after Stonewall] it didn't affect me at all."[6] This is the problem in most Sondheim musicals: letting someone else in. In *Anyone Can Whistle,* Nurse Fay can't loosen up and whistle; in *Company,* Bobby can't commit to another; in *Follies,* Ben and Buddy can't open up to their wives; in *Sunday in the Park with George,* Seurat can only reach out through his art; in *Passion,* Giorgio has to learn that love takes total commitment. Mary Rodgers says that Sondheim "was terrified, not of giving love, but of having to get it."[7] Sondheim may argue with autobiographical readings of his work, but this fear of someone breaking through the shell permeates his work:

> Someone to hold you too close
> Someone to hurt you too deep.[8]

This fear may be universal, but it has special import for gay men, educated within their own families that they are doomed to loneliness and unhappiness. It was particularly powerful for gay men brought up in a time when blackmail was a distinct possibility and exposure brought ruin. If you didn't dare trust anyone, how could you love? This lyric from *Company* shows that for Sondheim even the desire for love contains more than a hint of masochism. The desired someone "hurts too deep," both an emotional and a physical image, reflecting fear of intimacy and fear of penetration. This image only becomes more violent in *Passion* a quarter of a century later:

> A love that, like a knife,

Has cut into a life
I wanted left alone.[9]

The penetration now becomes violent. Is this surgery or stabbing, violent penetration or castration, or all of the above?

Underneath the wit and irony of Sondheim lyrics are anguish and terror. I have always been baffled by the cliched attacks on Sondheim's work as being too cool, too cerebral, too clever. I have always found the words passionate, naked in their presentation of a terror of intimacy combined with a desire for love. The music either soars with a mix of lyricism and anguish or is crabbed, tense, fearful. What is disturbing about Sondheim's works is not their coolness but their heat, made complex through irony and wit. Sondheim's emotional dramas are laid out in heterosexual patterns, but they also fit into the themes of closeted gay drama of the sixties. There is also a rage in Sondheim that bubbles up to the surface. His characters are angry. It's no surprise that he would write musicals about serial killers and presidential assassins. Such anger resonated with key moments in gay history of the past thirty years as much as the cleverness, camp, and irony. Perhaps that's what's gayest about Sondheim: the fusion of anger and irony once considered a crucial element of the gay stereotype.

It is good to have a biography of Sondheim like Secrest's that is not as offensive or defensive about his gayness as his critics have been, but if we are to believe the book, Sondheim was virtually a virgin when he met Peter Jones in 1991, which is unlikely. Moreover, in adherence to an old Freudian formula, the root of all evil is Sondheim's monster mother, Foxy. Those of us who know from monster mothers are aware that they cause a number of hang-ups but are at best a contributing factor to our homosexuality. Believe it or not, many straight men also have monster mothers. There are even, I am told, some straight men who have problems with intimacy. While Sondheim's homosexuality may have been a problem for him, it may also have enabled him to break the theatrical conventions set and maintained by his straight predecessors. It may have made it easier for gay artists like Arthur Laurents to want Sondheim as a collaborator on three important musicals: *West Side Story, Gypsy,* and *Anyone Can Whistle.* Would his core audience have been as devoted if he had been straight?

MEMORIES

West Side Story was not a smash hit in 1957. *My Fair Lady, The Pajama Game, Damn Yankees, Bells Are Ringing,* and *The Sound of Music* were the big hits of the fifties. *West Side Story* broke what were fairly hard-and-fast rules about

Broadway musicals. It was a show for young people, but Broadway audiences were middle-aged. I saw the original production of *West Side Story* at the Winter Garden on my sixteenth birthday and was ravished by this show about how kids feel, about adolescent energy defined by dancing. We didn't have rumbles in the suburbs, but we sure loved to dance. *West Side Story* was certainly the sexiest show I had ever seen. All those cute young men in their tight jeans dancing away and forging strong male bonds. In his book *The Gay Metropolis,* Charles Kaiser devotes a fair amount of space to the 1957 musical *West Side Story* as an event for gay men. It is the only musical Kaiser discusses at length:

> To many gay adults coming of age in the sixties, the romance, violence, danger, and mystery so audible on the original cast album all felt like integral parts of the gay life they had embraced. The lyrics of "Somewhere" in particular seemed to speak directly to the gay experience before the age of liberation.[10]

For me, Larry Kert's plaintive singing of "Something's Coming" seemed to define the hopes of the fifties adolescent, particularly one who knew that he wanted something that seemed impossible, even unspeakable, in 1957. Then, a few years later, we had Richard Beymer playing Tony in the film, whose performance only magnified the sense that the possibilities Tony sang of might include me.

I felt the same way when I sat in a box at the Imperial Theater in 1960 watching *Gypsy* with a college friend I had a crush on—something, of course we never talked about. Years later, long after college, we both admitted we were gay. As a matter of fact, both of us have spent our careers writing about gayness, but then it was something to be hidden and, one hoped, overcome. *Gypsy* is a great show under any circumstances, but particularly under those. In the fifties, and 1960 was still the fifties, simply being with the object of one's affection was, if not enough, all we thought possible. Ethel Merman barreled down the aisle with the force of a freight train and gave us a brilliant version of the fierce, brave, but terrifying mothers we both had lived with, combined with a joyous, scary celebration of the tacky but seductive world of showbiz.

A few years later, I howled through *A Funny Thing Happened on the Way to the Forum* (1962) with another Object of My Affection, a beautiful young man who was constantly telling me that his friends thought we were having a homosexual relationship (something one didn't say in 1962). It was wishful thinking on both our parts, but we'll always have *Forum*. Three decades later a more-or-less openly gay performer would star in a revival of *Forum* that would be a bigger hit than the original production. He would be replaced by a black woman in male drag (Whoopi Goldberg).

Forum was the first Broadway show with a Sondheim score and that was a shock in 1962. It didn't sound like Jule Styne, for me at twenty the model for what a Broadway score should sound like. It was quirky, totally original. The ballads were more ironic and hilarious than the patter songs, the rhythms and intervals of which were constantly surprising. Those weird intervals at the top of the overture made this twenty-year-old "expert" wonder if Sondheim knew what he was doing.

Anyone Can Whistle appeared during the period in which Tennessee Williams and even William Inge were following Edward Albee's lead and turning to absurdism and a more flamboyant theatrical style. They and other gay artists were trying to move the theater out of the straitjacket of psychological realism and straight critics were screaming bloody murder.

Anyone Can Whistle contains one of those parade songs that seemed necessary to musicals at the time. Sondheim's evil diva, Mayoress Cora Hoover Hooper, sings a parade song about being out of the loop, unhappily out of step with the rest of society:

> Tell me, while I was getting ready
> Did a parade go by?[11]

Everyone in *Anyone Can Whistle* is an outsider who wants to be included, acknowledged, loved. The show is a celebration of what in the mid-sixties would still be called the abnormal. No one amongst this crop of abnormal people admits to being homosexual (this is a pre "gay" show), but the crypto-gay subtext is clear. "Everybody says don't," Hapgood, the hero, tells us, "Well I say do."

Could two straight men have written *Anyone Can Whistle* in 1964? It not only built on earlier groundbreaking shows like *On the Town* (eccentric characters and lots of dance) and *Lady in the Dark* (psychotherapy and act-ending mini-operas) but constantly gave the finger to normalcy, though never openly questioning compulsory heterosexuality. Was there any woman on stage in 1964 more camp than villainess Cora Hoover Hooper? She makes Dolly Levi, unveiled on Broadway a few months before, look positively staid. Dolly Levi, a benevolent cartoon, sang Jerry Herman songs, which are pumped-up versions of Jule Styne songs, generic show tunes. Cora, a comic book meanie, more Mama Rose than Dolly, sang parodies of jazzy nightclub tunes, complete with manic doo-wah male backup quartet. The style was pure camp. Cora had no boyfriend in the show, which took her out of the context of heterosexual romance and allowed for a gay reading. She also sashayed through much of the show in pants. One song that was cut from the original production was "There's Always a Woman," a supremely bitchy cat fight that's also laced with the misogyny that tainted gay culture in the years before Stonewall:

> She almost looks human—
> It must be the lighting.
> Whatever it is, it's a woman.[12]

At one point in the song's name-calling, Cora's nemesis, Nurse Fay, calls her a "fish," the old nasty gay term for a female—a telling one-word peep from the closet.

Anyone Can Whistle has never had a major revival, though in 1995 a concert version, a benefit for the Gay Men's Health Crisis, was a gay A-list event complete with adoring audience and, like the famous 1985 benefit concert version of Follies, recorded. Angela Lansbury narrates, Madeline Kahn does her Madeline Kahn schtick, and Bernadette Peters, who has become to Sondheim what Callas was to Bellini, took on the role of Nurse Fay Apple in which Lee Remick was beautiful but bland. Peters is over the top from her first lines of dialogue and the audience loves it. In his extremely homophobic book on musical theater, Broadway Babies Say Goodnight, Mark Steyn spends a chapter attacking Sondheim and his fans in which he says:

> It's a strange experience to take a "normal" person to a Sondheim gala, and
> watch the mystified looks as the first line of, say, "There Won't Be Trumpets"
> is greeted with delirious applause. "There Won't Be Trumpets" was cut from
> Anyone Can Whistle. . . . To be cut from a Sondheim flop is as high praise as
> you can get.[13]

Steyn, being "normal," doesn't get the gay adulation of Sondheim. Nor does he get the appropriateness to a gay man of Nurse Fay Apple's song of hope for the man of her dreams. Yes, that song was cut from a flop, but like that of Hart and Porter, Sondheim's success often comes in spite of the shows his songs were written for. Many of his songs are what might be called "gay standards," songs with particular meaning for gay men. Before Sondheim there was the all-time locus classicus, "Over the Rainbow." In the fifties we had Doris Day singing "Secret Love," a few years later "Strangers in the Night" ("doo bee doo bee doo"). Now we have Sondheim, whose songs allow space for gay men to find their own experience. So, yes, Bernadette Peters, who began at the legendary gay coffee house Caffe Cino, singing Sondheim gets cheered in ways "normal" people wouldn't understand.

Yes, I did see Anyone Can Whistle one-and-a-half times during previews in 1964 (I snuck in at one of its intermissions the second time). I thought it was brilliant, though one was very lonely in the balcony of the Majestic Theater during those previews. There was no TKTS booth then to sell discount tickets and to lure folks who otherwise wouldn't see a particular show. I had gone into New York to find the young man with whom I had had my first passionate affair, a person with whom I had nothing in common except sex, but something in my genetic makeup or my totally inadequate sexual education told me that you loved forever the person you had sex with. I discovered this young man was having sex with a lot of people, often for pay. I was traumatized. So I went to have a drink with one of my best friends from high school who was working in New York. He clearly was traumatized about something too, but we didn't talk about it. Actually, he too was traumatized about the loss of a boyfriend. All those years of friendship and we never talked about *it!* I left him moping at the bar of the Four Seasons—if you're going to mope, do it in style—and went to see *Anyone Can Whistle.* If we could have talked we could have commiserated, but you didn't talk unless you knew for sure. So between the Four Seasons and the Majestic Theater I decided that day that gay life was not for me. I would bury myself in my graduate studies and figure out after my Ph.D. what kind of life I would have, if any. When the time came to look for jobs, I avoided offers from California and New York (lead us not into temptation) and settled in Durham, North Carolina. "Once you see, you can't stay blind,"[14] but who knew that then? While I am making this momentous, silly decision, Sondheim is having a romance of sorts with his gorgeous leading lady, Lee Remick. After *Anyone Can Whistle,* Sondheim disappeared from view and so did I. Into the bowels of the Harvey Firestone Memorial Library, followed by the depths of Durham. A couple of years later, I would marry.

> Oh, how gently we'll talk,
> Oh, how softly we'll tread.
> All the stings, the ugly things
> We'll keep unsaid.[15]

Cut to May 1970, the day after the National Guard did some killing on the campus of Kent State University. A few weeks before, I had separated amicably from my wife of three years. Marriage and the prospect of a child had thrown me into a depression. However wonderful my wife was, heterosexual marriage and the thought of dwindling into the gray, unhappy couples we saw in Durham, North Carolina, horrified me. All this was set off by a powerful, unrequited crush on a male student. I was still under thirty and the lure of his . . . whatever (I don't now know or remember what lured me) was the most important thing in my psychic life at the time. In general, my psychic life was turbulent. I had come under the ministration of an elderly German psychiatrist, Heidelberg dueling scar and all, who would "treat" me and help me decide what sort of love life I wanted as long as I had none while he was treating me. Big loss. What sort of love life could I have in Durham in 1970? When I would mention my desire for men he would ask, "Do you vant to be like ze old men in ze park?" Which park? He wasn't particularly helpful.

Anyway, said beloved young man and I—as "pals"—went to New York and got standing room tickets to *Company,* which a few weeks before had received some of the most euphoric notices I had ever read. To make the trip more fun, we were being trailed by a detective hired, not by my wife, but by her brother, who was not happy with the concept of an amicable settlement. Real soap opera.

Company is about the relationship of a thirty-five-year-old bachelor, Bobby, with his married friends. Bobby avoids anything but sex and limited friendship with the women in his life. The women are painfully aware of Bobby's limitations:

> You impersonate a person better
> Than a zombie should.[16]

But Bobby fears anything resembling total commitment to someone who might know him "too well."

The couples who are Bobby's social life all have their own problems. At best, marriage is a mixed bag, causing the men to be "sorry-grateful, regretful-happy." At worst, marriage is a kind of mutual torture, filled with verbal or physical sparring. Fear of love is compounded by the fear that, even if one found a partner, one has nothing positive to offer. Amy's hilarious "Getting Married Today" is really a song of self-hatred:

> A wedding, what's a wedding?
> It's a prehistoric ritual
> Where everybody promises fidelity forever,
> Which is maybe the most horrifying word I ever heard.[17]

Amy can't believe Paul can possibly love unlovable, crazy her. Her sense of inadequacy is one with which gay men of the period, "carefully taught" self-hatred, resonated. The horrifying word in Amy's cry of terror is not "fidelity" but "forever." Sondheim's musicals are not love stories, but marriage stories, about the possibility of love through time, of love lasting, yet his focus is on men who cannot commit to another person.

Eventually, through the help of cynical Joanne, a Vera Simpson for the seventies, Bobby is scared into realizing what he is missing. Joanne propositions Bobby and tells him she'll take care of him, which leads him to ask: "But who will I take care of?"[18] Then, in one of the great eleven o'clock songs of musical theater, "Being Alive," Bobby moves from fear to longing. In a frightening, lonely world, love is the only saving possibility, though love itself, according to the lyric, is bound to be qualified, violent, and claustrophobic. Sondheim's first songs for Bobby's final number were far from affirming. *Company*'s first director, Hal Prince, remembers:

> We had a song for Robert to sing called "Happily Ever After." It was the bitterest, most unhappy song ever written, and we didn't know how devastating it would be until we saw it in front of an audience . . . If I heard that song I wouldn't get married for anything in the whole world.[19]

"Being Alive" isn't one hundred percent convincing. What got Bobby to this qualified epiphany? A cautious proposition from a male friend, and a more overt one from the drag queen surrogate. After "Being Alive," Bobby disappears to start a new life apart from the world of his married friends. Gay men read Bobby's disappearance as a move from the world of compulsory heterosexuality, the usual world of the musical, to an uncharted, unseen world of homosexuality. Otherwise, why cut all ties? In 1970, coming out often meant cutting ties with one's straight friends—or we thought it did. And the society of those friends— being the third at dinner, the baby-sitter to their kids—was often a way of staving off loneliness and the feared plunge into what was still a mysterious, frightening gay possibility. Bobby, we thought, left one world to come out in another. Did Sondheim write this in? No, but come on, Robert (note he's never butch Bob; he's diminutive Bobby or Robert. Who but gay men in the seventies used their formal first names instead of a nickname?) is thirty-five, a zombie emotionally with the women he beds, but the safe best buddy of half a dozen wives. In "You Could Drive a Person Crazy," Bobby's girlfriends sing:

> I could understand a person
> If a person was a fag.[20]

Exactly. Gay men in 1970 and since read Bobby as gay. A few years later, an openly gay Bobby could still dish with the wives but have a romantic life of his own, or a bisexual Bobby would be sleeping unproblematically with April and Peter. But to those of us who knew how hard it was to face the Great Unknown in 1970, *Company* was Truth. And there were, as one of my friends called signs of gayness, "hints of mint" in *Company*. Flight attendant April's male roommate, never seen, must have been gay. And, of course, there was Elaine Stritch dominating the proceedings with her whisky baritone voice. Stritch stood out in *Company,* the diva in an ensemble show who gets the big diva number, "The Ladies Who Lunch." Like the diva performances I describe in Chapter 3, there is a drag queen quality to Elaine Stritch's Joanne. I have seen other actresses play Joanne better (particularly Sheila Gish in Sam Mendes's 1996 London production), but the part is forever identified with Stritch's over-the-top-camp performance. Night after night her "The Ladies Who Lunch" got the sort of wild ovation one usually hears in the opera house. How could you not read a gay subtext when Stritch is the dominating presence? Coincidentally, Stritch played Martha at the matinees of Edward Albee's *Who's Afraid of Virginia Woolf?*

But that's my reading—and the reading of many of my contemporaries. Sondheim, wedded to the mores of Broadway, avoided the subject in 1970 or denied any gay reading. Yet even straight writers like William Goldman could exclaim: "I remember seeing *Company* five times and I loved it, and I had a huge, fucking problem, which is that the main character's gay but they don't talk about it."[21]

There is good reason for Sondheim's caution. He came of age in the theater when the critical establishment, on whom the success of a show often depended, were virulently homophobic. In 1963, the year before Sondheim and Arthur Laurents brought *Anyone Can Whistle* to Broadway, Howard Taubman, then drama critic of *The New York Times,* wrote a Sunday "Arts and Leisure" feature titled "Modern Primer: Helpful Hints to Tell Appearances from Truth." The play on a line from *Who's Afraid of Virginia Woolf?* made Taubman's principal target clear. Taubman wasn't interested in epistemology; he was interested in warning his audience about "intimations and symbols of homosexuality in our theater."[22] Ironically, Taubman's catalogue of signs of homosexuality in a play would place *Company* and *Follies* on the suspect list:

> Look out for the male character who is young, handsome, remote and
>   lofty in a neutral way.
> Beware the husband who hasn't touched his wife for years.
> Beware the woman who hasn't been touched by her husband for years.
> Look out for the baneful female who is a libel on womanhood.
> Look out for the hideous wife who makes a horror of the marriage relationship.
> Be alert to scabrous innuendo about the normal male-female sexual relationship.

The price for placing any signs of gayness on the stage other than a comic travesty of a sissy or a sensitive, suicidal young man was critical censure. Of course Sondheim and his collaborators would be cautious. The question is: Why is Sondheim still cautious?

Not surprisingly, some critics saw the queer potential in *Company* as its weakness. Martin Gottfried, at one time the critic for *Women's Wear Daily,* sounded the alarm in his review of *Company*. He warned that Dean Jones, the original Bobby, "can seem sexless and must watch it or the show's theme (and honesty) will be confused by hints of homosexuality."[23] This is typical of the sort of homophobic criticism Broadway shows—and gay men—faced even after Stonewall. Seeming "sexless" was a sign of homosexuality. A hint of homosexuality confused a show's "honesty" rather than made a show more honest. In 1970, critics could still insist that nature and honesty were only heterosexual. Sondheim, a gay man raised in the commercial theater, knew he had to accommodate this attitude. If the critics felt this way, so would much of the audience. Ironically, straight Dean Jones was replaced by gay Larry Kert whom, according to Sondheim and Prince, audiences liked more. Nine years later, Gottfried would write:

> It is such pessimism toward marriage and the hero's inability to love that makes
> his heterosexuality suspect. Depending on one's sensitivity toward this, a subtle
> element of homosexuality might be considered a distracting element of
> *Company.*

Again, interesting assumptions. Heterosexual men never are unable to love or never are pessimistic about marriage? As late as 1990, in her rather superficial book on Sondheim, *Art Isn't Easy,* Joanne Gordon vehemently denied any gay subtext to *Company:* "Critics who dwell on Robert's possible homosexuality are clearly uncomfortable with the show's, antiromantic unsentimental depiction of marriage."[24] The astute Gerald Mast sees and does not criticize that "subtle, distracting element" of homosexuality, though he does subtly "out" the show's creators:

> Perhaps Robert has discovered [at the end of the show] that he needs company—
> but not with heterosexual couples and female companions. The gay subtext of
> the show—Sondheim and Furth know about unmarried men in a coupled
> world—peeks out of the closet at its conclusion.[25]

Homophobe or homosexual, everyone but *Company*'s creators see that Bobby only makes sense as a gay character. As D. A. Miller vividly puts it, they repudiate "the possibility of gay representation with an emphasis that couldn't be firmer if they were organizing a St. Patrick's Day Parade. We, then, end up falling into the same furious incomprehension as Bobby's other girlfriends: we could understand a person if a person was a fag, but if he was not, he must be as crazy as he makes us."[26]

When *Company* was revived in 1995 in a disappointing, unimaginative production by Scott Ellis, the director, in interviews in the gay press, proclaimed his gayness but maintained Bobby's straightness, thus outing himself while closeting his production. Witnesses who saw Boyd Gaines (I saw his understudy who played Bobby as an affable, vacuous "straight-looking and -acting" guy but sang the music magnificently) tell me his Bobby seemed obviously gay. The revival foundered nonetheless.

The excellent 1996 London revival, directed by Sam Mendes, interpolated a scene in Act II between Bobby and Peter that had been cut from the original production. The dialogue at least raises the possibility of a homosexual relationship. Peter, you may remember, is the man who could only live happily with Susan after they divorced. Alone on the terrace, Peter asks Bobby if he has ever had a homosexual experience:

> ROBERT: Well, yes, actually, yes, I have.
>
> PETER: You're not gay, are you?
>
> ROBERT: No, no. Are you?
>
> PETER: No, no, for chrissake. But I've done it more than once, though.
>
> ROBERT: Is that a fact?
>
> PETER: Oh, I think sometimes you meet somebody and you just love the crap out of them. Y'know?
>
> ROBERT: Oh, absolutely, I'm sure that's true.
>
> PETER: And sometimes you just want to manifest that love, that's all.
>
> ROBERT: Yes I understand. Absolutely.
>
> PETER: I think that sometimes you can even know someone for, oh, a long, long time and then suddenly, out of nowhere, you just want to have them—I mean, even an old friend. You just, all of a sudden, desire that intimacy. That closeness.
>
> ROBERT: Probably.
>
> PETER: Oh, I'm convinced that two men really would, if it wasn't for society and all the conventions and all that crap, just go off and ball and be better off for it, closer, deeper, don't you think?
>
> ROBERT: Well, I—I don't know.
>
> PETER: I mean like us, for example. Do you think that you and I could ever have anything like that?
>
> ROBERT (*Looks at him for a long and uncomfortable moment. Then a big smile*): Oh, I get it. You're putting me on. Man, you really had me going there, you son of a gun.[27]

I think the writers inserted this scene to close off the speculation that Bobby will end up with a man, but the dialogue is too ambiguous for that. What does Bobby's long silence mean? That Bobby is seriously considering Peter's question/offer? If so, what stops him? That Bobby isn't interested in Peter, or in an affair with a man, or in an affair with half of a couple he's friends with? Or does Bobby come close to accepting Peter's offer but simply can't step over that line into homosexual sex with someone he likes and who truly likes him? Most important, if Bobby has had relationships with men, why isn't one of them in the cast of characters along with or in place of Marta, April, and Kathy? *Company*'s book writer, George Furth, always conceived of Bobby as straight—someone like Warren Beatty.[28] Nonetheless, the end product raises a lot of questions.

Bobby has always been a problem for performers. Dean Jones was constantly frustrated during his short run in the part. He told Tony Perkins on opening night, "Man, I really tried. I tried to make this part mine, but I couldn't."[29] How could he be the star when Stritch was on stage? Jones was bland, but so is Bobby. The trouble with *Company* is the same as with *Follies*. The show centers on the dilemma of a man who isn't a very interesting character for a musical. Audiences—as usual—cared far more about the women than about Bobby. Only Sam Mendes's London production with the charismatic black actor Adrian Lester as Bobby literally kept Bobby in the foreground. We were to believe that most of the show took place in Bobby's memory or imagination as he decided whether to attend the surprise party. Would Bobby be more interesting if he were gay and on the verge of belatedly coming out? It would at least give him a more definite problem.

There I stood, in May 1970, at the back of the then Alvin Theater, sweet (I thought then) young man at my side, absolutely emotionally rocked by this musical, seeing myself as Bobby and, like the musical, seeing no real option for my life except a heartfelt cry for love. I was in pain at that point and *Company* seemed another cry of pain that resonated powerfully. Bobby walks off the heterosexual stage and into the unknown at the end of the show. I felt I was on the verge of doing the same thing.

Like many show queens, I became a devotee of Sondheim because of *Company,* so much so that when I finally fell head over heels in love in 1976, the year of *Pacific Overtures,* I fell for a Bobby the night he told me how strongly he identified with that character. Oops!

> Knock, knock, a zombie's in my arms.

Nineteen seventy-one, a year after *Company,* and I had to see *Follies*—for me up there with *Gypsy* as one of the greatest of musicals—even before it formally opened. *Follies* was not a commercial success in its 1971 New York production nor in its 1987 London revival, but it is a cult show for show queens.

I know, from the number of cheering gay men in the audience that Saturday afternoon in 1971, that from the beginning it had a personal significance for lots of us. The 1998 revival at the Paper Mill Playhouse also had a large, mostly middle-aged gay contingent. A British friend of mine flew over to the States to see this *Follies.* He asked friends in New York how he would find the Paper Mill Playhouse when he reached the Millburn train station. They said, "Don't worry. Just follow the procession of queens." Sure enough, the train was filled with gay men on a pilgrimage to *Follies.*

Follies is a lament for a lost age of female star glamour and a celebration of the survival of formerly glamorous women. It is also an examination of failed heterosexual romance set in juxtaposition to youthful romantic fantasy, all laden with the sort of irony that was central to gay culture of the time. *Follies* is set at a revival of "Weismann Girls" (read "Ziegfeld Girls") just before the theater in which Weismann's lavish revues were staged is to be torn down. There the women reenact their star turns, sing of their unhappiness in the "real world" and of their survival. Weismann's theater is filled with ghosts of the characters' former, young selves. The two leading women, the sophisticated Phyllis and the simpler Sally, are at turning points in their own unhappy marriages. Phyllis is totally dissatisfied with her childless marriage to her successful, unhappy husband, Ben. Sally still pines for Ben, while Sally's husband, Buddy, cannot choose between his wife, whom he idolizes, and his mistress. Present conflicts alternate with flashbacks as their unhappy encounters alternate with their courtships, enacted by the ghosts of their younger, idealistic selves. Just as things come to a head, the show switches into a lavish Follies in which Sally, Buddy, Phyllis, and Ben perform elaborate star turns that depict their present unhappiness, punctuated by the optimistic tunes of their younger selves. Some audiences found the originally intermissionless three-hour musical too dark and bitter, but show queens read their own show and their own lives into *Follies,* particularly into its brilliant musical numbers.

Phyllis and Sally, the two women whose unhappy marriages are the focus of the musical, were never divas on stage. They were among the "beautiful girls," not the stars. They were chorus girls who married men who became "successful" in the material sense in which American success is usually measured. Unfortunately, their husbands are experiencing crippling versions of male menopause.

The many editions of the *Ziegfeld Follies* and its clones, the Shuberts' *Passing Shows,* the *Earl Carroll Vanities,* were glorifications of women as ornaments. The shows were named after their producers, not the directors or designers who created them (more important in spectacle than the authors), the writers or composers, or the women who paraded in those headdresses. These shows, named after men, were created for men to look at women in the context of a night's easy entertainment. The women, like those in Busby Berkeley's grand extravaganzas, were faces and bodies. Irving Berlin's "A Pretty Girl Is Like a Melody" is the song we most associate with those grand parades of leggy chorines: a "melody" but no words to suggest a brain or an individual personality. In Sondheim's pastiche of the Berlin song, the inevitable tenor sings a hymn to "Beautiful Girls." In this celebration, women are ornaments but also naughty, available—a male fantasy. Yet Sondheim is celebrating another aspect of women that didn't interest Ziegfeld, women's strength:

> This is how Samson was shorn:
> Each in her style a Delilah reborn.[30]

The only thing that can threaten these women is the American malaise, a sense of emptiness, a gut feeling that there is nothing under their beautiful appearance as their husbands feel there is nothing under their success:

> In the depths of her interior
> Were fears she was inferior
> And something even eerier.[31]

This malaise only occurs to those who risk love, which replaces the mirror with the face of the partner, which can be seen to be judging even when it isn't. Underneath *Follies* is a love-hate relationship with love—on the part of the characters and their creators. In the "Loveland" sequence, Young Buddy and Young Sally sing "Love will see us through till something better comes along." Unfortunately, nothing better does come along and love is impossible if one doesn't love oneself. Buddy's problem is cogently described in the refrain to his Follies number:

> I've got those
> "God why don't you love me oh you do I'll see you later"
> Blues.[32]

Sally and Phyllis, the ex-chorines, are tortured by regrets. The former stars of the Weismann Follies, however, have no such laments about their past lives. As former soprano Heidi Schiller sings in the Lehár-like aria, "One More Kiss," "Never look back." Heidi has survived intact by living for her art: "Facts never interest me. What matters is the song."[33] Hattie Walker, like her younger self, still hopes for another grand moment on stage: "Hell I'd even play the maid / To be in a show."[34] Divas may age—gracefully like Heidi, or flamboyantly like Carlotta Campion—but they survive. They are no longer the "Beautiful Girls" Roscoe sings of. Beautiful girls aren't divas. Divas are survivors, proud of their battle scars. Carlotta's hymn of survival through decades of show business, "I'm Still Here," became a classic and represents the credo of the diva, a strong contrast to the women who are in crisis because of the men in their lives. Carlotta moves from one young boy-toy to another, taking what she wants and moving on. Phyllis has also slept with young men, but more out of anger at her husband than a sense of sexual freedom. It isn't the divas in *Follies* who live in a time warp; it is the women who live through men, reliving their past romance because the present isn't happy. Divas adapt. They live out Sondheim's notion of the show's theme: "It's about how all your hopes tarnish and how if you live on regret and despair, you might as well pack up, for to live in the past is foolish."[35]

The original cast of *Follies* was a bizarre mix. B-movie actress Alexis Smith, who had a lesbian following, made a triumphant Broadway debut as the wry Phyllis. *Your Hit Parade* radio and TV star Dorothy Collins was Sally. These leading women were supported by Broadway old-timers like Mary McCarty and Ethel Shutta. In London, where glamorous Diana Rigg played Phyllis more as high comedy than American tragedy, Carlotta's "I'm Still Here" was sung by Dolores Gray, herself a survivor of forties and fifties stage and film musicals, replaced by Eartha Kitt. Perhaps the most famous *Follies* performance was the 1985 AIDS benefit concert version in Avery Fisher Hall with Lee Remick and Barbara Cook as Phyllis and Sally. Cook's Sally is absolutely brilliant, truly the savvy ex-ingenue. Carol Burnett plays Carlotta and the indomitable Elaine Stritch sings a characteristically bizarre, over-the-top "Broadway Baby." Stritch may have been a Broadway star of sorts, but never a Broadway "baby." In Robert Johanson's 1998 revival, the old-timers (Ann Miller, Kaye Ballard, Phyllis Newman) were bigger stars than Sally (Donna McKechnie) and Phyllis (Dee Hoty), which created a proper balance. The divas should be aging stars, Sally and Phyllis less well known.

Phyllis's problem is her unhappy marriage to Ben. Sally is still in love with Ben, which is one of Buddy's problems. Even Carlotta had an affair with Ben. In Act I, Ben gets one of the most self-perceptive songs in the show, "The Road You Didn't Take." Ben even gets the final number, in which he has an onstage nervous breakdown. Yet who cares about Ben? In the original production, I blamed John McMartin for the fact that Ben just didn't stand out as much as he should. Nor did Daniel Massey in London in 1987. Nor did the able Laurence Guittard in the 1998 revival. It wasn't their fault. Despair isn't very musical and Ben is in despair:

The yearnings fade, the longings die.
You learn to bid them all goodbye.[36]

Ben is a creation popular in song, but not viable in the theater: the self-pitying but stoic straight man in mid-life crisis. The late Frank Sinatra built the last half of his career on singing songs of this man, but Sinatra's persona mixed straight self-pity with courage and self-assertion as in the yucky "My Way." Like the divas, he was a survivor. Ben can't stand on his own but can't stand his wife. The 1987 London revival cut "The Road You Didn't Take" (Daniel Massey couldn't sing it) and replaced it with a witty duet for Ben and Phyllis, "Country House." By removing Ben's first-act solo, some of the focus was taken away from Ben. His new final number, "Make the Most of Your Music," was more upbeat but less dramatic. However, nothing one can do can make audiences see Ben as more important, even *as* important, as the women in the show. Book writer James Goldman admits, "It's a woman's show, I'm afraid."[37] What musical isn't? With a stage full of divas, who zeroes in on Ben or Buddy? With the women displaying such strength, who cares about a weak man?

The 1998 revival countered the emptiness with one happy marriage, that of the elderly song-and-dance team, Emily and Theodore, who would periodically dance across the stage oblivious to the discord around them. Their harmony is not in words, but dance, the ideal of the Fred Astaire–Ginger Rogers movies come to life.

From the informal survey of the men around me at various performances of *Follies,* the show seems to baffle straight men. The heterosexual men on stage are basket cases, the women castrating—and why are all these men in the audience screaming over those old women on stage? During the intermission at the Paper Mill Playhouse, the straight men behind me were loudly proclaiming their preference for "Andrew Lloyd Webber's *Blood Brothers.*" Women and gay men "get" *Follies.* The women can identify with the wives and we've got Carlotta Campion.

It is easy to give *Follies* a gay reading. One can't ignore the camp element of trotting out a gaggle of aging leading ladies to sing parodic songs. Moreover, the musical raised questions of particular importance to gay men two years after Stonewall. The sense of emptiness and self-hatred the two couples demonstrate isn't far from that exhibited by the gaggle of unhappy queens in Crowley's *The Boys in the Band.* The question of the value of loving relationships, of the validity of the discourse of marriage for gay men, and of the necessity of monogamy in such relationships were pressing questions for many gay men in 1971—as they are in a different sense now when many gay men want the right to marry.

"Could I Leave You," Phyllis's brilliant song of defiance to her husband, Ben, got a different twist two years later when David Kernan sang it in the 1975 hit revue *Side by Side by Sondheim:*

> Could I bury my rage
> With a boy half my age
> In the grass? Bet your ass.[38]

Kernan was doing what many gay men did while listening to Alexis Smith sing the song, making it ours, as we had silently made many heterosexual narratives ours, but Kernan's performance signaled a time when gay men wanted to switch from gay readings of straight narratives to gay narratives. A gay man would be more interested in singing Phyllis's irony and resiliency than her husband's self-pity. For us, the women in the show were far more interesting than Ben's version of male menopause or Buddy's self-loathing. Kernan's queering the song made literal what we had already done while hearing it. On Cameron Mackintosh's tribute to himself, *Hey, Mr. Producer!* (the title taken from "Broadway Baby," a song from *Follies*), in the parade of divas, between Judi Dench turning "Send In the Clowns" into *King Lear* and Bernadette Peters wailing Bobby's eleven o'clock song from *Company,* "Being Alive," Michael Ball stopped the show with Sally's torch song, "Losing My Mind." Ball is the best male singer in musical theater these days and the only one willing to go over the top with a song the way the great female divas have done. His "Losing My Mind" was the surprise of the gala and as great a rendition of this classic song of obsessive love as has ever been performed. Ball, intentionally or not, gave the gay men in the audience (and watching the video or listening to the recording) a Queer Moment.[39] He reminded me that my boyfriend in 1971 was impelled to memorize "Losing My Mind" after he first heard it. (Between *Company* and *Follies,* I finally came out.)

Sondheim was forty-one when *Follies* opened. From this point on, much of his work will focus on the frustrations, compromises, and losses of middle age. Women triumph and survive, but men are haunted by the roads they didn't take and pay the price for the ones they mistakenly do follow, chief of which is the route of an unhappy heterosexual marriage. How much of this was Sondheim and how much his Albee-influenced book writers? James Goldman's one Broadway non-musical hit was *The Lion in Winter,* which was *Who's Afraid of Virginia Woolf* in medieval drag except that his bickering couple had three sons, including a bitchy gay one. Both Goldman and Hugh Wheeler, the book writer for *A Little Night Music, Sweeney Todd,* and *Merrily We Roll Along,* had written plays including gay characters before collaborating with Sondheim.[40] Did the move to musical theater, more popular entertainment, involve compulsory heterosexuality?

If *Follies* doesn't offer much hope for coupledom, *A Little Night Music* (1973), the most romantic of Sondheim's works, allows at least two of its couples happy endings. Still, it was an odd project for musical theater at the first crest of the youth culture. Sondheim and his colleagues did not opt to write for a young audience who didn't much care for Broadway musicals anyway. *Pippin* opened the same season as *A Little Night Music* and offered its version of youthful idealism glitzed up with Fosse razzmatazz. It ran 1,944 performances to *A Little Night Music*'s 600. Sondheim's celebration of youth had come sixteen years earlier with *West Side Story*. Nor was he interested in the kind of contemporary relevance of *Pippin*. *A Little Night Music* is blatantly reactionary for the Vietnam War era, a waltz operetta set in Europe at the turn of the century. The young are impetuous and naive, their elders even more foolish.

I was thirty-two when I first saw *A Little Night Music,* two years into my first long-term relationship with a brilliant, turbulent young man. If I was chronologically older, I was as inexperienced in gay relationships as he and far more innocent about them—it was my desire to maintain some innocence that led to the demise of the relationship some years later. I wasn't crazy about that green first Hal Prince production. It was well cast, but chilly. I prefer to remember openly gay director Sean Mathias's warmer, more passionate 1995 London revival starring four of the divas of the British stage: Judi Dench, Patricia Hodge, Sian Phillips, and Joanna Riding. It privileged Sondheim's humane words over Hugh Wheeler's earthbound dialogue in which characters tend to give speeches about their feelings that are unnecessary because the songs have done it better.

My favorite character in *A Little Night Music* is Charlotte, the most unhappy, worldly-wise of the women. Charlotte has the one queer moment in *A Little Night Music* as she sings of the "little deaths" that make up her marriage in one of Sondheim's best lyrics. In French, an orgasm is a "little death," and the lyric is filled with sexual innuendo, but Charlotte's marriage to her vain, unfaithful husband, Carl-Magnus (a reference to his ego and his genitalia, no doubt), does diminish her. There would be no problem if Charlotte didn't love her boorish, wayward hunk of a husband. Being intelligent, she is painfully aware how foolish that is.

> My husband, the pig.
> I loathe and deplore
> Every bone I adore.[41]

Here, in a nutshell, is Charlotte's marriage: intense sexual desire for a man she doesn't like. Also in a nutshell is the problem with Sondheim musicals. When the songs so succinctly define a relationship, who needs dialogue? In the original production, this superb song was cut to retain some dialogue. The London revival wisely reversed the priorities and cut some of the dialogue to retain the song.

If anything, *A Little Night Music* is a score in 3/4 time about the foolishness of love. Love is not the object of terror it is in *Company,* nor the source of anger and frustration it is in *Follies.* Love is the subject of farce, but a necessity that shouldn't be taken too seriously:

> And a person should celebrate everything
> Passing by.[42]

Petra's message in "The Miller's Son" was the byword of the seventies for many gay men and some swinging heterosexuals:

> And there's many a tryst
> And there's many a bed
> To be sampled and seen. . . .[43]

At the end of *A Little Night Music,* the old baroness dies, but we know she has lived life to the fullest and regrets the loss of the more elegant world she knew, a world in which a beautiful, shrewd woman would make romance pay. Her daughter, Desiree, involved with two married men, is "untidy." The Baroness and Petra are the voices of two types of sexual revolutionary—the woman who learned that sex paid very well and the young woman who knows that she had better get all the thrills she can before she settles down and marries for material security. While they voice their philosophies, they stand outside the romantic action of the musical. The messy variable in the equation is love. At the end of *A Little Night Music,* the right couples are united, but they are untidily married to other people. In that seventies period of chic wife-swapping, this seemed more fashionable than immoral.

The problem in *A Little Night Music* is the typical Sondheim problem. The women have the interesting voices. The men are cardboard, seen best through the women. The men's songs depict their vanity and illusions, the women's, their perceptions and experience. Of course, the women all win. They all get the men they want.

I missed *Pacific Overtures* on and off Broadway and in London, yet the album is probably my favorite Sondheim score. I don't want dialogue interfering with the pleasure of the music, which to me sounds like Mahler's evocation of Chinese music, *Das Lied von der Erde* ("and one for Mahler"). Here, too is the presence of Sondheim's most important collaborator, orchestrator Jonathan Tunick, who finds the perfect texture for each score. *Pacific Overtures* shimmers. Do I care that I never saw it? Not really. I have my own sense of the play. It doesn't need performance to come alive for me. Is that because it doesn't call for the kind of performance I relish in a musical, a diva or divo star turn, the thrill of a larger-than-life performance? Is it because there are no women in the cast, a necessity in a musical? How can I say my favorite Sondheim score is from a musical I have no desire to see? Yet Sondheim's widest audience are those who know him from cast recordings, televised gala performances, concerts by and recordings of star turns by divas like Bernadette Peters and Betty Buckley. Theatrical productions are only the tip of the iceberg of the Sondheim phenomenon.

Sondheim is, as Ethan Mordden has proclaimed, one of the "four supreme melodists in the American musical." He is also the theater's greatest lyricist, combining the mordant wit and inventiveness of Lorenz Hart with Oscar Hammerstein's sense of character. The richness in a Sondheim musical is in the music and lyrics, which do a far better job at defining character and conflict than the dialogue. Perhaps Sondheim musicals are the best argument for the through-sung musical—if the talk can't match what is sung, dump it. It's not that Sondheim's book writers are bad. It's just that he's better. Recordings give us the best of the shows.

I have seen numerous productions of *Sweeney Todd:* the overproduced Hal Prince original twice, with a set that dwarfed the show; the New York City Opera version, also by Prince; the smoky, orchestraless Susan Schulman production at the Circle in the Square; and the reduced London revival directed by Declan Donellan with the greatest Mrs. Lovett, singer-director Julia McKenzie. It's Sondheim's most ambitious, most operatic score, though, as he admits, from the first ear-shrieking whistle (echoes of *Psycho*) and restless orchestral introduction, the ghost of Bernard Herrmann looms over the proceedings, but only the way Ravel and Mahler are in the atmosphere of *A Little Night Music* and *Pacific Overtures.*

Why is *Sweeney Todd* so important to Sondheim queens? It does not overtly deal with love, sex, and relationships the way his earlier successes do. Somehow, in the midst of this Victorian Grand Guignol, there is something deeply personal. Sondheim has gotten inside Sweeney's monomania and Mrs. Lovett's ruthlessness and loneliness. When Hal Prince's wife, Judy, first heard parts of the show, she cried to Sondheim, "It's the story of your life." When she recounts this story, Sondheim biographer Meryle Secrest, cautious not to let us get too close to her subject, only hints at why. There is something of the monster mother in Mrs. Lovett, taken here to macabre dimensions well beyond Mama

Rose. There is that sense of revenge on the corrupt, hateful "straight" world represented by the forces of legal authority, Judge Turpin and the Beadle. Ultimately, Sondheim seems to respond to Sweeney's dark, bitter version of human experience. Sweeney, the obsessive visionary, could not accomplish anything without the Sondheim heroine, Mrs. Lovett, a ruthless survivor, who conceives of the means of getting rid of the bodies and providing cheap meat for her pies.

In *Sweeney Todd,* the most beautiful songs are saved for the most menacing moments. "Pretty Women" is foreplay for cutting the Judge's throat. "Nothing's Going to Harm You" is a pretext for silencing innocent Tobias—as in *Gypsy,* a mother betrays her child. How seriously should one take *Sweeney Todd?* Is it merely Grand Guignol fun or an attempt at serious musical theater? Sondheim has said that melodrama and farce are his favorite dramatic genres. Neither probes very deeply, unlike his lyrics. Both maintain a safe distance from the consequences and implications of their material. Yet *Sweeney Todd* seems to be more because the music aspires to so much and because of moments, particularly in Sweeney's soliloquy toward the end of Act I, when Sondheim loses his usual ironic distance and gets painfully close to his central character.

Sweeney Todd was never a big, long-run hit. It did well for a while, but it died as soon as Angela Lansbury left the cast. Yet it was enormously influential. More than any other musical of its time, it found a voice for contemporary musical theater. Here was a highly melodramatic nineteenth-century period piece about a homicidal misfit presented in quasi-operatic musical language. *Sweeney Todd* is the progenitor of *Phantom of the Opera* (also a Hal Prince opus), *Les Misérables,* and lesser works like the Frank Wildhorn epics *Jekyll and Hyde* and *The Scarlet Pimpernel.* Compare Sweeney with the Phantom, the poor Victorian ensemble with the ensemble of *Les Misérables.* Compare the Thernardiers with Sweeney and Mrs. Lovett's humorous duets, Marius and Cosette with Anthony and Johanna. Then, to understand Sondheim, ask why *Phantom* and *Les Misérables* are hits and *Sweeney* was a highly respected non-hit. The answer is sentiment. We can cry over the deaths in the hits; *Sweeney Todd* elicits horror. We can moon with the soaring duets of the young lovers in the hits. In *Sweeney Todd,* Johanna is given "Green Finch and Linnet Bird," a beautiful mock operatic aria that is musically beautiful, lyrically very clever, but far from sentimental. Johanna and Anthony's duet, "Kiss Me," could be out of *A Funny Thing Happened on the Way to the Forum.* It is funny, not sweet like the duets of Marius and Cosette, Christine and Raoul. The Phantom is redeemed by his love for sappy Christine and Jean Valjean is unbelievably good. Sweeney Todd is crazy and homicidal like the Phantom, but without his sexual allure. His duet with Mrs. Lovett is about murder, not love.

The passion of the music can carry one along in *Sweeney Todd* only if one is ignoring the words. In *Phantom* and *Les Misérables* one has to ignore the words. There are few moments in *Sweeney Todd* in which passion is not protected by irony and they all belong to the men: Anthony's "Johanna," an oddly serious aria for a love affair that is otherwise presented in comic terms; the Judge's self-flagellation while singing his own version of "Johanna;" and Sweeney's "Epiphany." Anthony's song is serious to set it in ironic contrast to the Judge's, which is a brilliant depiction of a man caught between his sexual desire and the guilt and punishment his society imposes and that he, as judge, is bound to administer. Judge and sexual man in one song who can be read as a figure for the internalized homophobia many men of Sondheim's generation (and still) feel and act upon. Sweeney wants to kill the Judge for the same kind of lust the Judge punishes himself for. In "Epiphany" Sweeney moves from single revenge to revenge on all of society.

Sadly, *Sweeney Todd* lets us down exactly where the more popular, lesser works disappoint—at the end. The end of *Sweeney Todd* demands musical treatment but sinks in verbiage the way the end of *Les Misérables* sinks in weak reprises and bad recitative. Why is it that composers—good and mediocre— refuse to write strong musical endings to their works? Do they really believe we stop listening at about ten o'clock? This may be a legacy from Rodgers and Hammerstein who tended to have musically rich first acts and talky second acts with a few reprises. Musically the final scene of *Sweeney Todd* is a major disappointment. Having left the conventional musical filled with popular song for the operatic musical, Sondheim jettisoned the eleven o'clock song in favor of underscored dialogue. That is the bad influence of *Sweeney Todd*. Nonetheless, I've seen every production in New York and London, whereas one trip to *Phantom* was enough.

Merrily We Roll Along (1981), Sondheim's return to a conventional musical score—actually his most commercial theater score—has one of the great eleven o'clock songs in musical theater. It is the night the first Russian spaceship, Sputnik, is orbiting. Three idealistic kids are on a New York rooftop watching and, in that wonderfully warm and runny way kids can get, see their rosy future in that light in the sky. Given the backward progression of the narrative, this is the beginning of the story. Two guys and a girl meet on a New York rooftop and watch Sputnik soar over New York. The rest of the story is of the slow dissolution of the friendships forged that night. The narrative, ostensibly, is a heterosexual one, of course. Franklin Shepard, talented composer, sacrifices his art and his lofty ambition by becoming a successful Hollywood composer and producer. (What had he dreamed of, commercial failure?) He also betrays his first marriage and his principles by marrying an ambitious, rich second wife. His lyricist and best pal, Charley Kringas, can't deal with Franklin's selling out. The friends become estranged. Female pal Mary becomes an alcoholic. No matter how many rewrites *Merrily We Roll Along* has had, and it has had quite a few, it doesn't work as a heterosexual narrative. Who cares if Franklin is a Hollywood success? Why are Charley and Mary so upset? Back to the rooftop. Frank sings to Charley:

> And you and me,
> We'll be singing it like the birds,
> Me with music and you with words,
> Tell 'em things they don't know.[44]

Frank sings of artistic collaboration, but what can he tell "them" they don't know? When he and Charley sing together it seems to be about more than music:

> Our turn, we're what's new,
> Me and you, me and you.[45]

Merrily We Roll Along only makes sense as a tale of unrequited love. Mary and Charley love Frank, who cannot return their devotion. Everything Frank does is a betrayal not of their values, which are never clear, but of their love. Mary knows that what she mourns "never ever was," but it haunts her nonetheless. The "friendship" Charley wants back never really existed. Franklin didn't sell out; he moved on. If Charley had listened to his own lyrics, he would have understood his problem with Frank:

> And if I wanted too much
> Was that such
> A mistake
> At the time?
> You never wanted enough . . .[46]

Charley's words aren't about some fictional love affair. They're his repressed feelings about Frank back in 1962. Charley may have married, but we know he still discusses Frank with his shrink in 1975.

That's not the show George Furth (who created the unconvincingly heterosexual Bobby in *Company*) and Stephen Sondheim wrote, but it's the show one can read into the album. It's the show they would have written if they had been honest with the implications of their material—an intimate show about unrequited love. *Merrily We Roll Along,* however, was also a Harold Prince production, one of his most disastrous, and therefore had to have a grand concept rather than a character-driven narrative. *Sweeney Todd* had to have that giant set that dwarfed everyone and led to a decade of giant anti-actor sets. *Merrily We Roll Along* had to be about selling out one's dreams, even if that didn't quite make sense for the characters. And there are only three characters in the show. Franklin's wives are cardboard, the supporting players cartoons. This is why the smaller revivals have fared better.

Despite a great score, *Merrily We Roll Along* makes little sense without some acknowledgment of the closeted gay subtext. That subtext is a piece of history—one expression of unrequited gay love circa 1957 when unrequited love for straight men was more prevalent than now.

FOSCA'S PASSION AND BILLY'S KISS

The two Sondheim shows that were conceived by him and not his book writers were the two nineteenth-century quasi-operatic pieces, *Sweeney Todd* and *Passion*. These are the most daring of his works in terms of dealing with characters at emotional extremes. If Sweeney Todd is not mad at the beginning of his show, he certainly is at the end, but, as Sweeney, his deranged wife, and the maddened Toby demonstrate, madness is a valid response to the jungle in which they live. In *Passion* (1994), we hear Fosca's mad screams long before we see her, and during the course of the intense one-act work, Giorgio is maddened by his relationship with Fosca. The choice of these works shows that Sondheim was attracted by operatic properties. He said, "*Passion* is not an opera because there is so much dialogue, but it is an opera in its attitude toward people. If it were all sung and done at the Metropolitan Opera House nobody would laugh because this is the way Salome behaves and . . . Electra behaves and you accept it."[47] Sondheim was responding to the fact that the unsophisticated members of New York audiences laughed at key moments in *Passion*. Why? First, because *Passion* is operatic in the best demented sense, but James Lapine's clunky, prosaic book reduces its emotions to bathos. We buy the music and lyrics, but not the dialogue. In the scene in which we are introduced to Fosca, we have this exchange between her and the handsome young soldier, Giorgio:

> GIORGIO: Well, now you seem to be feeling more normal.
> FOSCA (*Laughing tensely*): Normal? I hardly think so. Sickness is normal to me, as health is to you. Excuse me. I shouldn't speak of my troubles. I have been going through a period of deep melancholy.[48]

It is not easy to keep a straight face through lines like that. Lapine makes Fosca a self-obsessed kvetch, the sort of person who answers at great length when you politely ask "How are you?" In contrast, Sondheim makes Fosca's obsessiveness and dark vision vivid:

> A love as pure as breath,
> As permanent as death,
> Implacable as stone.[49]

Passion makes the strongest case for an album of the score with just enough of the dialogue for continuity, as on the superb cast recording of Jeremy Sams's 1996 London production. It is, as Sondheim admits, a "chamber opera." If the characters are, as he acknowledges, operatic, they should just sing. Salome and Electra don't talk. If the work is indeed a "chamber opera," it doesn't belong on Broadway, where only Sondheim's devotees appreciated it, or London's West End, where it played to near-empty houses. Even star Michael Ball's many fans stayed away, missing his greatest stage triumph and Maria Friedman's riveting performance, which far surpassed Donna Murphy's in New York. What is the venue for a work like *Passion?* It certainly isn't for the same audience that flocks to *Beauty and the Beast,* which opened the same spring.

    Passion also needs to be queered to be appreciated. It is, after all, dedicated to Peter Jones, the young man with whom Sondheim was having a somewhat turbulent relationship at the time. Here, at a moment in which love enters Sondheim's life, he writes a musical about obsessive, queer love. *Passion* opens where many romantic works end—with an orgasm shared by two beautiful people, Giorgio and his lover, Clara, who sing a post-coital duet of their happiness. Sondheim aficionados all know that such a song of joy means trouble ahead—there are no non-ironic songs of happiness in Sondheim. What attracted Clara to Giorgio was "the sadness in your eyes" the day she first saw him: "How quickly pity leads to love." From the first, Giorgio is presented as sensitive. The relationship between pity and love will become crucial to the narrative. Giorgio's passion for Clara is a passion of the eyes, which see only her beauty. This story may take place in the nineteenth century, but the characters are infused by the late-twentieth-century belief that looks are everything. Giorgio and Clara seem to be normalcy itself. There is a hitch; she is married, with a child. Their happiness is limited to what Clara calls "matinees," afternoon performances of romantic love and sexual passion.

    Giorgio is sent away to a brigade headquarters in an aristocratic house in the country, miles from any real culture, where he meets the woman who will change his life, ugly, sickly, somewhat demented Fosca. In her first song, Fosca claims a realistic sense of proportion: "I do not hope for what I cannot have." Soon, however, she wants Giorgio's heart, soul, and body. She claims a kinship to Giorgio: "You and I are different."[50] How is Giorgio different? He is sensitive. He cries when upset. He is a soldier by family circumstance, not choice. He reads a lot and appreciates nature and art. When, at the doctor's behest, Giorgio goes to Fosca's room, she echoes the lines Giorgio earlier sang to Clara: "God, you are so beautiful." Here is a moment that echoes many early gay dramas, the presentation of the male as object of the gaze. Giorgio is polite to Fosca, considerate, but uninterested in her love for him. He loves Clara, after all.

Is it so hard to queer this story of unrequited love for a beautiful, conventionally straight but sensitive young man that gets out of control? Fosca finally gets Giorgio to her bedroom—he goes out of pity and duty—and she dictates to him a letter she wishes he had written to her:

> And though I cannot love you,
> I wish that I could love you.[51]

Cut to the delightful 1998 film comedy *Billy's Hollywood Screen Kiss,* a gay crossover movie about unrequited love. Billy, a gay romantic with serious hang-ups—an obsession with gayness as victimization and a lack of gaydar—falls in love with adorable, blond Gabriel, whom he thinks is straight. After all, Gabriel claims a girlfriend in another city, though he sends Billy maddeningly mixed signals that Billy reads inaccurately. Finally, after breaking up with his girlfriend, Gabriel, claiming drunkenness, gets in Billy's bed "to sleep." What follows is five hilariously agonizing minutes as Gabriel, feigning sleep, moves toward Billy. *Billy's Hollywood Screen Kiss* is hardly the moving romantic tragedy Sondheim offers in *Passion*. It is an interesting comic gloss, however, on gay unrequited love. Queer falls for straight (he thinks). Straight responds in complex ways. Gay becomes more obsessed and follows supposed straight around. In the ultimate fantasy, straight succumbs, at least for one night, or is converted altogether.

In *Passion,* Giorgio ultimately becomes as obsessed with Fosca as she is with him. He breaks off his compromise relationship with married Clara for the madness of Fosca's love:

> Love within reason,
> That isn't love.[52]

He admits his love for Fosca, though "Not the way that she loves me."[53] Fosca and Giorgio have one night in bed together, after which Giorgio must fight a duel with her cousin and protector, whom he wounds. Fosca dies content a few days later, but the anguish of his new passion and its aftermath sends Giorgio to a mental hospital. At the end of the musical he is echoing the words of the letter Fosca dictated to him: "Your love will live in me." It's more than an echo, actually—Giorgio has been taken over by Fosca's voice. He sings her words and her music.

Here is a kind of old-fashioned masochistic gay fantasy, the infatuation for the beautiful straight. In its nineties version in *Billy's Hollywood Screen Kiss,* the straight is really not straight, but not interested in Billy's anguish, tentativeness, or his lack of conventional good looks. Gabriel finds himself a gorgeous model and Billy finds himself with a more interesting, if less pretty, beau. No tragedy here. Everyone gets the right boyfriend. Sondheim is a child of an earlier era, the era of the closet; everything has to have that pleasurable anguish we know from classic gay fiction and drama of the day: James Baldwin's *Giovanni's Room,* Mary Renault's *The Charioteer,* Gore Vidal's *The City and the Pillar,* Tennessee Williams's *Cat on a Hot Tin Roof.* Sondheim's detractors giggled at *Passion* because all the Sturm und Drang seemed silly to them. You had to have been there—I was, at one time. *Passion* brought back memories of emotions I had felt. I also couldn't help thinking of the gay composer in his sixties in love for the first time with a good-looking young man, of the horrible sense of age as ugliness endemic to gay (and straight male) culture. The ugly duckling can offer his dark vision of experience and love to a young innocent. More than that, it's love as the total domination of one personality over another, a terrifying version of love that Sondheim now seems to accept and celebrate. To accept love, one doesn't just throw caution to the winds; one gives up oneself and becomes the other. Into Giorgio's beautiful body go Fosca's mind and voice.

Giorgio and Fosca's obsession is not new to Sondheim. It's akin to Sally's in *Follies* ("It's like I'm losing my mind"). *Follies,* too, ends with a man having a nervous breakdown. The difference here is an acceptance and celebration of this mad love: Fosca's joy realizing "I'm someone to be loved" echoed in Giorgio's exaltation at realizing and accepting Fosca's love:

> Love without reason, love without mercy,
> Love without pride or shame. [54]

I'm not sure the Gothic goes with the acceptance and reconciliation of the last twenty minutes of *Passion,* but, strange to say, this is one of Sondheim's happiest scores, though not happy the way *Billy's Kiss,* an homage to frothy fifties film comedies, is happy. Sondheim, whose career began in the fifties, still expresses the dark side of that decade, the side seen not in Doris Day movies but in Albee's

The American Dream. Passion is as close to "another love story" as he can get, but it's more Edward Albee than Doris Day.

BLEEDING CHUNKS

Ironically, one of Sondheim's longest running hits in London and New York was the 1975 revue *Side by Side by Sondheim,* devised and narrated with British camp panache by Ned Sherrin and featuring two women, Millicent Martin and Julia McKenzie, and a seemingly gay man in a white suit, David Kernan. The show offered two hours of Sondheim songs, some cut from their shows, others familiar to Sondheim fans. Sherrin's narration and some of Kernan's interpretations gave Sondheim's work a more openly gay dimension than they had in their original settings. This seemed to help the revue's popularity, not hurt it. It was the swinging seventies, and Sondheim was being sung by a British cast. Anglophilic New Yorkers felt that Sondheim had somehow been validated by this English tribute. Sondheim in this form also briefly resuscitated a lost Broadway genre, the intimate sophisticated revue. A few years later, in 1980, Off-Broadway gay writer and performer Craig Lucas and his collaborator Norman Rene, later the creators of the gay film classic *Longtime Companions,* created a musical revue of Sondheim outtakes, *Marry Me a Little.* Though Lucas and Rene presented their show as a heterosexual romance of sorts, this was a gay tribute to Sondheim.

In 1992–93, there was another Sondheim revue, first at Oxford (with Diana Rigg) and later at the Manhattan Theatre Club in New York, *Putting It Together* (conceived and directed by Sondheim diva Julia McKenzie). With a larger cast than the earlier revues (five performers and a small band rather than pianos), this show still adhered to the premise that excerpted Sondheim songs were "sophisticated" material—the show was set at a chic Manhattan cocktail party. *Putting It Together* was the vehicle for the return to the New York stage of Julie Andrews, one of Broadway's great divas of thirty years before. Among the men in the cast were singer Michael Rupert, who was best known for playing Marvin in the gay musicals *March of the Falsettos* and *Falsettoland,* and gay playwright-performer Christopher Durang. This, too, signaled a gay presence and subtext, if not text, to Sondheim's songs. A new version of *Putting It Together,* directed by openly gay Eric D. Schaeffer opened in Los Angeles in 1998 and on Broadway in the fall of 1999, marking Carol Burnett's return to musical theater. Like Julie Andrews, she had been away since the sixties. Schaeffer's version was no more successful than its predecessors. The young director has made a specialty of Sondheim musicals at his small theater in the suburbs of Washington, D.C., including a charming, if lightweight, Sondheim revue of his own devising. His theater is also known for good productions of gay plays. What ambitious small theater isn't these days? They know their core audience.

Despite my reservations about the dialogue in Sondheim musicals, these revues present a defanged Sondheim: hip, sophisticated, terribly clever, but no longer dangerous. They make him another Cole Porter or Noël Coward, gaily chic and chicly gay. This, of course, is a misreading of Broadway's darkest, though wittiest, composer/lyricist. It makes Sondheim the kind of gay wit my generation of queens aspired to being in the fifties and sixties. That's what we performed in our best moments. But Sondheim also is the bard of the terror and anguished self-loathing some of us—many of us—had been taught to feel and that in many ways we triumphed over. If he has any spiritual kin, it is Lorenz Hart. Which is why for many of us of my generation, our anthem isn't Jerry Herman's "I Am What I Am," but Sondheim's "I'm Still Here."

FAIRY TALES: GAY MUSICALS

Gay men have always known how to open that door into the other
world that waits so close to ours.

—AIDS: The Musical!

What's a gay musical number? A number written and/or performed by gay people? A number that acknowledges or sings about the feelings of gay people? A number with the kind of flamboyant excess gay people at one time responded to? Case in point: a film considered to be one of the great turkeys, *Can't Stop the Music* (1980), directed by, of all people, comedienne Nancy Walker, fresh from her triumphs as Rhoda's mother on *The Mary Tyler Moore Show* and *Rhoda.* Walker had been a great stage comedienne, one of the original stars of *On the Town.* Her singing of "I'm Still Here" stopped the show at the first grand Sondheim gala benefit at the Shubert Theater in 1973. I don't recall that she was asked to direct another film after this one. *Can't Stop the Music* was made to exploit the disco craze (best done in discos, not movie theaters), and to spotlight a group called The Village People. As any gay person over thirty-five can tell you, The Village People was a disco singing group who dressed outlandishly in gay drag, the same kind of outfits male strippers would later start their routines in: leatherman, construction worker, policeman, clone, cowboy, and scantily clad native American. *Can't Stop the Music* was produced by Allan Carr, who later would give Broadway *La Cage aux Folles.* Supposedly, Carr told the mostly gay Village People to keep closeted while he raised the money for the film, which presents them as not so much straight as sexless, which is the biggest giveaway to a gay character in film or on television.

Can't Stop the Music is no worse than a score of other films made to highlight recording stars, though the leads are nauseatingly perky, but the critics went out of their way to savage it as irredeemably awful. It's not good, but I can't help thinking a lot of the fuss was about the film's inability to keep its potentially gay subject matter closeted. The film should have replaced Valerie Perrine with Bette Midler or Paul Lynde and gone all the way. The odd thing about this film is that it has zero erotic charge, even with Steve Guttenberg, king of bad movies, and Bruce Jenner, making a rum try at a film career. There's a lot about *Can't Stop the Music* you don't need to know—rent the video if you must, or borrow my copy. The Village People's biggest hits were songs that celebrated places where one was likely to see/meet/have sex with a "Macho Man," songs like "In the Navy" and "YMCA." The group gently mocked the new hypermasculine clone look of the early eighties. The film tries inanely to present them as a mainstream group for straight audiences until "YMCA," which explodes any sense that *Can't Stop the Music* is a straight film. Suddenly, for no reason, Steve Guttenberg, Valerie Perrine, and The Village People walk into a YMCA and we get the gay version of a Busby Berkeley number, four minutes of scantily clad men in various geometric arrangements while "YMCA" beats on in the background (it comes one hour and twelve minutes into the film if you want to rent it just for that moment). The director tries to throw Valerie Perrine in a few shots with the hunks, but she looks like a fag hag playing with the boys, as she does through most of the film. The boys are about as interested in her as the muscle men are in Jane Russell in "Ain't There Anyone Here for Love?", the canonical queer moment in the film of *Gentlemen Prefer Blondes*. "YMCA" is funny, exuberant, campy, ironic, and filled with display of male bodies. It's gay—the high point of the film, not just because it is full of male flesh. It's gay because it knows it is silly, that it is queering all those musical films full of display of the female body. For that four minutes, this mindless film, futilely trying to pass off The Village People and their audience as straight, recognizes its gay audience. Remember Eve Sedgwick's definition of camp as asking the question, "What if the right audience for this were exactly *me?*" Gay theater states that gay folk are the audience for this work; no apologies, no compromises.

Ideally, I'd say that if we're going to have a gay musical theater, created by and for us, it's going to be outside the mainstream, but what kind of theater can it be? I want to look in this chapter at a variety of musicals written for gay audiences, and a couple that weren't, to explore the possibilities of the gay musical. My conclusions are going to be pessimistic and nostalgic. For the most part, openly gay musicals are less "gay," in all senses of the word, than their closeted Broadway predecessors.

To sing to a wide variety of people, a musical has to universalize, to generalize. There are three basic ways in which one can generalize about a "gay experience" within the shorthand of a musical, which relies to some extent on types and stereotypes. The first way is to posit a generic or paradigmatic gay experience. There are things most gay men have lived through—for instance, dealing with external and internalized homophobia, coming out to oneself and to one's family and peer group, and being introduced to institutions within the gay community and elements of current gay styles. There is also a gay history with heroes and martyrs, as well as historic turning points, one of which is AIDS. Finally, one can posit to some extent a gay performative style, once called camp but now known as "fabulous." I'm going to focus in this chapter on representations of gay experience using shows and films we can share through original cast albums, published scripts, or video. This offers only the tip of the iceberg, of course.

Before *La Cage aux Folles* demonstrated that you could make a hit musical about gay men as long as they were middle-aged and domesticated or, if, as *Kiss of the Spider Woman* does, you played to old, familiar stereotypes, gay musicals existed, as they still do, in smaller venues that cater to predominantly gay audiences. There are many small theaters all over the United States whose core audience is gay. Every city has at least one. The fact is that small theaters do best at the box office with gay-oriented plays that anchor their seasons. If these theaters do musicals, they have to be small scale—or Sondheim.

The first gay musical to be published and to have a cast recording of sorts was the Off-Broadway production *Boy Meets Boy* (1975; music and lyrics by Bill Solly, book by Bill Solly and Donald Ward). The text was published in William Hoffman's groundbreaking anthology, *Gay Plays: The First Collection* (1979). Compared to current Off-Broadway fare, *Boy Meets Boy* was a low-budget, amateurish production, typical of much coterie gay theater of the time.

Up to this point the gayest musical theater wasn't on stage; it was circulated through artifacts like Ben Bagley's fabulous series of albums of lesser-known Broadway songs by major composers, released on Painted Smiles Records. Strange but interesting collections of singers performed the more camp output of Gershwin, Hart, Youmans, and so on. A Gershwin album has Barbara Cook, Elaine Stritch, Anthony Perkins, and Bobby Short (an ideal *Norma* cast) sing songs like "Virginia, Don't Go Too Far" and "Under a One Man Top (with a One Man Girl)." The liner notes were as camp as the performances ("George Gershwin and his lovely wife, Ira"). Here was true musical camp, esoterica by well-known composers, silly songs by people usually taken seriously, performed by artists with a gay following. Gay theater was dominated by the practitioners of the ridiculous, particularly Charles Ludlam, whose camp extravaganzas often had music.

The dominant influences on *Boy Meets Boy* are Noël Coward and the Fred Astaire–Ginger Rogers films. The setting is London in 1936, but this isn't the real pre-Wolfenden London of draconian policing of homosexuality, but rather a fantasy London in a parallel universe where men can be openly gay and even marry. Frumpy Guy Rose, a minor British aristocrat, leaves arrogant American millionaire Clarence Cutler waiting at the church and is discovered unconscious under the bed of devil-may-care newspaperman Casey O'Brien after one of Casey's wild parties in his room at the Savoy Hotel. Casey was unconscious through the major media event, King Edward's abdication, and he needs a good story to redeem himself as a reporter, like finding out why Guy Rose didn't appear at his wedding to the American millionaire. In true Cinderella style, Guy transforms himself into a handsome young man, Casey falls in love with him, and they get married and live happily ever after. What is interesting about *Boy Meets Boy* are its assumptions about a fantasy gay life, or the life musicals might present, and the style the authors choose in the swinging 1970s. The show takes the kind of story line one might find in a Fred and Ginger musical—lovers meet, but one isn't interested; mistaken identity; foolish rivals for the affections of one; lovers reunite in a dance number—and unproblematically queers them. The world of *Boy Meets Boy* isn't the real world: it's the world of musicals. No social problems intrude here. Homosexuality is a non-issue for all of the characters. A gay man and a straight man can sing a duet against "Giving It Up for Love." Gay marriage is accepted. However, it's also a world where "straight looking and acting" wins. Guy isn't frumpy at all, but cute. Casey and Guy first find they have something in common when they sing a duet about their happy times in the Boy Scouts. At the finale, the chorus boys are all dressed "as boy scouts in pure white." There's some camp irony here, more now that the Boy Scouts of America are frantically guarding the crumbling citadels of heterosexism and Christianity from the onslaughts of homosexuals and Unitarians. In *Boy Meets Boy*, Guy and Casey's love of the Boy Scouts is another sign they aren't effeminate.

For the most part, the pleasant songs sound like minor versions of Noël Coward, a retro style in the mid-seventies, but the show celebrates the enabling fantasies of musical theater and the sophistication of thirties musicals as a style many gay men found attractive. Gay men no longer have to read themselves into the conventions of a heterosexist musical—it's done for them. The romance is queered and there's plenty of male display in the Paris nightclub strip show in the second act—something for everyone (gay).

Listening to the cast album of *Boy Meets Boy* is like listening to the recording of an amateur musical. The score is serviceable, the lyrics actually quite good, but clearly a gay musical couldn't attract the best performers in those relatively closeted times. Being in a gay show in Greenwich Village in 1975 was probably not a good career move. Nor did our best gay composers and lyricists want to touch gay material. We have come a long way. *Boy Meets Boy* did not speak directly to what was going on around it in the Village or the burgeoning urban gay ghettoes across the United States. It kept the musical in the realm of fantasy, perhaps where it belongs. Our place in American society, and thus in cultural productions, was still uneasy in 1975. The gay reality and fantasy was in the discos and baths, where the Divine Bette Midler reigned in the early seventies.

"A LITTLE SONG, A LITTLE DANCE . . ."

I wonder what a future anthropologist would make of the crop of gay musicals written in the late 1990s, what sort of picture of gay life in the late twentieth century she would tease out of shows like *Fairy Tales, The Ballad of Little Mikey,* or *The Gay 90s.* She might see that gay people are committed to fighting opposition and living out their domestic arrangements with integrity and love, but basically are pretty bland and a bit confused, proclaiming difference and sameness simultaneously. We can be clever at times, but not ironic; sentimental, but not very self-critical. If this is not our private reality, this is the public face presented in these shows, written for us. Maybe we did better as theater artists with a little more anguish. No wonder that for our gala, large-scale theatrical events, we still get a diva or two together and listen to Sondheim.

Flashback to 1997 for a case in point. It is a lovely June night in Chelsea. Along "the strip"—Eighth Avenue from 14th to 25th Street—rainbow flags are hanging from every lamppost in preparation for Gay Pride festivities. In the early evening, Chelsea is still quiet, not quite the buff showplace it becomes later on. Chelsea, in case you don't know, is one of Manhattan's gay neighborhoods. Such "ghettoes" in major cities or summer resorts like Provincetown and Fire Island were created as safe spaces for gay men who wanted to avoid being frowned upon by disapproving straights or bashed by the more pathological young version of same. Here gay couples can engage in the sort of public displays of affection usually reserved for straights and in general gay men can be proudly open about who we are with a minimum of hassle. Are such places still necessary in our more enlightened (in some places) times? My favorite upscale Baltimore grocery store, in a more or less suburban area far from the traditional gay ghetto, has copies of *The Advocate* displayed by each cash register where *People, TV Guide,* or the wacky tabloids are placed in most stores. Times have changed. The gay left can't stop assimilation any more than the Christian right can. There are, however, lots of gay men who still see the city ghettoes as their goal, their safe haven, or their paradise. Older coupled gay men may choose the suburbs, but the city is still the sexually charged place for traditional gay culture. One can at least watch the parade of male pulchritude pass by. Even we middle-aged folks can feel that sense of sexual possibility that makes gay ghettoes exciting, though age takes us out of the game.

My partner and I are headed West on 23rd Street and across Tenth Avenue, where the strips of pretty brownstones occupied by gay writers are replaced by parking lots and truck depots and where the WPA Theater is located, to see a preview performance of a new gay musical revue, *Fairy Tales*. Cabaret and revue are back in the smaller venues in New York, and satirical revue is an ideal form for gay musical theater, as the uptown success of *When Pigs Fly* proves. Clearly the producers believe *Fairy Tales* is a ready-made entertainment for Gay Pride month in Chelsea.

When we enter the shabby lobby of the WPA to pick up our tickets, we find a line of senior citizens purchasing discount tickets. It seems that the theater has a special rush ticket price for area senior citizens. They're not sure exactly what they're seeing, but it's cheap theater and they seem to like the ratty couches in the lobby upstairs and the air conditioning. These senior citizens constitute the majority of the small audience that will watch this preview performance of *Fairy Tales*. There are a few gay couples here as well. One sweet young man, newly arrived in the Big Apple from somewhere in the Deep South, sits next to us. He has come to New York to study acting and to become a star. "Someday, I'll be up there," he says without irony. I look around the filthy black hole of a theater and at the rather sad-looking handful of people in it and think of George Gaynes singing to Roz Russell in *Wonderful Town,* "Go home, go home / Go back where you came from / Oh why did you ever leave Ohio?" It takes a dedicated dreamer to make a silk purse out of this sow's ear of a theater and audience, but this young man just played Franklin Shepard in the South Something State University production of *Merrily We Roll Along* and he's ready for stardom. I could imagine him singing "It's Our Time" and believing it was written for him. What happens to an extremely good-looking innocent like that young man? One can't help but look at him and listen to him and think, "He'll be eaten alive." Thinking of his drama to come made the ensuing couple of hours more interesting, thank God.

Fairy Tales is a revue written by a Chicagoan, Eric Lane Barnes, who is active in gay singing groups in the Windy City. Barnes is a fair, derivative composer and a competent lyricist. His vocal arrangements are excellent and make his own material sound better than it is. His show comprises two-dozen songs about being gay with a couple of lesbian songs thrown in. The songs are performed by five talented young performers who work very hard to sell the show to this small, far from dynamic audience. The direction is effective, if unimaginative. Occasionally, as in the song "Garbage," in which three men do a Supremes-like number about their trashy lover who makes them want to be garbage men, or "The Letter Song," in which the men complain about the bad grammar in the "Dear John" letters they have received, the show is witty and amusing. The problem with the show is that it seldom is "gay" in the old sense of "keenly alive and exuberant." A couple sing a song called "You're the Bottom," obviously an attempt at Cole Porter wit, but all one can think about during the song is that this writer can't do Cole Porter—he doesn't understand the clash of high and pop culture that makes "You're the Top" work. Who does anymore? "You're the Top" is witty, combining names and things that one would never think of combining. "You're the Bottom" is labored. And there's no set-up to the song. Why are these people singing this to each other? The first act ends with a Gay Pride march that only made me think of the truly witty Pride march that ends the first half of *When Pigs Fly:* "You can take the sissy out of Mississippi . . ."

At the intermission, I thought, "I want to enjoy this, but why are they doing these numbers?" A good revue is self-justifying. It has an overall concept, a point of view toward its material. A good gay revue has an underlying political philosophy. *Fairy Tales* had neither. More important, it lacked a gay style. Irony was in short supply and the camp quotient was perilously low. Are these essential to a gay musical? Absolutely!

"God, I want to be up there with them," our young neighbor said. God, was I ever that young? Yes, but when I was nineteen I almost got kicked out of the Lunt-Fontanne Theater for laughing loudly and uncontrollably at *The Sound of Music.*

Nothing prepared me for how wrong *Fairy Tales* would get after the intermission as it moved out of an attempt at a witty revue toward a maudlin book musical. A couple of numbers in the first act were about a dysfunctional religious-right family whose young son is obviously gay. Mother sang a too predictable song, "God Hates Fags," and the family performed a contrapuntal dinner table grace during which the butch daughter sings of how she can't wait to leave home and the son sings of his crush on Tom Cruise. The song does not hit the target. The satire is not specific enough. It would have been funnier if the son's crush were on someone gayer (George Michael? Nathan Lane? Barney Frank?), or if the mother's song were wittier. The show needed some of the wry irony of the love songs to Newt Gingrich and Strom Thurmond in *When Pigs Fly,* which opened the same month. The second act offers us another dinner table scene. Son has now brought his lover home for Thanksgiving and son also hints that he has AIDS. The older gay folks in the audience know where this is heading. We're back in the days of linking gayness and AIDS and heading down into the land of clichés. We dread what is likely to ensue—and does. A couple of numbers later, the gay son and his lover are celebrating their fifth anniversary, the wood anniversary. Son has made his lover a wooden hummingbird feeder (won't it leak?). The young performer playing the son is doing his best "Mimi in the fourth act of *La Bohème*," frail-but-adoring bit. In the next scene, son is writing his father a letter asking for love and acceptance. The letter is out of ten 1980s made-for-TV movies. The more cynical gays in the audience (everyone but the young man sitting next to us) have made it this far with a bit of rolling of the eyes and squirming. Some already look like they're watching an accident. Then the *Titanic* hits the iceberg. Holding the hummingbird feeder, the lover sings his song of loss (the son has died without benefit of death scene—it was probably cut after last night's preview). It's a terrible, sappy quasi-folk song about how he will cherish the hummingbird feeder his lover made for him. One couple in the audience lost it at that point and began to laugh uncontrollably. It was one of those moments like Mary Tyler Moore breaking up at Chuckles's funeral ("A little song, a little dance, a little seltzer down your pants"). They tried not to laugh and then would explode loudly. No matter how hard I felt for the young man bravely singing away about the hummingbird feeder, I thought the laughter was an honest response. The show would have been one hundred percent better if the writer and director had realized the song was funny and gone with it. Once you have "Springtime for Hitler" on your hands, go all the way. What could possibly follow this embarrassingly awful moment but a mawkish through-sung memorial service in which religious-right mother blames her son's lover for his death and father sings of his love for his son and lover gets mad. It was so horribly predictable and predictably horrible that it could only inspire more barely suppressed explosions of laughter.

The young man sitting next to us, raised in the era of musicals awash in sentiment, was crying. Clearly this child does not have enough irony to survive in show business or in Chelsea. The show closed with the inevitable Les Mizzy hymn "Keepers of the Light." The audience gave the brave performers a sympathetic round of applause. They deserved purple hearts. Cole Porter and Noël Coward whirled in their graves.

What adjective could describe *Fairy Tales?* Unsophisticated, perhaps. The New York gay men in the audience have lived through too much to be satisfied with mawkish sentiment. The glitz and camp of *Kiss of the Spider Woman* or playful defiance of *When Pigs Fly* is more to their liking. The best response to bigotry and death is fury, not tears, and the best gay theatrical response is ironic wit, not sentiment. Though it would be difficult to be stylish in the gloomy WPA Theater, *Fairy Tales* lacked style. It plodded where it should have soared. It was earnest rather than playful. The irritating phrase out of personal ads—"straight looking and acting"—kept going through my mind.

I thought I had seen the end of *Fairy Tales* but, sure enough, it showed up in London at the Drill Hall, a venue for gay theater. I didn't check it out again. As someone who also writes gay theater, I couldn't help but be angry that this played the Drill Hall while more worthy work remains veiled in obscurity. Nor could I imagine what British gay men would make of it. No one I know went.

Fairy Tales raised a lot of questions for me about gay theater. Obviously at some point this show played successfully in Chicago or producers would not have gambled on New York success. Is the Chicago gay audience that different or has gay history moved quickly on, thanks in part to protease inhibitors and the progress of gay assimilation? The boy next to us from the Deep South obviously felt something about the plight of these young men on stage that I didn't feel. He had made the courageous move to the Big Apple, armed with his dream of stardom—and his looks—perhaps to get away from the kind of religious and familial intolerance the musical dramatized. Chelsea must seem like heaven to him—or at least Oz. I never had to deal with family rejection or that kind of religious bigotry. Nor have I ever dealt with the death of a lover from AIDS. Nor, for that matter, has a lover ever given me a wooden hummingbird feeder. I prefer clothing or jewelry. *Fairy Tales* didn't seem to be about me. I don't think my laughing neighbors thought it was about them either. There was something Middle American about the show that made me think it would play better in Peoria. It wasn't Chelsea. Or was it?

I found the combination of self-congratulation and reveling in victimization nauseating, an example of the worst of contemporary gay culture, the kind that makes me want to join with "post-gay" and "anti-gay" critics in decrying what they see as a gay "culture of official mediocrity."[1] Underlying *Fairy Tales*'s attacks on our detractors' claims of moral superiority was a claim of gay people's moral superiority. The show presents gay people as young, cute, somewhat clever, and noble urban sophisticates who have transcended Middle-American, inferior backgrounds. We're "Keepers of the Light." And we have not a jot of self-criticism or irony about our claims. The guys on the barricades in *Les Misérables* are fighting for the poor and disenfranchised. The gays in *Fairy Tales* sing of their innate superiority.

Meanwhile, out in Los Angeles, Celebration Theater, which specializes in gay drama and musical theater, produced two other musical definitions of What It Means to Be Gay, both of which were recorded. *The Gay 90s,* another small-scale cabaret revue, is a varied bunch of songs by different composers sung by a genial, talented group of performers. Like *Fairy Tales, The Gay 90s* speaks (sings) to lesbians as well as gay men. In his notes for the compact disc, director David Galligan proclaims his apolitical status (Welcome to L.A.) and general indifference to such events as Gay Pride parades. The focus of his production is on the personal and domestic, a celebration of the variety of lesbian and gay individuals and of the variety of domestic arrangements these people invent and maintain.

The strength of *The Gay 90s* is in its narrative songs, which make up the bulk of the score, songs that in old-fashioned ballad form tell stories about a variety of gay people—and seagulls. These songs echo the sort of narrative or patter song Coward and Porter did so well, but the premise of the show seems to be that songs have to have a gay message, so they tend to be preachy rather than cleverly diverting. The best are satiric without being too didactic. The cleverest songs are written by Kirby Tepper: in the first, a trio of men sing of their dependence on phone sex in "976":

> I want commitment but I'd rather
> Commit myself into a horny lather.

In the second, "Lookin' at Me," a soldier in the shower obsesses about being watched by another soldier, then anguishes over not being watched. In another, "And the Ship Sails On," two lesbian seagulls on Noah's ark are outed ("that seagull's wearing flannel") but eventually triumph over their homophobic adversaries. While satirizing lesbian stereotypes, the song makes its preaching fun. God tells the homophobic animals: "If gulls like muff, it really doesn't matter." After hearing these three hilarious numbers, I can only wish for an evening of Kirby Tepper. A couple of the other songs almost match Tepper's. "All the Good Men Are Gay" crystallizes the problem of the urban straight woman, and "Well-Spoken Woman," a masterpiece of double entendre, is an aria celebrating a woman who is a "cunning linguist" who works miracles with her tongue.

The only specifically Los Angeles song is John Bucchino's classic "Sweet Dreams," about the Hollywood dreams and harsher reality of a young man and woman. In fact, what's missing here is a sense that this is anything more than a collection of gay-themed songs. That may be enough for a midnight show at a nightclub, but not for a theatrical revue. Some of the serious songs, particularly Naomi Caryl's "Mirror Image," are mawkish. Caryl's song manages, unintentionally I think, to celebrate without irony same-sex desire as narcissism—but, hey, this is L.A. The show ends, as all these events do, with the obligatory self-congratulatory anthem.

There is a little more insight, transgressiveness, and anger in another Celebration Theater production, Mark Savage's *The Ballad of Little Mikey* (1994), which wittily chronicles the life of a gay activist. Savage knows how to balance irony and satire with political zeal. His music sounds like he listened to *Sunday in the Park with George* twice too often, but he's a good lyricist, defining character and situation aptly. The strongest scenes are flashbacks to Mikey's coming out at college. Mikey's sex life begins in the bathroom, cleverly dramatized in the song "Tap," where Mikey finds lots of sex "while sitting on the toilet," but not the "true love" he craves. Mikey moves on to the gay activist group, but at first, wanting to be a "regular guy with a difference," he finds the activists "like something out of the Twilight Zone." Eventually he comes to realize that "Coming out is more like coming in" to a world of unique individuals, and he becomes a political firebrand. Since *The Ballad of Little Mikey* is a Los Angeles production, it is not surprising that the defining political moment in Mikey's life is leading a protest against the film *Cruising*. What could be more radical in L.A. than protesting a movie on political grounds? Twelve years later, Mikey remembers his coming-of-age as he decides whether to take a high-paying legal position. Of course, he opts to remain an activist and his partner, a real homey, picket-fence type, blesses his decision but sees it in domestic terms: Mikey is just fighting for a life like his parents. In true Hollywood style, *The Ballad of Little Mikey* manages to valorize gay radicalism and Middle-American domesticity with one theatrical gesture. Steve, Mikey's partner, is more Donna Reed than nineties gay. The satire rings truer than the artificial balance of radicalism and assimilationism or the show's sentimental moments. The show's final anthem is a combination of "love conquers all" and "to the barricades."

Combining the personal and the political is necessary in gay politics. After all, what we are fighting for is the right to privacy in our bedrooms and respect from those around us for our private choices. Still, I'm not sure queer radicalism and assimilation are quite as easily combined as *The Battle of Little Mikey* makes us think. The show hits home in its presentation of the sense of loss felt by a former radical who finds himself uncomfortably ensconced in middle-class affluence and values. If we are to believe the conclusion, Mikey will hold on to those values while rekindling his radicalism. Moreover, if we are "just like our parents" (God forbid!), why do we need musicals about our lives and experiences?

Celebration's 1998 hit, *Naked Boys Singing,* shows the direction commercial gay theater is taking. The title does not tell us what the naked boys are singing because it is of secondary importance. *(Naked Boys Singing Sweeney Todd?)* Only nudity seems to attract a large gay audience to gay theater, so we are deluged with extravaganzas like *Making Porn* or *Two Boys in a Bed on a Cold Winter's Night,* excuses for nudity. Occasionally, as in David Dillon's *Party,* there's an enjoyable play as well as naked bodies. With all the skin on the Internet it seems odd that some gay men only will go to the theater to see naked male bodies. Nonetheless, the aptly titled *Naked Boys Singing* is enjoying a long run Off-Broadway. Another gay show keeping the revue tradition alive, it has clever songs as well as nudity.

WITH STYLE

Our anthropologist will have a different set of impressions when she studies the two Howard Crabtree revues, *Whoop-Dee-Doo!* (1993) and *When Pigs Fly,* which began its two-year run in 1996. Howard Crabtree was known in the New York gay community for the outlandish costumes he put together to cheer up friends who were ill with HIV-related infections. The shows are built around Crabtree's costume designs. The unique visual style of these revues, tied to song and dance celebrating and commenting on issues of concern to a particular community, is reminiscent of a tribal ritual. They are celebrations of a gay style lacking in these other shows, as well as musical versions of gay experience.

Howard Crabtree's revues are prime examples of Tony Kushner's Theater of the Fabulous: "Irony. Tragic history. Defiance. Gender-fuck. Glitter. Drama."[2] There is as much, if not more, political statement in Crabtree's revues as there is in a show like *Fairy Tales,* but the playful, ironic presentation, the overt theatricality, the drag, the tacky glamour, inspires laughter. There is no appeal to pity here or easy sentimentality, no wooden hummingbird feeders (if there were, the actors would have worn them, not sung about them). Like the other revues we have discussed, Crabtree's shows assume a community between cast and audience—that we're all gay. The heterosexuals in the audience are the outsiders. They may enjoy the show, but it isn't being done for them.

Crabtree's revues emphasize the very tactics many contemporary gay men have trouble with—camp and drag. The shows are shoestring versions of the grand revues of the past, complete with grand, outlandish costumes. There's also an echo of the Judy Garland–Mickey Rooney "let's put on a musical in Dad's barn" movies. In the Howard Crabtree revues, the costumes are the center of the show—Crabtree was famous for his fabulous but tacky costumes. Though the lyrics are in themselves witty, they are a complement to what the audience sees. In *The Gay 90s,* Kirby Tepper satirized the issue of gays in the military in a funny song without theatrical trappings. The first act of *Whoop-Dee-Doo!* ends with a production number entitled "A Soldier's Musical," the title a parody of Charles Fuller's *A Soldier's Play,* which was turned into the film *A Soldier's Story.* Everything in the Crabtree musicals links the world of gay experience and politics to theater, itself a metaphor for much of gay experience and political expression. In "A Soldier's Musical," the sergeant is costumed as a steak, his recruits as potatoes:

> Real meat and potatoes men
> Who date tomatoes now and then. [3]

Enter Private Banana, garbed, of course, as a Chiquita banana, who throws the meat and potatoes men into a panic: "The new recruit is a fruit." In the ensuing food fight against unhealthy foods (cupcakes), Private Banana loses his life saving Sergeant Sirloin, which brings the healthy food groups together:

> From now on fruits and veg'tables will weather
> All the horrors of the cuisinart together.

"A Soldier's Musical" looks like an elementary school extravaganza gone awry. By the end, the stage is filled with men garbed in oversized costumes as potatoes, oranges, apples, grapes. The silliness and childishness of the presentation underscores the silliness of the homophobia that causes the purging of gays from the military. At the same time, the number mocks movie clichés of military bonding and heroism.

Often the Crabtree musicals celebrate gay stereotypes. A song in *When Pigs Fly,* "Light in the Loafers," has two men dancing with garishly illuminated loafers, turning an anti-gay epithet into a visual pun. In "You Are My Idol" (*Whoop-Dee-Doo!*) an anthropologist shows what happened to the natives on a small Pacific island when a show queen's cassette player and collection of show albums fell from the cargo hold of a 747 onto the island. Scantily clad native men talk like Carol Channing and a Polynesian ritual turns into a drag show of gay divas, garbed in a South Sea Islander's idea of the diva's appearance. In *When Pigs Fly,* the inevitable gay revue anthem makes gay mincemeat out of the names and initials of the states ("You can't take the Mary out of Maryland. . . . You can try to take the KY out of Kentucky") as a statement of the lunacy of legislating against homosexuals.

Howard Crabtree revues are presented as a show queen's fantasy of what a musical should be. Howard himself is the central character and master of ceremonies, the earnest costume designer and impresario suffering cast egos and various backstage calamities. Some humorless gay brethren might complain that these revues present stereotypes of effeminate sissies. In fact, the shows defiantly celebrate sissihood and camp as central elements of gay theatrical culture. *Whoop-Dee-Doo!* and *When Pigs Fly* are no more camp than *Kiss of the Spider Woman* or *La Cage aux Folles,* but they certainly outcamp *Fairy Tales* and *The Gay 90s.* The style here celebrates theatricality as a means of gay self-presentation and refuses to express sentiment or victimization. In their flamboyant silliness, they are actually more defiant than most gay revues. It's an old-fashioned gay response—turning the stereotypes and epithets against the enemy by overacting them. On stage it still works. This is, after all, classical gay performative style—what Howard sings about in the finale of *When Pigs*

Fly, "Over the Top." It's what we gave straight musicals and what we do best in gay musicals. Without it, our shows are "straight looking and acting."

HISTORY

The eleven o'clock song in *When Pigs Fly* is "Laughing Matters," about the need for laughter in chaotic, unhappy times. In the show, the song had a special poignancy and meaning since Howard Crabtree died of AIDS on June 28, 1996, just as his work on *When Pigs Fly* was finished. He played himself in the original New York cast of *Whoop-Dee-Doo!* In the second Howard Crabtree extravaganza, which opened after Crabtree's death, "Howard" was a more fictional character played by an actor. The show became a grand memorial to the imagination of the man who conceived it. It's a sad irony that Crabtree died just at the moment in medical and gay history when AIDS seems to be a condition one lives with rather than an infection one dies from. Because of his death, the show became not only a hit celebration of gayness, but a celebration of the spirit of Howard Crabtree and the many theater artists who died from this horrible, ludicrous infection, which is one of the saddest chapters in gay history. That history is the grist for a number of gay stage and film musicals.

OUR HERO

Every civil-rights movement needs a martyr and Harvey Milk is ours. Harvey Milk was the first and foremost gay activist hero-martyr, a Long Island Jewish boy who grew up to be a military veteran and successful New York stockbroker, but who gave it all up to go to San Francisco where he first became a countercultural character in a new gay neighborhood, the Castro, but eventually, after two electoral defeats, became the first openly gay male publicly elected city official. Milk's life spans the crucial phases of American gay history during his lifetime: the closet, sexual liberation, and political activism. Dan White, the man who murdered both him and the mayor of San Francisco served four years of a criminally lenient seven-year jail sentence (he later committed suicide).

In addition to a superb film documentary, *The Times of Harvey Milk,* our hero has been the subject of two very different musical theater works: an Atlanta-born musical, *The Harvey Milk Show* (1991), and an opera performed in Houston, New York, and San Francisco, *Harvey Milk* (1995).

The musical was written by two southern writers, composer Patrick Hutchison and librettist-lyricist Dan Pruitt. It was a big success for a small, ambitious Atlanta theater, Actor's Express, but it has fared less well with critics and audiences elsewhere. This is a southerner's Harvey Milk. We see the hero through the eyes of Jamey, a young man from Texas who was thrown out of his home when he came out to his father. Jamey found his way to San Francisco and survived by hustling until he was beaten up by fag-bashers. Saintly Harvey meets Jamey not by procuring his services but by taking him home to tend to his wounds. This Harvey is more Christ-like than sexual revolutionary, more cute than angry. His first song after being elected is about the "pooper scooper" law.

Harvey wins over the old inhabitants of the Castro through his charm and dedication. He and Jamey are a committed couple, idealistic kid and realistic older man. The villain of the piece is not Dan White, but an evil "Mr. Jones," the personification of homophobia and social conservatism, who tempts White to do the killing. Jones ties the gay invasion of San Francisco to the influx of ethnic minorities. Hating gays is part of hating "wags and wogs and wops and Guineas." This is simplistic politics even in Atlanta. Homophobia has more to do with gender issues than with race and ethnicity. At the end of the show, the spirit of Harvey appears to a drunk, disillusioned Jamey, urging him to keep up the fight. What's at stake in the fight are southern personalities and issues. Anita Bryant's "Save Our Children" campaign, which was based in Miami, not San Francisco, looms large in the action. Harvey responds to Bryant's campaign by pointing out the young people her hatred endangers:

> What of the kid from West Virginia
> Who now turns away from suicide?
> And what of the kid from eastern Texas
> Who tries to find his place—
> The grace he's been denied.[4]

Harvey wants to save southern kids. Watching *The Harvey Milk Show* at Actor's Express, I became confused as to where this show was taking place. It seemed far more Atlanta than San Francisco. The two most rousing songs in the show sound like old-time Protestant hymns—one is even called "Anthem." Christ-like Harvey dies and, sure enough, gets resurrected for the finale, just like all the martyrs in *Les Misérables*. This sweet, southern Harvey, singing stuff that sounded like it could have come from Nashville or the Gospel Hour, appealed to folks in Atlanta. The show was winning and endearing and offered the Harvey Atlanta could accept.

Shortly after the curtain rises on Stewart Wallace and Michael Korie's opera, *Harvey Milk* (1995), a fifteen-year-old Harvey makes his debut in the standing room of the old Metropolitan Opera House. His mother has warned him of the danger that could befall him there:

> Watch out for men who are different.
> Don't take their apples.
> Don't take their lemon drops.
> This is a world full of Golems.[5]

The importance of Harvey's Jewishness has been established from the first vocal utterance, a Hebrew prayer for the dead. He'll discover his gayness at the opera. As a huge blowup of Maria Callas's face slides into view (a bit anachronistic. It's 1945 and Callas didn't make her Met debut until a decade later) and the orchestra thunders a variation of Scarpia's chords from *Tosca,* the well-dressed men in the standing room section line up facing the audience. "Who are these men without wives," young Harvey wonders as he stands with the men. In the first act of the opera—set, according to the program, in "The Closet"—the Met standing room represents closeted pre-Stonewall gay culture. Well-dressed, affluent men for whom the opera represents a twilight zone between their daytime assimilation into straight society and their nighttime, secret gay lives cheer their favorite diva. Coming out is joining this elite, cultured society. It is also subjecting oneself to the police. Harvey is arrested the first time he tries to have sex in Central Park. This moment is presented in musical counterpoint to his mother's narrative of what happened to the Jews during the Holocaust and her admonition,

> Never forget who you are.
> Remember: Never again.

His activism will come from his Jewishness as much as his homosexuality. Flash forward a few years and Harvey has grown into a successful New York stockbroker, closeted homosexual, and opera queen. One side of the raked pink triangle on which the action is played in Christopher Alden's staging of *Harvey Milk* in the joint production of the Houston, New York City, and San Francisco Operas is a row of closet doors. The closet is maintained not only by the fear and wish to maintain privilege of those within, but also by the brutal, homophobic police keeping those doors closed. To come out of the closet one must fight the police as well as oneself. In Harvey's mind—and on stage—there is a symbolic joining of the well-dressed, closeted opera queen and the Holocaust victim as Harvey realizes he must be as open and proud of being "a man who loves men" as he is of being a Jew. At the rear of the stage a giant six-pointed star is made from the joining of a pink triangle and a yellow triangle, two images of Nazi oppression and extermination of gays and Jews. Out of this synthesis of Harvey the homosexual and Harvey the Jew comes Harvey the gay activist who will join the drag queens fighting the police at the Stonewall riots, which provide the climax of the opera's first act. Like the grandest of grand operas, each act of *Harvey Milk* contains a historical spectacle: The Stonewall rebellion in Act I, San Francisco's first Gay Pride parade in Act II, and in the final act the candlelight procession the night of Milk's murder.

The beauty and power of *Harvey Milk* is this theatrical distillation of ideas underlying gay history, particularly its combination through the title character of opera, Jewishness, and gayness. Those Scarpia chords identify a brutal chief of police, and the opera queen turned gay revolutionary must stop cheering Tosca the diva cop killer and become her. At the end of the opera, after Harvey has been murdered, his mother returns to place candles at either side of his corpse as Tosca does for Scarpia. In this opera, as in *Tosca,* the police still win.

Opera in the age of the closet was diva worship—cheering Callas, Tebaldi, or Milanov as they sang their suffering and offered images of women who are powerful but also victims. Off stage and on, the diva is a triumphant creature (Callas's lonely death happened after Stonewall), but she portrays the maddened Lucia, the noble, suffering Aida, or the passionate suicide, Tosca. There are no more operatic divas, nor is there the same closeted gay culture to worship them. Perhaps an interpretive community has also been lost—a group of men capable of reading their experience into the soprano's sufferings and high C's. *Harvey Milk* outs opera, or at least one element of opera audiences. In the opera, Harvey moves from standing room in Act I to a box he shares with his lover, Scott, in the last act. There Harvey becomes the diva, cheered by the lesbians and gay men in the audience. Perhaps opera in the nineties has to be an uncloseted celebration of opera's place in gay culture—like *Harvey Milk.*

Opera in the age of the closet was often conducted, staged, and designed by closeted gay men. Now it is to a lesser extent. Many of our talented artists are dead of AIDS-related infections and many are now out of the closet. Leonard Bernstein came out before his death and was outed by biographers. Conductor Thomas Schippers was the subject of a cautious outing in *Opera News* more than twenty years after his death. Press reports on *The Ghosts of Versailles* made clear that composer John Corigliano and librettist William M. Hoffman were gay. In reviewing *Harvey Milk* for *New York* magazine, music critic Peter G. Davis outed himself, partially as a means of establishing his credentials to review the opera and raising the question of whether a straight critic would review the opera fairly or whether a straight reviewer's reservations about the piece would be seen as anything but homophobia.

Stewart Wallace, the composer of *Harvey Milk,* is straight. The music is good—not great, but good—certainly equal to many of the standard repertory verismo operas that used to be the vehicles for the divas of yore (*Cavalleria Rusticana, Andrea Chenier, La Gioconda*). We ask too much if we demand that all opera scores be great, and not all the great scores are the most enjoyable theater pieces. We've lost some of the grand old tub-thumpers, not because they're not thoroughly enjoyable or worth hearing, but because there are no big, great voices around to sing the hell out of them as there were in the fifties and sixties. Wallace is better with the lyrical moments than the grand ones, but he orchestrates extremely well and his solos for the principals are good, effective musical theater writing. *Harvey Milk* is a successful theater score, the best I've heard mixing the styles of contemporary American music, from John Adams's minimalism to Lou Harrison's orientalism to Leonard Bernstein's jazziness. It also consciously aims for a fusion of grand opera with Broadway, which is easier now that so many musicals aspire to the status of opera. If anything, the score for *Harvey Milk* is less nineteenth century, more aggressively rhythmic and jazzy, verging on rock at times, than what is heard in the scores of hits like *Titanic* and *Ragtime.* I'm not sure the more contemporary styles and the contemporary libretto mix well with unamplified, operatic voices (actually there was some amplification in New York). I would have preferred a Broadway vocal sound. It's not gay music—there's no such thing. It's terrific theater music, which may be as close to gay music as you can get.

Michael Korie's libretto for *Harvey Milk* is a celebration of gay pride fought for and earned by a generation who grew up in households in which "homosexual" was the dirtiest of words. In his aria before being killed, Milk sings to his Jewish mother:

> Mama, I've slept with over a thousand men.
> If you don't know by now,
> I'm gay, queer, fegelah, different.
> But I never had the guts to tell you.
> Never had the balls to say it out loud,
> me and my whole generation.
> We were born too soon and we saw no choice,
> 'til a warm night in June when we found our voice,
> And the lies we told our mothers turned to shame.
> And shame to rage.
> And rage to pride.
> And pride to hope.
> And hope will never be silent.
> If a bullet should enter my brain

let it shatter every closet door.

This is a new role for opera, this political exhortation, but one that makes the art form serious, akin to drama, rather than frivolous, like the gay-created *The Ghosts of Versailles,* which is beautiful and fun but totally a diversion—theatrical dessert—very camp, but nothing much else. Somehow this earnestness and didacticism works better in grand opera than it does in intimate revue. *Harvey Milk* is about many of my generation of opera-goers. There's a sense of vindication and triumph in the second-act love duet between Harvey and Scott. After all those male-male duets of homosocial friendship (*The Pearl Fishers, Don Carlo, La Bohème*) that were mediated by love of a woman, here we have two men singing of their love for one another. This isn't the tortured, thwarted love of Benjamin Britten's central characters, but the passion of two openly gay men. *Harvey Milk* is of a piece with much contemporary American opera in being based on characters out of contemporary history, in looking for an immediacy and relevance not found anymore in Broadway musicals.

The excellent recording of *Harvey Milk* is accompanied by many pictures of Milk and the key moments of his life and death, as if the opera were a documentary. It isn't. It does what the musical stage can do so well—create meaningful symbolic actions. As the notes for the album tell us, the opera is "unapologetically mythic." Moreover, the opera acknowledges itself as a moment in gay history—the outing of opera and opera queens. I can only imagine what the audience reaction was like at the San Francisco Opera.

A footnote. We went to *Harvey Milk* at the New York City Opera a few months after seeing Britten's *Death in Venice*—a gorgeous, haunted opera, but hardly a testimony to gay pride—at the Met. The audience for *Death in Venice* was not large, but it was like one of those gay reunions at which you see every gay person you know from all over the country. When we arrived at our seats on the second tier at the New York City Opera for *Harvey Milk,* we were surprised that we weren't surrounded by other gay men. Not only did the audience around us look pretty straight, it looked like a housewives' convention, or so we thought until the Dykes on Bikes wheeled down the stage in the Gay Pride parade finale to Act II. The well-dressed women around us all started cheering. Duh! Housewives indeed!

STONEWALL

If Harvey Milk is our hero, Stonewall is our Boston Tea Party. This battle between denizens of a Greenwich Village gay bar and the police, a fun-house mirror reflection of a number of sixties battles between rebels of various kinds and the police, was one of a number of local victories won in that decade—for instance, the legislation resulting from the 1957 Wolfenden Report in England that led to the decriminalization of homosexuality in 1967 (We Americans are way behind. Many American states still have sodomy laws on the books and the Supreme Court in 1986 upheld a state's right to make and police such laws against consensual private acts between citizens), and legislation in San Francisco that eliminated many anti-gay statutes and the police's violent actions against free assembly by gays and lesbians. Still, Stonewall represents a group of citizens fighting against injustice. Britain's Gay Sweatshop, a theater group active in the seventies and eighties, made it the crowning moment in their dramatic chronicle of gay history, *As Time Goes By* (1977). In another Gay Sweatshop production, Philip Osment's *This Island's Mine,* a character recalls:

> Then came the rumors from New York
> Of riots in Greenwich Village,
> And a new sort of Pride was born
> Which quickly spread to Europe.[6]

This conceives of Stonewall as a second American Revolution. Stonewall has also been dramatized effectively in *Harvey Milk* and Doric Wilson's play *Street Theater* (1982). A British filmmaker, Nigel Finch, turned the Stonewall riots into a musical film that offers a capsule history of American gay activism in the 1960s. Though loosely based on historian Martin Duberman's book *Stonewall,* the film is far from a documentary. Like the musical theater pieces about Harvey Milk, it turns history into a myth of gay liberation. The Stonewall finale of Act I of the opera *Harvey Milk* is built from the actual chants and songs that are part of the history of Stonewall, particularly the "ta-ra-ra-boom-di-ay" kick line of the drag queens:

> We are the Stonewall girls
> We wear our hair in curls
> We have no underwear
> We show our pubic hair
> We wear our dungarees
> Above our nelly knees.

Harvey is converted to radicalism the night of the Stonewall uprising by young radical Scott Smith. Stonewall is their *Liebesnacht,* the background and corollary to their romance. In Nigel Finch's film *Stonewall* (1996), the history of the uprising is tied to the relationship of a southern country boy with radical leanings, Matty Dean, and a Puerto Rican drag queen, La Miranda. The songs the drag queens lip-synch between episodes of the film and as cross-cut commentaries on some sequences provide a kind of Greek chorus. The dominant voice of the film is that of the black and Latino drag queens, the true radicals, contrasted with the cautious, bourgeois voice of the Mattachine Society and the carefully policed gay white middle-class social interactions on Fire Island. Actually, the most vibrant voice is that of the black fifties and sixties girl groups the drag queens lip-synch to. Matty Dean (a pseudonym as fictional as the names of the drag queens) finds his own voice in his protest song to the tune of the "Battle Hymn of the Republic." He gets the well-dressed members of the Mattachine Society to sing his song, albeit cautiously, on the way back from their proper, ineffective demonstration in front of Independence Hall in Philadelphia, but they're not going to fight the battles. Rather than participating in the Stonewall rebellion, the Mattachine Society posts a plea for peace and quiet on the wall of the Stonewall Inn. At the Stonewall rebellion, the drag queens find their own voice as they do their kick line and sing "We are the Stonewall girls." No more lip-synching. The film also underscores the connection between the death of Judy Garland and the rebellion. As the police invade the Stonewall Inn, Bostonia, the black drag queen who is the lover of the closeted owner of the bar and Mother Superior to the drag queens, insists that Judy's voice be kept on the jukebox.

Stonewall is a film filled with music, but not really a musical film. It demonstrates the problem of defining genre in many gay shows and films. It's tricky talking about gay musicals, because so much gay drama and film have verged on being musical. Mart Crowley's groundbreaking *The Boys in the Band* (1968) had a musical title echoing Judy Garland and Cole Porter's "Anything Goes" played under the opening credits of the film version. Terrence McNally's *The Ritz,* the first unabashedly gay comedy to reach Broadway, had Rita Moreno's Googie Gomez, a combination Charo and Bette Midler, singing show tunes in a gay bathhouse. This put Moreno on the map as a minor Broadway diva after years of film. Harvey Fierstein's hit *Torch Song Trilogy* has a musical title and a first act whose scenes are punctuated by mock torch songs. Jonathan Harvey's play *Beautiful Thing,* turned into a successful film, has Mama Cass's voice and music as a metaphor for the liberation the gay teenage boys are experiencing. A critic friend of mine describes the 1998 gay film comedy *Billy's Hollywood Screen Kiss* as a musical in disguise. Like *Stonewall,* it has musical interludes performed by lip-synching drag queens. As music, dancing, and musical performance have been so much a part of gay culture, it sometimes is difficult to make clear distinctions as to what is a musical and what isn't. In

Stonewall, we know the "straight-looking and -acting" members of the Mattachine Society are ineffectual because they can't sing or dance. To be gay is to live out the old stereotypical epithet "musical."

To be gay in *Stonewall* also means having the courage to be queer. Matty Dean dons his Puerto Rican drag queen lover's drag to take her draft psychological examination for her. As he makes her affirm both masculinity and femininity, he must do the same. His lapse from political correctness comes when he rejects La Miranda for a more conventional "straight-looking and -acting" gay male: "Is it my fault I wasn't born with a permanent sissy gene?" However, in *Stonewall,* the sissies are the fighters, and Matty Dean leaves his closeted middle-class butch lover to return to gutsy La Miranda.

The Stonewall rebellion was mostly carried out by drag queens, but in musical theater in general, drag equals gay. We have drag queen heroines in *La Cage aux Folles* and *Kiss of the Spider Woman,* as well as the quasi-musical *Torch Song Trilogy.* In Tony Kushner's *Angels in America,* Louis, who is filled with left-wing theories he can't act on, sees drag queens as politically incorrect, the gay world's "Stepnfetchits," but the most noble characters are drag queens. Insofar as drag queens liberate all of us from entrapment in conventional gender roles, they are terrific. What's the downside? That straight people might think we're all "like that"? What's so bad about that? Better a drag queen than Jesse Helms. Perhaps this is why the Australian quasi-musical *Priscilla, Queen of the Desert* was so exhilarating. It reminds us that we have the potential to be fabulous, even in the various literal and metaphoric outbacks we travel through.

SINGING AIDS

In discussing the drag performer Lypsinka, David Román notes that her performance "serves as a fantasy for a certain gay spectatorship yearning for the 'simplicity' of life before AIDS."[7] *Stonewall,* like the Harvey Milk musicals, is far from apolitical but it does take us back to a time before AIDS, when there were clear-cut heroes and villains. After the last image of "The end" in *Stonewall,* we are shown a vivid reminder of a darker, more ambiguous time to follow, an epitaph for its maker, Nigel Finch, who died of AIDS-related infections at thirty-five years old just after his film was finished. The epitaph— a marker of yet another talented young artist's unjust, untimely death—makes *Stonewall* a reminder of the necessity of anger and activism in the age of AIDS, a reminder that the members of ACT UP, whatever their attire, are the descendants of the Stonewall girls.

Remember the wooden hummingbird feeder? It was an attempt to sing about the experience of AIDS, not a very musical subject. It sang of AIDS in the way the infection was generally treated on stage and in music during the first decade of the epidemic. In *Stonewall,* Ethan, the handsome young member of the Mattachine Society, in defending the "illness" explanation for homosexuality, says, "At this point, sympathy would be a huge step for us. Pity's better than hate." For a while, popular AIDS cultural productions, like made-for-TV movies, presented the young gay man (gay = AIDS) as someone to be pitied. He was young, handsome, noble, played by straight cutie pies like Aidan Quinn, Hugh Grant, or Tom Hanks, and the straight audience could weep for him, feel sympathy, but know that this gay person would be dead at the end of the film. Too easy! Gay artists and audiences quickly tired of the tearjerker model of AIDS melodrama, which is why some of us laughed through the hummingbird feeder number in *Fairy Tales.* ACT UP reminded us what some of us older folks had forgotten since Stonewall and some younger gays never had to learn, that anger often is more useful than tears. Moreover, gay theater, like much of mainstream America, tended to present AIDS as a gay disease, ignoring its effects on the poor. Two small musicals present a more complicated response to AIDS.

AIDS: The Musical! (1991; by Wendell Jones and David Stanley, music by Robert Berg), a Los Angeles production, is a more direct gay response to AIDS. In their preface, the authors state that they didn't want to write "another tired tired tired boring tragic AIDS play" but rather something that would dramatize the more upbeat and activist ways the gay community was dealing with AIDS: "Being part of and witness to this transformation—and because we're fags—we couldn't help but chronicle and musicalize it, taste be damned."[8] A musical version seemed the most appropriate *gay* expression of the new responses to AIDS. At the beginning of the second act, a character says to the audience: "You know, a lot of people have been asking us, 'Why don't you have any straight people in your show?' The answer is really very simple. 'Because we don't have to.'"[9] If the media has been ignoring homosexuals, this musical can ignore heterosexuals. Like the best gay AIDS theater, *AIDS: The Musical!* manages to be ironic, satiric, and earnest simultaneously. Its manner is not the flamboyant, old-fashioned camp of the Howard Crabtree musicals; rather, it celebrates contemporary gay flamboyance and irony. While celebrating activism, for instance, the show gently satirizes ACT UP meetings: "ACT UP people aren't hostile to newcomers—just to each other."[10]

The musical begins where early AIDS dramas inevitably ended, at the deathbed of a young man, Bob, who is surrounded by his caregivers. Here, though, the caregivers, representing different points of view toward Bob's illness and the crisis in general, squabble. Luis is an angry activist who wants to change the system of health care delivery, Christian a New Age spiritualist who is wearing himself out as an AIDS buddy. Lisa, who has just broken off with her lover, Penny, wants to get away from the chaos of Los Angeles and settle in a women's commune in Northhampton, Massachusetts. Thomas, Bob's lover, is also sick. In the midst of this emotional turmoil, Bob announces: "I'm a theatre queen. I always wanted death to be like a big musical with angels and songs," which heralds an opening number for principals and chorus. From this point, the musical chronicles Thomas, "our good-natured but tortured leading character," on his adventures as a Person With AIDS: from a brief stay in an overcrowded hospital where he finds his insurance company has canceled his policy, to his workplace where his boss orders him to take "a long [unpaid] rest," to a New Age meditation group, a safe-sex club, an ACT UP demonstration, and a celebration of Radical Faeries. The final scene is another ACT UP demonstration demanding more health care for Persons With AIDS. For all the need for love and spiritualism, *AIDS: The Musical!* is a call for social action. The musical numbers serve a variety of purposes from social commentary to emotional outburst. In the first act, the principals sing of their conflicts with their parents, who say they accept their children, but with a qualification:

> And I love you
> And I love you but
> Just don't talk about it
> We don't want to hear it.[11]

The various social organizations are defined through song, from rousing anthem to ACT UP rap. Many of the songs are expressions of anger, from dying Carlos wishing for a gun to kill his enemies, a challenge to the sweet, passive victim of earlier AIDS representations, to the activists painting the city red. In a show that is also a celebration of sex in the age of AIDS, there are also love songs and celebrations of sexual ecstasy. Ultimately, *AIDS: the Musical!* is a celebration of gayness and the gay community's refusing guilt or shame, expressing anger and passion, and living heroically in the face of AIDS.

    elegies for angels punks and raging queens (1989; by Bill Russell, music by Janet Hood), set in New York but, like many new American plays, performed more in London, is a series of poetic self-descriptions of a variety of Persons With AIDS interspersed with songs. The show is intended to be a verbal counterpart to the Names Project Quilt, attempting stylized memorials. The rhyming, sometimes forced (injection/infection), gets tiresome at times; the music (eight of the "elegies" have been turned into songs) is insistently, well, elegiac (piano, cello, and harp accompaniment), until the obligatory "We Are the World"–style final anthem. Russell's cast of characters comes out of a specific locale, a past Greenwich Village filled with "junkies and hot-to-trot teens" and "angels, punks, and raging queens." Like *Rent,* this is a picture of a kind of bohemia ravaged by AIDS, and, to Russell's credit, the thirty-six voices present a real cross-section of urban society, gay and straight, though over half are gay—it is Greenwich Village—and of responses to the virus. Not all the characters are sympathetic; their anger takes many forms, including infection of others as a kind of revenge. To Russell's credit, his elegies do evoke both specific characters and familiar types. There is Billy, the boy who fled the insularity and prejudices of North Dakota to live as a gay man. When Billy dies, his body is returned to North Dakota for burial, to "the town which I despised." After he receives the grim news of his HIV status, Nick leaves the doctor's office and goes to the baths "and fucked every jerk I could." Joe hates his AIDS Quilt panel:

> at least
> I was remembered
> but I requested
> fabulous.[12]

elegies acknowledges the AIDS memorial and political movements, from the quilt to ACT UP, but when the show was written, the end was still, inevitably, terminal. The last song is "Learning to Let Go."

In London, *elegies for angels, punks and raging queens* had an interesting performance history. It began at the King's Head, a famous small pub theater in bohemian Islington, with a cast of twenty-nine actors and four singers. I saw it first when it had been remounted at the Drill Hall, a traditional venue for queer performance. There doesn't seem to be much separation between performer and audience at the Drill Hall, and this intimacy really worked, as did the Spartan atmosphere of the large black room. Some mad soul got the idea to move the show to one of the West End's gaudiest theaters. Here, given West End union regulations, the number of actors was halved, and West End name singers Kim Criswell and Simon Green were brought in. On a proscenium stage in a pink Victorian monstrosity of a theater, the show was embarrassing—a lesson in the importance of appropriate venue for a theatrical work.

CROSSOVERS

William Finn's *Falsettos* and Jonathan Larson's *Rent* represent two different types of musical theatrical response to AIDS. Both started in small Off-Broadway theaters and took years to complete. Both became works accepted by mainstream audiences—though *Falsettos* was never the megahit *Rent* has become, it did have a respectable Broadway run, particularly for a small, nonspectacular musical about a gay man. Like the leads in the other successful Broadway shows about gay men and AIDS, Marvin, the central character of *Falsettos,* is gay and Jewish. In the first of the two one-act musicals that make up *Falsettos,* written and first produced a decade apart, Marvin has left his wife, Trina, and eleven-year-old son, Jason, for a handsome young man, Whizzer. Trina takes up with the psychiatrist she and Marvin have been seeing, which Marvin takes, as he takes most things, as a monumental betrayal. Meanwhile, Marvin and Whizzer have nurtured a dysfunctional gay marriage. At a time in which gay people policed positive images of homosexuals, William Finn was courageous in writing a show about a dysfunctional gay man, a sort of homosexual Woody Allen. For Finn, it is Marvin's Jewishness, which he shares with the other characters, that defines him more than his sexuality. The first number in *March of the Falsettos* (1981) is "Four Jews in a Room Bitching," which seems to be the operative participle for these males. Marvin expects to remain the center of the life of wife, son, and lover and explodes when they have other ideas. Trina is supposed to remain faithful to him; Jason is supposed to be the adoring son. Whizzer is supposed to be a male version of the ideal wife, looking lovely, cooking gourmet meals, and always sexually available. By the end of *March of the Falsettos,* Trina has married the psychiatrist, Mendel; Jason is in therapy to get over his fears of being gay; and Whizzer has packed his bags and left. *March of the Falsettos* is relentlessly clever in its post-Sondheim way, but the audience understands why everyone has left Marvin. Despite Marvin's centrality, our sympathies are with everyone else.

Falsettoland (1990), the second part, which can stand on its own brilliantly, is a picture of the building of intentional families in the face of AIDS. Jason has remained friends with Whizzer, the sanest adult he knows, as well as the best baseball coach. After a reunion at one of Jason's Little League games, Whizzer moves back into Marvin's apartment, next door to a lesbian couple. Charlotte is an internist, Cordelia a kosher caterer. This time, Marvin and Whizzer, somewhat older and wiser, are a happy couple. However, Dr. Charlotte sees that "Something bad is happening." Men come to her office with new diseases: "Something so bad that words have lost their meaning." Whizzer is the next target of the "something bad," and in the process he becomes the focus of the love and caring of his and Marvin's family. Trina, Marvin's ex-wife, realizes that Whizzer is part of her family and her life. Jason, who adores Whizzer, wants his Bar Mitzvah, catered by Cordelia, moved to Whizzer's hospital room. Whizzer dies shortly afterward, and the show ends with Marvin and Whizzer singing a duet celebrating their love:

Once I was told

That all men get what they deserve.

Who the hell then threw this curve?

There are no answers

But what would I be

If you had not been my friend?[13]

"Friend" may seem a weak word for what Marvin and Whizzer were to each other, but perhaps it's the most important one for an audience unaccustomed to seeing gay couples. In *March of the Falsettos,* Marvin and Whizzer are lovers, spouses of a sort, but not really friends. Growing up is seeing the person you share a bed with as a friend. In the face of AIDS, William Finn presents an assimilationist ideal: Marvin, gay man and father in an intentional family of lesbians, gay men, and heterosexuals. All three couples—heterosexual, gay male, lesbian—are presented as loving marriages. The gender politics of the *Falsettos* is not as enlightened as its gay politics: men are grown-up children who need to be taken care of by women, who are the nurturers: wife and mother, doctor, cook.

AIDS in *Falsettos* is presented as a horrible thing that happens to nice people who happen to be gay men. Whizzer is never an abject victim. His final song, "You Gotta Die Sometime," presents his vision of death as an erotic object, feared but attractive, a ravisher:

He puts his arms around my neck and walks me to the bed

He pins me up against the wall and kisses me like crazy

The many stupid things I thought about with dread

Now delight.

Then the scene turns to white.[14]

Despite Whizzer's tempting vision of death, Dr. Charlotte is right: "AIDS stinks."

Like *March of the Falsettos, Falsettoland* was first presented separately at a nonprofit theater, then moved to a commercial run Off Broadway. Despite rave reviews, *Falsettoland* didn't last long on Christopher Street in Greenwich Village. In 1990, gay people who had suffered through the ravages of this disease didn't want a musical about it, no matter how good. A couple of years later, the two pieces were put together as *Falsettos* and performed on Broadway for about a year. *Falsettos* always seemed to be written for a straight Jewish audience more than a gay audience. Marvin's coming out and family tribulations are presented as a crisis for a Jewish family. I had seen a moving production of *Falsettoland* at a small

theater in Washington, D.C., that convinced me this was a brilliant little show. I
was horrified by what happened on Broadway in front of a predominantly straight
audience. At the first mention of the word, "homosexuals," the audience laughed.
Marvin's homosexuality was played as something alien to the characters on stage
as well as to the audience. All sympathy went to the straights. I have seldom felt
so alienated in a theater as I did that night. In 1998, The National Asian-American
Theater Company in New York revived *Falsettoland* to rave reviews.

Jonathan Larson's *Rent* is *Hair* and *A Chorus Line* for the nineties. A
group of kids, mostly from affluent middle-class suburban backgrounds, live a
fashionably dissident life in New York. Like the tribe in *Hair,* these kids are
decidedly countercultural; like the kids in *A Chorus Line* a number of them are
aspiring artists, but unlike the kids in *A Chorus Line* they seem to have no talent,
no particular dedication to their art, and no self-discipline. Many of them have
AIDS, either through sexual transmission or drugs (many are also drug addicts).
The show irresponsibly romanticizes heroin abuse in a way common in rock
music but unusual in the commercial theater. The ultimate message of *Rent,*
much like that of *Hair* but with much better music, is live for today and love.
"Let the sun shine!" *Hair,* like most of the sixties counterculture, was not
particularly enlightened about homosexuality. *Rent* acknowledges the existence
of queerness at the margins of a marginal society. *Rent* seems at first to be more
radical and anti-assimilationist than most gay musicals. Collins, the black genius
computer whiz who uses his knowledge to redistribute wealth in ways Marx
never dreamed of, is in love with Angel Shunard, the Puerto Rican drag queen
who is the antithesis of "straight looking and acting." This is a gay counterculture my suburban students don't know. Yet the formula isn't much different from
that of *Kiss of the Spider Woman,* in which a nelly Latino queen got to have sex
with a macho man, or *A Chorus Line,* in which Paul, the abject gay, was a Latino
drag queen. In *Rent,* Angel doesn't carry the baggage of guilt and shame Paul
carries and the macho man is gay, but this is a small step forward. Of all the
characters with AIDS in the show, guess who dies? Poor Angel, the drag queen,
of course. We still have a gay character alive at the end, but the transgressive
one, the one Mother in Long Island would have the most trouble accepting, is
killed off while the heterosexuals with AIDS are alive at the final curtain. This
quasi-bohemian community has been created by a straight white male. Lesbian
novelist Sarah Schulman, who has her own personal issues with *Rent,* has written
a book-length critique of the show's representation of lesbians, gay men, and
AIDS. She is spot on about straight-audience reception of Collins and Angel:

> They kiss on stage while the transvestite is wearing a dress. The audience is
> reconfirmed in their own sense of how tolerant they are. Gay men wear dresses.

They die. How sad. What a relief. Well, that's what happens to gay people, I guess. They're secondary subplots. That's their place, even in the story of AIDS.[15]

David Román notes that "AIDS in *Rent* is normalized to such a degree it can't help but be, if not overlooked, at least, unexamined."[16] More than normalized, AIDS, like heroin addiction, is kinda cool. Lovers exchange AZT the way they pass on their stash. It's all part of being bohemian. The audience does see the communal rituals of AIDS: an AIDS support group, though without fear or anger, and an AIDS memorial service. We get the death of the drag queen, but the miraculous recovery of the dying Mimi for a happy ending for the heterosexual lovers. AIDS is not a gay disease in *Rent* as it is in *Falsettos*. It's a disease of the poor, but poor is chic in *Rent,* like the emaciated, drugged-out-looking fashion models of recent years sporting expensive clothing that looks like it was picked up in a thrift shop for a buck.

Rent is a fascinating phenomenon. I have students who have seen it dozens of times. A young man I know who was publisher of Duke's nasty right-wing rag loved the show. How could an ultraconservative Republican kid love a musical filled with dope addicts, lesbians, and drag queens, and whose villain is a yuppie real estate tycoon? Like rock stars of the last generation, *Rent* has become a means of rebelling vicariously, even for kids who are anything but rebels. After all, the leading characters are from the suburbs and aren't too impoverished to have answering machines. It's interesting that the British, who are used to more sophisticated representations of class politics, don't get *Rent.* British gay friends who work in musical theater and love everything with a tune simply don't like it.

We saw the show early in its Broadway run, when the audience still contained a fair sampling of typical Saturday matinee theatergoers. The distin-guished-looking elderly couple behind us made it through all of the drug stuff and gay stuff without a hitch, but walked out in a huff toward the end of the show during the most overtly political number, "What You Own." It's expected nowadays that a musical will give you gay people and people different from those in Westchester, but politics is the great American taboo. What the straight middle-class kids who flock to *Rent* buy now is the racial assimilation the show represents and the hipness of being anti-homophobic, if not particularly pro-gay.

Rent also raises questions about gay reality and gay representation. While in the original cast the two gay men were played by straight performers, Mark, the straight filmmaker whose girlfriend, à la Woody Allen's *Manhattan,* becomes a lesbian, was played by an openly gay performer, Anthony Rapp, who sees his celebrity as a means of helping gay kids. Yet, as usual, the performers who originally played Collins and Angel were advertised as straight.

The opera queen in me found *Rent* an extremely witty riff on *La Bohème*. The more one knows Puccini's depiction of la vie bohème," to my mind one of the most thoroughly successful musical theater works ever written (even Franco Zeffirelli can't destroy it), the more one enjoys Jonathan Larson's cleverness. The music is an interesting mix of rock and Broadway. Like most theater composers of the past generation, Larson admired Sondheim, but he was more eclectic, mixing the best in contemporary theater music with rock and avoiding the easy listening of recent Broadway pop operas.

David Román writes that "more than anything else in our theater right now, *Rent* has become a vehicle for what the times tell us about AIDS."[17] It may also be a vehicle for where we are about gayness in the Broadway theater. Television offers us tidy, affluent, asexual gay men in just about every show. Straight-created (though gay-directed) *Rent* avoids any traditional mode of theatrical representation (is it a musical? a rock concert?) and offers a world without prejudice (and, for kids, an ideal world in which parents are only voices on the answering machine). In this world, gays are exotics, safely distant from suburban experience. Sarah Schulman notes the double bind gay people encounter in this marketing of homosexuality.

> What it really means is that, while in the past we could not be represented because the fact of our existence would mitigate the supremacy of heterosexuality, marketing and the commodification of our experiences has now made it safe for us to be represented and have that fact reinforce the superiority of heterosexuality.[18]

Rent has gay characters, but it isn't really gay.

AIDS, LACAN, AND BUSBY BERKELEY

The film *Zero Patience* (1993) by the brilliant Canadian director John Greyson uses the form and freedom of the musical to attack the popular myths surrounding AIDS and to valorize the anger and tactics of ACT UP. The story is as follows: Sir Richard Burton, the Victorian naturalist and sexologist best known for his translations of the Kama Sutra and Arabian Nights but also responsible for some writings on sexual practices, is still alive and working as a curator in a Toronto museum. Burton is creating a Hall of Contagion, exhibiting characters like Typhoid Mary and creatures like the African Green Monkey, supposedly responsible for the transmission of AIDS to humans. What the exhibit needs to be complete is a display on Patient Zero, the Quebecois flight attendant who supposedly brought AIDS to North America. Patient Zero emerges from limbo and begins a romance with Burton, whom he helps to see the foolishness of prejudiced, simplistic causal narratives. This imaginative story is told as a musical with an excellent score (by Glenn Schellenberg) of nine songs plus reprises. With one exception, the songs are commentaries on the political ramifications of the narrative. In one way or another, the songs are basically about sexual pleasure that is not to be denied because of AIDS. Some, like "Pop-a-Boner," a guide to bathhouse etiquette, or the duet of Burton's and Zero's talking and singing sphincters, are defiant stands against prudery and celebrations of sources of gay sexual pleasure. Some focus on AIDS narratives. In "Just Like Scheherazade," Zero sings of his desire to be kept alive through the telling of his story, but truthfully, "Why do they need someone to blame?" Zero wants to be remembered his way—"I'm not the first, but the best." Burton's exhibit of the African Green Monkey and other jungle creatures comes to life to mock the idea that they are "contagious." The real story of AIDS, according to the HIV virus, a drag queen, is one of "greed, ambition, and fraud." In the final number, the issue is not Patient Zero, but "zero patience"—"for accusations, for all blame, for hollow proclamations." The exception to the choric songs is a duet between Zero and Burton about the love they can never really have. Yet it too is a song about language, about the "Six or Seven Things" they did not tell each other.

In *Zero Patience,* Greyson combines anger against AIDS Pharisees with a rekindling of a politics of pleasure. The film is filled with beautiful images of nude men, a celebration of the male body. Musical numbers recall everything from Busby Berkeley to MTV. The brilliant colors echo past musicals. Zero introduces the Victorian Burton to the pleasures of sex and the joy of love. This version of Zero is a rebuttal to Randy Shilts's version in *And the Band Played On.* Zero brings beauty, joy, and love, not disease and death. The perverse cautionary narratives of mainstream social institutions are based on falsification of evidence. Greyson brilliantly balances anger with life celebration without belying the horror of AIDS. For him, AIDS as a source of cautionary, homophobic, anti-pleasure narratives is a vestige of Victorianism that must be erased. Burton's exhibition is sabotaged, first by ACT UP, but finally, miraculously, by Zero with Burton as an accomplice.

Zero Patience is, to my mind, the great musical theater piece about AIDS, created by an artist with a mastery of film, but who also has read much of the theoretical and political writing about AIDS as well as some postmodern theory. Even the songs have echoes of intellectual figures like psychoanalytic theorist Jacques Lacan and critic Leo Bersanyi. Yet the film is anything but arid. Like the best theater works I have discussed here, *Zero Patience* combines the new—

gay politics developed over the past half-century of activism—with the old—gay style, honed and refined by another of our saints, Oscar Wilde. As I recall, Wilde's most camp work, *Salome,* was turned into a musical.

EASILY ASSIMILATED

On stage we have been better served by musicals that include homosexual desire within a wider spectrum of sexuality, thus avoiding the superficial self-congratulation of the gay musical. In these works we find a far more complex treatment of love and desire, those powerful human experiences the musical treats best.

Michael John LaChiusa's *Hello Again* (1994) is a musical adaptation of Arthur Schnitzler's *La Ronde.* Whereas Schnitzler's oft-revived play (as I write this, a new version is on Broadway with Nicole Kidman) was a turn-of-the-twentieth-century Viennese picture of sexual mores and manners, LaChiusa's work is a picture of longing for connection that sex doesn't satisfy that spans the twentieth century. Like Schnitzler's play, the musical is a series of sexual encounters in which a character from the first scene has a rendezvous with a new character in the second scene who beds another new character in the third scene until, in scene ten, the last character encounters a character from the first scene. Scenes six and seven feature encounters between men and an androgynous but male character, the Young Thing (played originally by John Cameron Mitchell, who created Hedwig). The first is set in a stateroom on the *Titanic* on its last night. The Husband, a middle-aged man, has picked up the Young Thing from steerage and seduces him as the ship sinks. The Husband claims that marriage is "the greatest adventure a man and woman share," but on this sinking ship, he seeks an angel, a figure of youth and innocence, for a more romantic adventure. The boy, more worldly than he looks, wants a sugar daddy to help him get settled in New York. He is not bright enough to comprehend why the stateroom is tilting and why the passengers outside are screaming. The Husband's seduction of the Young Thing becomes a dance of death, accompanied by the screams of the passengers and the cracking of the ship. The androgyny of the Young Thing that the script calls for suggests that for the Husband the gender of the angel in unimportant. It is youth he desires.

In the next scene, it is the seventies in a chic New York disco. The Young Thing is picked up by a screenwriter who also sees him as an angel. In this incarnation, the Young Thing is a vapid creature, a temp worker with no aspirations or interests. He's also a shipwreck survivor looking for "somewhere safe."

> Anywhere, anywhere safe.
>
> With someone who won't fall apart
>
> When the world begins to fall apart.
>
> Someone single, not too dull or smart
>
> But safe;
>
> Decently, honestly safe.[19]

For a brief moment, the Writer and the Young Thing can fantasize that safe place in each other's arms, but it doesn't extend past one night. Like the Writer's screenplays, it is safely in the realm of romantic fantasy. The scene shows the dark side of the sexually liberated seventies in which emotional needs and romantic dreams are not fulfilled by sexual encounters. The Young Thing sums up the disillusionment: "Got no expectations. / Used to, now I don't."[20] LaChiusa wants us to see this as a universal experience not limited to gay men; thus the lack of specific gender identity for the Young Thing.

These scenes with the Young Thing are bittersweet moments in a work full of disappointment and loss. These male-male encounters are part of the larger picture *Hello Again* presents. The androgynous Young Thing is male and female (though played by a male), the Husband and Writer are neither hetero- nor homosexual. The gender configuration is not as important as the search for connections that seem to be impossible.

The original production of *Cabaret* (1966) belied the ambiguous sexual politics of its source, Christopher Isherwood's *Berlin Stories,* to present the heterosexual romance Broadway audiences of the time expected. American writer Cliff Bradshaw and erstwhile performer Sally Bowles had a relatively conventional Broadway romance (boy meets girl, boy loses girl, without the happy ending) set within an unconventional musical framework. Though there was an androgynous quality to the emcee, originally played by Joel Grey, his numbers were decidedly heterosexual. Bob Fosse's film version made the Isherwood character, Cliff, bisexual, turning the romance of the stage musical into a love triangle. In the 1987 revival, also directed by Prince, Cliff was an unhappy gay man seeing in Sally a way back into the closet:

> His earnestly willed affair with Sally is a subterfuge, a commercially shrewd
> cover-up of the non-sexual attachment of Isherwood's odd couple, a homosexual
> and a woman unlucky in love who turns to Clifford-Christopher as a refuge from
> heterosexual catastrophe.[21]

Since the only homosexuals the revival offered were the mincing queens, Bobby and Victor, Clifford's desperate re-entry into the closet was justifiable. In Joe

Masteroff's 1988 revision, Cliff seems to be reluctantly bisexual, though in John Benjamin Hickey's totally uncharismatic performance in the 1998 Roundabout Theater revival, he seems to have no sexual drives at all. Sally clearly is the instigator in any sexual encounter she has with this passive lump.[22] While every man in the show seems to want to bed Cliff, he shows no interest, though in this production the bisexual Nazi, Ernst, and Bobby and Victor are no longer stereotypes. Ernst's expression of his Nazism is a transfer of affection from Cliff to the seedy whore, Fräulein Kost. Victor and Bobby are handsome, talented performers. Bobby knew Cliff in London and is surprised at his reluctance to enjoy gay sex.

If Cliff rejects the fabulous but doomed world of the cabaret, the production is clear in its insistence that the cabaret is not merely the place of escape from reality Sally desires, but a site of sexual liberation. The 1998 Roundabout Theater production, directed by Sam Mendes and Rob Marshall, and adapted from Mendes's 1993 London revival, paints a grand, black-and-white picture of omnisexual desire. Same-sex desire is not just an element of chic decadence in this production of *Cabaret*. It is presented as a necessary part of the musical world *Cabaret* celebrates. The world of the cabaret show is actually more politically aware than the characters are off stage. Sally Bowles does not see the implications of the show in which she performs, and Cliff, who seems uncomfortable and out of place in the cabaret, cannot allow himself to express his homosexual desire freely. The cabaret is not just one setting among many in this production. The show takes place in a cabaret with the audience seated at tables drinking. Only the lack of cigarette smoke renders the performance inauthentic, but smoke machines create an illusion of a smoky nightclub.

Even more than in the original Harold Prince production, the center of this rethinking of the show is the emcee, an even more androgynous figure than Joel Grey's celebrated incarnation. First appearing shirtless with red sequined pasties on his nipples, the emcee alternates gender performances. In the first act, he is the naughty, oversexed boy of burlesque comics, but his burlesque performances of desire are directed at both the cabaret girls and the cabaret boys. During his opening number, "Willkommen," he is constantly framing his crotch with his hands like a burlesque dancer when he isn't fondling the crotches of the men and derrieres of the women on stage with him. During "Two Ladies," one of which is obviously a man in drag, the emcee and his two companions perform a shadow show that, in about thirty seconds, offers an entire Kama Sutra of hetero- and homosexual positions. As Frau Schneider and Herr Schultz sing a reprise of their ballad celebrating marriage, the stage fills with couples tenderly slow dancing. One of the couples is the emcee and Bobby. They are not mocking the heterosexual couples or the idea of marriage but proclaiming their right to dance on the stage with them and share their idealization of romantic love.

In the second act, the emcee is more insistently in drag, first unrecogniz-
able in the cancan performed by the cabaret girls, then, in a sequined dress,
singing a beautiful torch song, "I Don't Care Much." If the original book focused
on Nazi anti-Semitism and the coming of the Holocaust, this production is as
concerned with the doom about to befall homosexuals in Berlin. In the original,
the emcee was a figure for the encroachment of Nazism. As Prince described
him, "He starts out as a pathetic, self-deluded entertainer who gradually turns
into an emblem of the Nazi mentality."[23] Here he represents the world the Nazis
will destroy. At the end of the first act, in an act of mockery of the encroaching
Nazi movement, the emcee drops his trousers to reveal a swastika painted on
his ass. The final image is of the emcee in a concentration camp uniform
ornamented with both the yellow star and the pink triangle. The cabaret setting
flies out revealing whitewashed brick walls and a gunshot rings out as the lights
black out. The joyous, raunchy era of the cabaret and its liberating polymorphous
perversity will be destroyed by Nazi anti-Semitism and policing of any deviation
from conventional masculinity.

Ute Lemper's fascinating album of Berlin cabaret songs from the 1920s
shows the real models for the sort of numbers Kander and Ebb created for
Cabaret and the political spirit found in Sam Mendes's production. Lemper
sings a lesbian duet first performed by Marlene Dietrich and Margo Lion in
1928, a line from which became a theme song of German lesbians of the period,
"Oh, you're my favorite girlfriend." "The Lavender Song" (*Das Lila Lied*) is an
angry marching song that could have been written in the 1990s, containing in
its chorus the defiant lines "We're not afraid to be queer and diff'rent."[24]
Mendes's production captures the spirit of these songs.

Six months into its run, *Cabaret* moved into the old Studio 54, the
setting for seventies chic decadence and glamour in New York. For those of
us who remember Studio 54, where Liza and Truman Capote and the beautiful
people cavorted, where gays and straights partied together, the site adds
resonance to *Cabaret*.[25] Another era of sexual liberation, wiped out by greed
and AIDS, echoes in the production, which also insistently echoes the sexual
politics and style of its own era. The outfits the cabaret girls and boys wear
are not period-specific as they were in the original, which echoed George
Grosz's paintings. Now, like those in the revival of *Chicago,* they could be
contemporary. The handsome cabaret boys have obviously spent a lot of time
in the gym. As the emcee I saw the brilliant Robert Sella who, with his
platinum blond hair and sexual posturing, could be a rock star as much as a
twenties Berlin cabaret compère. Like the glitter-rock characters in Todd
Haynes's film *Velvet Goldmine,* Sella created an androgynous figure who
evoked a number of eras, including our own.

At the beginning of the second act of this *Cabaret* the master of ceremonies brings two people out of the audience to dance with him: first a woman, then a man. At that moment, the audience is not in a Berlin nightclub in the 1920s; it is in Studio 54 in the late 1990s. The insistence on the equality of heterosexual and homosexual desire through these two dances, contemporary interpolations into a three-decades old musical, does more to include us in the world of musical theater than the vapid celebrations offered by shows like *Fairy Tales* and *The Gay 90s*. Sam Mendes may be straight, but he, like Neil Bartlett, knows that gay men are a crucial part of what the musical is about.

REPRISE: QUEERING THE CD

On the cover of the CD *Stage 1: How I Love You* are two cute young men in bed. One looks adoringly at his partner. The other looks alluringly at the camera, as if inviting the viewer to join them in bed for a threesome. The subtitle to this album is "A Passionate Musical Experience." On the back cover is a picture of the two men, shirtless, embracing. Inside are pictures of the couple in bed in various states of undress. Lift out the CD and the picture underneath it of the two men in bed, one behind the other, suggests that something sexual may be happening.

The sequel is *Stage 2: The Human Heart.* The cover is graced by another male couple posing for the camera. The back of the CD offers us a shot of them in bed, one undressed except for briefs, looking out at the viewer. The brochure is full of pictures of the couple in domestic bliss: moving into their new house, sitting together in the living room, showering and shaving, plus more shots in bed. Lift up the CD and you have them nude on a raft in the pool. The pictures look like they're commercials for something: bed linens perhaps, or a real estate agent who caters to gay clientele. They're not glossy enough for *Out* magazine but might pass muster for *The Advocate*. What these young men are selling is an image of the generic gay: white, cute, young, middle class, domestic, and coupled.

What's on the CDs, you might ask? Show tunes, of course. The albums are cheaply produced, the tracks competently crooned by men who probably are in the chorus of musicals, to keyboard accompaniment (the second album adds a few other instruments). The only gimmick is that the love songs are sung by men ostensibly to men. The brochure notes of *Stage 2* present this as "an occasion of some subversiveness and a part of an ongoing revolution." You can't help noticing that more money has been put in the visual material than in the CD. In an age in which some of our major rock stars have written and recorded male-male love songs and gay Rufus Wainwright has brilliantly adapted the show tune genre for the nineties, a cheaply produced compact disc of guys singing anemic versions of show tunes hardly seems revolutionary. The music misrepresents the spirit of the musical. Every song is wanly crooned. There's none of the spirit of defiance, of optimism and self-assertion in the face of impossible odds that characterizes the best of show music, no "I Have a Dream" or "I'm Still Here." Above all, there's no irony, the red cells in the blood of musical theater. Guys in piano bars belt the numbers with the gusto of gospel hymns—for show queens these numbers are our hymns. The singing on the recordings is as bland as the faces on the photos.

The albums are, in essence, self-contained shows. The pictures in the brochure are a visual accompaniment to the songs, creating a gay fantasy environment for them. As usual, that fantasy is one of youth, good looks, and availability, as well as one of love. I'm sure there are sentimental young people coming out for whom this album represents an important symbol of gayness and openness—perhaps our young neighbor at *Fairy Tales*. It doesn't play to us show queens who not only "lived through all of last year" but actually made it through *Fanny* and *The Boy Friend* as well as *Ragtime* and *Titanic,* not to mention the bombs along the way. Now we're more connected to the fabulous survival of the divas than these bland pretty boys posing for the camera. I hoped that when Larry Kert sang "Something's Comin'" and David Daniels (the Broadway baritone, not the countertenor) sang "Follow Your Heart" they saw me, a gay cocoon, out there in the Winter Garden audience. I didn't need them in their skivvies on the dust jackets of the cast albums (though I wouldn't have minded). Seeing them in the spotlight on a great stage in a theater was my idea of an erotic fantasy. The trouble with the fantasies provided by the performances and the printed material of the *Stage* compact discs is that they're small-scale, domestic, not at all fabulous enough to represent the musical. The cardinal rule of the musical, like the cardinal rule of gay culture when I came out, was above all, No Blandness. Whoever produced this album thought of these show tunes as quiet background music for a candlelight dinner or make-out session. Ethel Merman would not have approved of domesticating show music this way.

Tennessee Williams's greatest character, Blanche DuBois, she of the colored lights and "paper moon hanging over a cardboard sky," who knew as any diva or show queen does that life is at its best when it approximates theater, cried, "I don't want realism. I want magic!" In Andre Previn's 1998 opera of *A Streetcar Named Desire* (libretto by Philip Littell), Blanche's big aria is "I Want Magic." The opera, inspired by our greatest and most operatic of playwrights, opened in the fall of 1998 in what is still symbolically the gay capital of the United States, San Francisco. As the musical has moved closer to opera and, by focusing on spectacle rather than character, lost its personality, it may be opera, still celebrating larger-than-life characters, that takes the lead in creating

American musical theater and in celebrating its gayness. Who would have thought that at the turn of the twenty-first century, American opera, celebrating gay artists and heroes, would be in the ascendancy and that the musical comedy, our own art form, would be represented by revivals of past classics as vehicles for aging divas?

So far, much of openly gay musical theater is gay in name only as many gay men fear the camp, drag, and flamboyance of the gay men who were invested in musical theater. Even the Howard Crabtree musicals are purposely tacky evocations of a gala past theatrical genre, memorial services for a dead theatrical form and a past era of gay history. The magical moments in the musical theater I know and love are extravagant allegories of our experience: Tony singing of a longing for something he cannot name, Lola in Latina drag in the locker room combining seduction and self-parody as only a queen can, Rose refusing to accept straight suburban boredom, Carlotta proudly singing a hymn to her survival. Yes, three out of four of the songs have lyrics written by a man who denies their gayness, but what's one man against all of us in the audience who know better. No matter how ardently those cute, scantily clad boys in the chorus sang "There Is Nothin' Like a Dame," we knew better about them, too. Yet we share these moments with the rest of the audience who also found ways to read them—or to not think about them at all.

Gay critics can lament the ostensible heterosexism of the classic musical, but these shows offered an opulent world in which desire could go in a number of directions and could be read simultaneously in seemingly opposite ways. The old musicals better represented the complexity and fluidity of gender than simple-minded pap like *Fairy Tales* or narcissistic dreariness like the *Stage* compact discs. For show queens, musicals are fun house mirrors, offering us wonderfully bizarre, exaggerated pictures of our loves, desires, and appetites. They are life in drag.

A SELECTIVE DISCOGRAPHY
(WITH SOME VIDEOS THROWN IN)

Here are recommended albums for the scores I couldn't live without. I am aware that these lists go out of date very quickly as new recordings are made and others pulled off the shelves, but this will give you a sense of what is out there and what I think are the most interesting recordings of shows discussed in this book—a complete list of show albums I think are essential would be a book in itself.

* = available on video

NOËL COWARD

THE MASTER'S VOICE (EMI). Coward's songs are best sung by their creator. The most important collection of Coward performances is the four-CD set *The Master's Voice* from Coward's many HMV recordings. Most of his famous songs are here, performed in various arrangements, plus some excerpts from his plays. Coward's performance style will not be to everyone's taste. He doesn't have much of a singing voice and aims for an "effortless" effect, as if really trying to sing would be simply too strenuous, so the effect is classic British passive-aggressive. This is the best record of one of the most celebrated performers of the twentieth century. He's an excellent comic playwright, a clever lyricist, a competent composer, and, though an acquired taste, a polished performer. That's not bad for one person to claim.

BITTER-SWEET (TER). Coward's classic operetta lovingly performed by a British cast.

SAIL AWAY (Angel) has been re-released. Elaine Stritch's best performance on record in songs written for her. The score is pallid and dated. The same can be said for a musical of the same period, THE GIRL WHO CAME TO SUPPER (Columbia) with a less lively cast.

If you can find the original cast album of a British Coward revue of the early 1970s featuring Patricia Routledge, COWARDY CUSTARD (RCA), it's a terrific collection of truly funny performances of Coward, far better than the American revue OH, COWARD.

JERRY HERMAN

Herman hasn't been revived or re-recorded as much as others on this list, so one compares original cast albums for all the shows.

LA CAGE AUX FOLLES (RCA). Only one choice—the original cast. Gene Barry is kind of droopy, but it's a good record of an historic show. I thought Walter Charles (West Coast tour, then Broadway) was a funnier, more characterful Albin/Zaza than the original George Hearn, but Hearn sings well on the album.

HELLO, DOLLY! (RCA) has lots of cast albums. I prefer Pearl Bailey and Cab Calloway in the well-sung all-black version, but Mary Martin is delightful and Channing does her patented Dolly with a supporting cast as over the top as she. If you want Channing, get the 1964 recording, not the sad 1994 revival.

MACK AND MABEL. The cult favorite. Herman's best score saddled with an impossible second act. The original cast album (MCA) has Bernadette Peters (terrific), Lisa Kirk (ditto, in a thankless role) and Robert Preston (charming, but something's missing). The eagerly awaited but disappointing 1995 London revival (Westend), better sound and more of the score, has Caroline O'Connor, excellent but not as good as Peters, and Howard McGillin, who really sings Mack's music. On stage there was zero chemistry between McGillin and O'Connor, partly the script's fault. Mack keeps saying he really can't love Mabel, but you've got to feel he wishes he could. The wonderful Kathryn Evans takes the Lisa Kirk role. As an album, I prefer the Westend, though I can't forget the production's flaws (poor direction, ugly design, and still in desperate need of a better book).

MAME with Angela Lansbury (Columbia), a delightful recording, but maybe the BBC will release its 1997 broadcast with Julia McKenzie as a terrific Mame and Donald Pippin conducting a solid supporting cast. BBC 2 records a number of musicals complete with dialogue for broadcast. The casts are inspired and the excellent BBC Concert Orchestra is used. There's some staging and props and an audience to give the performances a real sense of theater.

KANDER AND EBB

CABARET. Textual problems here, so fans need more than one album. The 1966 Broadway cast (Columbia) records an historic moment, a show trying to stretch the limits of the conventional musical, but much is still conventional. Critics didn't like her, but I think Jill Haworth's Sally Bowles is appropriate for the character, bumptious but sexy. The best Sally, Tandy Cronyn (daughter of Hume Cronyn and Jessica Tandy), who played Sally on tour and later in New York, never got to record her perfect performance. The great Judi Dench, London's Sally, did, and it's worth having (Sony). A 1993 studio recording from TER has Dench as Frau Schneider, the radiant Maria Friedman as Sally (too good), and all the songs written for the various versions. The Bob Fosse movie* has a lot of new songs written for Kander and Ebb's favorite singer, Liza Minnelli, and cuts everyone else's music but Sally's and the emcee's and the Nazi hymn "Tomorrow Belongs to Me." I'd get the video instead of the CD. The 1998 revival is a mix of the two scores. The performances are brilliant. Alan Cummings's emcee, raunchier and more emotionally complex than Joel Grey's, is brilliant. Natasha Richardson's Sally is radiant even on disc and Mary Louise Wilson makes Frau Schneider's numbers little dramas. The producers have wisely given the cabaret numbers a sense of live performance with audience noise and cheers to provide the crucial intimacy of this magnificent production. A document of one of the great musical productions of the century.

CHICAGO. Three albums as of this writing. The original 1975 recording with Gwen Verdon, Chita Rivera, and Jerry Orbach (Arista CD) is a must. So is the more complete 1998 London cast recording (RCA Victor) for its two female leads (Ute Lemper and Ruthie Henshall) and the best band, under the manic Gareth Valentine. The cast album of the New York revival is good, but not as good as the London cast.

KISS OF THE SPIDER WOMAN. If only you could put together the two cast recordings. Chita Rivera's performance is a must (RCA). You need that ageless, androgynous quality rather than Vanessa Williams's sexy, youthful performance (Mercury). Aurora is a dream and a myth, not just a good singer. Of the men, I like Howard McGillin as Molina on the second recording. For once, McGillin's over-the-top, slightly eerie quality works. He's not as charming as Brent Carver, but more passionate. Brian Stokes Mitchell is a better singer than Anthony Crivello as well as the cellmate of any queen's Genet fantasies.

COLE PORTER

ANYTHING GOES. The 1935 score (rather than the collection of Porter hits usually served up) is on EMI conducted by John McGlinn with the original orchestrations and characterful performances. The usual melange can be heard on the cast album of the Broadway revival (RCA) with Patti LuPone belting Reno (sorry, I've never been a fan of Lupone) and Howard McGillin sounding like a real thirties radio crooner.

FIFTY MILLION FRENCHMEN (New World). McGillin excellent again and in good company with talented leading ladies Kim Criswell and Karen Ziemba, and the fixture of recent recordings of classic musicals, Jason Graae.

KISS ME, KATE. There are three complete versions. Two are studio recordings with the original orchestrations. Both cast opera types as Fred and Lili. Thomas Hampson on EMI knows how to sing theater music better than Thomas Allen, but Diana Montague on TER is more idiomatic and charming than stentorian Josephine Barstow. I prefer Kim Criswell (EMI) for the comic numbers. The original cast recording of the 1999 Broadway revival (DRG) is the most vibrant. The orchestrations are better and the cast is ideal. The original cast album, recently remastered, is heavily cut, but a document of one of the great casts of the 1940s (Alfred Drake, Patricia Morison, Lisa Kirk, Harold Lang). The MGM film* with its usual cast (Howard Keel, creepy Kathryn Grayson, Ann Miller) goes through the usual MGM revisions but is fun.

NYMPH ERRANT. Not one of Porter's best-known scores, but one of the wittiest and most exuberant. EMI has a live concert performance recorded at the Theatre Royal, Drury Lane, in 1989 with a host of female stage stars including Elizabeth Welch doing "Solomon," which she performed on the opening night in 1933! The cutesy arrangements make the score sound at times like Jerry Herman (Donald Pippin, the musical director, served in that capacity for *Mame* and *La Cage*), but this album is still a favorite of mine. There are a number of over-the-top performances in this parade of second-string divas (Liliane Montevecchi, Kaye Ballard, Maureen McGovern, Patrice Munsel, Larry Kert)—it's almost a parade of mad scenes—but they're all great fun.

OUT OF THIS WORLD. Both the 1950 original cast (Sony Broadway) and the much more complete 1995 New York concert version (DRG) (including "From This Moment On," insanely cut from the original, though it shows up as an Ann Miller number on the film *Kiss Me Kate*) are available. A toss-up, but I think the original cast is better. If you like the score, get both. Ken Page on the new one has a hard time with Jupiter's music while the original, George Gaynes, sounds like Wotan, and Andrea Martin on DRG isn't as good a Juno as veteran Charlotte Greenwood.

COLLECTIONS. Ella Fitzgerald's *Cole Porter Songbook* (Verve) is a classic. So is *Bobby Short Loves Cole Porter* (Atlantic)—brilliant high-class saloon singing. *Kiri Sings Porter* by Kiri Te Kanawa (Angel) is in the Fitzgerald tradition with lush arrangements. Thomas Hampson with John McGlinn (Angel) is trying for something more like theater music with some of the original orchestrations. Good choice of songs, but somewhat monotonous. The Los Angeles AIDS benefit tribute to Porter has David Hyde Pierce doing a brilliant "Thank You So Much, Missus Lowsborough Goodby" with a queer twist, Matt Zarley's "Love for Sale," and Jamie Anderson doing a divo turn on "In the Still of the Night," high points in a mixed bag. A 3-CD compilation of original recordings with some more modern versions, *You're the Top: Cole Porter in the 1930s* (Koch), is essential for Porter fans.

RODGERS AND HAMMERSTEIN

CAROUSEL.* Though I prefer a better singer as Billy than Michael Hayden, someone who is young but has a legit voice, the RCA recording of the 1993 London cast has Joanna Riding as Julie, terrific new orchestrations, and most of the music. The album of the New York cast (also RCA) of this revival (also with Hayden) has Audra McDonald's radiant Carrie. TER should do a complete version. The Fox film with the usual gang (Gordon MacRae, Shirley Jones) is heavy-handed.*

THE KING AND I.* The original (MCA) gives you some idea of Lawrence and Brynner in their prime. Doretta Morrow and Larry Douglas sing the love duets well. The score isn't complete. The 1992 (Philips) recording with Julie Andrews and Ben Kingsley gives you the lush film orchestrations and excellent performances of the two leads. Lea Salonga is a good Tuptim, but Peabo Bryson is not the singer for Lun Tha. No ballet. The 1996 (Varese Sarabande) recording has Donna Murphy's characterful Anna (I preferred her replacement, Faith Prince) and the charismatic Lou Diamond Phillips with an excellent supporting cast. No overture, no ballet, and no "Western People Funny." If you can find a copy, the 1964 Lincoln Center production (RCA) has the overture and ballet and good performances all round except for the Anna. There's also a (Columbia) studio recording with Barbara Cook, the best Anna of all. The film has terrific performances by Brynner and Deborah Kerr lip-synching to Marni Nixon's voice.

OKLAHOMA!* The 1998 London revival was so absolutely perfect in every way that the album of same (TER) is the clear first choice. John Owen Edwards, the maestro of the TER recordings, conducts a terrific orchestra, and the cast, particularly Curly and Jud, are ideal. The film (MacRae and Jones) is slow and heavy and not much fun.

SOUTH PACIFIC.* The Mary Martin–Ezio Pinza original, with a superb supporting cast, is not complete, but essential (Columbia). There's a bizarre recording with Kiri Te Kanawa (good) and José Carreras (strained) and awful support from Mandy Patinkin as Cable and woefully miscast Sarah Vaughan ruining Bloody Mary's music—good for a laugh or cry (Sony). JAY has a complete recording that's well conducted and full of personality, once you get past the overture, which sounds like *Parsifal.* Paige O'Hara is a perky, youthful-sounding Nellie. Justino Diaz is wooly as Emile. I miss a real singer like William Tabbert as Cable; Sean McDermott, fresh from *Miss Saigon,* sounds wimpy where you need passion and anger. Pat Suzuki (where has she been?) is a fine Bloody Mary. The film is well cast, but like having a drug flashback.

RODGERS AND HART

BABES IN ARMS (New World). A terrific recording of a consistently fine score with Judy Blazer and Judy Kaye. You know the classics like "Where or When," "Johnny One Note," and "The Lady Is a Tramp," but who can resist gems like "Way Out West (On West End Avenue)"? Better yet is the 1999 recording of the Encores City Center concert version (DRG). Other than the always charming David Campbell, no big names, but terrific individual performances from a young cast.

THE BOYS FROM SYRACUSE. No cast recording of the original, but there is one of the 1963 revival (Angel), cut but with a dynamic young cast and a small band. There's also a 1950s Columbia studio recording conducted by Lehman Engel with new orchestrations, and a fine cast featuring Jack Cassidy. The best is the 1997 City Center concert version (DRG) complete and very well sung with the original orchestrations conducted by Rob Fisher.

ON YOUR TOES. The 1983 New York revival (JAY) has the original orchestrations, good performances and all the music. The cast album of the 1954 Broadway revival (Decca) has fifties-sounding orchestrations by Don Walker, cuts, the interpolation of "You Took Advantage of Me" (from *Present Arms*) for Elaine Stritch (a characteristically bizarre rendition, but a showstopper in 1954), but a more interesting cast.

PAL JOEY.* You need two: the 1950 studio recording (Columbia) under Lehman Engel that inspired the 1952 revival. Harold Lang sounds like Joey and Vivienne Segal recreates her original Vera (she was Hart's favorite performer) and the 1995 New York concert version (DRG) with the original orchestrations under Rob Fisher, who knows just how this music should go. Patti Lupone (menacing rather than sophisticated) and Peter Gallagher are not as well cast as Segal and Lang but there's more of the brilliant score and a better supporting cast. A desecration of a film with Frank Sinatra.

COLLECTIONS. I wouldn't be without Dawn Upshaw's collection (Nonesuch) or Ella Fitzgerald's (Verve). I also like Frederica von Stade's *My Funny Valentine* with the original arrangements under John McGlinn (Angel). It sounds like what the music was supposed to sound like in the twenties and thirties, a show tune version of original instrument recordings of nineteenth-century music. Von Stade has the most interesting collection of music. If you can, find Ben Bagley's Rodgers and Hart compilations (6 volumes on Painted Smiles).

SONDHEIM AND COLLABORATORS

ANYONE CAN WHISTLE. Neither of the single CDs is note complete. On the original (Columbia CD), Lansbury is radiant, Remick good, Guardino blah. The recording of the 1995 Carnegie Hall concert (Columbia) has Bernadette Peters's brilliant Nurse Apple. Madeline Kahn is no Lansbury. Scott Bakula is charming. There is more of the score here (including the cut songs "There Won't Be Trumpets" and "There's Always a Woman"), though some cuts in the ballet sequences (there's less of the climactic "Cookie Chase" than on the original cast album), and there's some dialogue as well as narration by Angela Lansbury. Lots of rapturous audience response. TER has recorded a note complete version on 2 CDs with the charismatic English divas Maria Friedman and Judi Dench. I can't wait to hear it.

COMPANY. Four recordings. The first two are of the 1970 cast, first with Dean Jones, then with Larry Kert (both on Columbia). The cuts without the Bobby are identical, but Kert is the better Bobby. The recording of the disappointing 1995 Roundabout Theater revival (Angel) is miserable. As essential as a recording of the 1970 cast is the 1995 London revival (First Night). It's the same reduced orchestration used at the Roundabout, but a really characterful cast. They don't sing as well as the 1970 cast, but this production has a point of view and complex, powerful performances, particularly from the charismatic Adrian Lester as Bobby.

FOLLIES. More textual problems on the recordings of this, one of the greatest of American musicals. The original cast recording (Angel) is heavily cut to fit on one LP, and the sound is tinny, but it is a memento of a fine original cast. The 1985 concert version* (RCA) has ups (Barbara Cook) and downs (Mandy Patinkin), some performances that are bizarre, like Elaine Stritch's way-over-the-top "Broadway Baby," and a few miscastings, like Carol Burnett's earnest "I'm Still Here," but it is pretty much note complete. Lots of ecstatic response from the show queens in the audience, but that's an integral part of any *Follies* performance.

The recording of the 1987 London production (First Night) contains some new songs ("Country House," a new "Loveland,'"Ah, but Underneath," "Social Dancing," and "Make the Most of Your Music") and cuts "The Road You Didn't Take" (essential for Ben's character), "The Story of Lucy and Jesse," and Ben's nervous breakdown, "Live, Laugh, Love." The tone is more dry, ironic, British than the darker American original. Supposedly Sondheim called this high-tech Cameron Mackintosh production "Hello, Follies!" Diana Rigg and Julia McKenzie are magnificent, David Healy is the best Buddy on record; Daniel Massey is Daniel Massey. Dolores Gray, who was London's Annie Oakley in the 1940s, does a brave "I'm Still Here." You believe her. The supporting cast is fine including the British diva Adele Leigh singing "One Last Kiss."

The recording of the highly praised 1998 Paper Mill Playhouse production (TVT) contains every song ever written for American productions of *Follies* but, other than "Ah, but Underneath," none of the London material. Dee Hoty and Laurence Guittard sing Phyllis's and Ben's music better than their competition. The slight strain in Donna McKechnie's voice seems right for Sally. Tony Roberts was his usual boring self on stage, but on the album he can sing his music. Kaye Ballard does the best "Broadway Baby," and Ann Miller's is the greatest "I'm Still Here," sounding old but determined and triumphant. Jonathan Tunick conducts his own classic orchestrations. The sound isn't great—the recording sounds like it was made in a small room, certainly not in a theater. Still, if you are only going to buy one *Follies,* this is the one. You really need all four recordings.

GYPSY (music by Styne). *Gypsy*, like *Follies*, belongs in any list of masterpieces of musical theater. If you're an aficionado, you need all the recordings. Merman's steamroller performance is a great memorial (Columbia). She's relentless, everything the same volume and intensity, but that's Rose, and "Rose's Turn" is still a revelation, a moment when a one-trick pony suddenly turns into an artist. The Lansbury is more nuanced (RCA). I don't know what I would think of the Tyne Daly if I hadn't seen her mesmerizing performance (Nonesuch). She flies off pitch and doesn't really have some of the notes, but it's still stupendous. There's such rage here, yet charm when she needs it. It's another "who would have thought" performance. Too bad Linda Lavin, Daly's replacement, didn't get a recording. All reports I have heard claim she was terrific. Betty Buckley, the greatest of Roses, recorded "Rose's Turn" twice. The Carnegie Hall concert (Sterling) is a superb one in which she is accompanied by her doting, cheering audience. This album, on which Buckley sings Sondheim, Rodgers and Hammerstein, and Weill, among others, is one of my favorites. I wouldn't totally dismiss the Roz Russell (with vocal help from Lisa Kirk) film.* The supporting cast isn't very good, the direction unimaginative in the Warner Bros. musical style of the time (at least that meant the films were faithful, if plodding, replicas of the Broadway shows), but you get the show and Russell's fierce and funny Rose. To me a small-screen *Gypsy* is a contradiction in terms, but CBS made one.* Bette Midler smirks too much for my taste. She can't lose herself in the role and doesn't really find Rose in her. It's Midler performing Midler doing a crowd-pleasing Rose. No comparison with the others.

MERRILY WE ROLL ALONG. The RCA original cast album gives the original score performed by a group of adenoidal voices accompanied by a band that sounds like it's on speed. You can hear why this production flopped. The recording of the York Theater Company production (Varèse Sarabande) gives Sondheim's revised and improved score and better performances, including Malcolm Gets's excellent Franklin (Gets is an excellent musical theater performer who plays a supposedly straight man on a TV sitcom), but with a little band.

PASSION. The original recording* (Angel) has Donna Murphy's Fosca, full of odd register breaks, which is what the part calls for. You can hear Fosca's ugliness. Marin Mazzie sings beautifully, as always, as Clara, but Jere Shea in the central role is bland. This cast performs on a video of the Broadway production. The London production (TER) rearranged some of the music for star Michael Ball, who gives an impassioned performance, proving once and for all that he isn't just another pretty face and voice. The show makes more sense when Giorgio is the central character instead of Fosca. There's more dialogue here, and a superb Fosca from Maria Friedman, less spooky and sweeter than Donna Murphy. If you only want one *Passion,* this is the one to have. One disappointment—Sondheim wrote a lovely Christmas chorale for the London production that is not on the CD.

SATURDAY NIGHT. There are two complete recordings of this early Sondheim score that prove Sondheim could write show tunes as well as anyone. The London cast, from the 1998 production (the first in London) at the Bridewell Theatre (First Night), offers a good stopgap recording, perfectly acceptable when it was the only one. But now we have the cast recording of the delightful 2000 New York production at Second Stage starring David Campbell (Nonesuch). As usual, musical director Rob Fisher has infused the project with both excellent musicianship and vitality. An essential recording for Sondheim fans.

WEST SIDE STORY (music by Bernstein). The 1957 (Columbia) original is essential. It's not complete, but the performances are terrific. Bernstein recorded a bizarre complete version (DGG) with José Carreras with a heavy Spanish accent as the Polish-American Tony (Anita maybe, but not a Tony). Accent problems aside, he just doesn't sound natural in this music. On the video* of the making of this album, you see Carreras laboring with the rhythms, which simply don't come naturally to him. Kiri Te Kanawa is closer, but too soprano-y. Kurt Ollmann, a good Riff, probably should have been Tony, and Tatania Troyanos is less off target than her colleagues, but Chita Rivera *is* Anita. Bernstein overdoes his own music—the orchestra overwhelms characters and story. Unidiomatic. There are a couple of British recordings, but we need a new, complete *West Side Story.*

GAY MUSICALS

THE BALLAD OF LITTLE MIKEY (Mark Savage) (AEI). The recording is a bit tinny, the singing not always in tune, but it's worth having for the clever musical numbers. I haven't seen this in U.S. CD stores—I found it at Dress Circle in London, the Mecca for show queens.

THE BOY FROM OZ. The Sydney original cast recording of this hit Aussie musical about gay entertainer Peter Allen is available in England (EMI Australia). Todd McKenney is even more relentlessly perky than Allen himself. Chrissie Amphlett's Judy Garland (Allen was a warm-up act for

Garland) and Angela Toohey's Liza Minnelli (Allen's wife at one time) are convincing imitations.

BOY MEETS BOY (Bill Solly) (AEI). The recording contains apologies for the bad technical quality. It sounds like one of those privately made recordings of an amateur production. The performances aren't very good, but the score is clever and charming.

ELEGIES FOR ANGELS, PUNKS AND RAGING QUEENS (Russell, Hood) (First Night). The London cast doing the dreary songs. Only for the curious.

FAIRY TALES (Barnes) (Firefly). The cast recording of the original Chicago production. Some songs were changed for the New York production.

FALSETTOS (MARCH OF THE FALSETTOS and FALSETTOLAND) (Finn). The two shows are available separately or as one two-CD set (DRG). Unfortunately Trina's hilarious new song for the Broadway production of *Falsettos,* "I'm Breaking Down," isn't included. The cast is terrific and the scores are superb, particularly *Falsettoland.*

THE GAY 90s. There is a widely distributed cast album on Varèse Sarabande, a label that should be praised for releasing so much good esoteric musical theater material. The material is well sung, the album well produced. Program out the dreary stuff and listen to the good comic material. Barbara Cook has a classic cut of "Sweet Dreams" on her album *Live from London* (DRG).

HARVEY MILK (Wallace and Korie). Teldec has released a superb recording of the San Francisco Opera production. By this time the cast had a lot of experience in their roles, having played them in Houston and New York, and the composer had made a number of major revisions in the score. Highly recommended. I hope someone made a video. The opera needs to be seen.

THE HARVEY MILK SHOW (Hutchison and Pruitt). A cast album was made to be sold at the Atlanta production, but never released nationally. Another recording that sounds like it was done underwater. It does not do justice to the fine performances of Chris Coleman and Brian Barnett as Harvey and Jamey. A memento for those who saw the production.

NAKED BOYS SINGING (Café Pacific). The cast recording of the original Los Angeles production.

WHEN PIGS FLY (Gallagher, Waldrop) and WHOOP-DEE-DOO! (Gallagher, various). The RCA cast albums gives you the clever lyrics, playful, parodistic music, and excellent performances, and the brochures give you some idea of what the show looked like, but you had to see them to believe them.

The films STONEWALL and ZERO PATIENCE are available on video and highly recommended.

ESSENTIAL MUSICALS

ANNIE GET YOUR GUN (Berlin, D. Fields). Merman's classic performance is available from the 1966 Lincoln Center revival (RCA), which includes some new material written for her ("An Old-fashioned Wedding") but cuts the two songs for Tommy and Winnie (no great loss). Merman in 1966 was a rawer version of her 1946 voice and relentless. Mary Martin and John Raitt are on an album of the 1957 television version, again cut, but Martin is charming. Two studio versions are both fine. John McGlinn gives us his usual carefully prepared "authentic" version with Kim Criswell, something of an ingenue as Annie (a refreshing change), and Thomas Hampson properly raffish (Angel). Judy Kaye is terrific on a note-complete recording from JAY with Barry Bostwick, who has left Broadway for television, as a good Frank. The 1999 original cast album starring Bernadette Peters is a major rearrangement of the score (Angel). Tom and Winnie's songs are back, but Annie has lost the supposedly politically incorrect "I'm an Indian Too." When will people learn that these shows have to be taken as historical documents? Frank loses his first self-descriptive number, "I'm a Bad, Bad Man." Does it make him too much of a sexist for the nineties? The cuts notwithstanding, this is a terrific album. Beginning with "There's No Business Like Show Business" (originally written to cover a scene change and reprised too often here) makes sense. The orchestrations are far better than the original saxophone-heavy ones. Most important, Bernadette Peters makes Annie's songs her own and sings them better than anyone. Listen to her on the one-note "I Got Lost in His Arms." She makes the song seem like one of Berlin's best. Sweet-voiced Tom Wopat sings Frank's music better than anyone. In this new recording, one realizes more than ever what a terrific score this is.

DAMN YANKEES (Adler and Ross). First recommendation—the video of the Warner Bros. film,* a very faithful reproduction of the stage production with most of the original cast. Tab Hunter plays Joe instead of Stephen Douglass, which queers the proceedings a bit. (Did anyone ever think Tab Hunter was straight?) Joe's ballads are either cut or reduced—too bad. But you get Fosse's choreography and a visual record of Verdon's performance. Otherwise, get the original 1955 cast (RCA) with Verdon's incomparable Lola and Douglass belting out the ballads magnificently. The other recordings pale by comparison.

EVITA (Lloyd Webber, Rice). Patti LuPone's performance on the cast album of the Broadway production (MCA) is a monument of a diva in her prime. Elaine Paige sings the music better in the London album, but there is such relentless drive in LuPone's performance it wins you over by sheer force of will, which is appropriate for Eva Péron. Patinkin, for once, isn't overly mannered. His Che is terrific. Though old-fashioned I was first put off by the insistent rock guitar in the opening Requiem, I like the film score (Warner Bros.).* Madonna's no LuPone or Paige, but she sings the music well. Banderas is very good as Che, Jonathan Pryce is cold and creepy as always in musicals. The film was a success and so is the album.

GENTLEMEN PREFER BLONDES (Styne, Robin). Channing's breakthrough role. On the cast recording (Columbia) there are moments when you think she's a real baritone. The 1953 film* has that classic number with Jane Russell and the gym boys.

LADY IN THE DARK (Weill, I. Gershwin). Three recordings. A strange radio broadcast with a lot of the dialogue and little of the music, but giving some sense of Gertrude Lawrence's veddy British performance (AEI). I'm not impressed. Then a rerelease of the Columbia recording with Rise Stevens wobbling through Liza's music and Adolph Green doing the Danny Kaye queen role. Appended are cuts of Kaye doing his numbers. Conductor Lehman Engel, as is his wont, soups up the orchestration (too bad since Weill did them himself), and there are many cuts. The essential recording is of the 1997 Royal National Theatre production with Maria Friedman (JAY). It's complete, Weill's orchestrations are restored, Friedman is terrific, and so is her supporting cast, including James Dreyfus as Russell, a celebration of true queenliness instead of a parody of it. There's an interesting film with Ginger Rodgers that cuts most of the music!

PLAIN AND FANCY (Hague, Horwitt). A favorite of mine and one of the best scores of the 1950s. The original cast album is available on CD and is terrific (Angel). Some beautiful ballads, particularly Katie's opening song, "It Wonders Me," and Barbara Cook's "This Is All Very New to Me." And, of course, David Daniels singing the hit ballads.

SHOW BOAT (Kern, Hammerstein). John McGlinn's reconstruction on Angel not only gives you all of the complete score, but even some of the great moments cut before the opening and the songs written for subsequent revivals and films. He chooses an operatic cast. Jerry Hadley is fine as Gaylord, though his dialogue scenes are a bit wooden. Frederica von

Stade sounds a bit mature. Teresa Stratas is a fine world-weary Julie. The rest of the cast is superb. Almost four hours of music and some of the dialogue. An essential recording of one of our masterpieces. The 1936 film and 1951 MGM film version (Keel, Grayson, Ava Gardner) are available on video.*

SUNSET BOULEVARD (Lloyd Webber, Hampton, Black). Too bad the best Norma Desmond and Joe Gillis, Betty Buckley and John Barrowman, didn't get to record their performances. You can get Buckley singing Norma's two big numbers on her CD *With One Look* and with a big orchestra on her Carnegie Hall concert (Sterling). Elaine Paige sang Norma very well. She too has recorded the two big numbers on her album *Encore* (Atlantic). The original cast albums (both Polydor) give you the entire score, one of Lloyd Webber's best. LuPone is overly mannered, more Judith Anderson in *Rebecca* than Gloria Swanson. Glenn Close is not a very good singer. Kevin Anderson sounds depressed as Joe, Alan Campbell, wan.

TOP HAT.* The video is available and addictive.

VICTOR/VICTORIA.* The video of the film is a must.* You can do without the original cast album of the show (Philips) which is droopy.

DIVAS AND DIVOS

I have already mentioned Betty Buckley's Carnegie Hall concert (Sterling), one of my favorites, and Barbara Cook in London, recorded live at Sadler's Wells (DRG). They demonstrate two approaches to singing theater music. Cook is Tebaldi, gorgeous of voice, restrained, but filled with integrity, always finding the right mood for the music. Buckley is Callas, always taking risks and making each piece a high drama in which important things are at stake. Bernadette Peters's Carnegie Hall album, *Sondheim, Etc.* (Angel), is also a great performance (another AIDS benefit). If one were to have one Judy Garland album, it would be the 1998 compilation, *Judy* (4 CDs, a video, and a 100-page booklet).

Two CDs by male singers deserve special attention. Brent Barrett's *The Kander and Ebb Album* (Varèse Sarabande) offers one of the best of Broadway male singers performing a variety of songs by this stellar writing team in excellent arrangements. Craig Rubano's *Finishing the Act* (Orchard) is a compendium of songs written to bring down the first act curtain. Many are diva turns, but Rubano makes the most of them. The album is a bit overwhelming for one listening, but a courageous, winning set of performances.

NOTES

OVERTURE

1. My favorite overviews are Gerald Mast's *Can't Help Singin': The American Musical on Stage and Screen* (Woodstock, N.Y.: Overlook Press, 1987), and Ethan Mordden's *Broadway Babies: The People Who Made the American Musical* (New York: Oxford University Press, 1983). Also recommended, the handsomely illustrated Amy Henderson and Dwight Block Bowers, *Red, Hot, and Blue: A Smithsonian Salute to the American Musical* (Washington: Smithsonian, 1996).
2. Mark Steyn, *Broadway Babies Say Goodnight: Musicals Then and Now* (London: Faber and Faber, 1997), p. 201.
3. D. A. Miller, *Place for Us: Essay on the Broadway Musical* (Cambridge, Mass.: Harvard University Press, 1998), p. 132.
4. Neil Bartlett, *Night After Night* (London: Methuen, 1993), pp. 22-23.
5. Ibid., p. 33.
6. Tony Kushner, "Notes Toward a Theater of the Fabulous," in *Staging Gay Lives,* John M. Clum, ed. (Boulder, Colo.: Westview–HarperCollins, 1996), p. vii.
7. My favorites: *Camp Grounds: Style and Homosexuality,* David Bergman, ed. (Minneapolis: University of Minnesota Press, 1993), and Philip Core, *Camp: The Lie That Tells the Truth* (New York: Delilah Books, 1984).
8. Bergman, ed., *Camp Grounds: Style and Homosexuality,* pp. 4-5.
9. Eve Kosofsky Sedgwick, *Epistemology of the Closet* (Berkeley: University of California Press, 1990), p. 156.
10. Miller, *Place for Us: Essay on the Broadway Musical,* p. 39.
11. The major works in this area are Wayne Koestenbaum, *The Queen's Throat: Opera, Homosexuality, and the Mystery of Desire* (New York: Poseidon Press, 1993), and Sam Abel, *Opera in the Flesh* (Boulder, Colo.: Westview Press), 1996.
12. See the discussion of Hollywood and Broadway musicals in the 1930s in Henderson and Bowers, *Red, Hot, and Blue: A Smithsonian Salute to the American Musical,* pp. 81-138.
13. Actually, one can hear the operatic sources for the shows in the scores: Verdi in the big numbers in *Les Misérables;* Puccini, particularly *La Fanciulla del West,* and Lehar in *Phantom of the Opera.*
14. Daniel Harris, *The Rise and Fall of Gay Culture* (New York: Hyperion, 1997), p. 37.
15. Larry Kramer, *The Normal Heart* (New York: New American Library, 1985), p. 114.
16. Alan Gurganus, *Plays Well with Others* (New York: Knopf, 1997), pp. 40-41.

CHAPTER I

1. George Chauncey, *Gay New York: Gender, Culture, and the Making of the Gay Male World, 1890–1940* (New York: Basic Books, 1994), p. 99.
2. Ibid., p. 105.
3. See Allan Bérubé, *Coming Out Under Fire: The History of Gay Men and Women in World War II* (New York: Free Press, 1990).
4. Dan Hulbert, "Outlaw *Oklahoma* Has to Toe the Mark." *American Theatre* 14, no. 5 (May/June, 1997): 40-41.
5. Daniel Harris, *The Rise and Fall of Gay Culture* (New York: Hyperion, 1997), p. 34.
6. Mark Levine, "Primo Uomo: The Next Pavarotti May Sound Like a Woman." *The New Yorker* (November 10, 1997): p. 94.
7. Levine, "Primo Uomo," p. 97.
8. *The Advocate* (October 14, 1997): p. 27.

9. Chauncey, *Gay New York,* p. 61.

10. Wayne Koestenbaum, *The Queen's Throat: Opera, Homosexuality, and the Mystery of Desire* (New York: Poseidon, 1993), p. 11.

11. D. A. Miller, *Place for Us: Essay on the Broadway Musical,* p. 69.

12. Ibid., p. 65.

13. Richard Dyer, for instance, writes: "In stereotyping, the dominant groups apply their norms to subordinated groups, finding the latter wanting, hence inadequate, inferior, sick, or grotesque and hence reinforcing the dominant groups' own sense of the legitimacy of their domination" ("Stereotyping," in *Gays and Film,* ed. Richard Dyer [New York: Zoetrope, 1984], p. 30).

14. I e-mailed a group of gay students who were show queens and asked them if they had thought about the connection between gayness and musical theater. They all answered that they had thought about it. Some of their comments will be quoted in this chapter. This one is from the talented young man who was my Fabian, a small-town Georgia boy who took my musical course last year because he felt he was out of the loop with his friends because he didn't know enough about musicals.

15. We are to believe, for instance, that thirty-five-year-old Ellen Morgan on ABC's *Ellen* has become aware of her gayness (to use her term) without ever having had a sexual experience.

16. When I began going to musicals in the 1950s, they weren't miked or were miked only by a few microphones placed in the footlights for general amplification. Up in the cheap seats, one strained to hear. Performers stayed as close to the footlights as possible. Delivery of the dialogue was anything but naturalistic. Now we get the amplified sound of a voice coming from the same source at the same volume no matter where on stage the singer is. We also get some electric effects to beef up the singers' voices.

17. How could anyone who had seen Julie as *Cinderella* sit through the amateurish performance of Brandy, in the recent remake of the same, singing off-pitch and exuding all the talent and assurance of the diva of a junior high musical. It at least inspired some vicious parodies from my show queen students.

18. In all fairness, it must be said that Raquel Welch had some success replacing Lauren Bacall in the 1981 musical *Woman of the Year.*

CHAPTER II

1. Mark Steyn, *Broadway Babies Say Goodnight: Musicals Then and Now,* (London: Faber and Faber, 1997), p. 67.

2. Jerry Herman with Marilyn Stasio, *Showtune: A Memoir* (New York: Donald I. Fine Books, 1996), p. 72.

3. See Gary C. Thomas, "'Was George Frideric Handel Gay': On Closet Questions and Cultural Politics," in *Queering the Pitch: The New Gay and Lesbian Musicology,* eds. Philip Brett, Elizabeth Wood, and Gary C. Thomas (New York: Routledge, 1994), pp. 155-203.

4. Charles Kaiser, *The Gay Metropolis: 1940–1996* (Boston: Houghton Mifflin, 1997), p. 17.

5. Richard Rodgers, *Musical Stages: An Autobiography* (New York: Random House, 1975), p. 88.

6. *The Noël Coward Diaries,* ed. Graham Payn and Sheridan Morley (London: Weidenfeld and Nicolson, 1982), p. 270.

7. Herman, *Showtune: A Memoir,* p. 227.

8. Quoted in Samuel Marx and Jan Clayton, *Rodgers and Hart: Bewitched, Bothered, and Bedeviled* (New York: Putnam, 1976), p. 237.

9. Quoted in Kaiser, *The Gay Metropolis,* p. 93.

10. These days it is harder to date musicals. *Ragtime* opened in Toronto in 1996, in Los Angeles in 1997, and had its formal opening in New York in January 1998.

11. Philip Core, *Camp: The Lie That Tells the Truth* (London: Delilah Books, 1984), p. 9.

12. Quoted in Marx and Clayton, *Rodgers and Hart: Bewitched, Bothered, and Bedeviled,* pp. 237-238.

13. Quoted in ibid., p. 171.

14. Quoted in Philip Hoare, *Noël Coward: A Biography* (New York: Simon and Schuster, 1995), pp. 477-478.

15. Quoted in Marx and Clayton, *Rodgers and Hart: Bewitched, Bothered, and Bedeviled,* p. 232.

16. It is interesting to note that Rodgers and Hammerstein did not produce the 1952 revival of *Pal Joey.* Another composer, Jule Styne, did.

17. Gerald Mast, *Can't Help Singin': The American Musical on Stage and Screen* (Woodstock, N.Y.: The Overlook Press, 1987), p. 166.
18. Ibid., p. l68.
19. William G. Hyland, *Richard Rodgers* (New Haven: Yale University Press, 1998), p. 268.
20. Quoted in Marx and Clayton, *Rodgers and Hart: Bewitched, Bothered, and Bedeviled,* p. 210.
21. *The Complete Lyrics of Lorenz Hart,* ed. Dorothy Hart and Robert Kimball (New York: DaCapo Press, 1995), p. 224.
22. Ibid., p. 252.
23. Ibid., p. 228.
24. Ibid., p. 224.
25. Ibid., p. 272.
26. Ibid., p. 273.
27. Ibid., p. 275.
28. Frederick Nolan, *Lorenz Hart: A Poet on Broadway* (New York: Oxford University Press, 1994), p. 31.
29. Quoted in Marx and Clayton, *Rodgers and Hart: Bewitched, Bothered, and Bedeviled,* p. 168.
30. Ibid., p. 116.
31. Ibid.
32. Nolan, *Lorenz Hart: A Poet on Broadway,* p. 221 (emphasis added).
33. Quoted in Marx and Clayton, *Rodgers and Hart: Bewitched, Bothered, and Bedeviled,* p. 236.
34. *Complete Lyrics of Lorenz Hart,* p. 275
35. A combination of quotes in Marx and Clayton, *Rodgers and Hart: Bewitched, Bothered, and Bedeviled,* (p. 224), and Nolan, *Lorenz Hart: A Poet on Broadway,* (p. 238).
36. Quoted in Boze Hadleigh, *Sing Out!: Gays and Lesbians in the Music World* (New York: Barricade Books, 1997), p. 57.
37. Quoted in Marx and Clayton, *Rodgers and Hart: Bewitched, Bothered, and Bedeviled,* p. 224.
38. Hyland, *Richard Rodgers,* p. 38.
39. Dorothy Hart, *Thou Swell, Thou Witty: The Life and Lyrics of Lorenz Hart* (New York: Harper, 1976).
40. Quoted in Nolan, *Lorenz Hart: A Poet on Broadway,* p. 309.
41. Ibid.
42. George Chauncey, *Gay New York: Gender, Culture, and the Making of the Gay Male World, 1890–1940* (New York: Basic Books, 1994), pp. 310-311.
43. John Loughery, *The Other Side of Silence: Men's Lives and Gay Identities: A Twentieth Century History* (New York: Henry Holt, 1998), p. 42.
44. *Complete Lyrics of Lorenz Hart,* p. 151.
45. Ibid., p. 33.
46. Ibid., p. 114.
47. Ibid., p. 152.
48. Cook sings the ballad on the album *Barbara Cook in London.* Dawn Upshaw also sings it beautifully on her Rodgers and Hart album.
49. *Complete Lyrics of Lorenz Hart,* 165.
50. Ibid., p. 58.
51. Ibid., p. 275.
52. Ibid.
53. Ibid., p. 282.
54. Ibid., 340.
55. Ibid., pp. 141-142.
56. Charles Schwartz, *Cole Porter: A Biography* (New York: DaCapo Press, 1977), p. 176.
57. William J. Mann, *Wisecracker: The Life and Times of William Haines, Hollywood's First Openly Gay Star* (New York: Viking, 1998), pp. 296-297. Mann's book is the richest account we have of Hollywood gay life in the first half of this century.
58. Hector Arce, *The Secret Life of Tyrone Power* (New York: William Morrow, 1979), p. 70.
59. Chauncey, *Gay New York,* p. 288.
60. Schwartz, *Cole Porter,* p. 98.
61. William McBrien, *Cole Porter: A Biography* (New York: Knopf, 1998), pp. 102-103.
62. Ibid. p. 252.
63. Ibid., p. 161.

64. *The Complete Lyrics of Cole Porter,* ed. Robert Kimball (New York: DaCapo Press, 1992), p. 145.
65. Ibid., p. 201.
66. Mast, *Can't Help Singin',* p. 186.
67. *Complete Lyric of Cole Porter,* p. 440.
68. Ibid., p. 119
69. Ibid., p. 207.
70. Ibid., p. 389.
71. Ibid., p. 114.
72. Ibid., p. 302.
73. Linguist Ronald R. Butters is skeptical of "gay" in our sense entering the language as early as some historians think. See his essay "What Did Cary Grant Know About Being Gay and When Did He Know It: The Etymology of the Popular Term *gay* 'homosexual.'" *Dictionaries* (Spring, 1998), pp. 188-204. I disagree with Butters and think that Cary Grant knew exactly what he meant when he improvised that famous line in *Bringing Up Baby,* "Because I just went gay all of a sudden."
74. *Complete Lyrics of Cole Porter,* p. 310.
75. Ibid., p. 125.
76. "Gay men also assembled in elegant men's bars like the Oak Room in the Plaza and, most famously, at the Astor, on Seventh Avenue at 45th Street . . . At the Astor's oval bar, gay men gathered on one side, heterosexuals on the other. While heterosexual patrons could touch each other as much as they wanted, whenever the gay customers became slightly outlandish, the bar's management would immediately warn them to tone down their behavior." Kaiser, *The Gay Metropolis,* p. 14. My high school health teacher, a man beyond senility who was a font of strange information, spent much of his one class on sex warning us boys to avoid the Astor Bar, where he claimed to have caught crabs!
77. *Complete Lyrics of Cole Porter,* p. 365.
78. Ibid., 64.
79. Stephen Citron, *Noël and Cole: The Sophisticates* (New York: Oxford University Press, 1993), p. 54.
80. *The Noël Coward Diaries,* ed. Graham Payn and Sheridan Morley (London: Weidenfeld and Nicolson, 1982), p. 260.
81. Quoted in Cole Lesley, Graham Payn, and Sheridan Morley, *Noël Coward and His Friends* (New York: William Morrow, 1979), p. 127.
82. Terry Castle, *Noël Coward and Radclyffe Hall: Kindred Spirits* (New York: Columbia University Press, 1996), p. 2.
83. *Noël Coward: The Complete Lyrics,* ed. Barry Day (Woodstock, N.Y.: Overlook Press, 1998), p. 114.
84. *The Noël Coward Diaries,* p. 508. Written in 1962. Earlier (1949) Coward mentions reading *De Profundis* and writes of Wilde: "What a silly, conceited, inadequate creature he was and what a dreadful self-deceiver. It is odd that such a brilliant wit should be allied to no humour at all." (p. 135)
85. Castle, *Noël Coward and Radclyffe Hall,* p. 10.
86. Noël Coward, *Present Indicative* (New York: Doubleday, 1937), p.198.
87. Philip Hoare, *Noël Coward: A Biography* (New York: Simon & Shuster, 1995), p. 140.
88. Quoted in Clive Fisher, *Noël Coward: A Biography* (New York: St. Martins, 1992), p. 69.
89. Quoted in Hoare, *Noël Coward,* p. 140.
90. Quoted in Fisher, *Noël Coward,* p. 70.
91. Hoare, *Noël Coward,* p. 276.
92. Ibid., p. 495.
93. Quoted in ibid., p. 276.
94. *The Collected Stories of Noël Coward* (New York: Dutton, 1983), p. 474.
95. Quoted in Hoare, *Noël Coward,* p. 509.
96. *Noël Coward: The Complete Lyrics,* p. 149.
97. *Noël Coward and Radclyffe Hall,* p. 37.
98. *The Noël Coward Diaries,* p. 266.
99. In Ray's case the heterosexual posturings didn't work. His homosexuality became common knowledge too quickly—boys like me in the 1950s knew he was gay, though I don't remember how—and he soon had something to cry about.

100. *The Noël Coward Diaries,* p. 641. It is interesting that Payn, who co-edited the diaries, would not censor Coward's very candid comments about Payn's professional failure and indolence.
101. Ibid., pp. 368-369.
102. Quoted in Hoare, *Noël Coward,* p. 123.
103. Letter to Roddy McDowall. Quoted in Hoare, *Noël Coward,* p. 491.
104. *Noël Coward: The Complete Lyrics,* p. 195.
105. Ibid., p. 160.
106. Quoted in Hoare, p. 245.

CHAPTER III

1. *The Complete Lyrics of Cole Porter,* ed. Robert Kimball (New York: DaCapo Press, 1992), p. 312.
2. Ira Gershwin, "Bride and Groom," *Oh, Kay!* Reprinted from booklet for Nonesuch recording of *Oh, Kay!* (1995), p. 42. Gershwin reused the lyric for *Lady in the Dark.*
3. *The Complete Lyrics of Cole Porter,* p. 241.
4. Ibid., p. 388.
5. Arlene Croce, *The Fred Astaire and Ginger Rogers Book* (New York: Galahad Books, 1972), p. 33.
6. Ibid., p. 33.
7. John Loughery, *The Other Side of Silence: Men's Lives and Gay Identities: A Twentieth-Century History* (New York: Henry Holt, 1998), pp. 63-64.
8. Vito Russo, *The Celluloid Closet* (New York: Harper & Row, 1987), p. 35.
9. Croce, *The Fred Astaire and Ginger Rogers Book,* p. 8.
10. John O'Hara (lyrics by Lorenz Hart), *Pal Joey* (New York: Random House, 1952), p. 4.
11. Gore Vidal, *Palimpsest: A Memoir* (New York: Random House, 1995), p. 131.
12. Frederick Nolan, *Lorenz Hart: A Poet on Broadway,* (New York: Oxford University Press, 1994), p. 172.
13. Martin Gottfried, *Nobody's Fool: The Lives of Danny Kaye* (New York: Simon and Shuster, 1994), p. 55.
14. Moss Hart and Ira Gershwin, *Lady in the Dark* (New York: Random House, 1941), p. 106.
15. Ibid., p. 167.
16. Ibid., p. 154.
17. Ibid., p. x.
18. Ibid., p. 174.
19. Ibid., p. 53.
20. Ibid., p. 158.
21. While there was no cast album of *Lady in the Dark,* Danny Kaye recorded a number of the songs with an orchestra conducted by the show's musical director, Maurice Abravanel, a month after the show opened. Clearly Kaye's clowning as gay Russellwas a reason for the show's success.
22. Gottfried, *Nobody's Fool,* p. 58. Recent writing on Kaye and his alleged lover, Laurence Olivier, have put the spotlight on the possibility of Kaye's bisexuality, which sheds a different light on his pansy act. See Donald Spoto, *Laurence Olivier: A Biography* (New York: HarperCollins, 1992).
23. Hart and Gershwin, *Lady in the Dark,* p. 47.
24. *Six Plays by Rodgers and Hammerstein* (New York: The Modern Library, 1959), pp. 517-518.
25. Much has already been written about director Harold Prince's decision to take "Why Do I Love You" from Magnolia and Gaylord and to give it to Parthenia to sing to her new granddaughter at the beginning of Act II (the song's rightful place in the score). It is a mistake. The lyrics make no sense in this context and the audience needs a reminder of Gaylord's love for Magnolia at the beginning of the thirty-year span of Act II. Having Kim reprise it with Parthenia at the end gives the act a musical symmetry, but little else.
26. "Lonely Room" was cut from the film (villains don't sing?). It was not on the first original cast album but was included later, sung not by the original Jud, Howard da Silva, but by Alfred Drake, the first Curly.
27. Ethan Mordden, *Rodgers and Hammerstein* (New York: Harry N. Abrams, 1992), p. 47.
28. *Six Plays by Rodgers and Hammerstein,* p, 153.
29. Ibid., 176.
30. When I saw an early performance of the Nicholas Hytner production of *Carousel* in New York in 1993, I was fascinated to hear how many of the middle-aged and older women in the audience

found Hammerstein's celebration of female masochism to be dated and offensive, yet a year later when Duke University mounted a production of *Carousel,* students were baffled and angered by attempts on the part of some of us on the faculty to link the musical to contemporary issues like domestic abuse. Like *Phantom of the Opera* and *Les Misérables,* the show gave them a good, sentimental cry. Why ruin it with analysis?

31. *Six Plays by Rodgers and Hammerstein,* 166.
32. Ibid., p. 202.
33. Ibid., p. 519.
34. Mordden, *Rodgers and Hammerstein,* p. 207.
35. Stacy Wolf, "Mary Martin: Washin' That Man Right Outta Her Hair," in *Passing Performances: Queer Readings of Leading Players in American Theater History,* eds. Robert A. Schanke and Kim Marra (Ann Arbor: University of Michigan Press, 1998), pp. 283-302. Martin's and her husband's sexuality is also mentioned in Boze Hadleigh's *Sing Out: Gays and Lesbians in the Music World* (New York: Barricade Books, 1997), pp. 268-269.
36. *Six Plays by Rodgers and Hammerstein,* p. 207.
37. Mordden, *Rodgers and Hammerstein,* p. 207.
38. Films by younger gay men suggest that *The Sound of Music* was important to them. In Tony Vitale's 1997 film, *Kiss Me, Guido,* gay Warren watches a video of *The Sound of Music,* Kleenex in hand. In Jonathan Harvey's 1993 play and 1996 screenplay, *Beautiful Thing,* the sixteen year old blossoming queen, Jamie, knows that Eleanor Parker played the Baroness. American gay friends have told me that she was a character they could identify with.
39. Ethan Mordden, *Coming Up Roses: The Broadway Musical in the 1950s* (New York: Oxford University Press, 1998), p. 8.

CHAPTER IV

1. Review of *Follies, The New York Times* online, May 9, 1998. Ben Brantley spends much of his rave review praising Ann Miller. In a later Sunday review (May 24, 1998), straight Vincent Canby, in his lukewarm review, spends almost as much time on Miller's inappropriateness. That Canby doesn't get what Brantley thinks is central to the success of the production is a reminder of the continued straight-gay split in the perception of vital elements of musical theater. One can't be too rigid in these formulations, however; famous homophobe John Simon wrote an even more ecstatic review of *Follies* than gay Brantley did.
2. The Paper Mill Playhouse is a lovely theater in suburban Millburn, New Jersey, that has specialized in revivals of musicals. When I was a kid, they were doing operettas in addition to recent musicals. The theater appeals to older suburbanites who don't want to go into the city. Now shows like *Follies* and diva events like Betty Buckley in *Gypsy* bring in fans from New York and earn reviews in the *Times.*
3. Jack Babuscio, "Camp and the Gay Sensibility," in *Camp Grounds: Style and Homosexuality,* ed. David Bergman(Amherst: University of Massachusetts Press, 1993), p. 24.
4. Philip Core, *Camp: The Lie That Tells the Truth,* (New York: Delilah Books, 1984) p. 7.
5. Scott Long, "The Loneliness of Camp," in *Camp Grounds,* p. 79.
6. James Goldman (lyrics by Stephen Sondheim), *Follies* (New York: Random House, 1971), p. 69.
7. This is not to say that all drag queens in the sixties and seventies did imitations of divas. However, the drag queens who became national celebrities, particularly Jim Bailey and Craig Russell, were also impressionists who specialized in female stars.
8. Richard Benner, *Outrageous,* 1977.
9. Daniel Harris, *The Rise and Fall of Gay Culture,* (New York: Hyperion, 1997), p. 13.
10. Tony Kushner's *Angels in America* has as its most sympathetic characters two "ex–ex-drag queens," Prior Walter and Belize.
11. LuPone opened Lloyd Webber's *Sunset Boulevard* in London. The show, which had flaws in casting and production, got mixed reviews. The powers that be blamed LuPone, who was overwhelmed by a set that looked like a giant red and gold jukebox as well as saddled with an uncharismatic leading man. The set was toned down, the staging improved, and a new leading man brought in, but LuPone didn't get a second chance. Glenn Close was announced for the Broadway version promised to LuPone. Supposedly LuPone read about it in the papers. She sued and won.

Faye Dunaway was fired from the Los Angeles production. She also played Callas in the touring company of *Master Class.*

12. Quoted in Marybeth Hamilton, *The Queen of Camp: Mae West, Sex, and Popular Culture* (New York: HarperCollins, 1996), p. 224.

13. Ben Brantley, review of *Lypsinka Is Harriet Craig, The New York Times* online, February 10, 1998.

14. If you are curious about the queer theory notion of gender as a series of performances rather than a fixed, "natural" identity, I recommend two concise treatments: Judith Butler, "Performative Acts and Gender Constitution: An Essay in Phenomenology and Feminist Theory," in Sue-Ellen Case, ed., *Performing Feminisms: Feminist Critical Theory and Theatre* (Baltimore: Johns Hopkins University Press, 1990), pp. 270-282; and Moe Myer, "Reclaiming the Discourse of Camp," in Moe Myer, ed., *The Politics and Poetics of Camp* (London: Routledge, 1994), pp. 1-22. The theoryspeak in these essays is less turgid than most.

15. I am focusing here on American drag. The British have a very different tradition of drag in theater, from Elizabethan boys playing women to the pantomime dames to Dame Edna Everage. The men in the highly popular 1970s television series *Monty Python's Flying Circus* could do drag without being considered gay. Drag in that show is both silly and, to some extent, misogynistic. British gay drag artists like Lily Savage and Bette Bourne play off their androgyny. Cheap, false glamor is combined with earthy male humor. You never forget there's a man inside that getup. On the brilliant and more politically correct Canadian television series of the early 1990s, *The Kids in the Hall,* the often very convincing drag turns of the mostly straight performers were considered loving comic performances of female characters—the kids actually made pretty women! Americans never pull that off very well.

16. Hamilton, *The Queen of Camp: Mae West, Sex, and Popular Culture,* p. 227.

17. Pamela Robertson, "'The Kinda Comedy That Imitates Me': Mae West's Identification with the Feminist Camp," in *Camp Grounds,* pp. 161-162.

18. One of the most fascinating aspects of *The Drag* is its catalogue of gay slang of the period. See *Three Plays of Mae West,* ed. Lillian Schlissel (New York; Routledge, 1997).

19. Boze Hadleigh, *Sing Out: Gays and Lesbians in the Music World* (New York: Barricade Books, 1997), p. 129.

20. In an episode of the NBC sitcom *Veronica's Closet,* Kirstie Alley is confronted with a drag queen who "does" her on a local cable television station. First horrified at the drag queen's performance, Alley at the end of the episode has the drag queen understudy her at a fashion show. Drag imitation becomes the sincerest form of flattery for this sitcom diva.

21. Quoted in Charles Kaiser, *The Gay Metropolis: 1940–1996,* (Boston: Houghton-Mifflin, 1997), p. 121.

22. Available on a video, *Judy Garland and Friends.*

23. Ethel Merman with George Ellis, *Merman* (New York: Simon and Shuster, 1978), p. 93.

24. Quoted in Boze Hadleigh, *Hollywood Gays* (New York: Barricade Books, 1996), p. 75.

25. Dennis McGovern and Deborah Grace Winer, *Sing Out, Louise: 150 Stars of the Musical Theater Remember 50 Years on Broadway* (New York: Schirmer Books, 1993), p. 155.

26. Hamilton, *The Queen of Camp,* p. 218.

27. Marjorie Garber, *Vested Interests: Cross-Dressing and Cultural Anxiety* (New York: Routledge, 1992), p. 158.

28. David Ehrenstein, *Open Secret: Gay Hollywood 1928-1998* (New York: Morrow, 1998), pp. 81-83.

29. Camille Paglia, "Judy Garland As a Force of Nature," *The New York Times* (June 14, 1998): sec. 2, p. 32.

30. Kaiser, *The Gay Metropolis,* 192.

31. Ibid.

32. Richard Dyer, *Heavenly Bodies: Film Stars and Society* (Basingstoke and London: Macmillan, 1986), p. 179.

33. Ibid., p. 180.

34. Ibid., p. 194.

35. Jack Babuscio, "Camp and the Gay Sensibility," in Richard Dyer, ed., *Gays and Film* (New York: Zoetrope, 1984), p. 46.

36. Ethan Mordden, "I Got a Song," *The New Yorker* 66 (October 22, 1990), p. 140.

37. Judith Crist, quoted in Kaiser, *The Gay Metropolis,* p. 196.

38. William Goldman, "Judy Floats," reprinted in *Rainbow: A Star- Studded Tribute to Judy Garland,* Ethlie Ann Vare, ed.(New York: Boulevard Books, 1998), p. 152.

39. Harris, *The Rise and Fall of Gay Culture,* p. 17.

40. "The street kids . . . who made up the better part of the mob on Christopher Street, were not the type to moon over Judy Garland records or attend her concerts at Carnegie Hall. They were more preoccupied with where they were going to sleep and where their next meal would come from." John Loughery, *The Other Side of Silence: Men's Lives and Gay Identities: A Twentieth-Century History* (New York: Henry Holt, 1998), p. 316.

41. Martin and Gray also wrote the musical version of Noël Coward's *Blithe Spirit,* titled *High Spirits,* in 1964.

42. The Garland video is in the *judy* set, produced by 32 Records (1998). Wainwright and family's haunting version of "What'll I Do" is on *The McGarrigle Hour* CD (Hannibal, 1998). Wainwright's first solo album of songs only a queen could write, including a tribute to ill-fated operatic heroines, "Damned Ladies," is on Dreamworks (1998).

43. One such interview is reprinted in Vare, ed., *Rainbow: A Star-Studded Tribute to Judy Garland:*

> Once, when she asked her manservant for a record "that *faggot* has"—her voice hissing the term for the unidentified homosexual; and once, as we were stretched across her bed, watching a Fred Astaire movie: "Astaire," Liza said, "is the only elegant American actor we've ever had." She mentions that a famous actor, also noted for his elegance "is really British—and a—*faggot.*" (p. 206).

44. An hour of selections from the concert are available on CD, *Barbara Cook at Carnegie Hall,* (Sony, 1975).

45. Michael Moon and Eve Kosofsky Sedgwick, "Divinity: A Dossier, a Performance Piece, a Little-Understood Emotion," in Eve Kosofsky Sedgwick, *Tendencies* (Durham: Duke University Press, 1993), p. 216.

CHAPTER V

1. Arthur Laurents (book) and Stephen Sondheim (lyrics), *Gypsy* (New York: Theatre Communications Group, 1994), p.11.

2. Ben Brantley, review of *Gypsy. The New York Times online* (September 21, 1998).

3. Laurents, *Gypsy,* p. 104.

4. Roger Baker, *Drag: A History of Female Impersonation in the Performing Arts* (New York: New York University Press, 1994), p. 203.

5. Ethan Mordden, *Broadway Babies: The People Who Made the American Musical* (New York: Oxford University Press, 1983), p.158.

6.   D. A. Miller, *Place for Us: Essay on the Broadway Musical,* (Cambridge: Mass.: Harvard University Press, 1998), p. 83.

7. Mordden, *Broadway Babies,* p. 159.

8. Stephen Sondheim (book James Goldman), *Follies* (New York: Random House, 1971), p. 57.

9. Baker, *Drag,* p. 203.

10. Jerry Herman (lyrics) and Harvey Fierstein (book), *La Cage aux Folles: The Broadway Musical* (New York: Samuel French, 1984), p. 81.

11. Jerry Herman with Marilyn Stasio, *Showtune: A Memoir,* (New York: Donald I. Fine Books, 1996) p. 226.

12. See, for instance, Bernard Slade's hit comedy, *Tribute.*

13. Herman, *Showtune: A Memoir,* p. 228.

14. Herman, *La Cage aux Folles,* p. 31

15. Fred Ebb (lyrics) and Terrence McNally (book), *Kiss of the Spider Woman: The Broadway Musical* (New York: Samuel French, 1997), p. 12.

16. Ibid., p. 28.

17. Ibid., p. 71.

18. Ibid., p. 51.

19. Ibid., p. 75.

20. Ibid.

21.   For a discussion of the power of the male-male kiss, see my *Acting Gay: Male Homosexuality in Modern Drama* (New York: Columbia University Press, 1994), pp. 7-18. Audiences still audibly groan, as I discovered at a recent performance of Noël Coward's *Design for Living*.

22.   Ebb and McNally, *Kiss of the Spider Woman*, p. 33.

23.   John Cameron Mitchell (book) and Stephen Trask (music and lyrics), *Hedwig and the Angry Inch* (unpublished mss., 1998), p. 20.

24.   Ibid., p. 37.

25.   Ibid., p. 72.

26.   Ibid., p. 3.

CHAPTER VI

1.   D. A. Miller, *Place for Us: Essay on the Broadway Musical,* (Cambridge, Mass.: Harvard University Press, 1998) p. 130.

2.   Betty Comden and Adolph Green (lyric by Lee Adams), *Applause,* in *Great Musicals of the American Theatre, Volume Two,* ed. Stanley Richards (Radnor, Penn.: Chilton Book Co., 1976), p. 467.

3.   Ibid., 474.

4.   Tommy Tune, *Footnotes: A Memoir* (New York: Simon & Schuster, 1997), p. 140.

5.   Quoted in Stephen Holden, "Focusing on Glam Rock's Blurring of Identity," *The New York Times* (November 8, 1998), sec. 2, p. 22.

6.   When Will Kemp, who alternated the role of the swan on Broadway, played the swan, there was a much more powerful contrast between swan and man in black than in Adam Cooper's performance. Kemp truly was two different personalities, more tender as the swan, more cruel as the man in black.

7.   Jann Parry, "Black or White, They're Birds of a Feather," *The New York Times,* (September 27, 1998), sec. 2, p. 29.

8.   John Lahr, review of Matthew Bourne's *Swan Lake, The New Yorker,* (October 19, 1998): p. 90.

9.   Quoted in Stephen Schaefer, "Bourne to Be Wild," *The Advocate* (October 27, 1998): p. 70.

10.   Ibid.

CHAPTER VII

1.   Quoted in Charles Kaiser, *The Gay Metropolis, 1940–1996* (Boston: Houghton-Mifflin, 1997), p. 188.

2.   Stephen Sondheim (lyrics) and Mary Rodgers (music), "The Boy From . . . "

3.   Meryle Secrest, *Stephen Sondheim: A Life* (New York: Knopf, 1998), p. 180.

4.   Secrest, *Stephen Sondheim: A Life,* p. 85.

5.   Mark Steyn, *Broadway Babies Say Goodnight: Musicals Then and Now* (London: Faber and Faber, 1997), p. 198.

6.   Secrest, *Stephen Sondheim: A Life,* p. 230.

7.   Ibid., p. 173.

8.   Stephen Sondheim (music and lyrics) and George Furth, (book), *Company* (New York: Theatre Communications Group, 1996), p. 114.

9.   Stephen Sondheim (music and lyrics) and James Lapine (book), *Passion* (New York: Theatre Communications Group, 1996), p. 114.

10.   Kaiser, *The Gay Metropolis,* p. 93.

11.   Stephen Sondheim (music and lyrics) and Arthur Laurents (book), *Anyone Can Whistle* (New York: Leon Amiel, 1976), p. 112.

12.   Quoted in brochure of Columbia CD of 1995 Carnegie Hall concert version of *Anyone Can Whistle.*

13.   Steyn, *Broadway Babies Say Goodnight,* pp. 135-136.

14.   Sondheim and Laurents, *Anyone Can Whistle,* p. 161

15.   Sondheim and Furth, *Company,* p. 70.

16.   Ibid., p. 43.

17.   Ibid., p. 59.

18. Ibid., pp. 110-111.
19. Quoted in Craig Zadan, *Sondheim & Co.* (New York: Harper & Row, 1974, 1986), p. 124.
20. There is some controversy about this line. To our ears, "fag" seems harsh and homophobic. It is also out of character for these women. Hip Marta and flight attendant April aren't likely to use such a homophobic, derogatory term. In the 1995 Roundabout Theater revival, the audience heard:

> I could understand a person
> If he happened to be gay.

This also appears in the most recent published version (p. 42). The 1996 Sam Mendes production went back to the "fag" line. At the Cameron Mackintosh gala, *Hey, Mr. Producer,* in 1998, the divas Maria Friedman, Ruthie Henshall, Lea Salonga, and Millicent Martin sang:

> I could understand a person
> If a person was a drag,

which doesn't make much sense at all.

21. Quoted in Secrest, *Stephen Sondheim: A Life,* p. 371.
22. *The New York Times* (April 28, 1963): sec. 2, p. 1. I discuss this and other examples of homophobia from mainstream critics in my book *Acting Gay: Male Homosexuality in Modern Drama* (New York: Columbia University Press, 1994), pp. 174-183.
23. This and the following quotes are reprinted in Joanne Gordon, *Art Isn't Easy: The Theater of Stephen Sondheim* (New York: DaCapo Press, 1992), p. 55.
24. Ibid.
25. Gerald Mast, *Can't Help Singin': The American Musical on Stage and Screen* (Woodstock, N.Y.: Overlook Press, 1987), p. 326.
26. D. A. Miller, *Place for Us: Essay on the Broadway Musical,* (Cambridge, Mass.: Harvard University Press, 1998), p. 125.
27. Sondheim and Furth, *Company,* pp. 102-103.
28. George Furth is still anxious about people reading Bobby as gay. Peter may be bisexual, but Furth insists Bobby is straight, the sort of man women and men want to confide in. Furth generously shared his view with me in a phone conversation.
29. Quoted in Zadan, *Sondheim and Company,* p. 129.
30. Stephen Sondheim (music and lyrics) and James Goldman (book), *Follies* (New York: Random House, 1971), p. 9.
31. From "Ah, But Underneath," a quasi–Gypsy Rose Lee number written for the glorious Diana Rigg in the 1987 London production of *Follies* in place of "The Ballad of Lucy and Jessie," a parody of Weill's "Saga of Jenny" from *Lady in the Dark.* The latter neatly defines the relationship of Sally and Phyllis, but the former is a better number and a more cogent self-analysis for Phyllis. "Ah, But Underneath" was also used in the 1998 Paper Mill Playhouse revival.
32. Sondheim and Goldman, *Follies,* p. 91.
33. Ibid., p. 18.
34. Ibid., p. 35.
35. Zadan, *Sondheim and Company,* p. 136.
36. Sondheim and Goldman, *Follies,* p. 40.
37. Quoted in Zadan, *Sondheim and Company,* p. 152.
38. Sondheim and Goldman, *Follies,* p. 74.
39. He isn't the first male singer to perform "Losing My Mind." Tim Curry does a version on the recording of a Los Angeles AIDS benefit concert.
40. Wheeler's *Look, We've Come Through,* about struggling young actors in New York, was a moderate Off-Broadway success in the early seventies.
41. Stephen Sondheim (music and lyrics) and Hugh Wheeler (book), *A Little Night Music,* (New York: Applause Musical Library, 1991), p. 208.
42. Ibid., p. 174.
43. Ibid., 173.
44. Stephen Sondheim (lyrics), *Merrily We Roll Along.* Quoted from brochure of Columbia CD.
45. Ibid.

46. Ibid.
47. Quoted in Secrest, *Stephen Sondheim: A Life,* pp. 387-388.
48. Sondheim and Lapine, *Passion,* p. 21.
49. Ibid., p. 61.
50. Ibid., p. 35.
51. Ibid., p. 61.
52. Part of one of the solos added to the London production for Michael Ball.
53. Ibid.
54. Sondheim and Lapine, *Passion,* p. 122. This is sung quietly in the New York production but is a real aria in the London production.

CHAPTER VIII

1.   Toby Manning, "Gay Culture: Who Needs It," in *Anti-Gay,* Mark Simpson, ed. (London: Freedom Editions, 1996), p. 108.
2.   Tony Kushner, "Notes Toward a Theater of Fabulous," in *Staging Gay Lives: An Anthology of Contemporary Gay Theater,* ed. John M. Clum (Boulder, Colo.: Westview Press, 1996), p. vii.
3.   Peter Morris (lyrics) and Dick Gallagher (music), *Howard Crabtree's Whoop-Dee-Doo!* (New York: Samuel French, 1995), p. 45.
4.   Dan Pruett (lyrics and book) and Patrick Hutchison (music), *The Harvey Milk Show,* in Clum, *Staging Gay Lives,* p. 49.
5.   All quotations come from the edition of Michael Korie's libretto accompanying the compact discs of *Harvey Milk* (Telarc Records, 1996).
6.   Philip Osment, *This Island's Mine,* in *Gay Sweatshop: Four Plays and a Company,* Philip Osment, ed. (London: Methuen, 1989), p. 94.
7.   David Román, *Acts of Intervention: Performance, Gay Culture, and AIDS* (Bloomington: Indiana University Press, 1998), p. 99.
8.   Wendell Jones and David Stanley, *AIDS: The Musical!* in *Sharing the Delirium: Second Generation AIDS Plays and Performances,* ed. Therese Jones (Portsmouth, NH: Heinemann, 1994), p. 208.
9.   Ibid., p. 239.
10. Ibid., p. 233.
11. Ibid., p. 224.
12. Bill Russell (music by Janet Hood) *elegies for angels punks and raging queens* (New York: Samuel French, 1996), p. 22.
13. William Finn, *The Marvin Songs (In Trousers, March of the Falsettos, Falsettoland)* (New York: Fireside Theater, 1993), p.245.
14. Ibid., p. 239.
15. Sarah Schulman, *Stage Struck: Theater, AIDS, and the Marketing of Gay America* (Durham, N.C.: Duke University Press, 1998), p. 148.
16. Román, *Acts of Intervention,* p. 275.
17. Ibid., p. 281.
18. Schulman, *Stage Struck,* p. 150.
19. Michael John LaChiusa, *Hello Again* (New York: Dramatists Play Service, 1995), pp. 56-57.
20. Ibid., p. 57.
21. Foster Hirsch, *Harold Prince and the American Musical Theatre* (Cambridge: Cambridge University Press, 1989), p. 66.
22. In all fairness to Hickey, I saw the production while Jennifer Jason Leigh was playing Sally. She was sub–community theater awful and paid no attention to anyone on stage with her, so it would be difficult to establish a convincing relationship of any kind with her.
23. Quoted in Hirsch, *Harold Prince and the American Musical Theatre,* p. 60.
24. Kurt Schwabach (lyrics) and Mischa Spoliansky (music), trans. Jeremy Lawrence. From the brochure to *Berlin Cabaret Songs* (London, 1998).
25. The lavishly illustrated text of the current *Cabaret* production includes a section on the transformation of Studio 54 into the Kit Kat Klub. Joe Masterhoff, John Kander, Fred Ebb, *Cabaret: The Illustrated Book and Lyrics* (New York: Newmarket Press, 1999), pp. 114-15.

INDEX

INDEX OF SHOWS

COMPOSERS, LYRICISTS, WRITERS